Book of

Paris Walks

Edited by Andrew White

Edited and designed by
Time Out Guides Limited
Universal House
251 Tottenham Court Road
London W1P 0AB
Tel + 44 (0)171 813 3000
Fax+ 44 (0)171 813 6001
guides@timeout.com
www.timeout.com

Editorial
Editor Andrew White
Editorial Director Peter Fiennes
Managing Director Paris Karen Albrecht
Managing Editor Nicholas Royle
Consultant Editor Paris Natasha Edwards
Researcher Katherine Spenley
Proofreader Tamsin Shelton
Indexer Kathy Grocott-Ward

Design
Art Director John Oakey
Art Editor Mandy Martin
Senior Designer Scott Moore
Designers Benjamin de Lotz, Lucy Grant
Scanning/Imaging Chris Quinn
Picture Editor Kerri Miles
Picture Researcher Olivia Duncan-Jones
Picture Admin Kit Burnett

Administration
Publisher Tony Elliott
Managing Director Mike Hardwick
Financial Director Kevin Ellis
General Manager Nichola Coulthard
Marketing Director Gillian Auld
Marketing Manager Christine Cort
Accountant Catherine Bowen
Production Manager Mark Lamond

The Editor would like to thank the following:
Lanning Aldrich, Peter Ayrton, Jonathan Bryant, Jonathan Cox, Simon Cropper, Juliet Gardiner, Sasha Goldman, Sarah Guy, Wally Hammond, Ruth Jarvis, Alkarim Jivani, Richard Joy, Arabella Keatley, Mandy Martinez, Georgia Mazower, Lesley McCave, Nana Ocran, Cath Phillips, Alex Poots, François Sergent, Robert Silman, Ricky Stein, Caro Taverne, Philippe Thareaut, Jill Tulip, Susanne Twerenbold, Kelvin White, Susan White.

Maps by Mapworld, 71 Blandy Road, Henley-on-Thames, Oxon RG9 1QB.

Photography by Adam Eastland except for: pages 19, 72, 130, 140, 229, 235, 279, 290 AKG; page 59 Magnum Photo; pages 83, 86-93 Jeanloup Sieff; pages 33, 34, 95, 196, 200, 203 Gamma/FSP; pages 240, 248, 249, 250 BFI; page 245 Essential; page 251 Artificial Eye.

Published by the Penguin Group
Penguin Books Ltd., 27 Wrights Lane, London, W8 5TZ, England
Penguin Putnam Inc., 375 Hudson Street, New York, New York 10014, USA
Penguin Books Australia Ltd., 487 Maroondah Highway (PO Box 257), Ringwood, VIC 3134, Australia
Penguin Books Canada Ltd., 10 Alcorn Avenue, Toronto, Ontario, Canada M4V 3B2
Penguin Books (NZ) Ltd., Private Bag 102902, NSMC, Auckland, New Zealand

Penguin Books Ltd., Registered offices: Harmondsworth, Middlesex, England

First published 1999
10 9 8 7 6 5 4 3 2 1

Colour reprographics by Precise Litho, 34–35 Great Sutton Street, London EC1.
Printed by Southernprint (Web Offset) Ltd, Upton Industrial Estate, Poole, Dorset, BH16 5SN

Contents

Using this book

We recommend that you read the entire text of any walk before setting out. Not only should this whet your appetite and give an overview of the journey ahead, it will also help you to plan stopping-off points according to opening times provided in the listings. Indeed, for the longer walks, it'll give you a chance to plan at which point you want to abandon the walk and stagger to the nearest café/bar.

In the interests of not interfering with the flow of the prose, we have avoided endless directions in the text. The text and the maps should be used alongside each other, so if one seems unclear, consult the other. That said, every one of the routes has been walked and scrupulously checked, so we hope you'll find it very hard to get lost…

Maps

The route is marked in red. Two thin red lines indicate that you will be required to retrace your steps. Short diversions from the main route are also indicated. The dotted lines mark suggested routes to the start and from the finish of the walk (for the Métro), and in some walks it indicates a possible diversion from the main route. Some, but not all, of the sites highlighted in the walk are marked on the maps. We have always indicated a route to and from the nearest Métro: apologies to bus travellers – free bus maps are available from Métro stations.

Distance

The distances given are to the nearest half-kilometre or half-mile.

Time

The timing of the walks obviously depends on the speed of the walker, and the length and frequency of stops. The times given are therefore approximate, and assume that there are no lengthy stops en route (though of course these are highly recommended), and that a healthy pace is maintained.

Notes

These are largely self explanatory and merely aim to help walkers plan the timing of the walk, and forewarn them of any peculiar features.

Listings

We have listed virtually every café, bar, restaurant, shop, museum, gallery, church, park and relevant organisation mentioned in the text of the walk that is open to the public. They are arranged by category and alphabetically, not following the chronology of the walk. They were all accurate at the time of writing.

For the eating and drinking sections at the end of each walk, we have listed the opening hours for the establishment, and where we can, included a brief summary of the venue. Those included that are not mentioned in the walks are taken from the annual *Time Out Paris Eating & Drinking Guide*. For those venues appearing in the *Eating & Drinking Guide* we have added a short description of the fare. All the remaining listings are taken from the text, and are divided, sometimes somewhat crudely, into categories. The final 'Others' category, where it occurs, may list organisations that readers might wish to contact should the walk inspire further investigation.

Walks' accessibility

Further information can be found in *Access in Paris*, an English-language guide by Gordon Couch and Ben Roberts, published by Quiller Press. It can be ordered from RADAR, Unit 12, City Forum, 250 City Road, London EC1V 8AF (020 7250 3222). The Office de Tourisme de Paris produces *Tourisme pour tout le monde* (60F). A freephone number

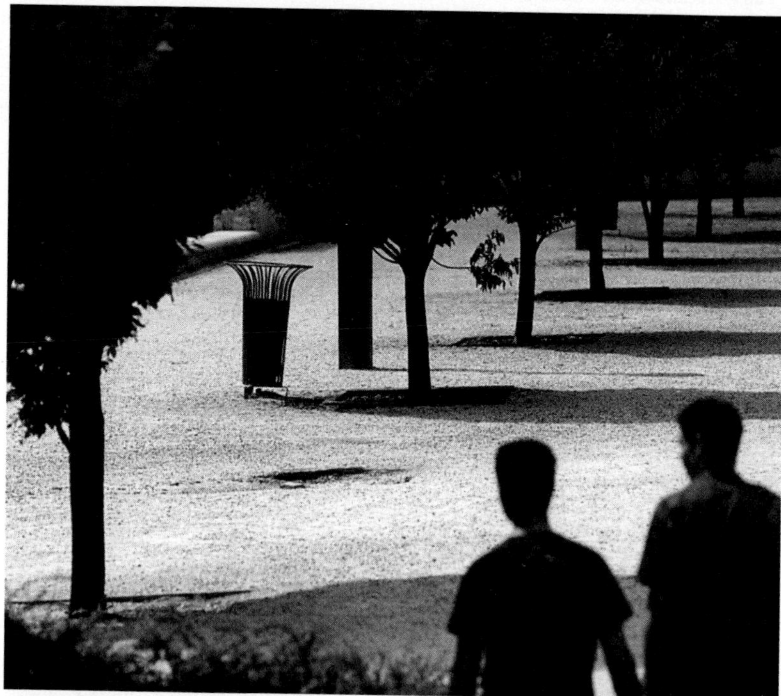

(08.00.03.37.48) offers advice (in French) to disabled persons living in or visiting Paris. Other sources of advice are:

Comité national de liaison pour la réadaptation des handicapés (CNRH)
236 bis rue de Tolbiac, 13th (01.53.80.66.63). Publishes *Paris Ile-de-France Pour Tous* (60F; 80F if ordered from abroad), an all-purpose tourist guide for the disabled.

Association des Paralysés de France
22 rue du Père-Guérain, 13th (01.44.16.83.83). **Open** 9am-12.30pm, 2-6pm, Mon-Thur; 9am-12.30pm, 2-5pm, Fri. Publishes *Où ferons-nous étape?* (85F), listing French hotels and motels accessible to those with limited mobility.

General tips

Paris is divided into 20 *arrondissements*, which feature in all addresses. In this book we have given a broad outline of the area covered by each walk in the contents by listing the arrondissements that the walks visit, and we supply an arrondissement map at the back of the book.

Most museums are closed on Mondays or Tuesdays, and public holidays – check the listings for details.

Most restaurants and many cafés close for some or all of either July or August (usually August). By law, prices listed and charged include a 10-15% service charge. It is polite to leave a few coins on the table if the service is good, but this is in no way mandatory.

Tourist information

Office de Tourisme de Paris
127 avenue des Champs-Elysées, 8th (01.36.68.31.12/recorded information in English 01.49.52.53.56). **Open** *summer* 9am-8pm daily; *winter* 9am-8pm Mon-Sat; 11am-6pm Sun.
Branches: *Eiffel Tower* (01.45.51.22.15). **Open** *May-Sept* 11am-6pm daily. *Gare de Lyon* (01.43.43.33.24). **Open** 8am-8pm Mon-Sat.

Espace du Tourisme d'Ile de France
Carrousel du Louvre, 99 rue de Rivoli, 1st (08.03.03.19.98./from abroad (33)1.44.50.19.98). **Open** 10am-7pm Mon, Wed-Sun. For visitors to Ile-de-France as well as Paris.

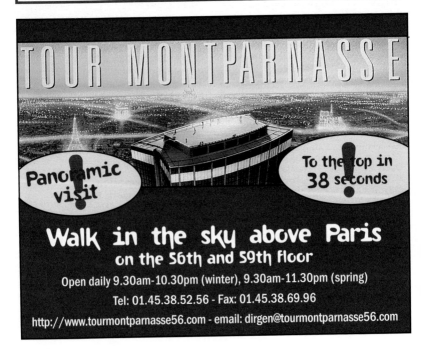

Introduction

Paris has led a charmed life. The city has often been threatened with destruction and devastation, but has somehow survived. Its beauty, culture and wealth have been a magnet for people from all points of the globe, sometimes those who have come to settle, often those who have come to visit, but also those intent on ruling.

In the fifth century Ste-Geneviève reputedly held off the rampaging Attila through prayer; in 1871 the Prussian advance reached the southern arrondissements before a treaty was signed; a rush to the front in taxis staved off the German advance in 1914; and von Choltitz couldn't bring himself to follow Hitler's orders to destroy the city as his army retreated in 1944. Ironically perhaps, the Parisians themselves have destroyed much of the city. The revolutions of 1789, 1830 and 1871 all had their architectural casualties, and it was Préfet Haussmann who changed the face of the city in the nineteenth century, destroying much of the medieval centre in the process. But the absence of sustained bombing, especially during the twentieth century, has meant that the city retains so much beauty and historic charm, from the medieval corners of the Latin Quarter to the boulevards of the Haussmann era, and it is still so small, that walking is both practical and rewarding. There are, of course, the truly mesmerising, but often crowded, buildings and monuments that we all know about, but there are also the quieter *allées* and *passages*, the street markets and mixed communities, where the locals are not in awe of the city in which they live.

These walks embrace many facets of Paris and explore it through the eyes of novelists, journalists, historians and comedians, all enthusiasts for a city that is part of their lives. They have each devised their own walk, drawing on historical, architectural and personal observation. We learn not only about Paris's past and present, but also about what delights and irritates the writer.

Liz Jensen takes us bouncing up the Butte Montmartre to the heights of the Sacré-Coeur; Alistair Horne guides us through the lives of some of those lying beneath grand monuments in Père Lachaise cemetery; Jeanloup Sieff illustrates an aimless wander among the sculpted tombs in Montmartre's cemetery with his own photographs; and Marie Darrieussecq passes a not uncritical eye over the statues in the Jardin du Luxembourg.

Several of the walks follow a theme. Paris's famous literary heritage draws Michael Palin to haunt Hemingway's shadow; Nicholas Lezard remembers Beckett; and Maureen Freely loops over the river in search of Simone de Beauvoir. There are also the more secluded walks: Geoff Dyer in search of his favourite bar, passing several others on the way; Abdelkader Djemaï visits the immigrant communities of Belleville and La Goutte d'Or; and Nicholas Royle takes us up to the spectacular Buttes Chaumont in all its glorious artificiality.

And so on. There are 23 walks in all, providing a mix of styles, outlooks and settings. The end result is a book that can be read with pleasure at home as a collection of commentaries on Paris, but above all as a thought-provoking guide to a series of *chemins* around the capital. And if you feel the slightest tremor of tendinitis, the merest flicker of fatigue or twinge of thirst, duck into a café and savour your surroundings. *Un demi, un crème*, perhaps even a *pastis* to fortify you for the road ahead.

Bonne promenade!

Andrew White

The sacred and the profane

Liz Jensen

Sex, art and death in Pigalle and Montmartre.

Start: Mº Pigalle, 18th
Finish: Mº Abbesses, 18th
Time: 2-3 hours
Distance: 4km/2.5 miles
Getting there: lines 2 or 12 to Mº Pigalle
Getting back: Mº Abbesses (line 12).
Note: this walk is not suitable for children. The sleazy side of Pigalle is best seen at night, but little else is open at this time. The wild garden only opens at very specific times. See Jeanloup Sieff's walk (p82) for a map of the Cimetière de Montmartre.

Years ago, when my sister lived in Paris, I would travel up from my home near Lyon to stay with her family in their dingy little apartment a short walk from the Gare du Nord. Sometimes with my young step-niece, or with the family's snuffling, dusty little Pekinese dog in tow, I'd meander in ever expanding circles from the small nexus of streets around their block, feeling like neither a real tourist nor a real native. It was in the course of these wanderings that I cooked up a walk that takes in three of life's great themes: sex, art and death.

This circuit – highly unsuitable, in fact, for young children and small dogs – takes in the best of the *quartier*, but it begins by giving you a little soupçon of the worst. Pigalle is well known as the sleaze district of Paris, but it's also an area where people live. Any side-street off the boulevard de Clichy will contain slices of normal everyday France in the form of bakeries, residential blocks, churches, schools and *tabacs*. However, to catch a fleeting glimpse of the notorious 'street of shame', leave Pigalle Métro and head left up the boulevard de Clichy. Pigalle is best seen at night, when the neon's alight and the hookers and transvestites are out in full regalia. By day, the almost triumphant tackiness of the district is less obviously displayed – but there's still plenty going on. Note the way most of the signs – LIVE SEX SHOW, SEX CENTRE, PEEP SHOW, INFLATABLES – are in English. *Hypocrite lecteur!* If you're in the mood for a more academic sex tour, sample the surprisingly tasteful thrills of the Musée de l'Erotisme, which is open both day and night, and boasts exhibits from all over the world, ranging from a 'cunnilingus chair' to decorated dildoes, Japanese erotic prints and contemporary erotic art. Just past Blanche Métro, you'll see the red sails of the Moulin Rouge, sequin-infested home of cabaret and cancan – but what exists now is aimed strictly at the tourist clientele, and is a far cry from the Moulin in its famous heyday. Just beyond is the hip MCM café, where you can stop for a drink; as you leave, notice the small cobblestoned alleyway marked cité Véron off to the right. This houses a small art theatre and a host of pretty, secluded little apartments with shady courtyards and a sleepy village atmosphere – in stark contrast to the urban touristorama just a stone's throw away.

English is the lingua franca of the neon lights that adorn the porn shops of sleazy **Pigalle**.

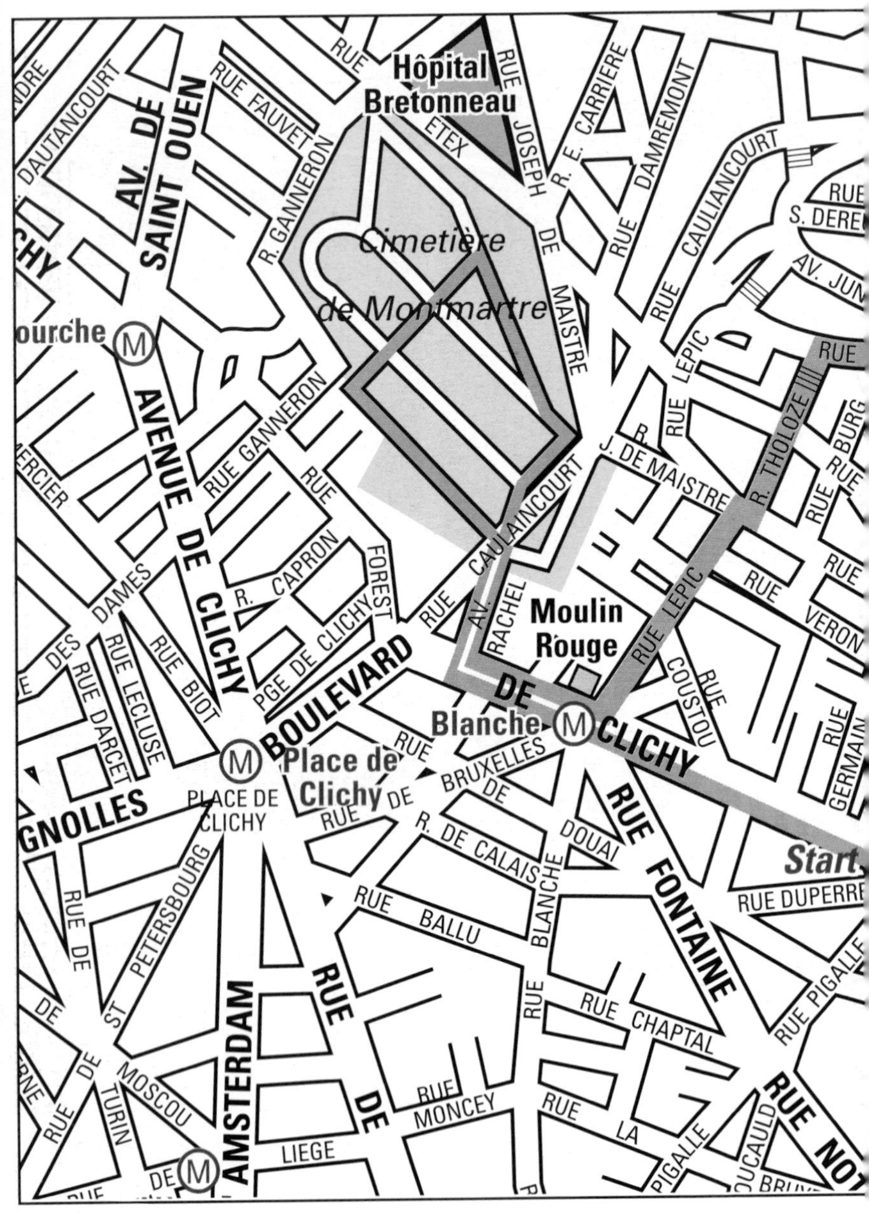
Hôpital
Bretonneau
Cimetière
de Montmartre
Moulin
Rouge
Start
Blanche
Place de
Clichy
PLACE DE
CLICHY
ourche
RUE
RUE FAUVET
ETEX
RUE
JOSEPH
DE
MAISTRE
R. E. CARRIERE
RUE DAMREMONT
RUE CAULIANCOURT
RUE
S. DERE
AV. JUN
DAUTANCOURT
AV. DE
SAINT OUEN
R. GANNERON
RUE GANNERON
RUE GANNERON
AVENUE
DE CLICHY
RUE LEPIC
RUE LEPIC
R. J. DE MAISTRE
R. THOLOZE
RUE CAULAINCOURT
AV. RACHEL
RUE
R. CAPRON
FOREST
PGE DE CLICHY
BOULEVARD
DE
CLICHY
RUE DES DAMES
RUE LECLUSE
RUE BIOT
RUE DARCET
GNOLLES
RUE DE BRUXELLES
RUE DE DOUAI
R. DE CALAIS
RUE BLANCHE
RUE FONTAINE
RUE COUSTOU
RUE GERMAIN
RUE DUPERR
RUE BALLU
RUE CHAPTAL
RUE LA
PIGALLE
RUE PIGALLE
RUE NOT
RUE DE ST PETERSBOURG
RUE DE MOSCOU
RUE DE TURIN
RUE AMSTERDAM
RUE DE LIEGE
RUE MONCEY
ERCIER
VERON
BURG

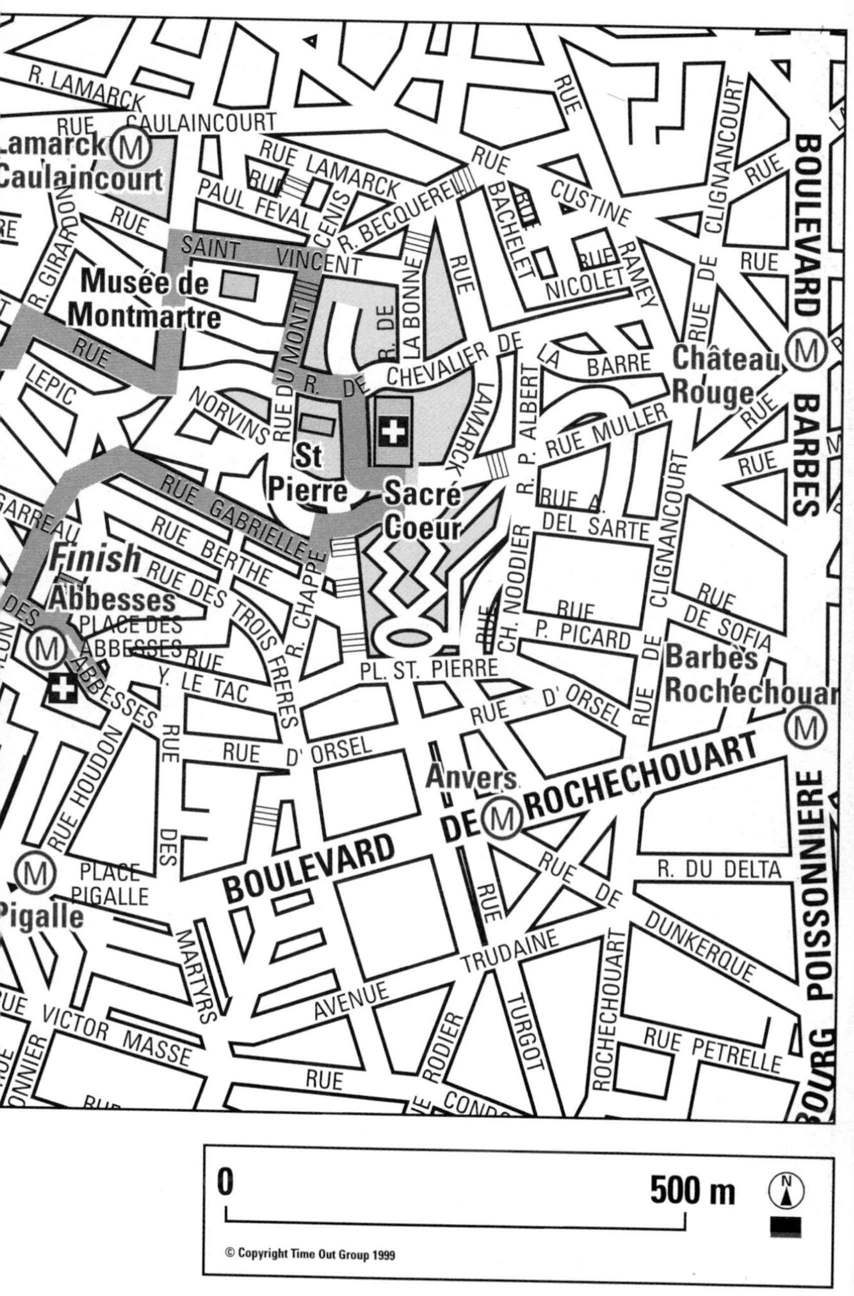
R. LAMARCK
RUE CAULAINCOURT
Caulaincourt
RUE LAMARCK
PAUL FEVAL
RUE SAINT VINCENT
R. GIRARDON
CENIS
R. BECQUEREL
RUE BACHELET
RUE CUSTINE
RUE NICOLET
RAMEY
RUE CLIGNANCOURT
RUE DE
Musée de Montmartre
RUE LEPIC
RUE DU MONT
R. DE LA BONNE
R. DE CHEVALIER DE LA BARRE
NORVINS
LAMARCK
R. P. ALBERT
RUE MULLER
Château Rouge
BOULEVARD BARBES
St Pierre
Sacré Coeur
RUE GABRIELLE
RUE BERTHE
R. CHAPPE
RUE A. DEL SARTE
CH. NOODIER
Finish
Abbesses
PLACE DES ABBESSES
RUE DES TROIS FRERES
RUE Y. LE TAC
RUE DES ABBESSES
RUE P. PICARD
RUE DE SOFIA
PL. ST. PIERRE
RUE D' ORSEL
Barbès Rochechouar
RUE HOUDON
Anvers
BOULEVARD DE ROCHECHOUART
RUE DES MARTYRS
PLACE PIGALLE
Pigalle
RUE DE DUNKERQUE
R. DU DELTA
TRUDAINE
AVENUE
RUE VICTOR MASSE
RODIER
TURGOT
ROCHECHOUART
RUE PETRELLE
POISSONNIERE
0
500 m
N
© Copyright Time Out Group 1999

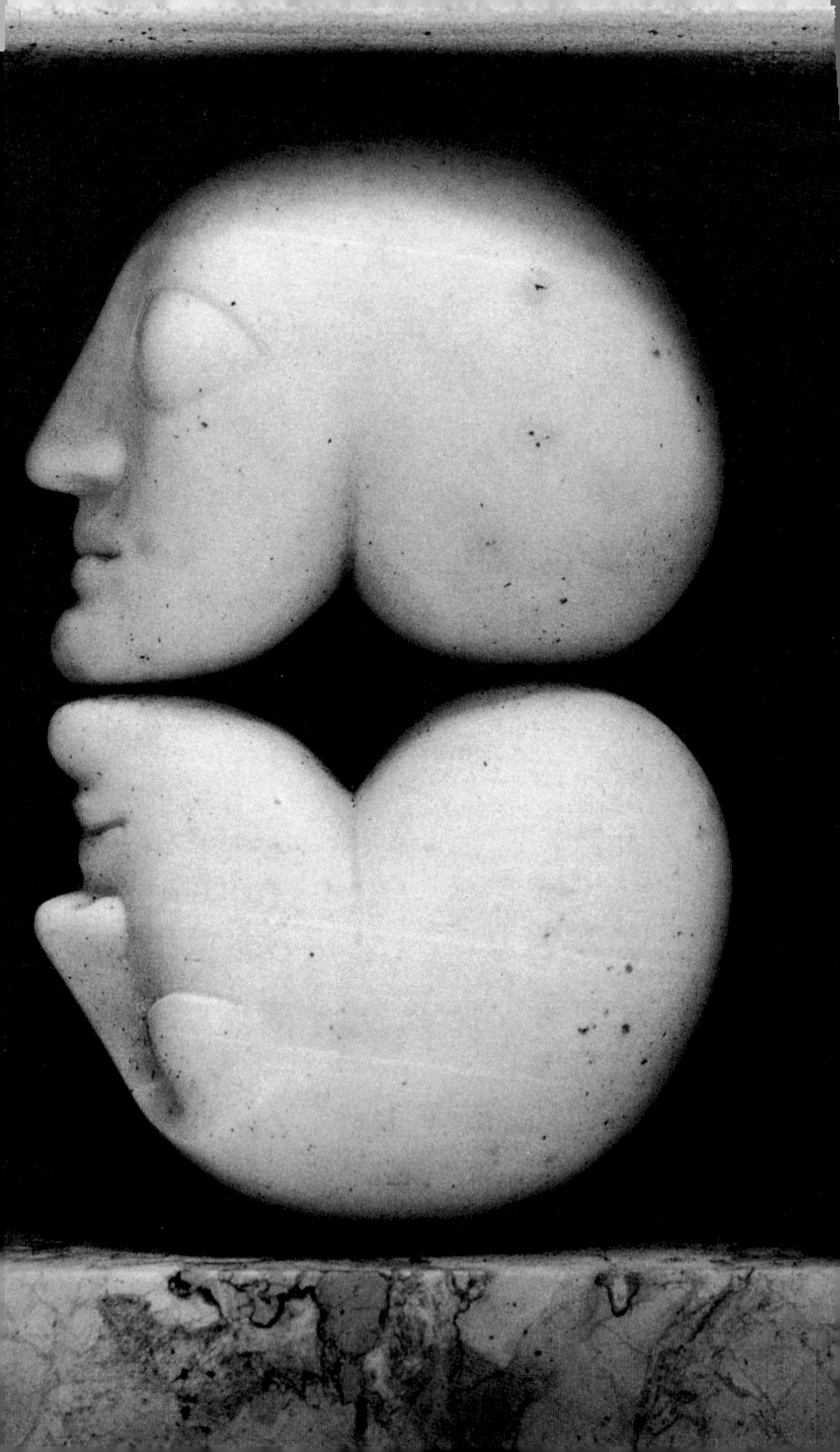

Death comes next – but in the nicest possible way.

Leave the boulevard, turn right at Corcoran's, a typical olde-worlde Irish pub, with its air-conditioning and big-screen TV, and enter avenue Rachel. This leafy residential avenue leads to the famous Cimetière de Montmartre, resting place of many of France's great and good, including Zola, the Guitry family, Foucault, Truffaut, Stendhal, Degas and Offenbach – and a few monsters, too, no doubt. Death, the Great Leveller! As you enter the gates, you can ask the guard for a map of the cemetery. This piece of paper isn't entirely worthless, as it will give you an idea of the layout of the avenues – but frankly, if you want to track down a particular grave, you'd be better off using a divining rod. Just past the gates you'll find yourself in the oddest and most dismal part of the cemetery, where once-dignified sepulchres huddle under an iron road bridge roaring with traffic – but the deeper you go, the more magical it becomes, an oasis of tranquillity in the frantic cacophany of the city. I don't have a great fondness for cemeteries as a rule, but I love this one. Some of the tombs, graves and sepulchres are tended with the bright flowers of recent grief, and others are dilapidated, flaking and blackening away, eroded by weather, pollution and neglect – but it's always seemed to me a peaceful, even happy, resting place. There's pomp and circumstance in abundance, but charm and grace, too.

The cemetery is criss-crossed with gravel walkways, but head first for the grassy roundabout just beyond the entrance. Directly opposite, you'll see a little flight of steps. Climb these, passing the Fragonard plaque as you go, and come face to face with the salmon-coloured marble of Emile Zola's tomb – complete with a verdigris'd bust of the man who left to posterity, among other things, the famous phrase, *'J'accuse!'* Then, returning down the same steps, head along avenue de la Croix. Just after it begins to slope downwards, turn right into the avenue de Montmorency – noting the gigantic, grandiose sepulchre of the Duke and Duchess of Montmorency and the tomb in the shape of Cleopatra's Needle – then take a left down the steps into avenue Samson, then right into the avenue du Tunnel. Just before this avenue turns right at the perimeter wall, you'll see on your left the tomb of Foucault, of pendulum fame. Continue right into avenue Montebello, up a dark tunnel of chestnut trees and discover that the road comes to an abrupt end, marked by a bench and a water-pump. Behind the bench, though, you'll see a narrow flight of steps – from the top of which there's a view of the cemetery that gives you a good idea of its huge scale and many levels. Next, descend the steps and turn left into avenue Cordier (note the surnames and the stars of David on the tombs to your left; this is the Jewish part of the cemetery) and continue along it, stopping to admire the simple white tomb of the artist Victor Brauner and his wife Jacqueline, which features a striking sculpture of two heads, one mirroring the other, and the celebratory inscription: *'Pour moi peindre c'est la vie, la vraie vie. MA VIE.'* ('For me, painting is life, true life. MY LIFE.') For a contrast to its white minimalism, continue along the avenue until it joins avenue Berlioz, where you'll see Berlioz's eerily dark tombstone adorned with his profile in bas-relief. Opposite, a double-headed tomb bears testimony to a more recent past. Here lie the children Yankel, Mala and Haia Krys, and Chaia and Rivka Chwer, deported and killed by the Nazis in 1942 simply *"parce que vous étiez juifs"'* (because you were Jews). Truffaut, too, is nearby. Avenue Berlioz returns you to the road bridge – beneath which more graves are unhappily crammed – and exit again on to avenue Rachel. Turn left and retrace your steps

'Painting is my life' is the sentiment mirrored in the sculpture gracing a grave in the magical **Cimetière de Montmartre**.

past the Moulin Rouge, then turn left again into rue Lepic, where the uphill struggle on the Butte Montmartre begins.

I always walk up the right-hand pavement of rue Lepic, because the shops on this side are the best: exquisite pâtisseries, butcher's shops with lolling ox tongues on display, fruiterers groaning with succulent plums and giant strawberries – oh, and if you look across the road from the hairdresser's, you can see the blackened little armature that marked an earlier entrance to the Moulin Rouge. If you're hungry, there is a choice of little cafés and takeaways on this section of rue Lepic – including the Délice Lepic, a very simple no-fuss Chinese food stop. Note, too, one of the idiosyncrasies of Paris street-cleaning: the gutter system that sluices water down the kerbsides. Its flow is channelled by rolled-up pieces of carpeting, repositioned at intervals. Typical French plumbing, you might think – but actually, crude though it is, the system works impressively on these urban hillsides.

In the old days, when this was all windmill-strewn countryside, the long, snaking rue Lepic used to be the pathway for carts carrying gypsum, the basic ingredient of plaster, down from the quarries in Montmartre. It's hard to imagine, but Montmartre contains a maze of underground tunnels, making it prone to subsidence – hence the tight building restrictions, which have allowed the area to keep a vestige of its rural past. Turn right at the fishmonger's on the corner of rue Lepic; you are now on rue des Abbesses – so called because it once led to the Women's Abbey of Montmartre, nicknamed 'the army's whorehouse on the hill' following the seduction of the Abbess in 1590 by the besieging Henri de Navarre. After a few paces, you'll see a wonderful, quirky little hat shop on your right called Têtes en l'Air, where you can buy a mad confection to balance on your head should you wish to draw attention to yourself during the rest of the walk. Immediately opposite this shop, looking across rue des Abbesses, you'll see rue Tholozé, the street you're headed for – and high above it, on the hillside facing you, a replica of the Moulin du Radet, immortalised by many artists, most

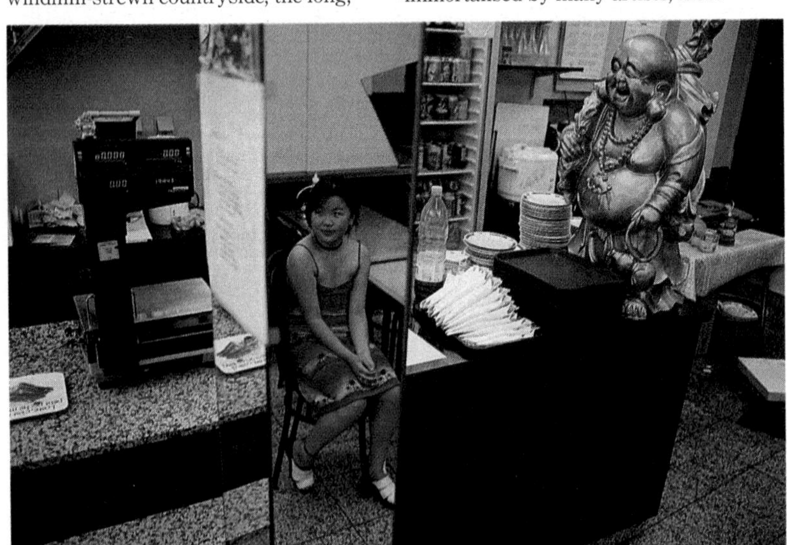

Dip into one of the little cafés on **rue Lepic** *– low prices, fine food and spiritual guidance.*

The Butte Montmartre has drawn artists over the years – here **van Gogh** *admires the view.*

notably Picasso and Renoir. It was on to the sails of the original mill that in 1814, during a particularly gory phase of Montmartre's history, a miller was nailed, in pieces, as punishment for having shot an attacking Russian soldier in the head. The miller's only surviving son later turned the mill into a dance hall.

Mount the steep rue Tholozé, and climb the stairs at the top to rejoin rue Lepic, taking a right at the mill. Soon you'll see the second of *les deux moulins, (*both replicas) – all that remain of the 40 or so mills that once stood on the hilltop (or *butte*) of Montmartre. Beneath this one, the Moulin Radet, there is now a restaurant. Cross and head up rue Girardon, then turn immediately right into rue Norvins, stopping at place Marcel-Aymé to look at *Le Passe-Muraille*, a witty, joyfully surreal sculpture of a man walking out of a wall, by Jean Marais (after Marcel Aymé's 1943 short story of the same name). This area is packed with quiet, charming little streets, and there's always a clamour of birdsong from the trees. But while there's still a hint of the countryside here, it doesn't last long. As you head up rue Norvins, the street begins to sprout easels and souvenir shops; you are nearing the Sacré-Coeur and the *butte*'s pinnacle. You can jettison yourself out of this small but vigorous tourist pocket by avoiding the rest of rue Norvins, which leads to the rampantly tacky epicentre of Montmartre's tourist trade, the place du Tertre. Instead, follow rue des Saules to the left – stopping to eat at the small but exquisitely sited La Maison Rose, which serves a terrific view along with its good food.

You may be reluctant, after all this climbing uphill, to head downwards – but allow yourself to be seduced into it by the prospect of seeing, in the middle of Paris, a real vineyard, just a little further down the same road. This is the famous Montmartre Vineyard, planted in 1933 in memory of the wine industry that thrived here, in the days when the Lapin Agile on the corner was the haunt of many a famous local drinker. The grapes are harvested and made into a wine that is said to double your urine output. (So, should that ever be your ambition…) The field itself may be minuscule, but it's lovingly tended; in summer its lush green is flecked with the mauve and white of delphiniums, lobelia, iris and saxifrage – and not a weed in sight. Which is all the more surprising when you see that right next to the vineyard, along rue St-Vincent (follow it) is the Jardin Sauvage St-Vincent, which as a designated conservation area is encouraged to sprout as many weeds as it likes.

After this little pastoral detour, it's time to head back uphill and into the thick of the *butte*, so turn right after the Jardin St-Vincent and head up the rue du Mont-Cenis, with its broad stairs decorated by iron banisters and lamp-posts. It's another steep haul, but you'll be rewarded by an extravaganza of a view from the top. You'll also see, to your left as you face uphill, a huge white water tower. This is a famous Paris landmark, stunted sister to the nearby Sacré-Coeur. It's surrounded by tree-shaded benches where street-artists gather to sketch portraits, making it a good place to stop for a rest and a bit of voyeurism. Along the rue Cortot opposite is the Musée de Montmartre, a charming seventeenth-century manor that pays homage to Montmartre residents such as Modigliani, Toulouse-Lautrec and the composer Charpentier.

It starts getting very tat-encrusted again round here, and this time there's no avoiding it, so head left down the rue du Chevalier-de-la-Barre (you can buy a stupendously good baguette sandwich to take away at Au Petit Creux on the corner) and emerge into the shadow of the great, eye-popping edifice that is the Basilique du Sacré-Coeur.

Buskers, cameras, hawkers, street theatre, accordions, tour buses, beggars, ice-cream, pickpockets – all human life and its myriad leisure accoutrements are here at the foot of the great white whale that is the famous basilica. Like many cathedrals, the Moby Dick of the Paris skyline emerged in the wake of a bloody piece of history – in this case, Paris's capitulation to the Prussians, followed by the 1871 Paris anti-government uprising called the Paris Commune. The Archbishop of Paris ordered work to begin in 1877, as a flamboyant act of Catholic contrition to apologise for the 'crimes' of the left-wing locals. Hardly surprising, then, that it has always fired controversy. While many see the monument's whole moral foundation as reactionary, others also object to it on architectural grounds, saying its dazzling whiter-than-whiteness renders it an excruciating eyesore. Infuriatingly for them, the stone of the basilica secretes calcium when it rains, enabling it to bleach itself automatically. (The same process also means that it is also very slowly dissolving, so there's hope for the building's critics in the long term.) 'A monstrous efflorescence' was how Emile Zola described its bulbous artichoke domes – which makes you shudder to think what he might have made of his own tombstone back at the cemetery. Personally, I've always been fond of the Sacré-Coeur's extravagant wedding-cake exterior – perhaps because wedding cakes themselves are such a thrilling gastronomic folly. But just as there is a stodgy downside to wedding cake, there's a stodgy downside to the basilica, too. Inside its massive portals, the grandiosity of the Archbishop's scheme is reflected in a gloomy, cavernous interior that holds you in its sombre thrall, but doesn't have the dizzy chutzpah of the icing. It is probably the perfect place, however, to light a candle and cleanse your soul after the profanity of Pigalle, should the need grip you. And to prepare you for the ordeal that is to come: the big climb up to the Dome.

Because yes, you can even be the plastic bride or groom on the top!

Some people will tell you it isn't worth climbing up the Sacré-Coeur, 'because you can see everything from the bottom'. But take my word for it that they are lying to you; whenever I have questioned such

The huge white wedding cake of the **Sacré-Coeur** *dominates the Paris skyline – climb up and look down on the cityscape.*

people – often locals – they've ended up admitting, shame-facedly, that they've never actually done it. Of course they haven't! But two words of warning, before you buy your 15-franc ticket at the small side entrance: don't attempt to go up if you are, er, 'chunky'. And similarly, if you find yourself in the queue behind a fattie, delay your start, because the spiral staircase to the top is punishingly narrow and mind-bogglingly long, and the last thing you want is to get stuck behind someone who looks like they might just peg out with the strain and come hurtling down the stairs to squash you. Even for someone relatively fit, it's a long schlep – but just remember, as the stairs twist upward, shuttle you across a parapet and begin again, that it's excellent toning for the thigh muscles. And that the vertiginous view from the top will be worth it.

Because it really is. From up on the Dome, all of Paris lies spread before you, and you can finally begin to get a real sense of the scale of the capital. What's more – and this is the real advantage of being at this height – you can actually see where the city ends, as the buildings give way to the green hills at the city's perimeter. What always strikes me is how beautiful Paris can be despite a notable absence of greenery at its centre. It really does appear, from up here, as though every square millimetre is built on. There are pay-telescopes all around the balcony of the Dome, and with them you can zoom in on any part of the city you like. But there are plenty of landmarks to see with the naked eye including, most obviously, the Tour Eiffel, the Arc de Triomphe, the Louvre, Notre-Dame and the massive, blocky rectangle of the Gare du Nord. When you've taken in the whole eyeful, descend the narrow staircase marked 'sortie' and you'll emerge – very dizzy – back in the basilica, where for 10F you can light a candle to give thanks for your safe arrival back on land.

Heading out of the front portals, climb down the broad flight of steps and get a wonderful view of the whole edifice of the Sacré-Coeur from square Willette – named impishly after the local artist who yelled 'Vive le diable!' at its inauguration.

We've had a bit of sex. We've had quite a lot of death. But so far, not a great deal of art – which is all wrong, because art is really what Montmartre is most famous for. To remedy this, begin your descent by heading past the funicular railway at the foot of the Sacré-Coeur and take the little passage called la Chappe, which consists of a flight of steps, then turn right into the quiet rue Gabrielle, and follow its curve. The shabby and unremarkable-looking No.49 – marked by a small plaque – is where Picasso had his first studio in Paris in 1900. From there, follow the path of the majestic painter into rue Ravignan, and find yourself in a sloping square, dappled with horse chestnut trees. This is place Emile-Goudeau, site of the famous Bâteau-Lavoir, the old piano factory where Picasso, Braque and Juan Gris invented Cubism. Although the original building no longer stands, the site itself still houses artists' studios. The stairs at the bottom of the square take you to the continuation of rue Ravignan; follow its right-hand pavement, pausing at the small flight of steps to look up and left, for your first sight of the final landmark of your walk, the peculiar church known to locals – for reasons that will become clear – as 'St-Jean-des-Briques'.

Head for this church (real name St-Jean-de-Montmartre) down rue des Abbesses, stopping to take in the full weirdness of its façade from the pretty, bustling place des Abbesses. When the church was finished in 1904 – well before the consecration of the Sacré-Coeur in 1919 – it must have looked like pure science fiction. As the first ever church to be constructed from reinforced concrete, it is an anti-symphony in man-made materials. Clinging to its brick façade there are cement sculptures, tile mosaics, and pillars and decorative balconies barnacled with glazed ceramic discs the dull sheen of which brings to mind the scales of a dinosaur. But it's a place that grows on you, and some prefer it to the pompous complacency of the Sacré-Coeur. Inside, it's stranger still; a rather doomy, theatrical atmosphere prevails in the brown cavern of the main hall, which is adorned with more ceramic studs, spiky iron chandeliers, and stained-glass windows, including one of the grimmest grim reapers I've ever met standing guard to the left of the organ above the door as you leave. Once again, in the midst of life we are in death!

Recover from that poignant thought by stepping out through the huge carved wooden doors, and into daylight, to find yourself facing the Abbesses Métro – one of the prettiest stations in Paris. Its art nouveau *joie de vivre* will put the spring back in your step for the final few paces of your walk, which ends by plonking you on a handy bench in the place des Abbesses close to a cluster of bars, cafés and brasseries.

From where another Paris beckons.

Eating & drinking

Au Lapin Agile
22 rue des Saules, 18th (01.46.06.85.87). **Shows** 9pmTue-Sun. **Admission** *show, one drink* 130F.

Au Petit Creux
8 rue du Mont-Cenis, 18th (01.46.06.39.61). **Open** 10.30am-11pm daily. Closed 29 Nov-24 Dec.

Corcoran's Irish Pub
110 boulevard de Clichy, 18th (01.42.23.00.30). **Open** 10am-2am daily.

Délice Lepic
14 rue Lepic, 18th (01.42.64.47.43). **Open** 10am-10pm daily.

La Maison Rose
2 rue de l'Abreuvoir, 18th (01.42.57.66.75). **Open** 10.30am-3.15pm, 6-11pm, Mon-Fri; 10.30am-11pm Sat, Sun.

MCM Café
92 boulevard de Clichy, 18th (01.42.64.39.22). **Bar** 9am-5am daily. **Concerts** 11pm Mon, Tue, Thur, Fri. The cable-music channel's flagship café.

Le Moulin de la Galette
83 rue Lepic, 18th (01.46.06.84.77). **Open** noon-3pm, 8pm-midnight, daily. French and Italian food, plus a charming courtyard garden.

Le Sancerre
35 rue des Abbesses, 18th (01.42.58.08.20). **Open** 7am-2am daily. A brash and busy café that attracts a young and bohemian crowd.

Le Trèfle
68 rue Lepic, 18th (01.42.54.44.11). **Open** noon-3pm, 7pm-12.30am, daily. Short but succulent menu of North African cuisine.

Churches

Sacré-Coeur
35 rue du Chevalier-de-la-Barre, 18th (01.53.41.89.00). **Open** *Crypt/dome Oct-Mar* 9am-6pm daily; *Apr-Sept* 9am-7pm daily. **Admission** *Crypt* 15F; *dome* 15F; *crypt/dome* 23F.

St-Jean-de-Montmartre
Open *winter* 8.30am-noon, 3-7.30pm, Mon-Sat; 8.30am-noon, 3-6pm, Sun; *summer* 8.30am-noon, 3-7.30pm Mon-Sat; 8.30am-noon, 4-7pm, Sun.

Museums

Musée de l'Erotisme
72 boulevard de Clichy, 18th (01.42.58.28.73). **Open** 10am-2am daily. **Admission** 40F; 30F concs.

Musée de Montmartre
12 rue Cortot, 18th (01.46.06.61.11). **Open** 11am-6pm Tue-Sun. **Admission** 25F; 20F concs.

Nightlife

Jardin d'Hiver
4 bis, cité Véron, 18th (01.42.55.74.40). **Open** *box office* 10am-1.30pm, 2.30-7pm, Mon-Fri.

Moulin Rouge
82 boulevard de Clichy, 18th (01.46.06.00.19). **Dinner** 7pm daily. **Shows** 9pm,11pm daily. **Admission** *with dinner* 750F, 790F, 880F; *with drink* 350F (at bar), 510F (9pm), 450F (11pm).

Parks

Cimetière de Montmartre
20 avenue Rachel, access by stairs from rue Caulaincourt, 18th (01.43.87.64.24). **Open** *summer* 9am-5.45pm daily; *winter* 9am-5.15pm daily.

Jardin Sauvage de St-Vincent
rue St-Vincent, 18th. **Open** *school term-time* 4-6pm Mon; *Apr-Oct* 2-6pm Sat.

Shopping

Têtes en l'Air
65 rue des Abbesses, 18th (01.46.06.71.19). **Open** 2-7pm Mon; 10.30am-7.30pm Tue-Sat. Closed Aug.

Walking for Godot

Nicholas Lezard

A personal pilgrimage in the footsteps of Samuel Beckett.

Start: Mº Denfert-Rochereau, 14th
Finish: allée des Cygnes, 15th
Time: 3-4 hours
Distance: 11km/7 miles
Getting there: lines 4, 6 or RER B to Mº Denfert-Rochereau
Getting back: RER Avenue du Président Kennedy/Maison de Radio-France (line C)
Note: this walk is equally suitable for committed Beckett fans and those seeking an introduction to his work. The allée des Cygnes, at the end of the walk, never closes, although it is probably wiser to walk it in daylight.

I am not particularly fond of literary walks. Once, because I was being paid to, I went on a Bloomsday Joyce Walk around Dublin – a depressingly middlebrow affair whose guide absolved anyone of the need to read, let alone begin to get the point of, Joyce's works, and which included at least one pub that Joyce never drank in but Brendan Behan had. We paid for our Guinnesses in fivers with Joyce's portrait on them; currency circulated by a state that had driven him into permanent, disgusted exile. The exercise gave off a faint smell of hypocrisy and literary bad faith, like the fine tang of urine in Leopold Bloom's breakfast kidneys.

A Beckett walk is another matter. His characters – those not wheelchair-, bed- or dustbin-bound – trudge with the weary, painful and circular inevitability of the damned.

And although you could do a Beckett walk in Dublin and environs, or London, or even Hamburg, a real Beckett walk would have to be in Paris; and while Paris is a city that is not exactly made for walking, it is one you always somehow end up doing a lot of walking in. And no one quite pretends to have read Beckett in the way they pretend to have read Joyce. You either have or haven't.

I also had personal reasons for leaping on this commission with gratitude: it was a chance to revisit my own past. I had arrived in Paris in 1981, aged almost 18, astonished by my first real taste of freedom from home and family, a copy of *Ulysses*, the Beckett trilogy (*Molloy*, *Malone Dies* and *The Unnamable*) and Deirdre Bair's recently published Beckett biography in my bag. From the biography I worked out the exact location of Beckett's current flat (he was, of course, still alive then, already my hero, and I young and foolish enough to think of Beckett's achievement as something, in theory at least, attainable, or worth aiming for). For days, or strictly speaking three days, I would skulk outside the nondescript modern block he lived in, whose glass front door gave me a tantalising, painful view of the letterbox in the hall with his name on it, wondering whether I should ring the bell and introduce myself. Of course, I knew, from both what was implicit in the work and explicit in the biography, that such an intrusion would be unforgivable and traumatic, if for different reasons, for both of us. I never did ring that bell – an accidental glimpse of him would have done – and I would be tormented for years afterwards by meeting people who had bumped into him on a Paris street, shaken his hand and talked with him, taken polite and respectful advantage of his unfailing decency. I only finally got round to pestering him after his death, which I learned about while waiting for a Paris Métro: a TV screen on the platform announced his ending, a sombre interruption in 1989's dreamlike cavalcade of tyrannical collapse in eastern Europe.

Shortly after his interment I went round to the Montparnasse cemetery he and his wife, Suzanne, are buried in, and stood, in mute and dutiful homage, at the stark grey, prone marble slab marked simply 'SAMUEL BECKETT', and next to his wife's name recording her death to be the same as his own. He had both courted and cheated death, and thought and written about it so much, that for a while it seemed as though the Creator ('the bastard! He doesn't exist!') had decided to play one last cruel joke on him by allowing him to live for ever. Of course not: that tombstone was the last absurd full stop, the death not only of the world's last indisputably great writer, but of my own hopes of speaking to him myself. His death put the seal on my own pretensions; for had I not, once, trudged around the same streets he had, as broke and hungry as he so often once was, read the same books he had? Did these forced coincidences not legitimise my own search for literary kudos? Of course they didn't – but that's what literary walks allow us to suppose. So I apologise for this sincerely, but only once: a Samuel Beckett walk will, for me if not for you, also be a Nicholas Lezard walk.

For me, Paris is now full of vacated spaces, flats where good friends once lived but don't any more, fleeing, or more accurately, regretfully packing up and then fucking off out of a city whose increasingly right-wing intolerance of the impoverished or the non-white had made it more and more tiresome to live in. Even in 1981, the sense of Paris as a place of sexual, artistic and alcoholic freedom was insultingly superior to London's; as soon as I got there I could see what all the fuss had been about, why writers from all over the world had made the place their home

'The last absurd full stop' – *Beckett's grave, and his wife's. He survived her by six months.*

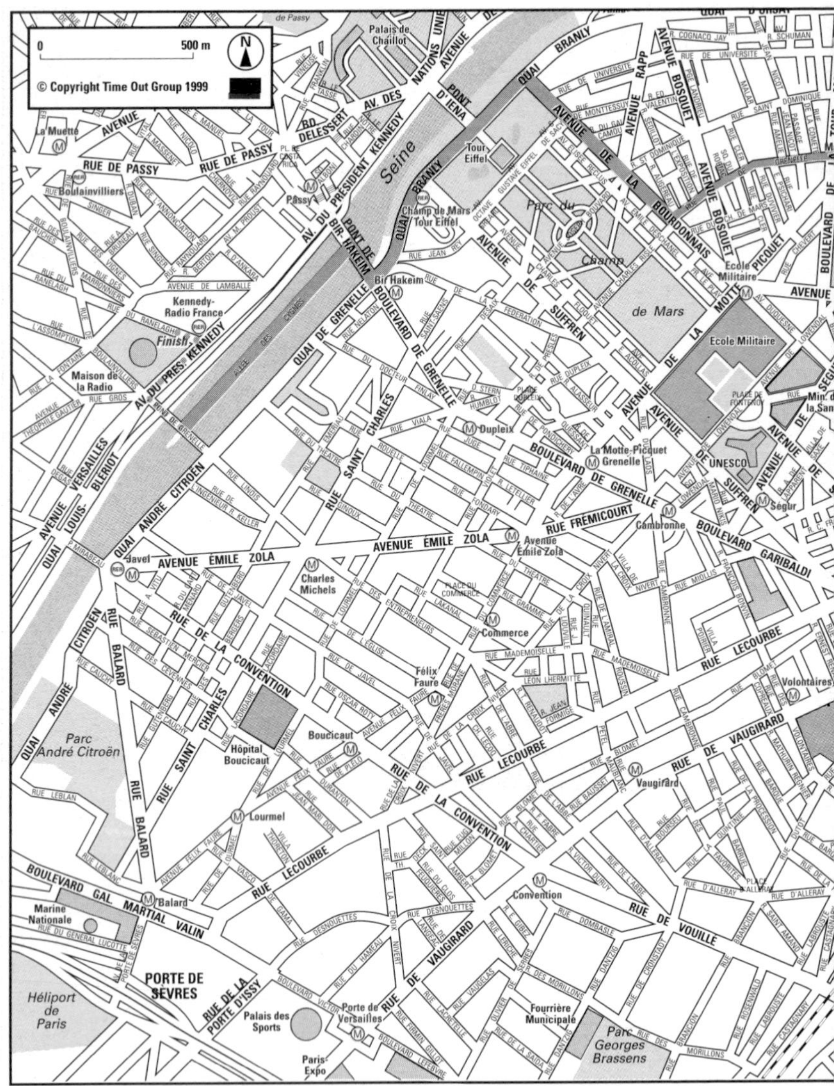

0
500 m
N
© Copyright Time Out Group 1999
Seine
Palais de Chaillot
Tour Eiffel
Parc du Champ de Mars
Ecole Militaire
UNESCO
Kennedy-Radio France
Finish
Maison de la Radio
Parc André Citroën
Hôpital Boucicaut
Héliport de Paris
PORTE DE SEVRES
Palais des Sports
Paris Expo
Fourrière Municipale
Parc Georges Brassens
Marine Nationale

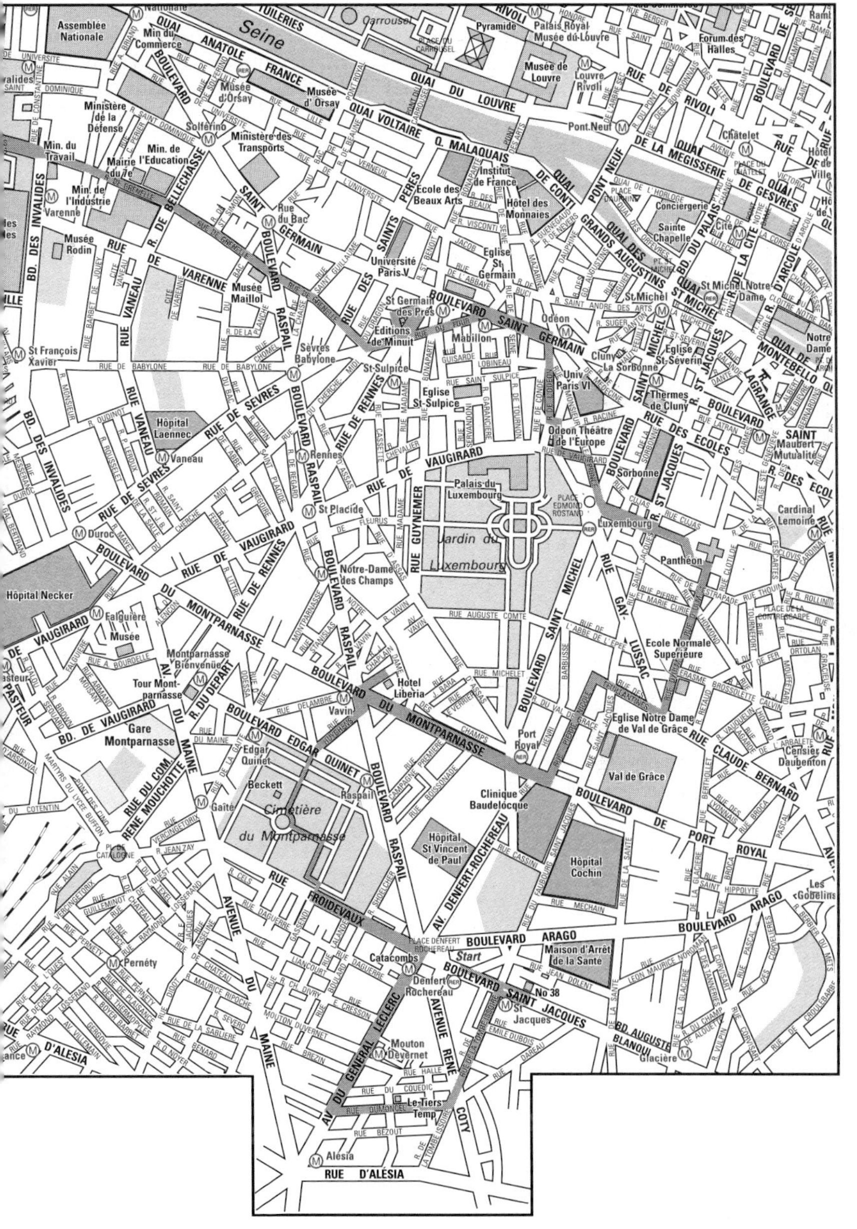
Seine
Assemblée Nationale
Tuileries
Carrousel
Pyramide
Palais Royal
Musée du Louvre
Forum des Halles
Quai Anatole France
Musée d'Orsay
Quai du Louvre
Louvre Rivoli
Musée de Louvre
Quai Voltaire
Ministère de la Défense
Solférino
Ministère des Transports
Pont Neuf
Châtelet
Min. du Travail
Min. de l'Education
Mairie du 7e
Min. de l'Industrie
Varenne
Q. Malaquais
Institut de France
Ecole des Beaux Arts
Hôtel des Monnaies
Quai de Conti
Quai de la Megisserie
Quai de Gesvres
Conciergerie
Sainte Chapelle
Cité
Rue du Bac
Boulevard Saint Germain
Université Paris V
Eglise St Germain
Grands Augustins
Quai St Michel
St Michel
Notre Dame
Musée Rodin
Rue de Varenne
Musée Maillol
St Germain des Prés
Editions de Minuit
Mabillon
Odeon
Cluny La Sorbonne
Eglise St-Severin
Quai de Montebello
St François Xavier
Sèvres Babylone
St-Sulpice
Eglise St-Sulpice
Univ. Paris VI
Thermes de Cluny
Rue des Ecoles
Maubert Mutualité
Hôpital Laennec
Vaneau
Rue de Sèvres
Rennes
Odeon Théâtre de l'Europe
Sorbonne
Rue de Vaugirard
Palais du Luxembourg
Place Edmond Rostand
Luxembourg
Cardinal Lemoine
St Placide
Duroc
Jardin du Luxembourg
Pantheon
Hôpital Necker
Notre-Dame des Champs
Boulevard du Montparnasse
Falguière
Musée
Ecole Normale Supérieure
Montparnasse Bienvenüe
Tour Montparnasse
Hotel Liberia
Vavin
Eglise Notre Dame de Val de Grâce
Gare Montparnasse
Boulevard Edgar Quinet
Edgar Quinet
Port Royal
Censier Daubenton
Val de Grâce
Beckett
Raspail
Clinique Baudelocque
Gaîté
Cimetière du Montparnasse
Hôpital St Vincent de Paul
Hôpital Cochin
Boulevard de Port Royal
Pl. de Catalogne
Rue Froidevaux
Les Gobelins
Boulevard Arago
Place Denfert Rochereau
Start
Maison d'Arrêt de la Sante
Catacombs
Denfert Rochereau
No 38
Pernéty
St Jacques
Boulevard Saint Jacques
Glacière
Mouton Duvernet
Avenue du Maine
Av. du General Leclerc
Avenue René Coty
Le Tiers Temps
Alésia
Rue d'Alésia

for a century or more. So when I went there to fill in the gaps in my memory and trace out the route of this walk, I was pleased to be able to see Jim Haynes, founder of *IT* and *Suck* (which once carried a photograph of Germaine Greer's anus), and a still-legendary host, publisher, facilitator, introducer and general charmer. He turned what would have been a melancholy and solitary day into one of intense amusement, not to mention information: over dinner he introduced me to John Calder, still mind-bogglingly hale, who has been Beckett's champion, friend and English-language prose publisher since *Malone Dies*.

Denfert-Rochereau Métro serves as the best way to get to Montparnasse cemetery and Beckett's last two homes. Having somehow negotiated place Denfert-Rochereau, follow east down the left-hand side of boulevard St-Jacques to No.38, the modern apartment block outside which I lurked in anticipation of seeing him. The letterboxes are still visible, but his name has long since gone.

Walking down boulevard St-Jacques I was astonished by the fallibility of my own memory: it may have been 18 years since I'd last stalked this street, but it had been at roughly the same time of year; so what were all these 100-year-old trees doing there, where none had been before? And that railway line down the middle of it? This won't bother you, happily, but reflect on not just the capriciousness of memory but the solipsism that it indicates; also the solipsism of both Beckett's writing and indeed of Paris, whose Haussmannian streets (designed in part so as to offer government soldiers the widest possible field of fire on potential mobs) have always seemed to me to be punishments, like the weals of a whip, inflicted on a surface softened by luxury, betrayal and hedonism. Paris features little in the interiority of Beckett's writings, except in his poetry, full of impenetrably private allusions; perhaps that's one of the reasons he moved and stayed there. Walking in Paris is a drag, I quickly rediscovered; you only walk there to get to a nice interior – a restaurant, a high-ceilinged flat, a bar. (Many bars.)

Follow the map to where he died, called with extraordinary frankness Le Tiers Temps, on rue Rémy-Dumoncel (not dissimilar to the place where Malone reminisces). They have just knocked down the room in which he spent his final days, in order to build an extension, but he is well remembered here. Nearby, the avenue René-Coty was where, during the war, he would deliver Resistance documents, at significant risk, to a man called Jimmy the Greek.

Return to place Denfert-Rochereau via avenue du Général-Leclerc, and continue under the merciful plane tree shade along the rue Froidevaux, turning right at the rue Emile-Richard. This takes you to the eastern entrance of the Cimetière du Montparnasse, where the guard can give you a map and will tell you, if you ask, where Beckett is buried (the 12th section, you'll work it out). I can't think of graveyards anywhere without thinking of Beckett's line in *First Love* ('Personally I have no bone to pick with graveyards'); I think of it here more than ever.

Along with literary walks, I have a mild bone to pick with literary and artistic graveyards, a kind of awkwardness; I've been to Père Lachaise and looked at Proust's grave, guiltily, for at the time I had hardly started *A la Recherche*...; mused over Oscar Wilde's grave – did he belong to the history of poetry or of publicity? – scribbled over with graffiti by followers of the band the Smiths; and sneered, snobbishly, at the morons paying inarticulate homage over the supposed grave of Jim Morrison. But what precisely did I think I was playing at when looking at these graves, or at Ezra Pound's, or Igor and Vera Stravinsky's in Venice? (He's not composing; he's decomposing.)

Eglise Val-de-Grâce, *the most Baroque of the city's churches; its monastic buildings are now in use as a hospital.*

IESV NASCENTI VIRGINIQ. MATRI

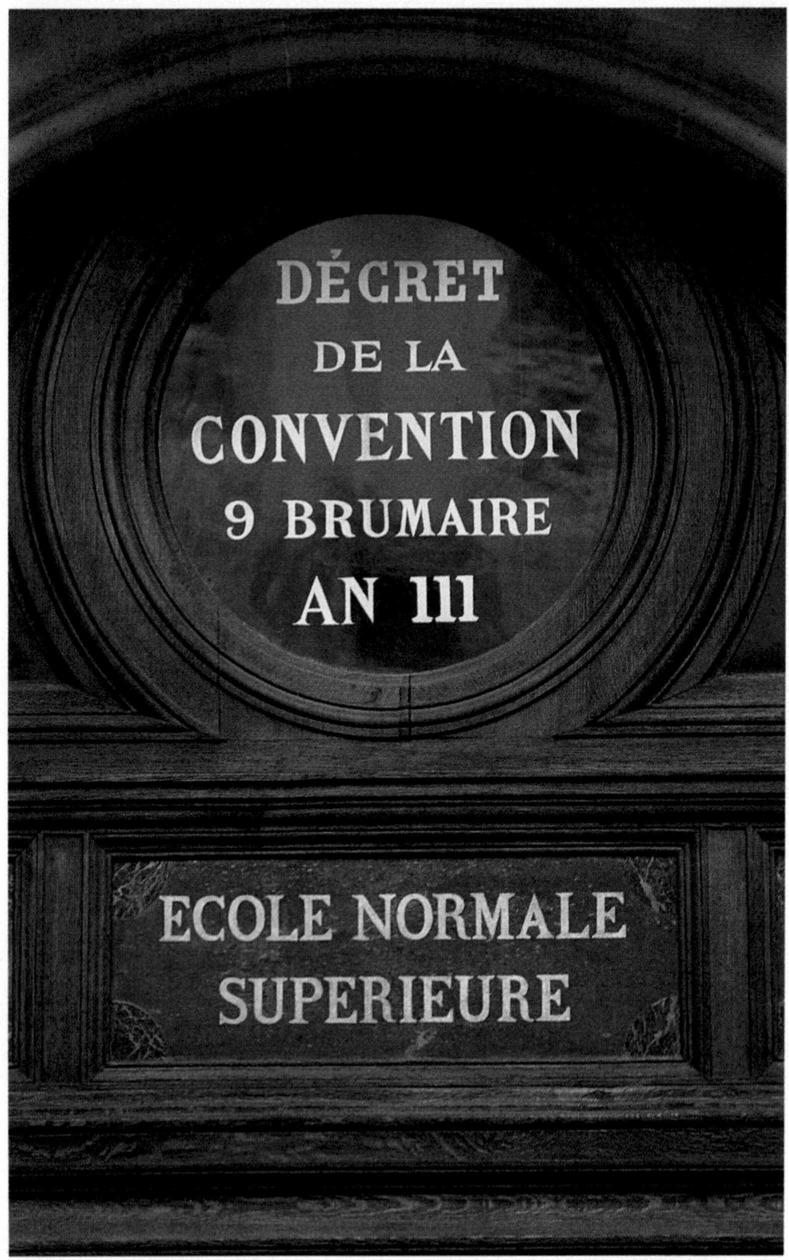

Beckett arrived in Paris aged 22 and got a job at the very superior **Ecole Normale Supérieure**.

Is this just high-class tourism, different only in degree to those who snap from the open-topped Routemasters in London or the Bateaux-Mouches along the Seine? The best that can be said for the awkward postures of respect you adopt by these sites is that they encourage humility.

Someone has placed some pebbles, in memory of Molloy's sucking stones it must be, on Beckett's tomb; that's nice, subtle; they look almost as if they're there by accident, and unlike graffiti can be removed by those with more austere standards. Think your own thoughts. Although as always it's better to think Beckett's.

That's enough depression. Best to get the last things out of the way first when you can; because now you can gird yourself for the road and go for a stroll through Beckett's beginnings in Paris, leaping back from his death at the age of 86 to his first (proper) arrival at the age of 22, when he became a teacher at the Ecole Normale Supérieure. This is important: the ENS took (and for all I know still takes) only about 28 students a year, the cream of the academic crop. Leave the north entrance of Montparnasse cemetery on the boulevard Edgar-Quinet. You've got a long walk ahead of you, so remember to get fully into the spirit of it by making sure you're in the same state as Beckett was for much of his time in Paris: broke, hungry, and in all probability hungover – although, like him, you won't have got up until noon at the earliest (students booked for earlier tutorials would open his door, see him asleep, and tiptoe out again). Your shoes are, in touchingly childish emulation of his hero Joyce, too tight, and you smoke French cigarettes almost continuously, which for some reason do not give you cancer the way Virginia cigarettes do – but they will get you with emphysema in your eighties. No drinking until five in the afternoon: after which point don't stop (white wine, mainly) for another fifteen hours. Seriously.

Turn down rue Huyghens to reach the boulevard du Montparnasse and catch sight of Le Dôme, Le Select, La Coupole and all the other big bars that really were popular places for intellectuals, even famous and intellectual ones – Beckett patronised them for ages. You can either go in now or save them up for later. (It's always amazed me that they let everyone in. Then again, their prices shoot you out again pretty quickly.) A quick left turn after Vavin Métro down the rue de la Grande-Chaumière gives you the site of the Hôtel Libéria, where Beckett lived just about cheaply enough until he found an apartment; it's now a Best Western (A la Villa des Artistes) and the cheapest room will set you back 690F a night. Regain the boulevard du Montparnasse, and after a quick browse at Librairie Tschann, which has a picture of Beckett accepting his honorary doctorate from Trinity, Dublin, turn left up the rue St-Jacques (where you can admire the unknowingly Impossibilist slogan of the Val-de-Grâce hospital – 'Iesu Nascenti Virginq. Matri'), right down the rue des Feuillantines, then left up the rue d'Ulm to the ENS. Beckett's room was on the first floor, to the right of the big central doorway to the building on your right. Don't the students look clever? (They used to shout pacifist slogans across the roofs to the military students in the Ecole Polytechnique: 'Sabre-wielders! Tigers thirsty for blood!' Let's face it, the French like any excuse to get out of a sticky situation [unlike Beckett, who hot-footed it from Ireland to France the moment war was declared], and these days paint idiotic anti-NATO slogans on the walls. And, on one white van on the rue d'Ulm, in English, 'Skateboarding is not a crime', which suddenly makes you think it is.)

Walk up the rue d'Ulm, keeping the towering Panthéon in sight, and then follow the map down to rue Corneille, where Beckett's favourite affordable restaurant, the Cochon de Lait, is now La Bastide-Odéon (three-course meal, 190F). You could, if you're dedicated enough,

Les Invalides, *seen from Pont Alexandre III – it's just a short hop to Joyce's former home.*

have carried down the rue de Vaugirard until you got to 6 rue des Favorites in the 15th, where Beckett lived both before, and to everyone's surprise including his own, after the war.

Whatever you do, you can walk down the rue de l'Odéon, site of the original Shakespeare and Co bookshop at No.12, the magnet for anglophone writers, and where Hemingway blew it, as far as Beckett was concerned, the only time they met, by saying that *Finnegans Wake* showed that Joyce had been finished by writing *Ulysses*.

Go left down boulevard St-Germain, then left up rue du Four, now a crazy, ongoing temple celebrating the intersection of Paris's fascination for clothes and money. Slightly further west on rue de Babylone, *En Attendant Godot* was premièred in January 1953 to an unprepared world at the now sadly departed Théâtre de Babylone. Then turn right at the rue Bernard-Palissy, still home to Les Editions de Minuit, Beckett's far-sighted and lucky French publisher. This leads to the corner of the tiny rue du Sabot, where according to Christopher Logue, 'a tall, gaunt figure in a raincoat handed in a manuscript in a black imitation leather binding, and left us almost without a word'. Logue, Paul Seaver, Alex Trocchi and others then spent half the night reading Beckett's *Watt* to each other, all but pissing themselves with laughter.

Cross over to the rue de Grenelle, one of the narrow but lengthy fissures running across Paris. Another long stretch lies ahead, along this quiet and picturesque street. Initially, it is all chic fashion shops, with artistic window displays and about three items for sale within. As you move westward, you are entering the political heartland of Paris – deserted on a Saturday late afternoon, it seems haunted by the memory of the Occupation; one can give oneself a nasty shock by imagining the swastika fluttering from the roof of the Mairie. The seventeenth- and eighteenth-century *hôtels particuliers* that line this street were once the homes of the aristocracy – now they house government ministries and embassies. Pass in front of the imposing Invalides, built as a nursing home for war veterans by Louis XIV, and where Napoléon now rests. Just before the

'I could not have gone through the awful wretched mess of life without having left a stain upon the silence.'

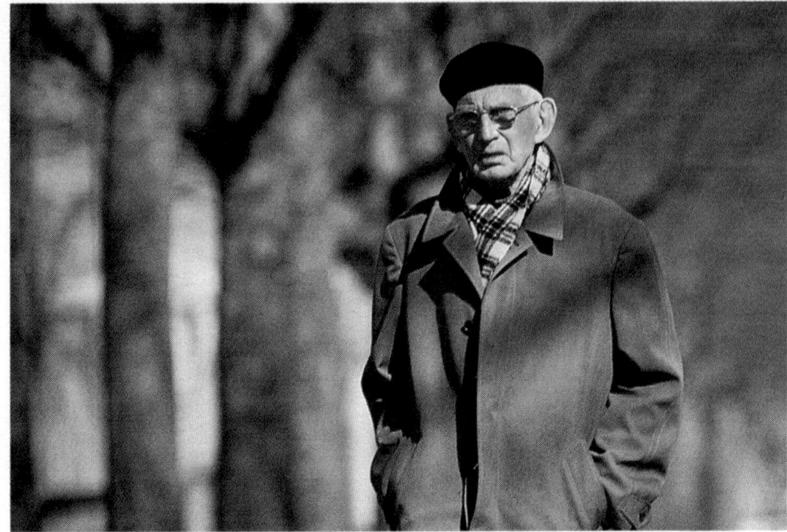

Samuel Beckett *as remembered by Christopher Logue – 'a tall, gaunt figure in a raincoat'.*

avenue Bosquet, turn right into the square de Robiac, as Beckett would have done when visiting Joyce at his apartment there (no plaque, number unknown) to help read texts out to the near-blind master as he composed *Work in Progress*, which became *Finnegans Wake*. The pair would then often – until Joyce's daughter, Lucia, enamoured of Beckett but quickly going mad, caused a break that was almost irreparable – walk up to the quai Branly before pacing the allée des Cygnes on the river in companionable silence. (I went via the avenue de la Bourdonnais, because that was where I lived when I first went to Paris, in a seventh-floor *chambre de bonne* at No.38 – the same number as Beckett's address!)

That, really, should do it. It did it for me; and I hadn't even visited Nancy Cunard's offices in the rue Guénégaud in the 6th arrondissement, where Beckett delivered his poem *Whoroscope* and bought himself, with the prize it won, enough funds to keep himself abroad for another few months in 1930; or the Hôpital Broussais, where he recovered after being stabbed by a pimp in 1937. (He never pressed charges; the pimp was incarcerated in the Prison de la Santé, the same prison Beckett's flat overlooked in the boulevard St-Jacques.) Nor did I take the Métro to Cardinal-Lemoine and hurl myself down the narrow *piste* of the rue Mouffetard, trying to trace the original for the bar he mentions in his poem *Sanies II* ('there was a happy land/the American Bar/in rue Mouffetard/there were red eggs there/I have a dirty I say henorrhoids/ coming from the bath'); but by this stage I was wild with literary cadences and cheap white wine.

You could rest by the Seine in silent contemplation, or make the long trek back to the Cimetière du Montparnasse. Either way, you are in the company of the dead.

Eating & drinking

La Bastide-Odéon

7 rue de Corneille, 6th (01.43.26.03.65). **Open** 12.30-2pm, 7.30-10.30pm, Tue-Sat. Closed three weeks in Aug. Contemporary Provençal cuisine.

La Closerie des Lilas

171 boulevard du Montparnasse, 6th (01.40.51.34.50). **Open** 11.30am-1am daily. Restored to its former glory, this institution gives especially good value in the brasserie rather than the restaurant. Get a 'Hemingway' cocktail here.

La Coupole

102 boulevard du Montparnasse, 14th (01.43.20.14.20). **Open** 7.30am-2am daily. Legendary Art Deco brasserie; reliable French fare.

Le Dôme

108 boulevard du Montparnasse, 14th (01.43.35.25.81). **Open** noon-2.45pm, 7pm-12.30am, daily. Closed Mon and Sun in Aug. Legendary Montparnasse fish house, also an upmarket café-bar.

Le Select

99 boulevard du Montparnasse, 6th (01.42.22.65.27). **Open** 7am-3am Mon-Thur, Sun; 7am-4am Fri, Sat. Hot food served 11am-closing time. Large, grand and historic self-styled 'American bar'.

Accommodation

A la Villa des Artistes

9 rue de la Grande-Chaumière, 6th (01.43.26.60.86).

Literature

En Attendant Godot Samuel Beckett
First Love Samuel Beckett
Malone Dies Samuel Beckett
Molloy Samuel Beckett
Unnamable Samuel Beckett
Whoroscope Samuel Beckett
Sanies II Samuel Beckett
Samuel Beckett, A Biography Deirdre Bair

Others

Cimetière du Montparnasse

3 boulevard Edgar-Quinet, 14th (01.44.10.86.50). **Open** *16 Mar-5 Nov* 9am-6pm daily; *6 Nov-15 Mar* 9am-5.30pm daily.

Ecole Normale Supérieure

45 rue d'Ulm, 5th (01.44.32.30.25).

Eglise du Val-de-Grâce

place Alphonse-Laveran, 5th (01.40.51.47.28).

Les Editions de Minuit

7 rue Bernard-Palissy, 6th (01.44.39.39.20).

Hôpital Broussais

96 rue Didot, 14th (01.43.95.95.95).

Librairie Tschann

125 boulevard du Montparnasse, 6th (01.43.35.42.05). **Open** 11am-8pm Mon; 10am-8pm Tue-Sun.

Le Panthéon

place du Panthéon, 5th (01.44.32.18.00). **Open** *Apr-Sept* 9.30am-6.30pm daily; *Oct-Mar* 10am-5.30pm daily. **Admission** 35F; 23F 12-25s; free under-12s.

Prison de la Santé

42 rue de la Santé, 14th (01.45.87.60.60).

Le Tiers Temps

26 rue Rémy-Dumoncel, 14th (01.40.64.18.20).

Beckett would pace the **allée des Cygnes** *in companionable silence with James Joyce.*

To she who is absent

Linda Lê

Down certain half-deserted streets in search of a lost love.

Start: rue de l'Echaudé, 6th
Finish: place St-Sulpice, 6th
Time: 2-3 hours
Distance: 6km/3.5 miles
Getting there: line 10 to Mº Mabillon
Getting back: Mº St-Sulpice (line 4)
Note: Louvre closed on Tuesdays.

There are streets whose names have the ring of fate, but a sort of bargain-basement fate, hastily sketched by the cruel pen of some caricaturist. The rue de l'Echaudé is one of those streets. If Hell were in the form of a city, you would enter it by a street with a name like this.

Echaudé. Burnt. Scalded. Taught a lesson. We always started our walks in this street, because it was here that I first met you. It's a narrow street that has its source in the boulevard St-Germain and flows into the rue de Seine. I remember seeing, one morning, the outline of a man, drawn in chalk. On the ground a wine bottle still lay, empty. No doubt a *clochard* had died in the night and been taken away. Homeless people abound in the streets around the rue de Buci crossroads. Some sleep off their drink in the doorways and others beg at the portals of the post office, which are impossible to pass without leaving an offering in the hands of some Charon, often flanked by a

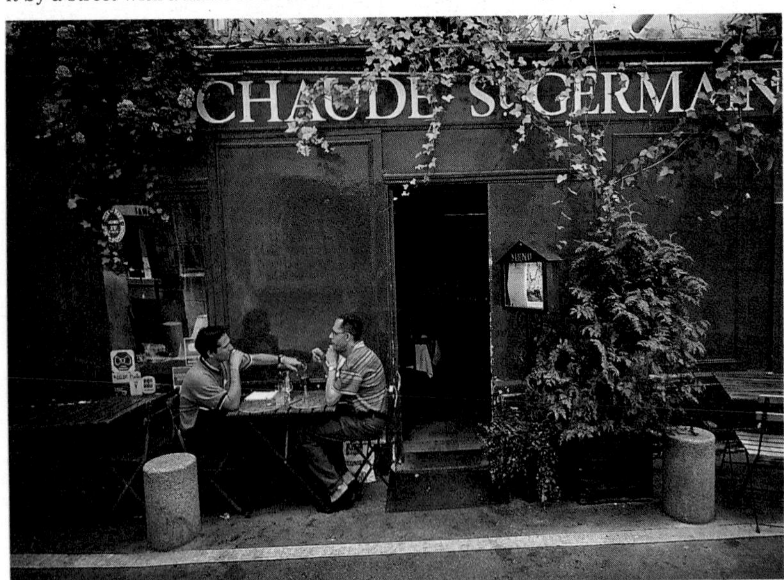

L'Echaudé St-Germain – *a charming French restaurant on rue de l'Echaudé, gateway to Hell.*

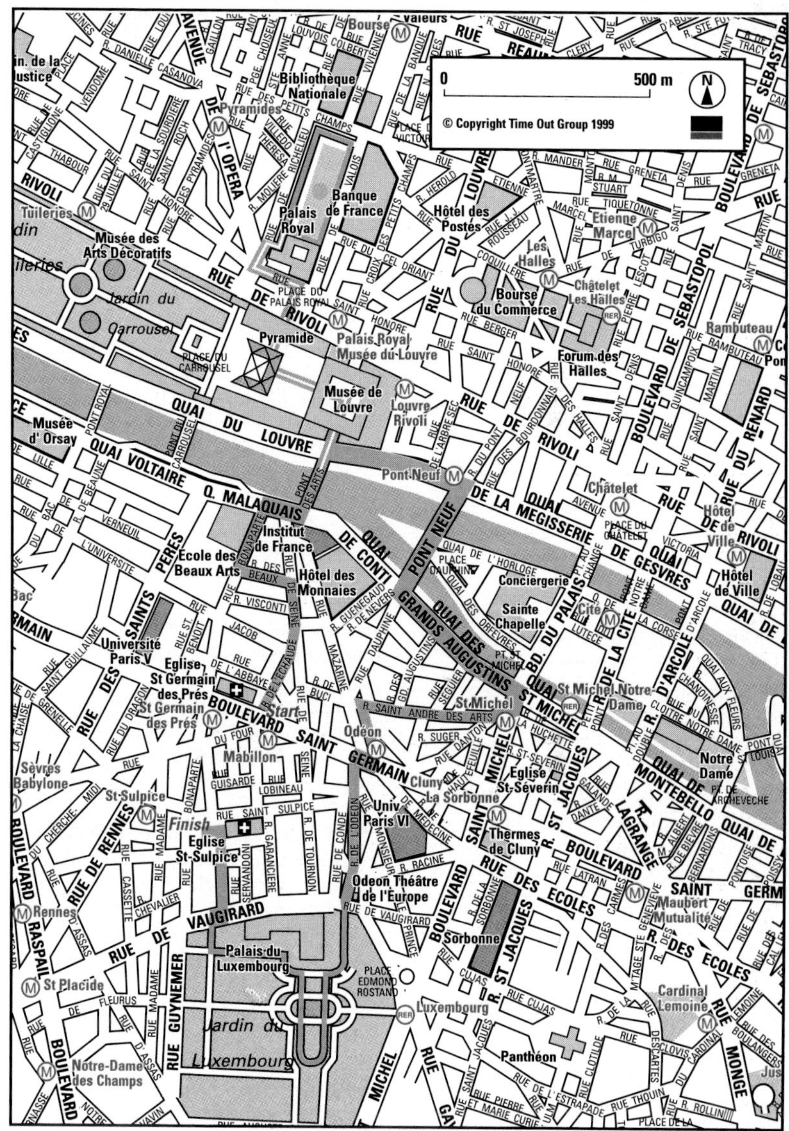

growling, threatening black mastiff. The rue de l'Echaudé, dark, deserted, in the middle of a neighbourhood teeming with crowds, is like a lame rhyme in the middle of a tumultuous poem. There is a sleepy bookshop there, called L'Or du temps, where the Surrealists still cast a long shadow. It was under this sign that I met you. I was looking for André Breton's *Entretiens*; you had just found, under a pile of sleeping books, an old edition of *L'Amour fou*. Bookshops function as churches once did: they encourage *amours*, love at first sight, secret meetings. Affinities call out to each other, correspondences are forged, a mystical understanding springs up between two beings who, a few minutes earlier, knew nothing of one another. You were wearing a black dress, your dark hair cascading down the small of your back. Words were superfluous: the book that you had bought, now grasped tightly against you, and our looks, timid but burning, revealed the birth of a passion. As irony would have it, it was born in this ill-named street, or so I thought then: now that you have left me, I think, each time I venture there, that nothing could better describe my sorry state. I am like a scalded cat, trailing its *nostalgie*.

The end of the rue de l'Echaudé leads into the rue de Seine, with its art galleries and the café La Palette, adorned with gilded youths; it's like turning from a widow's dark gaze to a fiancée's smile. Rue de Seine is triumphant, basking proudly in its refinement, to which the canvases of painters, well-known or obscure, lend a bohemian air. It's the street of patronage, kindling dreams in students from the nearby Ecole des Beaux-Arts. Often, during our walks, we would leave this street very quickly, turning left into the rue des Beaux-Arts to visit the Galerie Claude Bernard, where we once admired the works of Cremonini, the delicate painter of seashores whom Louis Althusser speaks of in his *Lettres à Franca*. Further along the same pavement, we would always pause in front of the hotel where Oscar Wilde died in poverty and disgrace, he whose tomb we had sought out at Père Lachaise, a simple white monument topped with a sphinx. After a glance into the mysterious house, its walls all draped in black, that is home to the sumptuous Italian art magazine *FMR*, we would turn right, taking the rue Bonaparte up to the quais and crossing the Pont des Arts. Lovers had carved their names into the parapet. A flautist always played the same heart-rendingly melancholy tune. Some afternoons, a snake charmer would spread his gear on to the wooden planks and hypnotise passers-by with his seductive little number. Opposite the Pont des Arts is the opening to the Louvre's Cour Carrée where, in season, platforms are erected in preparation for the fashion shows. In the middle of the courtyard, facing away from the St-Germain l'Auxerrois church, you can see Pei's pyramid shining like an alchemist's diamond. When the weather is fine, a large crowd lounges around the fountains and pools that surround the pyramid, dipping bare feet in the water. The faces, tired from having seen so many masterpieces file by, blinded by the light after having bathed in the dark rooms where each painting, closed in upon its own mystery, regards the visitor with the suspicion of a priest who will not divulge his secret to just any novice, revel in the sunshine and forget that they ever sought to probe the secrets of creation.

One should, you always said, go to the Louvre to admire just one painting, Chardin's *La Raie*, Bosch's *Nef des fous* or Breughel's *Mendiants*. We would go, you and I, with that ecstatic air that characterises lovers in search of things like unto themselves, to contemplate, in the Galerie Sully, George de la Tour's *Madeleine à la veilleuse*. Her face so resembles yours that now, since you are no longer by my side, I cannot raise my eyes to look at it without a sharp distress shaking my whole body. I imagine you, like her, garment falling loosely open, in a bedroom to which I no longer have access, lost in meditations of which I am no longer the object. Quickly, I want to flee; I seek refuge in the gardens of the nearby Palais-Royal. But there again, your image pursues me. I remember that we would walk under the galleries, harking back to

IM Pei's glass pyramid at the ***Louvre*** *– it shines 'like an alchemist's diamond' and its fountains draw the crowds.*

'Quickly, I want to flee; I seek refuge in the gardens of the nearby **Palais-Royal**.'

those pages of Balzac where a young Milanese count, exiled in Paris, follows through these gardens a woman whose appearance betrays her endless misery, and he learns that she is the companion of Gambara, a mad genius of a composer who has no choice but to become a street musician.

We would circle around the garden and retrace our steps to go for a drink at the Café Nemours, which overlooks place Colette. I am there, today like yesterday, like every day for the past year, chasing your shadow and ruminating over my own defeat. A musician with a hurdy-gurdy comes by, singing *Paris est cruel…* Everything in Paris comes down to old songs. I recall that when you and I would walk together we often came across a troupe of buskers belting out *La vie en rose*. Paris was sweet when you were hanging on my arm, laughing, a little weary, humming songs that everyone knows down to the last refrain.

Leaving the Café Nemours, we would take the same route, but instead of crossing the Pont des Arts, we walked down the quais to the Pont Neuf, where we always imagined we could make out the figure of the blind girl straight out of Léos Carax's film *Les Amants du Pont Neuf* – as if out of our own dreams of *amour fou*.

I never go out for a walk without a book in my jacket pocket. But there is no greater pleasure for the *promeneur* than to come back from a long walk with a book discovered during his or her wanderings. Between the Pont Neuf and the Pont St-Michel, the *bouquinistes* on the quai des Grands-Augustins have the best selection of old books. You can find, among the faded postcards and dated fashion magazines, the Shanghai edition of Victor Segalen's *Stèles*, a cheap edition of Conrad's *Nostromo* or Musil's *Journals*. It was at the stall of one of these *bouquinistes*, who loll on their lounge chairs listening to the radio, that we had managed, one stormy day, to find the poems of TS Eliot. The leitmotif of *The*

'… instead of crossing the Pont des Arts, we walked down the quais to the **Pont Neuf**…' *with its inevitable lovers, as in the film.*

Love Song of J Alfred Prufrock, 'Do I dare disturb the universe?', became our password, the sacred phrase of our love, which we thought, like all lovers, would by its very existence change the world and ignite the fires of revolution. Nothing can compare to the feverish excitement that gripped us as we dug through that dusty mess in search of a book that had accompanied our childhood, enriched our dreams, passed from hand to hand before coming to hide here, sleeping its peaceful slumber under an outdated cover and seeming to defy, with stony insolence, the city's ceaseless noise and agitation.

Feverish, a bit giddy, we would leave aside the books and continue our walk towards rue St-André-des-Arts, which always reeked of cooking smells from the restaurants and snack stands that line the top of the street. Here, Paris looks like a polyphagic monster that swallows up everything, meats and sweets, Brittany crêpes and Italian sandwiches, Chinese dumplings and American junk food. This belly, however, harbours a parasite, an old cinema, the St-André-des-Arts, which shows Bergman films every summer. How many times did we watch, sitting in clapped-out old seats, *Cries and Whispers*? Leaving the dark cinema, we would reaccustom our eyes to the light in passage St-André, at the end of the street. It's a narrow passage, littered with the tables that the *salons de thé* place in front of their doors. You can sample teas from around the world, and dream of living in one of the quiet little buildings in the Cour de Rohan, tucked into this passage between the ocean of punters in the rue St-André-des-Arts and the tide of vehicles in the boulevard St-Germain. Singing the Cour de Rohan would require a prose-poem. It is like a precious medallion hung around the neck of the candid young girl that Paris can sometimes be. It is under its windows that Romeo, had he lived on our shores, would have surprised Juliet, and it seems that from these houses the *marquises* still emerge at five o'clock, faces veiled, their feet clad in seraphic slippers. But once outside the Cour de Rohan, they become inhabitants of the capital, bearing a fierce look on their faces and walking with a hurried gait. We, too, scurried along the boulevard St-Germain to flee the mayhem, walking slowly up the rue de l'Odéon toward the theatre where Pushkin's *Chevalier avare* was performed at the turn of the century, and where, the year you and I met, Isabelle Huppert acted in Shakespeare's *Measure for Measure*.

Before walking around the back of the theatre to reach the Jardin du Luxembourg, we always tarried in front of 21 rue de l'Odéon. Cioran, whose aphorisms had lit up my long nights, lived out his last years here, in a modest apartment whose only embellishment was a rosebush blooming on the balcony. Cioran's shadow still haunts the Luxembourg's walkways, and it was always in search of his footsteps that we passed the garden gates. Did he stop at the Médicis fountain, where lovers often arrange *rendez-vous*, as in the suavely perverse films of Eric Rohmer? Did he look out there, as we did, for the arrival of that young woman, glimpsed one day near the statue of Laure de Noves, who was wearing a sign on her back that proclaimed her search for a lost love? She had affixed a large photograph of the man and inscribed beneath it the message of her distress and her waiting. Did she find him? At the time, we both laughed at the sight of that disconsolate and forlorn woman. Today, I wander alone between the shady Fontaine des Médicis and the impassive *Laure de Noves*, and I am seized with speechless sympathy for the abandoned woman who broadcast her despair. And it is alone that I head towards the Vaugirard exit to enter the tiny street almost opposite the gate, the rue Férou, which Balzac called the most

Rue St-André-des-Arts – *'always reeked of cooking smells from the restaurants and snack stands that line the top of the street'.*

The **Jardin du Luxembourg***, a place of games-playing, haunting shadows and rendez-vous.*

sinister in Paris – to our great surprise, for we both loved this mysterious street, whose buildings were slated, a few years back, for demolition. The residents' protests prevailed against the speculators, and the old houses, with their blackened façades, still stand, untakable, along the pavement that leads to the bookshop L'Age d'Homme. It was there that you had discovered Adam Mickiewicz and his long poem *Pan Tadeusz*, written in a house in the rue de Seine.

It was in front of this bookshop that our walks ended. We left one another in the shadow of St-Sulpice, which for me has always resembled some kind of sea-monster washed up here, waiting for the hour of the last judgement to swallow up the city around it. I had been told that Servandoni, having built the church, found it so ugly that he threw himself from the top of one of the towers in despair. We pretended to believe that it was just a legend, and it pleased us to say our *adieus* at the foot of a monument weighed down by such an evil spell.

Standing in the middle of place St-Sulpice, I watched you walk away, your hair floating in the wind. Paris resembled you, enigmatic, unpredictable, sparing with her secrets. Paris saw our love die, watched the wreck that I became after your departure sink into a heavy numbness. But Paris still beckons to me: its streets, honourable or disreputable, flashy or dingy, humble or proud, fierce or cheerful, are all enchanting. Paris saves and protects. Today, a fresh breeze is sweeping the autumn leaves out of place St-Sulpice, and a mocking voice emanating from the very entrails of the city whispers to the *promeneur*, 'And life goes on.'

Translated by Karen Albrecht.

'We left one another in the shadow of **St-Sulpice***, which for me has always resembled some kind of sea-monster washed up here.'*

Eating & drinking

Allard

41 rue St-André-des-Arts, 6th (01.43.26.48.23). **Open** 12.30-2.30pm, 7.30-11.30pm, Mon-Sat. Closed three weeks in Aug. French bourgeois cooking in a low-ceilinged and traditional setting.

Les Bookinistes

53 quai des Grands-Augustins, 6th (01.43.25.45.94). **Open** noon-2.30pm, 7pm-midnight, Mon-Fri; 7pm-midnight Sat, Sun. Reliably good dishes in a popular local venue.

Buvette des Marionnettes

Jardin du Luxembourg, 6th. **Open** *Sept-May* 8.30am-6.30pm daily; *June-Aug* 8.30am-7.30pm daily.

Café-Bar Le Nemours

2 place Colette, 1st (01.42.61.34.14). **Open** 7am-1am Mon-Fri; 8am-1am Sat; 9am-9.30pm Sun. Decent *croques* and light snacks in an ideal setting.

A la Cour de Rohan

Cour Commerce-St-André, 59-61 rue St-André-des-Arts, 6th (01.43.25.79.67). **Open** noon-7.30pm daily.

Crêperie des Arts

27 rue St-André-des-Arts, 6th (01.43.26.15.68). **Open** noon-1am daily. A generous and original collection of crêpes, including some stunning desserts.

L'Echaudé St-Germain

21 rue de l'Echaudé, 6th (01.43.54.79.02). **Open** noon-2.30pm, 7-10.30pm, Tue-Thur, Sun; noon-2.30pm, 7-11pm, Fri, Sat. A quintessential French restaurant, although well known by the tourist trade.

Lapérouse

51 quai des Grands-Augustins, 6th (01.43.26.68.04). Open noon-2.30pm, 7-11pm Mon-Fri; 7-11pm Sat. Closed Aug. A charming and historic traditional French restaurant, which recently has become less reliable, but in the past has been excellent.

La Palette

43 rue de Seine, 6th (01.43.26.68.15). **Open** 8am-2am Mon-Sat. Closed three weeks in Aug. Simple hot dishes in a classic artists' café.

Restaurant La Catalogne

4-8 cour Commerce-St-André (access 130 boulevard St-Germain), 6th (01.55.42.16.19). **Open** noon-3pm, 7.30-10pm, Tue-Thur, Sun; noon-3pm, 7.30-10.30pm, Fri, Sat. Either smart Spanish fare upstairs, or a tapas bar downstairs.

Yvan sur Seine

26 quai du Louvre, 1st (01.42.36.49.52). **Open** noon-2.30pm, 8pm-1am, Tue-Fri; 8pm-1am Sat, Sun. Acceptable but uninspired cooking in a snug on the banks of the Seine.

Books

L'Âge d'Homme

5 rue Férou, 6th (01.55.42.79.79). **Open** 9am-6.30pm Mon-Thur; 9am-5.30pm Fri; noon-6pm Sat.

L'Or du temps

25 rue de l'Echaudé, 6th (01.43.25.66.66). **Open** 1-7.30pm Mon-Sat.

Churches & gardens

Eglise St-Sulpice

place St-Sulpice, 6th (01.46.33.21.78). **Open** 8am-7.30pm daily.

Jardin du Luxembourg

place Auguste-Comte, place Edmond-Rostand, rue de Vaugirard, 6th. **Open** *summer* 7.30am-9.30pm daily; *winter* 8am-5pm daily. *Children's Playground* 10am-dusk daily. **Admission** *children's playground* 14F children; 7.50F adults.

Jardins du Palais-Royal

main entrance to palace place du Palais-Royal, 1st. **Open** *Gardens only* dawn-dusk daily.

Entertainment

Odeon, Théâtre de l'Europe

1 place de l'Odéon, 6th (01.44.41.36.36). **Open** *box office* 11am-6.30pm Mon-Sat; *telephone bookings* 11am-7pm Mon-Sat (Sun when plays are on).

Le St-André-des-Arts

30 rue St-André-des-Arts, 6th (01.43.26.48.18). 12 rue Gît-le-Coeur, 6th (01.43.26.80.25).

Galleries

FMR

12 rue des Beaux-Arts, 6th (01.46.33.96.31). **Open** 10am-1pm, 2.30-7pm, Tue-Sat. Closed Aug.

Galerie Claude Bernard

7 & 9 rue des Beaux-Arts, 6th (01.43.26.97.07). **Open** 9.30am-12.30pm, 2.30-6.30pm, Tue-Sat.

Le Louvre

entrance through Pyramid, cour Napoléon, 1st (01.40.20.50.50/recorded information 01.40.20.51.51/advance booking 01.49.87.54.54). **Open** 9am-6pm Mon, Thur-Sun; 9am-9.45pm Wed; *temporary exhibitions, Medieval Louvre, bookshop* 10am-9.45pm Mon, Wed-Sun. **Admission** 45F (until 3pm); 26F (after 3pm and Sun) concs.

Information

L'Hôtel

13 rue des Beaux-Arts, 6th (01.44.41.99.00).

Green tracks

Jean-Daniel Brèque

Peace and quiet, a glimpse into the past and future of Parisian railways – and a very odd police station.

Start: place de la Bastille, *sortie* rue de Lyon, 12th
Finish: porte de Montempoivre on the edge of the Périphérique, or Musée des Arts d'Afrique et d'Océanie, 12th
Time: 1-2 hours
Distance: 3.5km/2 miles
Getting there: line 1 to Mº Bastille
Getting back: Mº Bel-Air (line 6) or Mº Porte Dorée (line 8)
Note: check seasonal opening times of Promenade Plantée (see listings). There are not that many decent places to eat or drink en route.

Once upon a time, there was a railway station on place de la Bastille, and the line that started there took passengers far into the eastern suburbs, to Nogent-sur-Marne, Joinville-le-Pont, the banks of the Marne and the famous *guinguettes* (small restaurants with music and dancing) where Casque d'Or used to drive men wild. The line was closed in 1969 and its tracks outside Paris taken over by the RER, the new network of suburban trains. But no one seemed to know what to do with the tracks inside Paris. Left unattended, they fell slowly into decay. In 1986, the city bought the tracks and decided to transform them into a '*Promenade Plantée*'. The current mayor, Jean Tiberi, whose popularity is on the decline, has been cultivating the green vote for some time now.

This walk, as you'll see, is far from homogeneous. Much of it is closed at night (see listings for specific opening times, a typical example of French bureaucracy that would give Franz Kafka nightmares), and much of it is strictly forbidden to bikers, rollerskaters, skateboarders and dogs (though I have seen some feral cats). The best way to do it is, I think, as I've outlined it, but entrances are numerous (see map), and you can stop at almost any point to enjoy other sights.

Start by walking alongside the Opéra Bastille, but watch out: the walls of the building are bound in huge nets, meant to preserve you from bodily harm as some of the tiles occasionally fall off. So don't walk too close. Go to rue de Lyon, then turn left into avenue Daumesnil. Last time I was there, the hardhats were still at work, but they should be finished by the time you get there.

You are probably looking at the shops that have opened under the elevated walk. The place has been given the pompous name of Viaduc des Arts (Arts Viaduct), and some of the shops are pretentious and expensive, although still worth a look. According to a recent guidebook, there are 56 of them, mostly dealing in arts and crafts. Further along, you'll find a huge computer store, which has also spawned a lot of smaller shops. It's an uneasy mix at best, and not the last one we'll witness.

Walk along the avenue Daumesnil until you come to avenue Ledru-Rollin. On your left is a stairway – go up the stairs and you are there.

This was once an elevated railway, level with the second or third floor of the surrounding buildings. Later, as you leave

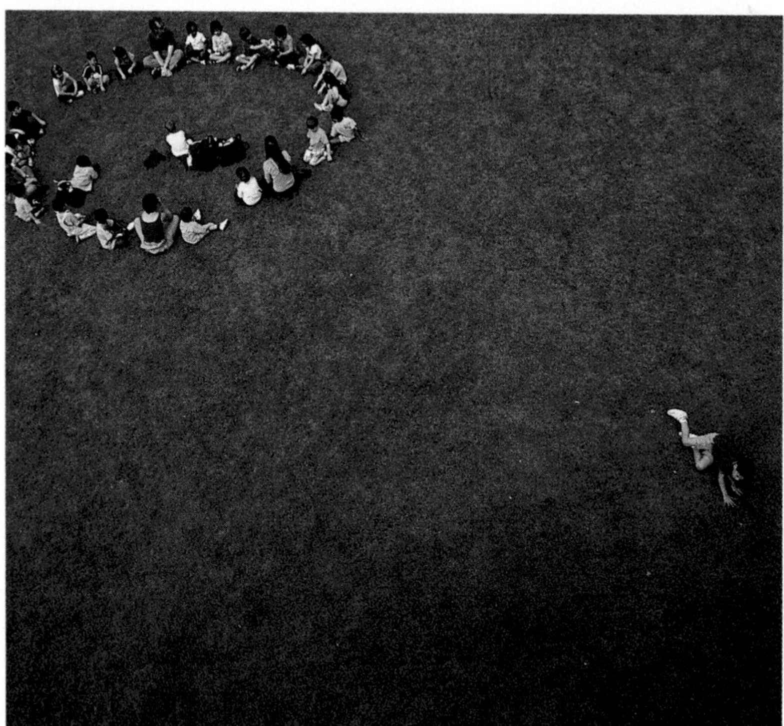

An all-round education on the circular lawn in the **Jardin de Reuilly** *– and other spin-offs.*

the Jardin de Reuilly, you'll go to ground level, and below ground level after that.

Take a look around and you'll notice another uneasy mix. On the south side, huge, solid buildings dating back to the end of the nineteenth century – down-to-earth bourgeois architecture, the product of quiet wealth, with some nice art nouveau touches from time to time. There are also numerous trees, which conceal some of the buildings during spring and summer. (You'll see later that this can be a blessing.) On the north side, a cityscape of backyards, rear entrances, roofs and chimneys. You are afforded the occasional view into private flats. Don't be too nosy: people live here. You'll also notice skylights along the sides, with views down into the shops.

After you've taken in the surroundings, have a close look at the Promenade itself. This is akin to an elongated walkway in a park. In spring (the best time), there are trees, bushes and flowers everywhere, from rose bushes to cherry trees, with water features and lots of benches. The fact is, most of the local people use this as they would a park. I overheard a lady telling her friend that she used to come here everyday at noon during spring and summer. You'll find many elderly people, young mothers and students colonising the benches, pushing prams or walking hand in hand, enjoying the sunshine and the scent of the flowers. Imagine this: you are a tourist walking in Paris, and there are no queues, no flashing cameras, no monuments. Nothing but quiet people leading quiet lives. I'm almost ashamed to reveal the secret.

An aside here: one day, I noticed two men talking quietly behind a tall bush. Probably gardeners, as this is not the place for illicit meetings – it's too open.

Go east and keep looking around you. Trees permitting, you can admire the beautiful building at 30 avenue Daumesnil, then, a bit further on, still on the south side, the Gare de Lyon. An interesting urban perspective, with wedge-shaped buildings like ships sailing on the asphalt.

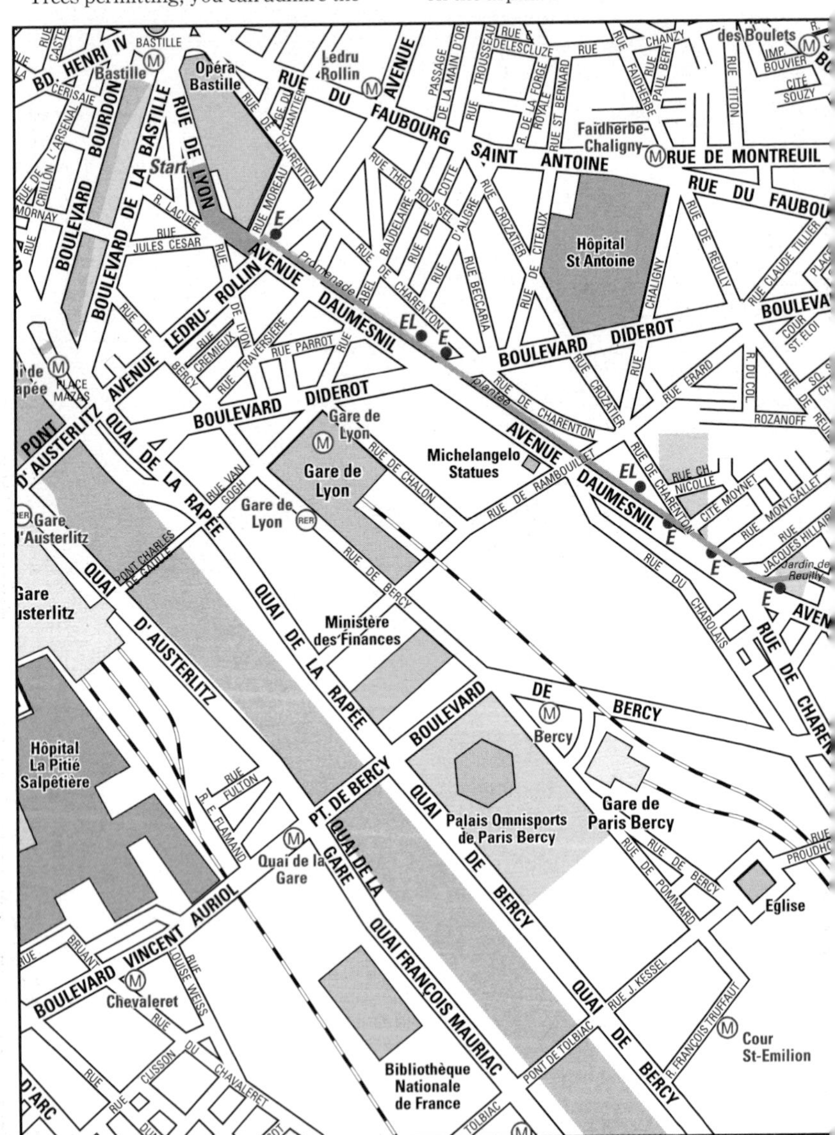

Above rue Hector Malot, there's another entrance, this one with a lift, which means that wheelchair users can access the walk. Take a look at the north side and gape, as I did, at the sinister-looking chimneys; do they make you think of an organ, as they did me? Or maybe rusted rockets…

And now we come to what is probably the highlight of the walk – unless you are faint-hearted. Go past the two rectangular ponds and it's on the south side. If the trees are in full bloom and obscure the view, you won't believe your eyes at first. Yes, it's Michelangelo's *Dying Slave*, agonising a dozen times over on a building's façade. Each of these cyclopean statues is graced with a triangular hole in its chest. You guess that there is supposed to be symbolic or allegorical meaning in this, and the mind reels. Michelangelo's work is also known as the *Dying Captive*, and this ludicrous building is a police station. I'm not making this up.

The first time I witnessed this eyesore, as I was driving along avenue Daumesnil,

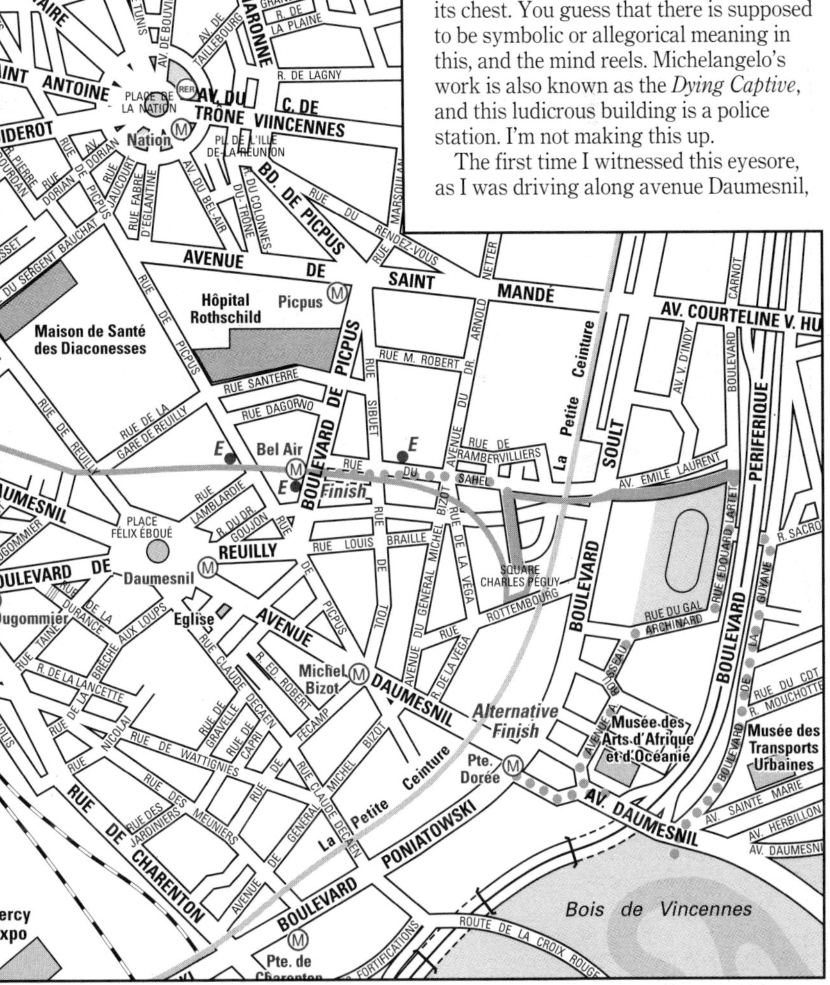

I was seized by a sudden dread. The feeling remains to this day. At some point I'll write a horror story about it.

The walk becomes a short corridor between two buildings, and you soon come across another entrance with a lift. The last time I was at this spot, a policeman was lecturing a skater and a man carrying a football. The policeman appeared in a bad mood; you would be, too, if you had to work where he does. Incidentally, the crime is signed: on the façade of the police station is a plaque that reads cryptically:

SAGI
M YUNEZ
YANOWSKI
1991

I can't keep this building from invading my thoughts. What is its meaning? Is it a case of subsidised art run riot? A crypto-gay statement (given his expression, Michelangelo's bodybuilder-slave could well be dying of pleasure)? A leftover prop from a Batman movie? Some mysteries are best left unsolved. Onward.

As you emerge from the corridor, you come to the end of part one of the walk. A small expanse of street – no cars, though – a sundial, and you are entering the Jardin de Reuilly, a pleasant, spacious park, complete with tennis court, kids' playground, fountain and circular lawn; on my last visit, a sunny day, sunbathers were out in force. You can either cross the bridge that goes over it, or walk down to the street and enter the park by one of several side entrances. Both routes eventually lead to the exit.

Caution, street ahead. Along allée Vivaldi you find restaurants and shops, a bakery, a shop selling Corsican cheeses. On the south side, what was once Reuilly railway station, an old-fashioned office building, totally without character. Now you come to your first tunnel, and starting here is an official bike path that runs alongside the walk.

At the end of the tunnel, signs inform you that walkers must take the left path (north) and bikers the path on the right (south). Good news for dog-fanciers: Fido is welcome here, as long as you have him on a lead. From time to time, you'll see sandboxes beside the path. Sadly, however, most of the dogs don't seem to grasp their meaning. Mind your step.

Part two of the walk might seem at first sight somewhat less interesting than part one. It's no longer elevated, more often than not below ground level, and since rollerskates and skateboards are permitted, tends to be busier. Be careful. At best, skaters may only bump into you; the odd one is also after your purse.

A nice touch is a small topiary maze, intended for children. A stairway leads nowhere other than to an observation point. That wailing noise you can hear is children crying once they realise they're lost. You might notice a sudden move in the bushes; relax, it's only a feral cat.

Go through two tunnels, and suddenly, you are in a street again – rue du Sahel. Now, pay attention, please. In front of you are three paths. The one on the extreme left (north side) is for bikers; the one on the centre left is for walkers; the one on the right leads to square Charles-Péguy, a little park. Take the one on the right.

This is a neighbourhood park, nice in its way but of little interest in itself, except to the people living nearby, who sit in the sun and watch the children at play. But, from here, you can catch a glimpse of another railway, which – hopefully – will become another *Promenade Plantée*.

The Petite Ceinture was once a circular line that went right around Paris. Passenger traffic stopped in 1934, after which the SNCF used it only for freight services. When I was living in the 20th arrondissement, there was a station behind my building, and I could hear train whistles blowing – mostly at night,

Michelangelo's **Dying Captive** *on the avenue Daumesnil police station endures a heartless death over and over again.*

unfortunately. Further north, in rue de Bagnolet, another station has been converted into a trendy bar, La Flèche d'Or (The Golden Arrow), with post-apocalyptic interior decoration.

Since the Petite Ceinture fell into disuse, two different groups have been lobbying to revive it. The first group wanted to get the trains running again, the second favoured another *Promenade Plantée*. It seems the latter option is going to win, mostly because of the impracticality of the first plan, the SNCF having sold parcels of land here and there.

Meanwhile, if you feel adventurous, you can jump over the fence and walk the wild tracks. I wouldn't recommend it, though. Firstly, it's illegal, and you may well bump into a policeman. Secondly, you might get a shock. There's little chance you'll be run over by a train, but there is still life on the Petite Ceinture. In the tunnel under the Hôpital Broussais, in the south-west of Paris, thrives what is probably the biggest bat colony in France.

It's thanks to the Petite Ceinture that, north of here, in rue de Lagny, we find the only level crossing in Paris – no longer active, of course.

On Saturday, 12 June 1999, an open day was held on the eastern part of the Petite Ceinture, with a train ride and picnics. There may be others in the months to come; during your stay in Paris, watch the papers.

Back to our walk. You can either retrace your steps or go to rue du Sahel by taking rue Marie-Laurencin by the 'amphitheatre'. At the end of the road, take a right along the hedged path on rue du Sahel to rejoin the *Promenade Plantée*. The walk goes under two bridges and becomes a small park. First, you think to yourself, 'This is very quiet,' but then you hear a murmur; we are nearing the boulevard Périphérique, the Paris ring road, and it's always busy.

Still, enjoy the surroundings. It's a pleasant, shady place – a bit wet, though – and the birdsong will soon make you forget the city around you. In a way, this place is like a microcosm of the whole walk: you are well below ground level here, and it's easy to forget you are in Paris. A closed, green world, an oasis of quiet. The same thing is happening all over the city: thanks to the rise of the greens, and to the mayor's pandering to them, a number of neglected places, rather than turning into high rises, car parks or malls, are being converted into small pockets of nature. Parisians and tourists alike come to enjoy them, as they do other more established parks such as the parc Monceau or the Buttes Chaumont. You could argue that these two parks, and others like them, are of historical interest, whereas this is not the case for our *Promenade Plantée*. But people come here neither because they want to make a stand for ecology, nor because it's a place where they can be seen. They come here because they enjoy it.

I hope you have enjoyed it, too.

You've come to the end of the line, so to speak, though you could extend your walk in order to drag weary limbs around the Musée des Arts d'Afrique et d'Océanie. It's a glorious building, its carved façade a jungle of detail, and a treasure trove of artefacts brought from afar. The room devoted to Aboriginal art is certainly worth a visit, as is the aquarium. Or you could pass under the Périphérique and head for the Bois de Vincennes. In the near future, the *Promenade* will be extended to take you there. A lot of trees will have to be planted to make this place secluded, and they won't be able to smother the noise from the Périphérique. Stick to the inside of Paris.

To return, go up to street level, in rue du Sahel, and walk to Bel-Air Métro.

And mind the cars. I'm sure you'll have forgotten there are cars in Paris.

The **Promenade Plantée** *is a long and narrow path lined with bushes and shrubs where the locals get away from it all.*

MUSEE
DES ARTS
D'AFRIQUE ET D'OCEANIE

The murmur of the **Périphérique** *grows to thunder as you approach the great ringroad.*

Thanks to Agnès Giard, Laurent Melikian and Christophe Mielle.

Eating & drinking

Le Janissaire

22 allée Vivaldi, 12th (01.43.40.37.37). **Open** noon-2.30pm, 7-11.30pm, Tue-Sun. Turkish cuisine.

La Mie de Pain

32 allée Vivaldi, 12th (01.43.40.50.50). **Open** 7am-8pm daily. Neighbourhood bakery: snack food, hot and cold drinks.

Au Père Tranquille

75 avenue Daumesnil, 12th (01.43.43.64.58). **Open** 7am-2am daily. An ideal pitstop for beer and fine, simple dishes.

Raimo

59-61 boulevard de Reuilly, 12th (01.43.43.70.17). **Open** 9.30am-midnight Tue-Sun. Closed Feb. Ice-creams and sorbets.

Le Viaduc Café

43 avenue Daumesnil (01.44.74.70.70). **Open** 9am-4am daily. Jazz brunch on Sunday 1-4pm. This bistro is a good place for a sophisticated *apéritif* or night cap.

Behind the detailed façade of the **Musée des Arts d'Afrique et d'Océanie** *is a wealth of artefacts and a fine basement aquarium.*

Parks

Jardin de Reuilly

entrance from avenue Daumesnil, 12th (01.43.43.78.51). **Open** 9am-9.30pm daily.

La Promenade Plantée

(01.43.41.98.43). **Open** as mentioned before, parts of the Green Walk are closed during night-time. But night-time varies throughout the year; here is the complete rundown. The walk opens every day, at 8am on weekdays, and 9am on Sat, Sun and Bank Holidays. For closing times, it's a bit more complicated…

1 Feb-1 Mar 6pm
2 Mar-Daylight Saving Time Switchday 7pm
DST Switchday-15 Apr 7.30pm
16 Apr-15 May 9pm
16 May-31 Aug 9.30pm
1-23 Sept 9pm
24 Sept-15 Oct 8pm
16 Oct-15 Nov 6pm
16 Nov-31 Jan 5.30pm

Museums

Musée des Arts d'Afrique et d'Océanie

293 avenue Daumesnil, 12th (information 01.44.74.85.00). **Open** 10am-5.30pm Mon, Wed-Sun.

Opéra National de Paris Bastille

place de la Bastille, 12th (08.36.69.78.68). **Open** *box office* 130 rue de Lyon 11am-6.30pm Mon-Sat. *Guided visits (01.40.01.19.70).*

Toporgraphy of Paris

Nicholas Royle

On the trail of the late artist and writer Roland Topor.

> **Start:** L'Occasion d'un livre, 10th
> **Finish:** Parc des Buttes Chaumont, 19th
> **Time:** 4-5 hours
> **Distance:** 8km/5 miles
> **Getting there:** five-minute walk from Mº Gare de l'Est (lines 4, 5, 7) or Mº Château d'Eau (line 4)
> **Getting back:** Mº Buttes Chaumont (line 7B)
> **Note:** opening times of relevant parks.

Roland Topor died in Paris in 1997, but he remains as much a vital part of Paris as any of the characters he wrote about, painted or drew, or any of the locations in which he lived, worked or raised a glass. A true polymath, Topor wrote short stories, novels and plays, he was a prolific painter and cartoonist, a set and costume designer for theatre and opera, an actor on stage and screen, and a filmmaker. His son, Nicolas Topor, also an artist, says that his father reacted against society's apparent need to stick him in a box. As soon as he felt he was being categorised as either this or that kind of artist, Topor would go off and do something quite different.

Born in Paris in 1938, Topor loved cities and disliked nature. The last two years of his life he lived with his son and daughter-in-law, but for 20 years before that he rented an apartment at 47 rue de Boulainvilliers in the 16th. There he had problems with a neighbour, who took exception to Topor's lifestyle simply because, in the opinion of Nicolas, it was unconventional. Topor may be best known, at least in Britain, as the author of *The Tenant* (1966; original title *Le locataire chimérique*, 1964), in which a harmless young man, Trelkovsky, finds being a tenant in a Paris apartment building a living hell. But the author's experience in rue de Boulainvilliers was not a case of life imitating art. Trouble with neighbours had been present right from the very beginning, as we will see.

This walk is structured around key locations from the earlier part of Topor's life and from *The Tenant* (in print in the UK in a handsome paperback edition from Black Spring Press), although reference will also be made to his last novel, *Jachère-party* (Editions Julliard, Paris, 1996), which has yet to be taken up by a British publisher. Any future translator will have to grapple with its awkward title; a literal, and probably unsuitable, translation would be 'Fallow Party'.

We start at L'Occasion d'un livre, a cute little second-hand bookshop on rue des Vinaigriers in the 10th. I don't think the bookshop was here when Topor lived in the area, nor the last time I was in the vicinity, staying with filmmaker Camillo Di Biase at No.22 (long since moved on).

Criss-cross the **Canal St-Martin** *thus.*

Roland Topor *pictured in the early 1970s.*

Rue des Vinaigriers offers one of the best approach routes to the Canal St-Martin. It's a very ordinary street and the effect of walking down it and finding such a beautiful part of the city hidden away at the end is quite stunning. Topor, a keen *promeneur*, often walked beside the canal.

I suffer from a condition that renders me incapable of walking past bookshops. L'Occasion d'un livre is dominated by *policiers*, crime novels, including some of Robin Cook's excellent Factory series. (Published in translation by Série Noir, Cook was allowed to keep his own name in France, while the same books in English are published under the pseudonym Derek Raymond to avoid confusion with two other well-known Robin Cooks.) The man behind the desk checks his records and confirms that he did have a copy of Topor's *Rêves de jour*, a collection of drawings made between 1964 and 1974, but that he has sold it. For now – although hopefully not by the time you visit – the shop is Toporless.

Rêves de jour is particularly noteworthy for bearing an illustration by Fernando Arrabal. Poet, artist, filmmaker and playwright Arrabal was one of three others with whom Topor founded the Groupe Panique in the early 1960s, the other founder members being Chilean-born filmmaker, theatre director and mime Alejandro Jodorowsky, and Belgian-born novelist and screenwriter Jacques Sternberg. The Groupe Panique had a major exhibition at the Palais Royal in 1972. Topor was later associated with the artistic movement Fluxus, working with artists Daniel Spoerri and Robert Filliou.

Rue des Vinaigriers stops at the canal and offers you a choice of left, right or up and over the first of a series of iron footbridges. The view up and down the canal from the mid-point of the bridge is so lovely you'll be pleased to know that this walk is also going to take you over the next five bridges 'downstream', that is heading south towards the Seine. Step off the bridge and cross into rue de la Grange-aux-Belles, then go right into rue Bichat. The huge building on your left is the Hôpital St-Louis, where Roland Topor was born on 7 January 1938. (He died on 16 April 1997, as the result of a stroke, in the Hôpital La Pitié-Salpêtrière, which, as the crow flies, is exactly the same distance from rue de Boulainvilliers, his home for 20 years, as is the Hôpital St-Louis – an odd but almost certainly meaningless coincidence.)

Go right down avenue Richerand to reach the canal once more. Double-back no more than a few yards to take the footbridge over the canal. The footbridges are important. Cross the wrong footbridge and you'll destroy the fragile balance of the walk, which I'm sure you wouldn't want to do. Now stroll down the quai de Valmy, and cross the next bridge back over the canal. Walk down the quai de Jemmapes and cross the *next* bridge over the canal and head down the quai de Valmy again. At rue du Faubourg-du-Temple, cross the canal one last time and, while doing so, stop to consider *La Grisette*. This statue of a flower-seller was one of Topor's favourite things in Paris; he loved her ordinariness.

Your indulgent criss-crossing of the canal is appreciated. In Topor's last novel, the heavily autobiographical *Jachère-party*, the narrator writes, 'My main concern has never been to represent the world, but rather to imagine it otherwise, to take the piss out of it…' I think that this repeated re-crossing of the canal is the kind of thing Topor would have done, partly because it could be interpreted as taking the piss, and partly because I suspect him of being disingenuous in *Jachère-party*: he is just as likely to find unusual beauty in the world as take the

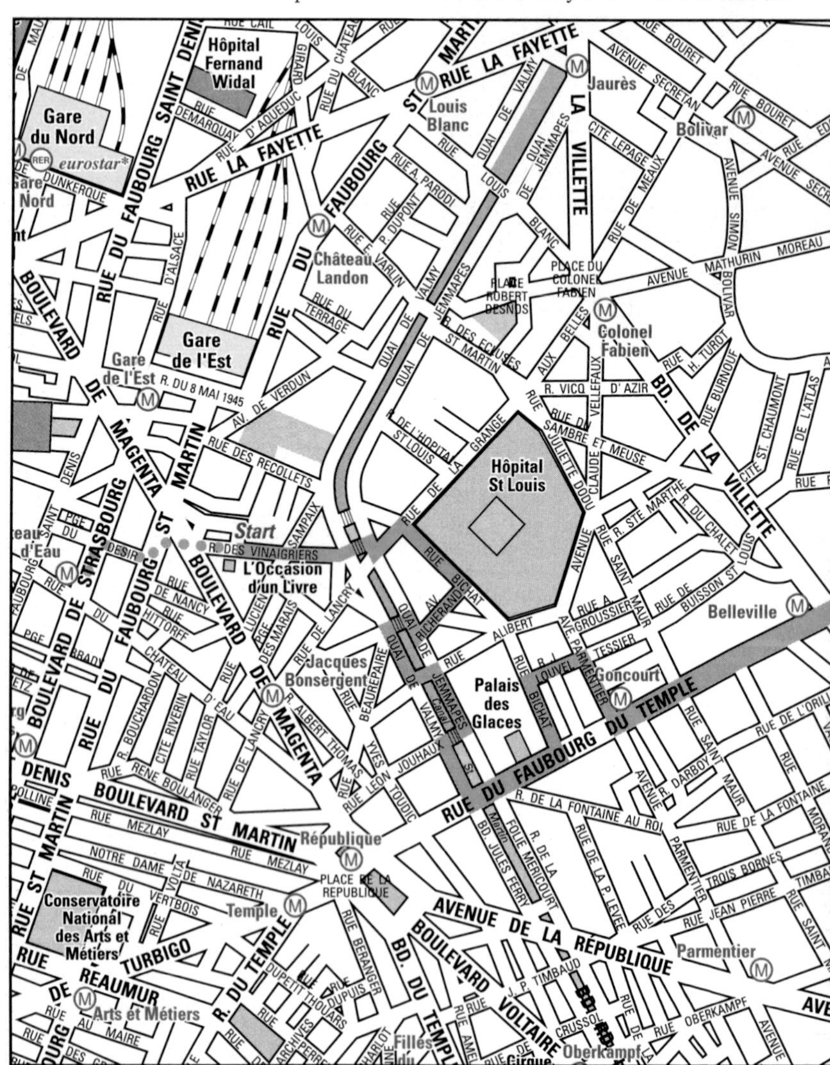

piss out of it. The following line from the same novel is prompted by the narrator's running a bath: 'When the taps cry, the pipes sing.' Perhaps it depends on your definition of taking the piss.

Now, follow further in Topor's footsteps up rue du Faubourg-du-Temple, against the traffic. Turn left into rue Bichat and right into rue Jacques-Louvel-Tessier. Topor and his sister and their parents, Polish Jewish refugees, lived on the left at No.11. This is where all the trouble with neighbours began, when fellow residents denounced the family as Jewish. Roland's father was forced into hiding and the children were sent away outside of Paris.

The Tenant is the compelling, delirious story of Trelkovsky and his vain attempts

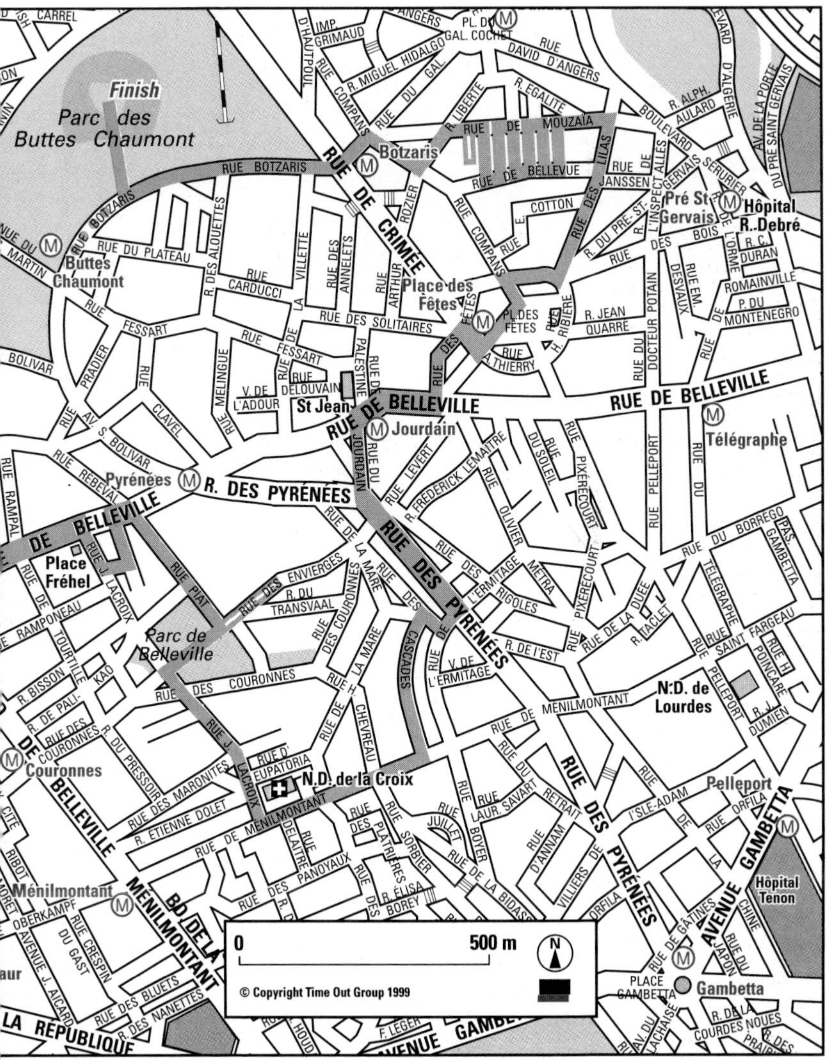

Shelley Winters and Roman Polanski in the latter's 1976 Topor adaptation, **The Tenant**.

to live a quiet life in a Paris apartment building on rue des Pyrénées (a street we'll come to). Maybe his mistake is renting an apartment previously inhabited by a young suicide, Simone Choule (the concierge proudly shows him the window out of which the woman jumped; Trelkovsky later discovers one of Simone's teeth in a hole in the wall). Maybe it's merely the bearing of a Polish name. (Another Pole, Roman Polanski, would not only direct the film of *The Tenant* [1976], but also play the lead role.) Trelkovsky takes great care to avoid displeasing the fearsome landlord, Monsieur Zy, but events – and the neighbours – conspire against him, and Trelkovsky is slowly driven mad. The novel is a *tour de force* of urban paranoia, although Topor, realising the potency of ambiguity, keeps us guessing: does the victimisation take place in Trelkovsky's head or are the neighbours really out to get him?

Turn right into avenue Parmentier. L'Odyssée, a second-hand bookshop, is across the street, but, on my last visit, there was no sign of anything by Topor. Go on down to the crossroads with rue du Faubourg-du-Temple. On the corner is Le Floréal, a favourite *café-tabac* of Topor's and the very first thing he painted. Turn left into rue du Faubourg-du-Temple and keep going until you reach Belleville Métro. This is where Jewish, African and Chinese communities rub shoulders in the *quartier ouvrier*, a low-rent, high-style riot of bright clobber and cheap merchandise. Synagogues and mosques stand side by side along boulevard de Belleville, the setting for a buzzing market on Tuesday and Thursday mornings.

Cross into rue de Belleville and stop for a breather in place Fréhel, a tiny bit of space gouged out of the city and decked out with benches and art. A sculpture by Ben, high up on one wall, consists of a life-size figure in a window-cleaner's cradle and a sign on which he has written the words: 'Il faut se méfier des mots.' ('Words must be mistrusted.') On the adjoining side of the square is a mural by Jean Le Gac. Both Ben and Le Gac are listed in one passage in *Jachère-party* alongside

Warhol, Klein and Adami as artists whose work deserves to be protected by curtains against the damaging effects of daylight – no chance of that here. The mural features a pulp-romance detective and the caption: 'Habitué au style allusif du peintre, le jeune détéctive comprit que le message lui indiquait de continuer la poursuite par la rue Julien-Lacroix.' ('Accustomed to the painter's allusive style, the young detective picked up the message that he should continue his pursuit down rue Julien-Lacroix.')

We hadn't intended to turn right into rue Julien-Lacroix, but it would be against the spirit of the walk to resist such an eloquent invitation. So turn right we do, but find little to detain us and so turn first left into rue Lesage and left again into rue Jouye-Rouve, then right to get back on to rue de Belleville. The right turn we do want is the next one: rue Piat. Topor had a studio a short way down on the right-hand side. Drawing was his first love. 'However,' he writes in *Jachère-party*, 'if I drew out of necessity, I ran the risk of becoming sick of it. I wrote in order to safeguard the pleasure I obtained from drawing.' Sadly, the studio is no longer there, so keep going and turn right into the Parc de Belleville.

This wonderful park barely existed when I lived in Paris 15 years ago (teaching, acting, writing). If it had, it would have been another good place to go for walks to work out plots and story ideas. First choice would still have been the Parc des Buttes Chaumont (which we will visit later), but the Parc de Belleville's stepped terracing, its many discrete sections and variety of views over a large swathe of Paris would have tempted me away from the 19th now and then. Possibly its obvious artificiality (both parks are man-made landscapes and proud of it) would have appealed even to nature-hater Topor, whose footsteps trailed endlessly between his rue Piat studio and Les Envierges, a café on adjacent rue des Envierges. To get to Les Envierges he would have negotiated the corner of rue Piat and rue des Envierges countless times. These days he would find it less easy, as there is a charming café on the corner called Rital & Courts, and Topor had a thing with cafés and bars similar to my thing with bookshops – he couldn't walk past them. Rital et Courts has been on this corner for ten years, so it opened while Topor was still alive but after he had moved out of the area and gone to live in the 16th. The tables outside boast fantastic views and it's a great place to stop for *un demi* – or, inside, to see one of the short films they screen.

L'Odyssée *bookshop, avenue Parmentier.*

Courts is short for *courts métrages* – short films. Topor's activities in film – as in all other art forms in which he engaged – were multifarious. As an actor he appeared in Werner Herzog's *Nosferatu the Vampyre* (1979) and Volker Schlöndorff's *Swann in Love* (1983). He art-directed as well as co-wrote Henri Xhonneux's *Marquis* (1989), and his talents as writer, set designer and graphic designer were employed on other films.

If you can drag yourself away from Rital & Courts and return to the park, make your way gradually down to rue Julien-Lacroix and follow it as far as place Maurice-Chevalier. On your left is the imposing edifice of Notre-Dame de la Croix, where Trelkovsky attends Simone Choule's funeral service. If it's a hot day, stepping inside for a few moments will cool you down. If it's raining, the church will provide shelter, although maybe, like Topor, you're happy to walk in the rain. 'I

Art for the people in place Fréhel by **Ben***…*

… and **Jean Le Gac***, both Topor favourites.*

love the rain,' he writes in *Jachère-party*, 'the different sounds as it falls on roofs, umbrellas and into puddles, the hissing of car tyres on the road surface, the groaning of windscreen wipers, not to mention the reflections that reveal the existence of an entire underground traffic network in an inverted city engulfed beneath our own.'

Once we've turned left on to rue de Ménilmontant, we could just keep going until we hit rue des Pyrénées, but rue des Cascades on the left is too intriguing to resist. When you reach No.55, take the steps opposite and turn left into rue de l'Hermitage, then left into rue des Pyrénées. This very long road, stretching all the way down past the Cimetière du Père Lachaise to near place de la Nation, is where Trelkovsky rents the apartment off Monsieur Zy. Topor never tells us where the house is exactly, but let's assume it was the top end he had in mind since he spent so much time around here.

Go right into rue du Jourdain and, astonishingly, there's a lovely little bookshop, Librairie l'atelier, just on the right. On my visit, they had one copy of *Jachère-party*. If you read French, buy it; if you don't read French, buy it for someone who does. Given the current priorities in fiction publishing in the UK, it's unlikely to get translated and find a British publisher, the author being neither a photogenic young woman, nor a stand-up comedian, but a deceased Frenchman, a genuine and unique talent who was never as successful in his lifetime as he deserved to be. Fame didn't elude him (at least not in France), but fortune did. We read in *Jachère-party*: 'Money, so concrete when it's gone or you only have a little, becomes light, almost gassy, as soon as it is amassed in great quantities… The zeros that indicate how much I am worth resemble the holes in my pockets, through which the other figures pass.'

The level of artifice of the dizzying **Parc de Belleville** *might have appealed to committed city-dweller and nature-hater Topor.*

Follow the map to place des Fêtes, out of Toporland and into the 19th. Cross the square, with its static herd of exoskeletal market stalls (unless you're here on market day), and head into rue des Lilas, which is dominated by huge, not unattractive apartment blocks. Do not turn left until rue de Mouzaia. Rue de Mouzaia and rue de Bellevue make an east-west ladder, with seven villas for rungs. A villa in French, as well as being what we understand as a villa in English, is a narrow little street like a mews. If you go up villa Félix-Faure, then down villa Sadi-Carnot, up villa des Lilas, down villa de Bellevue, and so on, you will find that, just as with the bridges over the Canal St-Martin, we end up just where we want to be. Sometimes life's like that. If you're doing the walk on a fine day, in spring or summer, you will be unable, as I was, to resist walking up the last alleyway, villa d'Alsace, even though it's a dead end (why is it a dead end? Of such questions are Toporesque stories born), because you will have become intoxicated by the scent of lavender and clematis spilling out from the front gardens of these tiny houses. Clouds of midges brush against you, and each villa has its own gaggle of children playing, children of all ages and races playing together happily. It is a vision of a love-thy-neighbour ideal that is the antithesis of Trelkovsky's (and to some extent Topor's) experience, and it is tempting to believe, probably naïvely, that as we move out of one century marked by barbarism and cruelty and into the next, we might be edging towards a more harmonious society.

At the top of each steep little villa you are dwarfed by gigantic apartment blocks on the other side of rue de Bellevue. All of the apartment windows have royal blue blinds that have been left open or closed in a deliberate pattern to spell out a message to the world. All we lack is the code to read it. Maybe all it's telling us is to go on. At the end of rue de Mouzaia, allow yourself to be drawn into rue du Général-Brunet, then cross at the lights and enter the Parc des Buttes Chaumont, without doubt the most beautiful and exhilarating space in the whole of Paris. It doesn't matter how much time you take to explore the park – its waterfalls and lake, the wooden bridge, the grassy slopes so steep you think you daren't sit down (but then you do) – you will never exhaust its possibilities. When I rented a damp, lonely studio at 5 rue Bouret in the mid-1980s, unconsciously gathering material for my first novel, *Counterparts*, with its Paris-based narrative of urban paranoia and spiralling madness, I only had to walk a few hundred yards to the park to shake off the shadow of Trelkovsky. I would conduct my own meandering surveys of the topography of the Parc des Buttes Chaumont, either circling the lake or crossing the wooden bridge, but without fail I would climb to the highest point, to the glorious folly of a gazebo with its superb view of the Sacré-Coeur. The process of climbing, then sitting and thinking, soaking up the view and contemplating your return to the streets below, puts everything calmly into perspective at the same time as freeing your mind to wander. From up here, it's tempting to believe that Roland Topor – rather than lying in the Cimetière du Montparnasse – is still walking the same streets, enjoying a glass of wine in his favourite cafés and bars, talking with friends, cursing his neighbours and dreaming up his fictions.

Thanks to Nicolas Topor and Gareth Evans.

Eating & drinking

Bar aux Folies

8 rue de Belleville, 20th (01.46.36.65.98). **Open** 6am-midnight Mon-Sat; 7am-11pm Sun. A truly cosmopolitan mix of people crowd into this café.

'... reflections that reveal the existence of an entire underground traffic network in an inverted city engulfed beneath our own.'

Topor, who lies in the **Cimetière du Montparnasse**, *left the world a more interesting place.*

Rital & Courts
1/3 rue des Envierges, 20th (01.47.97.08.40). **Open** *summer* 10.30am-11.30pm daily; *winter* 10.30am-11.30pm Tue-Sat, 10.30am-6pm Sun. Enjoy a drink, a meal or a short film.

Le Floréal
73 rue du Faubourg-du-Temple, 10th (01.42.08.81.03). **Open** 6.30am-9pm daily.

Parks

Canal St-Martin
For boat trips along the canal: Canauxrama *(01.42.39.15.00).*

Parc de Belleville
rue Piat, rue Julien-Lacroix, rue des Couronnes, 20th. **Open** 8.30am-9.30pm Mon-Fri; 9am-9.30pm Sat, Sun.

Parc des Buttes Chaumont
rue Botzaris, rue Manin, rue de Crimée, 19th. **Open** *May-Sept* 7am-11pm daily; *Oct-Apr* 7am-9pm daily.

Others

Hôpital St-Louis
42 rue Bichat, 10th (01.42.49.99.24).

Notre-Dame de la Croix
13 rue de Retrait, 20th (01.40.33.53.33).

Bookshops

Librairie l'atelier
2 bis rue du Jourdan, 20th (01.43.58.00.26). **Open** 10am-1pm, 2.30-8pm, Mon-Fri; 10am-8pm Sat; 10am-1pm Sun.

L'Occasion d'un livre
51 rue des Vinaigriers, 10th (01.42.05.30.15). **Open** 9.30am-7.30pm Mon-Sat.

L'Odyssée
160 avenue Parmentier, 10th (01.42.40.10.68). **Open** 11am-7pm Mon-Fri; 2.30-7pm Sat.

Books & films

Jachère-party Roland Topor (Editions Julliard)
Marquis (Henri Xhonneux, 1989, Bel/Fr) Philippe Bizot, Bien De Moor, Gabrielle Van Damme, Olivier Dechaveau. 83 min.
Nosferatu the Vampyre (Werner Herzog, 1979, WGer/Fr) Klaus Kinski, Isabelle Adjani, Bruno Ganz, Roland Topor, Walter Ladengast, Dan Van Husen. 107 min.
Rêves de jour Roland Topor (Le Chêne)
Swann in Love (Volker Schlöndorff, 1983, Fr) Jeremy Irons, Ornella Muti, Alain Delon, Fanny Ardant, Marie-Christine Barrault, Anna Bennent, Nathalie Juvet, Roland Topor. 111 min.
The Tenant Roland Topor (Black Spring Press)
The Tenant (Roman Polanski, 1976, Fr) Roman Polanski, Isabelle Adjani, Shelley Winters, Melvyn Douglas, Jo Van Fleet. 126 min.

Nadja's ghost

Antoine de Gaudemar

In search of André Breton's muse – and other Surrealists' inspirations.

Start: rue Lepic, 18th
Finish: Chartier, 9th
Time: 2-3 hours
Distance: 4km/2.5 miles
Getting there: five-minute walk from Mº Blanche (line 2)
Getting back: two-minute walk to Mº Rue Montmartre (lines 8, 9)
Note: Breton's meeting place with Nadja is a long walk east along rue La Fayette, and not really worth the detour.

Incorporated into Paris in 1860, the hotbed of the 1870 Communard uprising (plans for the Sacré-Coeur basilica were approved in 1873 in an effort to erase that painful memory), the Butte Montmartre so attracted the bohemians of the late nineteenth century that it became the archetype – indeed the stereotype – of the *quartier d'artistes*. At the time 30-odd windmills covered the Montmartre hilltop; just two remain today, the Moulin le Blute-fin and the Moulin du Radet, both replicas, and both located in rue Lepic. It was in the shadow of their spinning sails that the Impressionists, from Toulouse-Lautrec and Utrillo to Renoir and Van Gogh, liked to hang out, at Le Chat Noir, the Lapin Agile or in the neighbourhood's many other cabarets, or *guinguettes*, where circus acts drew great applause, the dance was French cancan and Aristide Bruant was the star singer.

In the early 1900s, a new generation of painters and writers moved in: Picasso and Braque, Juan Gris and Van Dongen, as well as Apollinaire and Max Jacob, Pierre Reverdy and Pierre Mac Orlan. It was at the Bateau Lavoir in 1907 (destroyed by fire in 1970 and replaced by an artists' studio complex) that Picasso painted Les Demoiselles d'Avignon, today considered the 'manifesto of Cubism'.

So it was not entirely by chance that the Surrealists in turn set up shop on the hillsides of Montmartre in the 1920s. This walk retracing their footsteps begins below the Moulin Radet, at the corner of rue Lepic and rue Tholozé. At No.20 of rue Tholozé, a narrow, quiet street that tumbles down the flank of the *butte*, is Studio 28, one of the oldest cinemas in Paris. Opened in 1928 – hence the name – on the site of a *guinguette* named La Pétaudière (bedlam), this cinematic shrine had its moment of Surrealist glory in 1930 with the *L'Age d'Or* scandal: one November day, the projection of Luis Buñuel's film was interrupted by protesters from the Ligue des Patriotes and the Ligue Antisémite. Ink bottles were hurled at the screen, smoke-bombs and stink-bombs thrown into the theatre; the gallery decorated by Jean Cocteau and hung with canvases by Joan Miró, Max Ernst and Salvador Dalí was sacked. The cinema was shut down, its reels impounded and the film banned. This pivotal incident contributed mightily to the legend of this place, which has survived the neighbourhood's many transformations. It is still an arthouse cinema, the gallery (with a little bar at the back) is still draped in red, photographs record its glorious history, the *livre d'or* out front bears the signatures of Montand, Signoret and Julien Carette, and the motto devised by Cocteau is still inscribed above

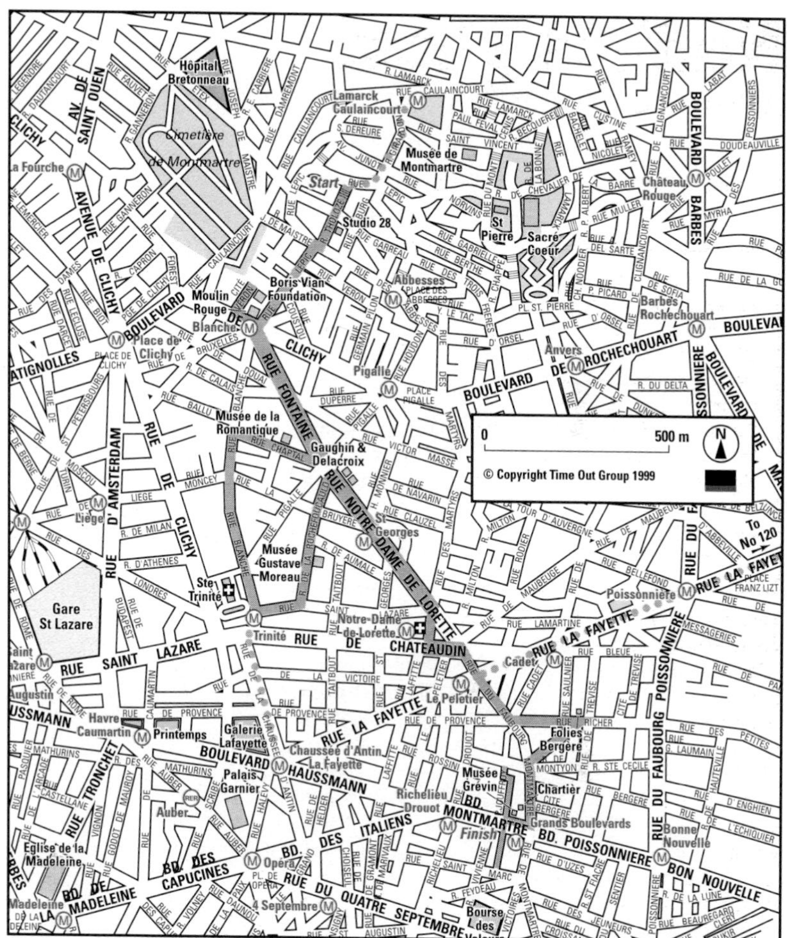

the entrance: 'The cinema of masterpieces, and the masterpiece of cinemas'.

Rue Tholozé ends near the crossing of rue des Abbesses and rue Lepic, a typically Parisian market street that zigzags down from the top of the *butte*. Always bustling, this part of rue Lepic has retained its village feel, in the cafés in particular, despite the incursion of a few trendy shops (the most notable being Rumba Records up the hill at No.45, with a fantastic stock of Caribbean and Brazilian music). At the foot of rue Lepic, in place Blanche, don't bother looking for the Cyrano, the large café where Breton gathered his friends from all over Paris for legendary conversations-cum-piss-ups. In its place, adjoining the famous Moulin Rouge (alongside the disco La Locomotive and the rock-café showcase of cable music channel MCM) is now a Quick fast-food joint: the building is topped by a gigantic neon Coca-Cola sign. Back then, Breton drank Mandarin-Curaçao, his friends Claquesin or Picon. These meetings, which took place nearly every evening at

André Breton – *inspiration and main protagonist in the Surrealist movement in Paris.*

l'heure de l'apéritif, were something of a ritual: Breton held court, newcomers were inducted, old-timers could be excommunicated (as were Antonin Artaud and Philippe Soupault in 1926), and the Surrealist movement's initiatives and manifestos were discussed – and sometimes decided – right there. You could run into Louis Aragon, Paul Eluard, Robert Desnos, Benjamin Péret, Jacques Prévert, as well as Max Ernst, Joan Miró, and Giorgio de Chirico.. These days it's hard to find local residents who still remember those days. The area is in constant flux, and there are fewer and fewer old folk around. Just one elderly man at a bar on the other side of the boulevard remembers, but advises, leaning over his beer and with his walking stick resting on the counter, 'Beware of the past, concern yourself with the present.' Now overrun with peep-shows and strip joints, the boulevard de Clichy still harbours two spots that would doubtless have pleased Breton and the Surrealists: the Musée de l'Erotisme, which sprawls over several storeys and includes some noteworthy antiquities, and, a bit further on at 6 bis cité Véron, a museum dedicated to that essential figure of 1950s Existentialist Paris, Boris Vian. The apartment where the writer, trumpet-player and singer lived from 1953 until his death in 1958 is filled with the books, manuscripts, records and belongings of the author of *L'Ecume des jours* (*Froth on the Daydream*) and *J'irai cracher sur vos tombes* (*I Spit on Your Graves*).

When Breton wasn't heading the table at the Cyrano, he was at his nearby home, just across place Blanche at 42 rue Fontaine. In this strange, gently sloping street, specialist music shops (instruments, stereo equipment) rub shoulders with seedy bars where half-dressed matrons hold court, theatres (La Comédie de Paris, Carrousel de Paris, Théâtre Fontaine) and a discotheque (Bus Palladium). No.42 bears no plaque recording the fact that Breton lived here for nearly 30 years. At the back of the arched hallway lies a paved courtyard with a concierge's lodge, geraniums and lace curtains. Looking up, you can see the

Moulin du Radet – *once peppered with windmills, Montmartre now only has two replicas.*

CITÉ VÉRON

windows of the poet's *atelier*. A high perch where, he liked to say, he was hanging in the sky. One evening, Breton stumbled and fell down the narrow spiral stairway that he climbed every day. Nothing was broken, except his enormous fountain pen, the nib piercing his wallet just over his heart. 'Stabbed with his own pen, what more fitting end for a writer?' joked his friend Prévert. According to Marcel Duhamel, founder of Gallimard's famous crime list Série Noire, who also witnessed the scene, Breton only half agreed. Continuing down rue Fontaine, you'll pass No.80, where the painter Toulouse-Lautrec lived, and, a little further on, La Table d'Isis bookshop specialising in astrology and tarot. Breton was a great fan of both.

Breton and his friends spent a good deal of time roaming the city, allowing themselves to be led by *le hasard* (chance). The streets, a 'mental landscape', provided inspiration. During one of these *dérives* (literally: drifts), while they were deep in conversation about poetry and the impossibility of living, ever in search of salutory inspiration, Breton and Soupault came up with the idea of 'automatic writing' – dreamlike sessions in which one wrote what one's pen seemed to dictate, heedless of style or narrative logic.

To reach the Opéra, another of the Surrealists' favourite *quartiers*, we, like Breton, have several options, though we shall follow a weaving course. Walk along rue Chaptal, dropping in on the Musée de la Vie Romantique. Here artist Ary Scheffer hosted the literary, musical and artistic set that included George Sand, Frédéric Chopin and Alfred de Musset. The villa set back in a courtyard displays some of Scheffer's work; his studio has also been maintained for exhibitions.

Continue along rue Chaptal to rue Blanche, which draws its name from its original colour (it was the route for dusty shipments of plaster from the Montmartre quarries). Simon Kra's Editions du Sagittaire published Surrealist works at No.6, near the fire station, which is still adorned with a grapevine. After passing the Eglise de la Trinité, typical of Second Empire religious art, you come upon place d'Estienne-d'Orves. Beyond lies the rue de la Chaussée d'Antin, increasingly bustling with shoppers as it approaches boulevard Haussmann and its cluster of department stores (Galeries Lafayette and, further down, Printemps). However, Breton would also have turned up into rue La Rochefoucauld via rue St-Lazare: at No.14 is the Musée Gustave Moreau (still open), a shrine to the symbolist painter the Surrealists adored, as recorded in Philippe Soupault's memoirs: 'We walked until we were out of breath, Breton and I, down the streets and the Grands Boulevards. The shop windows, the signs made us dizzy. One day Breton, always chasing after his memories, led me into the Musée Gustave Moreau. We were alone in this *belle époque* townhouse. No other visitors.'

In 1918, at the height of Cubism, the future Surrealists – who were then young men reeling from the butchery of the Great War – saw in symbolist painting, then forgotten, or perhaps ignored, the glimmerings of 'escape and emancipation'.

Continue up rue La Rochefoucauld to take rue Notre-Dame-de-Lorette. Gauguin was born at No.56, while Delacroix had his *atelier* at No.58. Further down, you find the Notre-Dame-de-Lorette church, built in the nineteenth century and modelled on a Roman basilica. It typifies this neighbourhood, known as La Nouvelle Athènes, constructed around 1820, when Greece and the ancient world were all the rage: opulent yet discreet buildings, numerous mansions with pilasters, columns and neo-Renaissance statues concealing rear courtyards and quiet gardens. Many writers and artists took up residence here: Géricault and Delacroix, George Sand and Chopin, sharing the quarter with impoverished

Every passage hides a secret – tucked in at 6 bis cité Véron is a museum dedicated to writer, singer and jazz trumpeter **Boris Vian**.

young girls – known as *lorettes* – who lived in rooms under the rooftops and peddled their charms down on the Grands Boulevards or the Champs-Elysées. Rue Notre-Dame-de-Lorette leads to place Kossuth, home of the large, austere building (facing you at No.13) that was for a long time the home of the French Communist Party (before its transfer to the current HQ in Brazilian architect Oscar Niemeyer's futurist bunker on place du Colonel-Fabien in the 10th). In the 1920s and even more in the '30s, many Surrealists, including Breton, Eluard and Aragon, were members or close companions of the Communist Party (founded in 1920 after a schism with the Socialist Party of the time).

Was Nadja one of the *lorettes*? In any event it was on rue La Fayette, a fair distance east of Notre-Dame-de-Lorette, that her fateful encounter with André Breton took place. At No.120 there was a militant bookshop, L'Humanité: just outside, on 4 October 1926, Breton, having just purchased Trotsky's latest work, met a poorly dressed stranger, curiously made-up but quite remarkable. 'She approaches, head held high, unlike the other passers-by. So frail that she barely touches the ground as she walks.'

'Who are you?' asks the poet before leaving her.

'I am the wandering soul,' replies the stranger, who was to inspire his greatest book, entitled simply *Nadja* (1928). The two agreed upon a rendezvous at the corner of rue La Fayette and rue du Faubourg-Poissonnière, at the Nouvelle France café, which only recently became a Chinese restaurant.

Between Opéra and the porte St-Martin lie the Grands Boulevards, a touch of bravado from Haussmann's great works and the nerve centre of Paris from the nineteenth century into the 1930s. The Surrealists were fond of these boulevards, planted with shady trees and lined with cinemas, cafés and theatres. Today, this area has lost much of its soul, and is struggling to recover its former prestige. Luckily, a few vestiges of *la belle époque* have survived. Continue down rue du Faubourg-Montmartre, taking a short detour to brush past the Folies Bergère music hall on rue Richer, another Surrealist hangout.

On boulevard Montmartre you'll find the Musée Grévin, with its wax figurines and ghosts of the past, and many covered passageways, an architectural invention of the nineteenth century so aptly described and analysed by the German philosopher Walter Benjamin. Glass-roofed galleries, an entanglement of shops, cafés, boarding houses, brothels: the urban underbelly, the subterranean arteries of the city. Sadly, the Surrealists' favourite, the Passage de l'Opéra, built in 1822, was demolished before the last war. In this passage stood the Certa café, renowned for its port, a gathering place for the Surrealists – and the Dadaists before them. It was Aragon who best described it in *Le Paysan de Paris*, partly written in the back room of the Cyrano and published in 1926: 'This is the place where one afternoon, towards the end of 1919, André Breton and I decided to bring together our friends, out of hatred for Montparnasse and for Montmartre, and also out of a taste for the passages' dubious reputation, and no doubt attracted by new surroundings that would become so familiar to us.' He goes on to explain his penchant for the passages: 'Everything is down to chance in my experience. I do not feel that the world has been laid at my feet. This handkerchief-seller or that little sugar bowl that I am going to describe to you, if you are not good, are the interior limits of my self, the idealised views that I have of my own laws, my ways of thinking, and I'll happily be hanged if this passage is anything other than a method to free myself of certain constraints, a means of

The **Folies Bergère** *on rue Richer – it's worth a little detour to see this Surrealist hangout and vestige of 'la belle époque'.*

BER

reaching beyond my own strength into a forbidden domain.'

To sample a bit of the atmosphere of these passages in the Surrealists' time, walk into the passage Jouffroy, at the corner of which Breton wrote that he saw Nadja passing by. All manner of shops, a hotel, a tearoom and, around a bend, a cluster of bookshops, one specialising in cinema, another more general-interest, with a large section dedicated to Paris and lovely vintage window displays. In the first portion of the passage, beyond the Musée Grévin's emergency exit (the main entrance is on boulevard Montmartre), is a quaint boutique selling walking sticks. A great fan as he grew older, Aragon was a customer and the *patron* still remembers his elegant figure. Cross over the boulevard and another passage opens up just next to the Théâtre des Variétés: the passage des Panoramas, very geometric, where you should seek out the boutique of the engraver Stern, *médaille d'or* in 1867 and still in business today. At the far end, leading into rue St-Marc, is a discreet sauna for men: it was in this quiet corner that 20 or so years ago Paris's first gay bars and meeting places sprang up.

A bit to the east, where Breton and his friends also frequented the cafés of the porte St-Denis and the porte St-Martin (for Breton 'their very moving aspect' was due to the fact that 'they were once a part of the walls surrounding Paris, which gives these two vessels, as if carried away by the city's centrifugal force, the appearance of being completely lost, which, for me, they share only with the marvellous Tour St-Jacques'), the boulevard Montmartre crosses rue Montmartre. At 7 rue du Faubourg-Montmartre, opposite trendy '80s club Le Palace (now closed) is Chartier, one of the least expensive restaurants in Paris – frequented by impecunious locals as well as intellectuals and artists – and one of the most beautiful. Opened in 1896 and now a listed monument, its décor has not changed. Many tourists know the place, but few notice the discreet plaque in the courtyard with the mysterious inscription: 'Who has opened the door to my death chamber? I had said that no one should come in. Whoever you are, get away from here!' Signed Comte de Lautréamont. It was in this house, then a hotel, that Isidore Lucasse, known as Lautréamont, the author of *Les Chants de Maldoror* and the hero and harbinger of Breton and his band of poets and revolutionaries, died on 24 November 1870.

Translated by Karen Albrecht.

Eating & drinking

Au Lapin Agile
22 rue des Saules, 18th (01.46.06.85.87). **Shows** 9pm Tue-Sun. **Admission** *show, one drink* 130F.

Au p'tit Creux du Faubourg
66 rue du Faubourg-Montmartre, 9th (01.48.78.20.57). **Open** 7.30am-8pm Mon-Fri; 7.30am-4pm Sat. Closed three weeks in July or Aug. Honest Gallic cooking at pauper-friendly prices.

Le Bistro de Gala
45 rue du Faubourg-Montmartre, 9th (01.40.22.90.50). Open noon-2.30pm, 7-11.30pm Mon-Sat; 7-11.30pm Sat. A friendly bistro with an excellent-value menu

Chartier
7 rue du Faubourg-Montmartre, 9th (01.47.70.86.29). **Open** noon-3pm, 7-10pm, daily. A Parisian institution.

Chez Jonathan
24 rue du Faubourg-Montmartre, 9th (01.48.24.23.04). **Open** noon-11pm Mon-Thur, Sun; noon-sunset Fri. A colourful Jewish salad bar, with good value dishes.

MCM Café
92 boulevard de Clichy, 18th (01.42.64.39.22). **Bar** 9am-5am daily. **Concerts** 11pm Mon, Tue, Thur, Fri.

Le Moulin de la Galette
83 rue Lepic, 18th (01.46.06.84.77). **Open** noon-3pm, 8pm-midnight, daily. Charming courtyard garden.

Nightlife & entertainment

Bus Palladium
6 rue Fontaine, 9th (01.53.21.07.33). **Open** 11pm-dawn Tue-Sat. **Admission** free for women Tue, 100F men; 100F Wed-Sat.

Breton wrote that he saw Nadja passing by the corner of **passage Jouffroy***; Louis Aragon shopped there for walking sticks.*

Carrousel de Paris
40 rue Fontaine, 9th (01.42.82.09.16). **Open** *Cabaret dinner* 8pm-12.30am daily; *disco* 12.30-5.30am Fri, Sat.

Comédie de Paris
42 rue Fontaine, 9th (01.56.31.31.80). **Open** *Theatre* 8.30-10pm Mon-Sat, 3.30-5pm Sun; *stand-up* 10-11.30pm daily.

Euro Men's Club
8-10 rue St-Marc, 2nd (01.42.33.92.63). **Open** noon-11pm daily.

Folies Bergère
32 rue Richer, 9th (01.44.79.98.98.). **Open** 9-11.30pm Tue-Sun.

La Locomotive
90 boulevard de Clichy, 18th (01.53.41.88.88). **Open** 11pm-dawn daily. **Admission** 55F Mon-Thur; 100F Fri, Sat.

Moulin Rouge
82 boulevard de Clichy, 18th (01.46.06.00.19). **Dinner** 7pm daily. **Shows** 9pm, 11pm, daily. **Admission** *with dinner* 750F, 790F, 880F; *with drink* 350F(at bar), 510F (9pm), 450F (11pm).

Studio 28
10 rue Tholozé, 18th (01.46.06.36.07).

Théâtre des Variétés
7 boulevard Montmartre, 2nd (01.42.33.11.41).

Théâtre Fontaine
10 rue Fontaine, 9th (01.48.74.74.40).

Shopping

Galeries Lafayette
40 boulevard Haussmann, 9th (01.42.82.34.56). **Open** 9.30am-7pm Mon-Wed, Fri, Sat; 9.30am-9pm Thur.

M&G Segas, Cannes de Collection Antiquités
Galerie 34, passage Jouffroy, 9th (01.47.70.89.64). **Open** 11.30am-6.30pm Mon-Sat.

Rumba Records
45 rue Lepic, 18th (01.53.28.10.40). **Open** 2-8pm Tue-Sat.

Le Printemps
64 boulevard Haussmann, 9th (01.42.82.50.00). **Open** 9.35am-7pm Mon-Wed, Fri, Sat; 9.30am-10pm Thur.

Stern Graveur
47 passage des Panoramas, 2nd (no phone). **Open** 9.30am-12.30pm, 1.30-5.30pm, Mon-Fri, Sun.

La Table d'Isis
3 rue Fontaine, 9th (01.48.78.38.60). **Open** 10am-noon, 1-7pm, Tue-Sat.

Churches

Eglise de la Trinité
place d'Estienne-d'Orves, 9th (01.48.74.12.77). **Open** 7.15am-7.30pm Mon-Sat; 8.30am-1pm, 5-8pm, Sun.

Eglise Notre-Dame-de-Lorette
8 rue Notre-Dame-de-Lorette, 9th (01.48.78.92.72). **Open** 4.30-6.30pm daily.

Museums

La Fondation Boris Vian
6 bis cité Véron, 18th (01.46.06.73.56). **Open** ring for details.

Musée de la Vie Romantique
16 rue Chaptal, 9th (01.48.74.95.38). **Open** 10am-5.40pm Tue-Sun. **Admission** 17.50F; 9F concs.

Musée de l'Erotisme
72 boulevard de Clichy, 18th (01.42.58.28.73). **Open** 10am-2am daily. **Admission** 40F; 30F concs.

Musée Grévin
10 boulevard Montmartre, 9th (01.47.70.85.05). **Open** *term time* 1-6.30pm daily; *school holidays* 10am-7pm daily. **Admission** 55F; 44F concs.

Musée Gustave Moreau
14 rue de la Rochefoucauld, 9th (01.48.74.38.50). **Open** 11am-5.15pm Mon, Wed; 10am-12.45pm, 2-5.15pm, Thur-Sun. **Admission** 22F; 15F concs.

Information

Parti Communiste Français, Fédération de Paris
120 rue La Fayette, 10th (01.44.83.85.15).

Books & films

L'Age d'or (Luis Buñuel, 1930, Fr) Gaston Modot, Lya Lys, Max Ernst, Pierre Prévert. 60 min. b/w.
Le Paysan de Paris Louis Aragon (1926)
Nadja André Breton (1928)
Les Chants de Maldoror Comte de Lautréamont (1868)
L'Ecume des jours (*Froth on the Daydream*) Boris Vian (1947/new UK edition Quartet Books 1996)
J'irai cracher sur vos tombes (*I Spit on Your Graves*) Boris Vian

Next to the Théâtre des Variétés lies the **passage des Panoramas** *where Stern Graveur has been in business for well over a century.*

PHIL
2000

Weeping widows

Jeanloup Sieff

A photographic tour of the Cimetière de Montmartre by one of the masters of the lens.

Start: Cimetière de Montmartre
Finish: Cimetière de Montmartre
Time: as long or short as you wish
Distance: as above
Getting there: line 2 to Mº Blanche, or lines 2 or 13 to Mº Place de Clichy followed by short walk
Getting back: short walk to Mº Blanche or Mº Place de Clichy
Note: the opening hours of the cemetery. Other walks visit this cemetery – Liz Jensen's and Elisabeth Quin's. Best places to eat and drink are towards Mº Blanche and rue Lepic.

I have always loved cemeteries, not for morbid reasons, but because I am drawn to their serenity – and to their statues.

'It's a beautiful day, let's go to the cemetery,' writer Emmanuel Berl's grandmother said to him when he was a child, and I did the same with my own children: each bike outing in Normandy was interrupted by a visit to the local cemetery, snoozing beside its church. We would even enjoy a picnic in the graveyard, sitting on a tomb, and my children learnt their mental arithmetic by working out the ages of the dead.

But far from recounting the story of my life, I am supposed to be telling you about the Cimetière de Montmartre and giving you the desire to discover it for yourselves.

First a little history. The Cimetière de Montmartre was officially opened on 1 January 1825 as the Cimetière du Nord. It covers an area of 11 hectares and has 750 trees, principally maples, which turn it into a forest of welcoming calm. In the sixteenth century, gypsum quarries occupied the land where the cemetery is now. During the Revolution the quarries' abandoned tunnels served as paupers' graves for the victims of various riots, probably including many of the 300 Swiss Guards killed in the Tuileries on 10 August 1792.

An initial attempt to create a cemetery, in 1798, failed because it was too small, taking up only one hectare. Only after the rebuilding of the *quartier*, between 1818 and 1824, was a new cemetery established, occupying ten times as much space. In 1825 it became the current Cimetière de Montmartre.

In 1888, during the extension of rue Caulaincourt, a metal bridge was built over the eastern part of the cemetery, allowing the walker to discover it from above.

Cemeteries will often provide visitors with a list of the famous personalities buried there, along with a numbered map to help you find them. This is a practice that has always bothered me, since I prefer to discover by chance the tombs of those I have loved, and not be like those crazed groupies who run from grave to grave, map in hand and without seeing anything, to be photographed in front of their idols' tombs.

It is in this way that, quite by chance, I have come across the tombs of Louis Jouvet and François Truffaut. Standing before Jouvet's grave, I tried a rendition, out loud, of the famous tirade from Jules Romains's *Knock*, in which I had seen him perform in 1949 at the Théatre de l'Athénée: '*Alors, ça vous chatouille, ou ça vous gratouille?*' ('So, does that tickle you, or "scratchle" you?'). And in front of François Truffaut's grave, in black marble

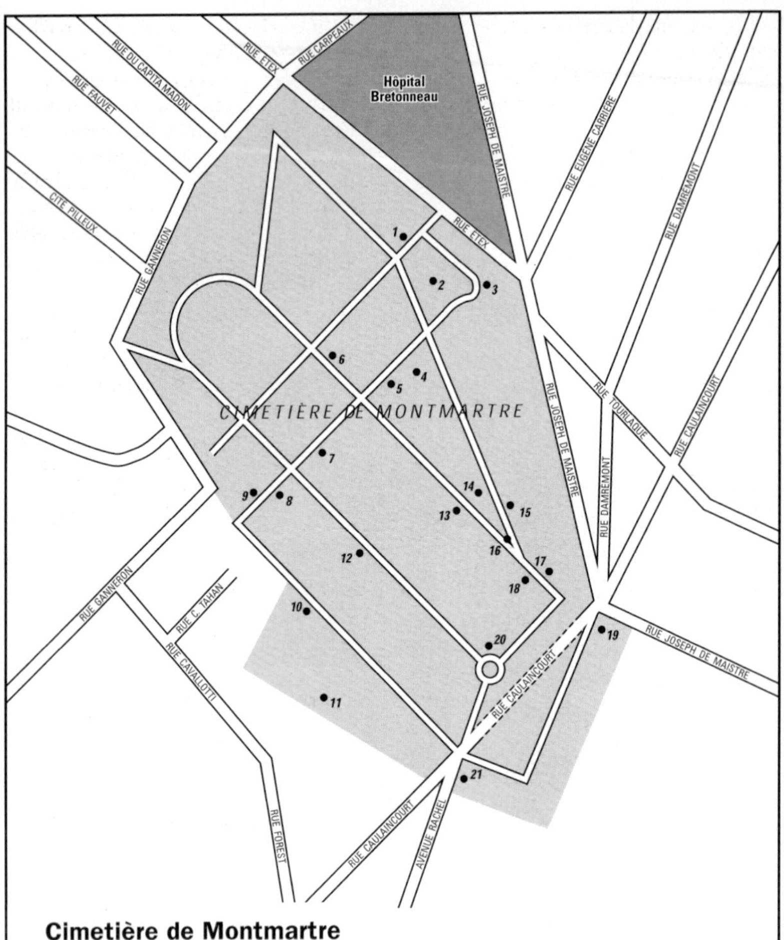

Cimetière de Montmartre

Jeanloup Sieff's walk

Plate 1	Herbillon family
Plate 2	Pierre Didsbury - No 4 on map
Plate 3	Pierre Didsbury - No 4 on map
Plate 4	Alexandre Dumas - 5
Plate 5	Alexandre Dumas - 5
Plate 6	Alexandre Dumas - 5
Plate 7	Henri Meilhac - 16
Plate 8	Guitry family -21
Plate 9	Dalida - 19

No photos

Henrich Heine - 13
Goncourt brothers - 9
Stendhal - 12
Alfred Vigny - 10
Edgar Degas - 3
Yaslav Nijinski - 6

Liz Jensen & Elisabeth Quin's walks

Léon Foucault - no 1 on map
Brauner family - 15
Jewish children - 17
Hector Berlioz - 18
Emile Zola - 20
Duke & Duchess of Montmorency - 7
François Truffaut - 14
Louis Jouvet - 11
Henri-Georges Clouzot - 8

0 250 m

bearing just the dates 1932-1984, I remembered our last meeting on a plane coming back from London where he was shooting *Farenheit 451*. I gave him a lift back to Paris, and we had promised to see each other again very soon… Then I recall doing a portrait of Catherine Deneuve, in my studio, the day after the announcement of his death. She was very sad, as was I.

Many other celebrities lie at rest in Montmartre. A few at random: Alexandre Dumas Jr, the Goncourt brothers, Henrich Heine, Stendhal, Vigny, Degas, the Guitrys, Nijinski… You'll also come across sculptures by Rodin and Rude.

For those who are interested, a map and a list are available at the entrance. Otherwise, I recommend chance encounters, and I will restrain myself from giving too much away, since it's better to let oneself be guided by the changing light, your own mood and the ever present birdsong.

According to statistics, women outlive their husbands by about ten years, which is probably the reason why one passes so many painstaking widows, watering can in hand, who, cleaning their tombs of pretty faded flowers and dead leaves, refuse to let their husbands lie in peace.

'Is there life after death?' wonder the disbelievers. 'Alas, yes,' I would be tempted to respond when I come across those pretentious mausolea that so often perpetuate pointless existences. They might be inscribed 'Mr X, Bureau Chief of the Gas Company' or 'General Y, decorated with the Medal of the Order of the Fertile Crescent'. You will also stumble across neo-gothic cathedrals where a dozen members of the same family huddle, united in death as they never were in life, and thus condemned to the most appalling lack of privacy for all eternity.

Fortunately, it is the ordinary graves, occasionally decorated with a beautiful allegorical sculpture, that are still the majority. Their lack of pomp and pretension makes it easier to feel that you are communing with the dead.

Around divisions 21/22 (all the help I'll give you) there's a superb bronze of a violated young woman, her eyes closed, face tense, lips forming a silent cry aimed at the Heavens. Youth and beauty conjure the inexorable, signal the denial and express the regret that all things must pass. That is why I like to walk in cemeteries, for I leave them soothed, relaxed, reassured as regards the ephemeral, which should not prompt anguish but give rise to serenity.

The Cimetière de Montmartre has all the charm of its age, like an old lady lost in her thoughts, or a yellowed photograph that recalls happy moments of times gone by. It is for you to discover it, at your own pace, and as you stand by the tomb of Henrich Heine, you may reflect on what he had to say about death: 'The worst of all illnesses is life, which only death can heal.'

Translated by Abigail Hansen.

Eating & drinking

Corcoran's Irish Pub
110 boulevard de Clichy, 18th (01.42.23.00.30). **Open** 10am-2am daily.

MCM Café
92 boulevard de Clichy, 18th (01.42.64.39.22). **Bar** 9am-5am daily. **Concerts** 11pm Mon, Tue, Thur, Fri.

Le Trèfle
68 rue Lepic, 18th (01.42.54.44.11). **Open** noon-3pm, 7pm-12.30am, daily. Short but succulent menu of North African cuisine.

Au Virage Lepic
61 rue Lepic, 18th (01.42.52.46.79). **Open** noon-3pm, 6pm-2am, daily. For a good-value, low-key meal after a walk in Montmartre.

Brasserie Wepler
14 place de Clichy, 18th (01.45.22.53.24). **Open** noon-1am daily. The best food on the square, particularly the seafood platters.

Information

Cimetière de Montmartre
20 avenue Rachel, access by stairs from rue Caulaincourt, 18th (01.43.87.64.24). **Open** *summer* 9am-5.45pm daily; *winter* 9am-5.15pm daily.

MADAME ALEXANDRE DUMAS
NEE HENRIETTE MARIE CECILE
REGNIER de la BRIERE
20 FEVRIER 1934

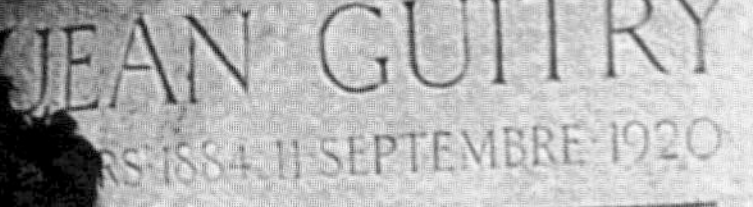
JEAN GUITRY
11 SEPTEMBRE 1920
GUITRY
13 DECEMBRE 1860 1er JUIN 1925
GUITRY
21 FÉVRIER 1885 24 JUILLET 1957
GUITRY

DALIDA

# of here
here

o the buzz of La Goutte d'Or.

Start: Mº Belleville, 20th
Finish: Mº Château Rouge, 18th
Time: 3-4 hours
Distance: 8km/5 miles
Getting there: lines 2 or 11 to Mº Belleville
Getting back: Mº Château Rouge (line 4)
Note: this is quite a lengthy walk, especially the stretch between Belleville and La Goutte d'Or – the line from Mº Belleville to Mº Barbès-Rochechouart is direct if you wish to skip the middle section.

It is from the hilltop it sits astride – like some cooper fashioning a barrel – that Belleville, which still remembers the old ways and the ancient gestures, has inherited its appearance: steep yet rounded, with hollows of greenery and sudden slopes. Along with the provincial aura that defines its charm, the *quartier* is a mass of ancient alleyways and cast iron railings, of cobbled lanes and inclined streets, of terraces and zinc roofs. It's a slice of Paris ripening, like the vines that once grew in neighbouring Ménilmontant.

Not long ago it was still a little village with its chicken coops, goats and garden plots, whose inhabitants came from all

Do this walk on market days (Tuesdays and Fridays) to see **Belleville** *at its busiest best.*

over, from France and elsewhere. Some, the peasants, labourers, artisans and vegetable merchants, came to do odd jobs; others, more illustrious, the writers, poets and musicians, came to a spot nearby to enjoy their eternal rest in the biggest garden in Paris, the Cimetière du Père Lachaise. There, the Irishman Oscar Wilde shares quarters with Frenchman Alfred de Musset, reminding us that genius – like geography – knows no borders. In any case, not in this neighbourhood, which has had a reputation as a pesky rebel since the Communards uprising, and where, in the area between the rues de Belleville, Jean-Pierre-Timbaud and Faubourg-du-Temple, North Africans, Asians, Jews, Greeks, Sri Lankans, Africans and Turks all offer up their shop-stalls, their versions of the East, their different languages and accents, and their culinary traditions.

As you emerge out of the Métro on to boulevard de Belleville you are met by a riot of sounds, colours and scents, the streets teeming with life. At certain times of day, on Tuesday and Friday mornings for example, when the esplanade hosts Paris's largest bazaar, the streets seem to palpitate like some giant blood vessel stimulated by spices, strong drink and the whiff of faraway travels.

As you wander down the broad boulevard de Belleville, observe the global village around you. This stretch of pavement is home to butchers both kosher and halal, white wine and mint tea, African produce and Mediterranean pastries, a modern gym and the Cléopâtra Turkish baths, travel agents and traditional clothing shops. You can also sit down at a terrace at Chez Lalou, at Maison Bénisti, or La Goulette, for an open-air feast of grilled meats, a good fish couscous with a *vin du pays*, or a succulent honey makroud, on the same pavement that also features the popular bar La Veilleuse, just opposite the Président, where Cantonese and Thai cuisines rule the roost.

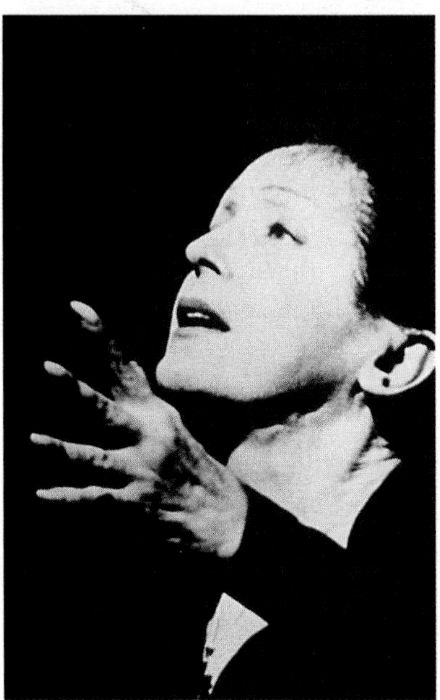

Edith Piaf – *one-time resident of Belleville.*

On the left, at No.120, a rundown building houses the Michkan-Yaacov synagogue. Not far from the synagogue rise the white-porcelain walls of the church of Notre-Dame Réconciliatrice, itself just a few metres from the alley leading to the modest Abou-Bakr mosque, named after one of the companions of the Prophet Mohammed.

Nearby lies a quieter corner. Proceed up rue de Pali-Kao to the bottom of the pretty Parc de Belleville, with its Maison de l'Air ('air house'), its outdoor theatre and its reflecting pools. Wander along the bottom, before mounting the steps under a colonnade of climbing plants, perhaps detouring to the right to cast envious eyes over the children playing in the wooden fort and on its slides. From the top of the park, Paris is spread out before you, including the Eiffel Tower, the Centre Pompidou and the Tour Montparnasse. It's in this area, which harbours the café-restaurant Le Vieux Belleville and Rital et Courts, that

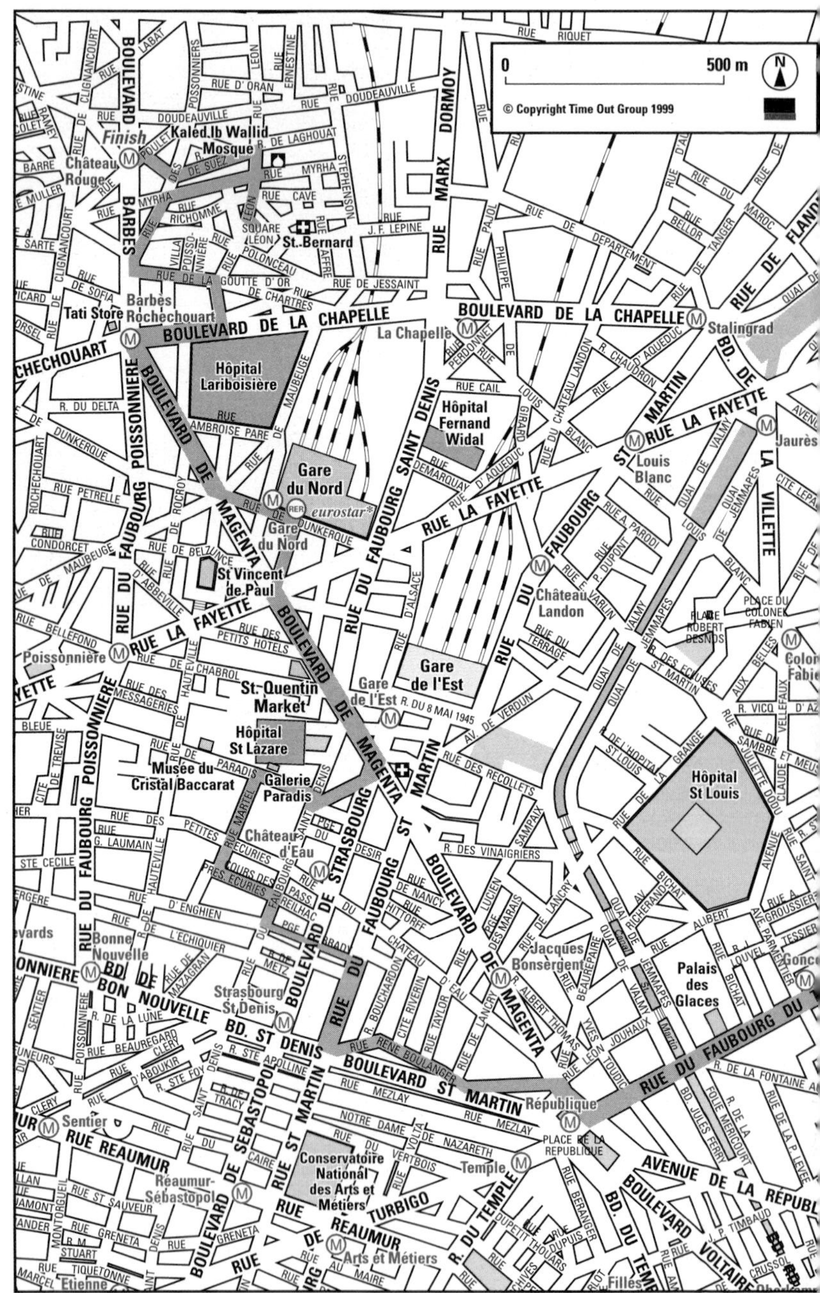
0
500 m
N
© Copyright Time Out Group 1999
Finish
Kaled Ib Wallid Mosque
Château Rouge
St. Bernard
Barbès Rochechouart
Tati Store
BOULEVARD DE LA CHAPELLE
La Chapelle
Stalingrad
Hôpital Lariboisière
Hôpital Fernand Widal
Gare du Nord
eurostar
Gare de l'Est
Louis Blanc
Jaurès
Château Landon
St Vincent de Paul
RUE LA FAYETTE
Poissonnière
St. Quentin Market
Hôpital St Lazare
Musée du Cristal Baccarat
Galerie Paradis
Château d'Eau
Hôpital St Louis
Jacques Bonsergent
Palais des Glaces
Bonne Nouvelle
Strasbourg St Denis
BOULEVARD ST MARTIN
République
PLACE DE LA REPUBLIQUE
RUE DU FAUBOURG DU TEMPLE
AVENUE DE LA REPUBLIQUE
BOULEVARD VOLTAIRE
Sentier
RUE REAUMUR
Réaumur-Sébastopol
Conservatoire National des Arts et Métiers
Temple
Arts et Métiers
BOULEVARD DE MAGENTA
BOULEVARD DE STRASBOURG
RUE DU FAUBOURG SAINT DENIS
RUE DU FAUBOURG POISSONNIERE
BOULEVARD BARBES
RUE MARX DORMOY
BD. DE LA VILLETTE
QUAI DE VALMY
QUAI DE JEMMAPES
BD. DE BON NOUVELLE
BD. ST DENIS
BOULEVARD DE SEBASTOPOL
RUE ST MARTIN
RUE DU TEMPLE
RUE DE TURBIGO
AV. DE VERDUN
RUE DE CHABROL
RUE DE PARADIS
RUE D'ENGHIEN
R. DU 8 MAI 1945

François Truffaut filmed scenes for his admirable *Jules et Jim*, in the narrow passageway of the villa Plantin.

And then there is all the music here, in this old-world neighbourhood that gathers together more than 40 nationalities of different creeds. Descend rue Piat to join rue de Belleville. Some 60 years ago the unforgettable voice of Edith Piaf (who was born in December 1915 at 72 rue de Belleville) rang out from street corners, alleyways and rear courtyards. Today, the accordion, the derbouka, the kora, the hurdy-gurdy, the sitar and the lute still keep the neighbourhoods, inhabitants and fans singing and dancing, here where the cabaret star Fréhel and Yves Montand used to perform.

Briefly retrace your steps and turn down rue Jouye-Rouve, where nothing seems to have changed: the old houses with their age-worn façades, the alleyways, the shops and the wine bars such as Le Baratin or Le Pataquès. These vintage hangouts, which have retained their furnishings and patina of yore, hark back to the Belleville of black-and-white photographs and of sepia postcards portraying coal merchants, knife-sharpeners, glaziers, upholsterers and furniture-menders. Artisans who did menial work and whose laborious lives exhibited a certain fondness for a job well done.

Follow the street round to rue Ramponeau. Belleville is also the little restaurants like Spanish-flavoured La Ramona further down the street, which doubles as a grocery store. Rue Ramponeau, also renowned for its beignets (fritters), houses, at the end of a blind and rubbish-strewn alley where the grass sprouts up between the cobblestones, La Forge, an old factory squatted by artists who work in metal, wood and other media with sometimes surprising results. You can visit and watch the artisans at work in the terrace of studios, or the large warehouse that forms its centre. Rather like Belleville itself, with its young and secular heritage, as it struggles to preserve its identity. The area has a history of subversion. It was the last *quartier* to surrender during the Commune – indeed, the very last barricade was held single-handedly for over a quarter of an hour on rue Ramponeau; it was the setting for some of the more enthusiastic rioting in the February riots of 1934 (against government corruption); and since the 1980s it has seen its heritage threatened by real estate speculation, such as has already invaded its sister neighbourhood La Goutte d'Or, in the 18th arrondissement.

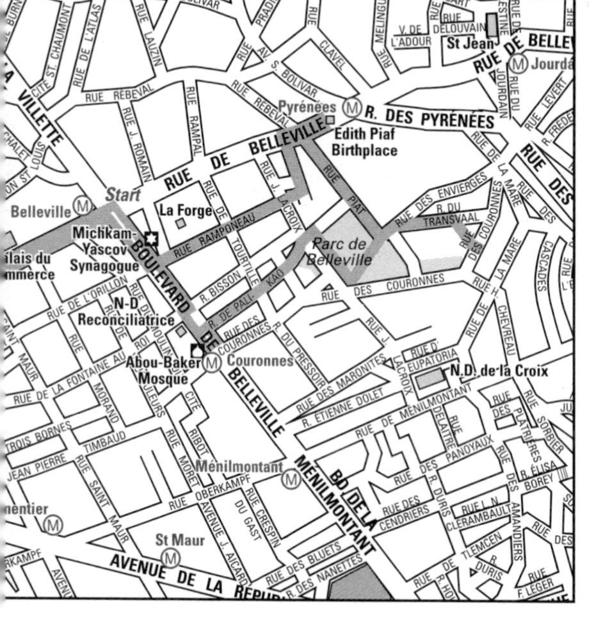

All the exotic fruit and veg you can eat at **Asie, Antilles, Afrique**, *rue du Faubourg-du-Temple.*

The walk to La Goutte d'Or is a long and winding road, arcing south of the Gare du Nord through buzzing passageways and along Haussmann boulevards, before joining the hectic hubbub of this corner of the 18th. You may choose to take the Métro, but then you lose the sensation of leaving one international *quartier*, rejoining bourgeois Paris, then re-emerging once again into that magical mix of people, sounds and smells that is La Goutte d'Or. The trek begins from the corner of the boulevards de Belleville and de la Villette. Head down the rue du Faubourg-du-Temple, which leads, after a ten-minute walk, to the place de la République. It's a genial thoroughfare, narrow and gently sloping, lined with a multitude of shops that reflect the cultural mix in this area, such as the one at No.88 that sells African, Caribbean and Asian groceries. The shop-front overflows with spiced meats and vegetables such as manioc, igname, gumbo, malanka, dachi and yams. Inside, rice, dried fish, condiments, dried fruits and peanuts fill the shelves.

Across the way, the old Palais du Commerce, with its outdated façade (currently under refurbishment), harbours the oldest dancehall in Paris, La Java, opened in 1922. It was once a Piaf haunt, but these days it has a decidedly Latino atmosphere, and salsa is the dance of choice. Further along, the Palais des Glaces puts on stand-up and other comedy shows. After the Goncourt Métro station and before arriving at place de la République, one of the greatest charms of the rue du Faubourg-du-Temple is its crossing with the quai de Jemmapes, bisecting the Canal St-Martin, which runs all the way through the 10th arrondissement. Its locks, footbridges, shady waterfronts and quaint boats, provide a great place for a leisurely stroll or quiet sit-down.

With its carousels, gardens and the greenish statue built by the Morice brothers and inaugurated on 14 July 1883, the place de la République is the traditional setting for public marches and meetings. It is an emblem of Paris and its sometimes agitated political and social past, a symbolic site that commemorates the abolition of the monarchy and the sovereignty of the people. It is also a traffic nightmare and should be carefully negotiated. Take the quieter rue René-Boulanger, past place Johann-Strauss with its diminutive statue of the composer, and join the rue du Faubourg-St-Martin. As you head north, ahead of you can be seen the imposing façade of the Gare de l'Est, behind you the porte St-Martin, one of the original gateways to the city. After about 50 metres on your left lies the passage Brady, where Pakistani and Indian restaurants with names such as Oh! Calcutta, La Route du Kashmir or Restaurant Pooja offer outdoor tables and intricately decorated interiors. In the evening, walking through the passage is like running a gauntlet of diners, as the tables and chairs form a long corridor along the alleyway. The windows of Le Sommier, also inside passage Brady, display a large variety of costumes and accessories for fancy-dress and other parties. (A few metres away in the rue Gustave-Goublier, the restaurant Les Barberesques serves up North African specialities amid noteworthy décor.)

Follow through both halves of the passage, and turn right briefly on to rue du Faubourg-St-Denis, before turning left through an archway into the Cour des Petites-Ecuries. As you turn in, look back across the road at the dainty little fountain just inside passage Reilhac.

Rue des Petites Ecuries is a quiet cobbled backwater with pleasant bars and cafés; it leads to the Galerie Paradis on the street of the same name. Unfortunately, this is no longer open to the public, but the grand entrance and tiled arches visible through the gates are a marvel in themselves and a fine testament to Monsieur Boulenger's Choisy-le-Roi tileworks. Rue de Paradis is the street of

Place de la République – *symbolic of France's merry-go-round of political and social change.*

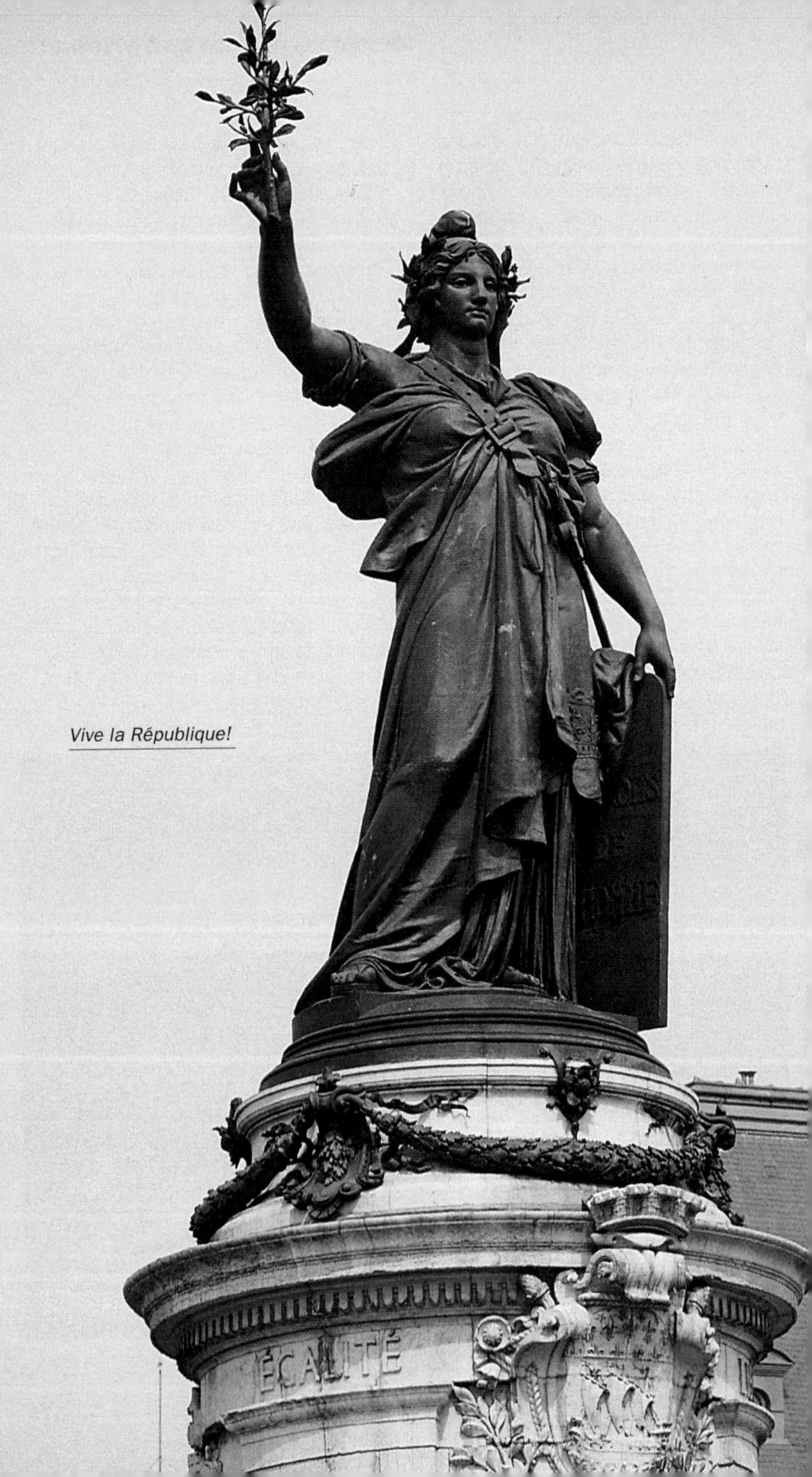

Vive la République!

china and glass, and at No.30 bis is the Musée du Cristal Baccarat, a museum and showroom of the celebrated glassmaker.

Follow up rue de la Fidélité where, at the end, the St-Laurent parish church flaunts its beautiful architecture. Further up boulevard de Magenta is the picturesque St-Quentin covered market, full of fruit and veg stalls, and one of the surviving covered iron markets built in the 1860s. Continue north, and take in the imposing Gare du Nord, its façade decorated with 23 monumental statues depicting French and foreign cities, and where the Eurostar train pulls in straight from London. Built by Haussmann's pet architect Hittorrf in the 1860s, the façade hides a huge glass and iron vault that shelters the platforms.

And now the last stretch up boulevard Magenta, and as the huge Tati sign hovers over the iron bridge, you know that you have arrived in the south-western corner of the area known as La Goutte d'Or ('the Drop of Gold'), named after the vineyard that existed here in medieval times.

Zola used this area as the backdrop for *L'Assommoir*, his novel set among the district's laundries and *absinthe* bars. But now this neighbourhood, like the heart of Belleville, sways to the beat of its immigrants, be it in the swarming markets like the one in rue Dejan, in the cafés, or in popular shops such as the unmissable Tati, known for its low prices and usually brimming with a multicultural clientele of limited means. This is also the place for *raï* music, which has unseated the more traditional Arabic *chanson*; for Tunisian sandwiches, for dodgy streetmerchants, for African and Arab fabrics, for jewellery sellers, butchers, shoeshops, carpet-peddlers and cagey purveyors of a game of three-card monte. Flimsy business cards vaunting clairvoyant mediums, marabouts and all

You don't have to look very hard to find bargains at **Tati**, *shopping focal point of Barbès.*

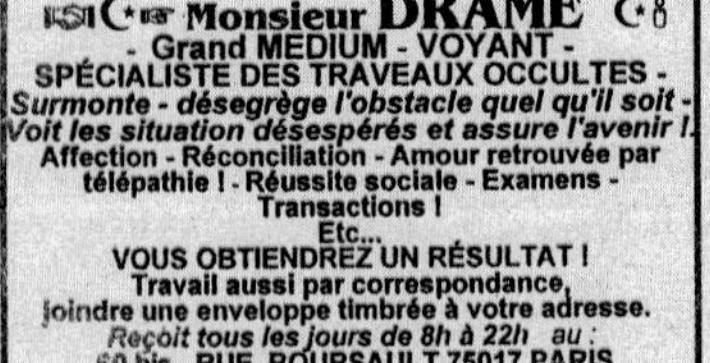

If you want to know what's lurking around the corner, take a walk through **La Goutte d'Or**.

manner of *guérisseurs* (spiritual healers) are thrust out at you at every turn. With their engaging style and approximate spelling, they promise you fortune, a good marriage, renewed sexual vigour, a speedy return of affection and good mental and physical health. The more audacious of these cards promise, even in these difficult times, a job and – miracle of miracles – a ten-year *Carte de Séjour* (resident's permit) to those who live here or come here to shop, or to go to the steam baths or the hairdresser's. At certain moments and in certain places, you could almost think that you were in the Belzunce or Panier districts of Marseille. A sort of Marseille-sur-Seine where only the boats and dockers are missing.

From the Barbès Métro station (where Le Louxor, le Palais du Cinéma, with its over-the-top façade, seems to have been shut down more or less since the time of Ramses II) head east along rue de la Charbonnière (there's a lively street market under the Métro tracks to your right on Monday, Wednesday and Saturday mornings). Turn left up rue Caplat to join rue de la Goutte-d'Or, where Zola's Nana grew up. Now this is a quiet and modern street, without the buzz of other parts of this *quartier*. Nevertheless, a quick glance up villa Poissonnière gives a tantalising view of the cobbled alleyways of Zola's time hidden behind the bland façades, made all the more enticing by the solitary lamplight on the path.

Join rue des Poissonniers, and the tempo picks up. Tiny restaurants specialising in *tajines*, or in Senegalese cuisine, such as Le Nioumre, tempt the visitor. African fabrics with bold designs, mosques hidden within anonymous buildings, and endless street chatter signal the cultural diversity.

Turn down rue Myrha, where to your left the Jewish Djerba café offers kosher food, whereas if you follow the road right you pass the Médina bookshop, full of Arabic textbooks for children and bound

A quick glance up **Villa Poissonnière** *and you could be back in the nineteenth century, a character in a Zola novel.*

Seek out **square Léon**, *just south of rue Myrha, for colourful murals and urgent graffiti.*

copies of the Koran. A little further on, behind a classic French doorway, lies the Kaled Ib Wallid mosque.

During the Algerian war for independence, which began on 1 November 1954, this neighbourhood became, especially at the end of the 1950s, the fiefdom of the FLN (Algeria's National Liberation Front). Bloody struggles ensued between them and the partisans of the MNA, led by Messali Hadj, the father of Algerian nationalism. Forty years later, in July 1995, the GAI (Groupe Armé Islamiste) assassinated Cheikh Sahraoui inside this mosque where he was the Imam. It was to be the first of a series of terrorist attacks that would throw Paris and all of France into mourning. This area has long been the focus of regular police raids, whether in pursuit of Islamic terrorists or seeking out the *sans-papiers*.

Behind rue Myrha lies the square Léon, nestling between two buildings whose fronts have been spruced up with bright murals. As you reach the square, you spy the elegant St-Bernard church down side-streets. Every June the square hosts *La Goutte d'Or en Fête*, a celebration of local talent, but whatever time of year you visit, it has its own lively, colourful charm. For the final leg, follow the map to Château Rouge Métro, taking in the Marché Dejean on the way, a buzzing market selling goods from, seemingly, all over the globe.

Translated by Karen Albrecht.

Eating & drinking

Le Baratin
3 rue Jouye-Rouve, 20th (01.43.49.39.70). **Open** 11am-1am Tue-Fri; 6pm-1am Sat.

Les Barberesques
1 rue Gustave-Goublier, 10th (01.40.18.10.85). **Open** ring for details.

Chez Lalou
78 boulevard de Belleville, 20th (01.43.58.35.28). **Open** noon-3.30pm, 6pm-midnight, daily.

Chez Ramona
17 rue Ramponeau, 20th (01.46.36.83.55). **Open** 7.30am-2am Tue-Sun.

Le Djerba
76 rue Myrha, 18th (no phone). **Open** noon-4pm, 7pm-midnight, Mon-Fri, Sun.

La Goulette
88-90 boulevard de Belleville, 20th (01.43.66.89.86). **Open** noon-3pm, 6pm-midnight, daily.

La Java
105 rue du Faubourg-du-Temple, 10th (01.42.02.20.52). **Open** 11pm-6am Thur-Sat. **Admission** 60F-80F Thur; 100F Fri, Sat.

Maison Bénisti
108 boulevard de Belleville, 20th (01.46 .36.87.88). **Open** 8.30am-11.30pm Tue-Sun.

Le Nioumre
7 rue des Poissonniers, 18th (01.42.51.24.94). **Open** noon-midnight Tue-Sun.

Oh! Calcutta
6 passage Brady, 10th (01.40.18.08.42). **Open** 6.30-11.30pm daily.

Le Pataquès
8 rue Jouye-Rouve, 20th (01.40.33.27.47). **Open** 4pm-midnight Mon-Fri; 10am-midnight Sat, Sun.

Le Président
120 rue du Faubourg-du-Temple, 11th (01.47.00.17.18). **Open** noon-3pm, 7pm-1.30am, daily.

Rital & Courts
1/3 rue des Envierges, 20th (01.47.97.08.40). **Open** *summer* 10.30am-11.30pm daily; *winter* 10.30am-11.30pm Tue-Sat, 10.30am-6pm Sun.

La Route du Kashmir
4 passage Brady, 10th (01.42.40.44.86). **Open** 7-11.30pm daily.

La Veilleuse
132 boulevard de Belleville, 20th (01.43.58.06.38). **Open** 6am-9pm Mon-Sat; 7am-9pm Sun.

Le Vieux Belleville
12 rue des Envierges, 20th (01.44.62.92.66). **Open** ring for details.

Shopping

Asie, Antilles, Afrique
88 bis rue du Faubourg-du-Temple, 11th (01.43.57.24.63). **Open** 10am-7.30pm Tue-Sun.

Librairie Médina
47 rue Myrha, 18th (01.42.64.06.04). **Open** 10am-8pm daily.

Marché St-Quentin
Open 8am-1pm, 3.30-7.30pm, Tue-Sat.

Le Sommier
4 passage Brady, 10th (01.42.39.25.05). **Open** 10am-7pm Tue-Sat. Closed Aug.

Tati
4 boulevard Rochechouart, 18th (01.55.29.50.00). **Open** 10am-7pm Mon; 9.30am-7pm Tue-Fri; 9.15am-7pm Sat.

Religion

Abou-Bakr mosque
39 boulevard de Belleville, 11th (no phone).

Kaled Ib Wallid Mosque
28 rue Myrha, 18th (no phone).

Masjid Al Fath Mosque
55-57 rue Polonceau, 18th (01.42.58.64.17).

Notre-Dame Réconciliatrice
57 boulevard de Belleville, 11th (01.40.21.71.11). **Open** 5-7pm Tue; 4-6pm Wed; 11am-noon Fri; 2-6pm Sat.

St-Bernard
12 rue St-Bruno, 18th (01.42.64.52.12). **Open** 2.30-7pm daily. Closed Aug.

St-Laurent
119 rue du Faubourg-St-Martin, 10th (no phone).

Arts & crafts

La Forge
21-23 rue Ramponeau, 20th (01.47.97.93.89). **Open** depends on who is in the studio.

Galerie Paradis
18 rue de Paradis, 10th (01.42.46.43.44).

Musée du Cristal Baccarat
30 bis rue de Paradis, 10th (01.47.70.63.30). **Open** 10am-6pm Mon-Sat. **Admission** 15F; 10F concs.

Other

Canal St-Martin
For boat trips along the canal: Canauxrama (01.42.39.15.00).

Cléopâtra Turkish Baths
53 boulevard de Belleville, 11th (01.43.57.34.32). **Open** 10am-6.30pm Tue-Sun.

Parc de Belleville
Open 8.30am-9.30pm Mon-Fri; 9am-9.30pm Sat, Sun.

Théâtre Palais des Glaces
37 rue du Faubourg-du-Temple, 10th (01.42.02.27.17).

The writing on the wall

Sasha Goldman

What with the *tau*, the *cense* and 1790s graffiti, Paris stone bears close scrutiny.

Start: place St-Paul, 4th
Finish: rue de Rivoli, 4th
Time: 1-2 hours
Distance: 2.5km/1.5 miles
Getting there: line 1 to Mº St-Paul
Getting back: short walk to Mº St-Paul (line 1)
Note: north of rue de Rivoli is quieter on Saturdays, south of rue de Rivoli quieter on Sundays.

Man, a curious beast, stands apart from other living creatures by his capacity to perceive time, making a distinction between that which has been and that which is to come. Memory, individual or collective, is the driving force behind his action: living memory, that which is in perpetual change, the memory that works, corrects, finds; and the memory that guides and teaches us.

At St-Paul, in the heart of the Marais, ready to start off on our stroll, let us pause and acknowledge the fact that we are standing at a key historical crossroads. The paths of two worlds run through this spot. Those who came from afar, from the eastern reaches of the globe, crossed through here to go to the ends of the earth, to the west: Finistère in Brittany, on the Atlantic coast… at that time, there was nothing beyond. And the Romans also took this path, which crossed to the regions outside the walls of the old city of Paris.

Paris blossomed and flourished on this site. Today, the eastern path enters contemporary Paris via Montreuil, by way of the Faubourg St-Antoine and Bastille, through St-Paul, and carries on westward to lose itself in the rue de Rivoli and the Champs-Elysées.

Before starting off, then, here on place St-Paul, a moment of silence for the past, a moment of silence, and of wisdom, to remember that phrase dear to observers of current events in eastern Europe: 'The past is becoming more and more unpredictable.'

We head down the neighbourhood's oldest surviving street, the rue du Prévôt, as if it were a secret passage of initiation, and pierce into the past – as the street's former name, la rue de la Percée, suggests. At the end of the street we see that former name carved in stone (with the number 12,

Village St-Paul – *north of the Ile St-Louis.*

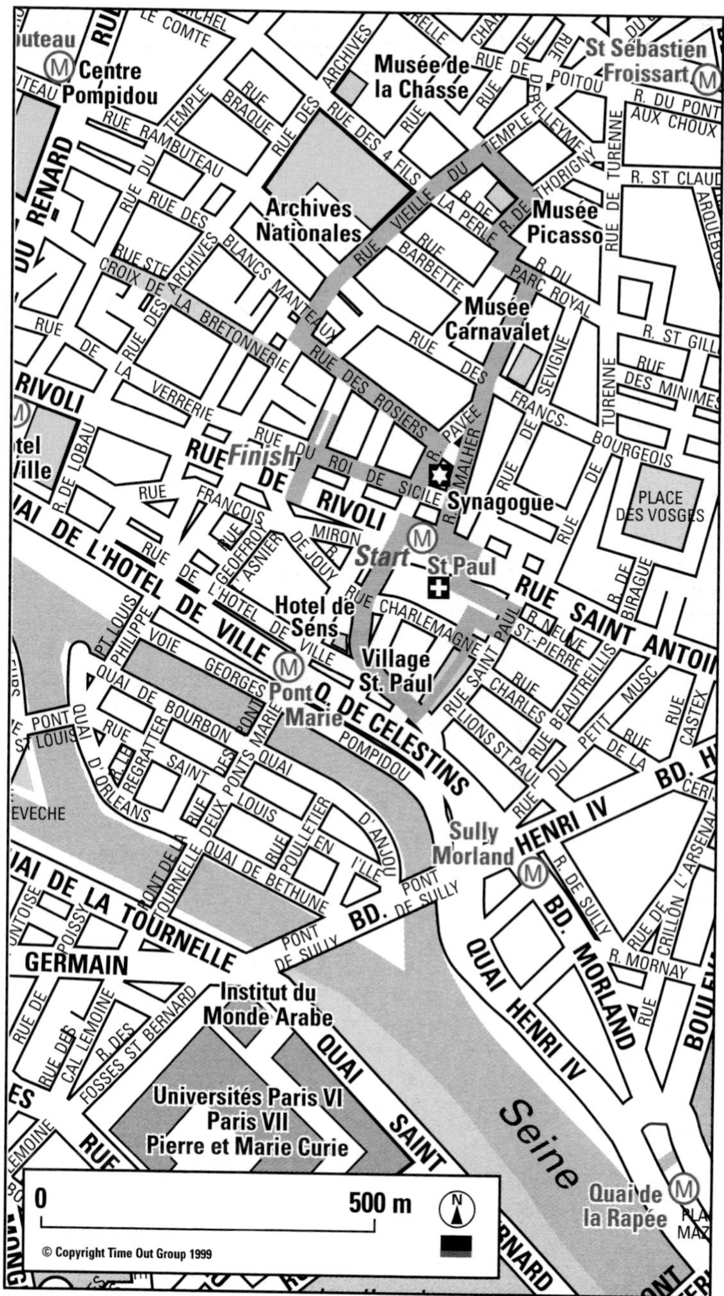
Centre Pompidou
Musée de la Chasse
St Sébastien Froissart
Archives Nationales
Musée Picasso
Musée Carnavalet
Finish
Synagogue
Start
St Paul
Place des Vosges
Hotel de Sens
Village St. Paul
Pont Marie
Sully Morland
Institut du Monde Arabe
Universités Paris VI Paris VII Pierre et Marie Curie
Seine
Quai de la Rapée
Rue de Rivoli
Rue Saint Antoine
Quai de l'Hotel de Ville
Q. de Celestins
Bd. Henri IV
Quai Henri IV
Bd. Morland
Quai de la Tournelle
Quai de Bourbon
Quai d'Orleans
Quai de Bethune
Rue des Rosiers
Rue Vieille du Temple
Rue des Francs-Bourgeois
Rue de Sevigne
Rue de Turenne
Rue du Temple
Rue Rambuteau
Rue de la Verrerie
Rue Ste Croix de la Bretonnerie
Rue du Roi de Sicile
Rue Pavée
Rue Malher
Rue Charlemagne
Rue Saint Paul
Rue Saint Louis en l'Ile
0
500 m
N
© Copyright Time Out Group 1999

indicating the twelfth quarter of the former division), round the corner from the old inscription for the adjoining street, rue des Prestres (in Old French: priests), today rue Charlemagne. These markings in stone, along with many others, have always fascinated me, guiding me like a forester's signs on the trees flanking a mountainside.

There is a special kind of pleasure, a sort of excitement, in finding these symbols of minor history so often on the periphery of scholarly studies. A walk through old Paris combines mainstream history with the discovery of the little signs that feel like personal messages.

Our walk continues along rue du Figuier, the name recalling the fig tree that stood at the intersection with rue Fauconnier, just in front of the splendid Hôtel de Sens. The tree was cut down on the orders of Queen Margot, since it impeded the passage of carriages. Today, however, one magnificent fig tree graces the top of the street, two others stand at the entrance of the Hôtel de Sens' pretty, pseudo-medieval garden, and the last, at the edge of the intersection, casts its shadow over the site of the original tree.

In the stone, high on the front wall above the principal entry of the Hôtel, a cannonball lodged itself on 28 July 1830, during the uprising against Charles X in the second Parisian revolution. It is still visible there, high up to the left, whereas Charles X himself was banished to history, overthrown by the rebels.

Rue de l'Ave Maria and rue des Jardins-St-Paul run along the vestiges of the ancient city wall built under Philippe-Auguste around 1190. This wall protected the megalopolis of the time and its inhabitants, who numbered almost 200,000. To the north, the city ended along the line of rue Rambuteau, to the west at the Louvre. Beyond the walls was 'the outside', with its swamps, its outlaw-ridden roads and the dark danger of the encroaching forests. A few convents were established outside the city, followed by nobles, who had their properties built 'away from the city'. Once the wall was finished, King Philippe-Auguste won the famous battle of Bouvines; the boundary of Paris was rendered redundant on that Sunday, 27 July 1214.

On the remains of the walls are stone workers' marks identifying the amount of work to be paid for. These marks, called *le tau*, are simple geometric figures carved by the humblest contract labourers who did the stonecutting.

Following through the Village St-Paul, we reach the secret enclave of the diminutive rue Eginhard, a cul-de-sac harbouring an exquisite hidden fountain in a style that dates from the transition between Louis XIII and Louis XIV.

Admiring the secret signs left in the stone by time, we turn into the tiny passage St-Paul, bordered by kerbstones called '*chasse-roues*' that protected against the carriage-wheels of the time, to find the hidden, almost secret side door into the St-Paul-St-Louis church. There, scurrying like a conspirator, and passing before works by the great masters (such as Delacroix's romantic *Christ au Jardin des Oliviers*), we discover a large piece of faded graffiti, its clumsy, hurried scrawl decorating the second column to the right of the aisle. What? Graffiti in a church? Sacrilege! The matter is far more complex: during the Revolution, the church was besieged, pillaged, laid bare to the events of the period. And here an anonymous zealot pounced upon this column to commit his slogan to stone: '*La République Française ou la mort*.' This inscription, dating from around 1793 and still there as a historic sign, invites the passer-by to sit down and meditate piously upon this minor monument.

Leave St-Paul-St-Louis. One imagines there was some mistake in the naming of rue Malher, but in fact the name is not a misspelling of the composer Mahler but

Passage St-Paul – *bordered by kerbstones called 'chasse-roues' that provided protection against carriage-wheels.*

the name of a lieutenant who fell here upon the barricades of the 1848 revolt. The street leads us into the Marais of the Renaissance, with its nearly 200 existing or former *hôtels particuliers* (mansions) and their majestic gardens.

Rue Pavée, rue Payenne, rue des Francs-Bourgeois, rue de Sévigné, rue de Thorigny and their *environs* hold some of the most beautiful, such as Hôtel de Lamoignon (now a library devoted to the history of Paris), the Hôtel Carnavalet and the Hôtel Salé (which houses the Musée Picasso). The Marais had its heyday in the seventeenth century: enormous wealth coexisted with abject poverty. The decree of 2 November 1789 declared the area's assets national property. The Marais was thus relegated to history, and here we are, centuries later, meandering through it.

Sticking with our theme of signs in the stone, we pass more vestiges of Philippe-Auguste's city wall. At the corner of rue Pavée and rue des Francs-Bourgeois, look out for a mark on the wall of the Hôtel Lamoignon: it is the semi-secret and barely visible mark of the *cense*, from the Latin *census*, indicating the boundaries of buildings paying property taxes to the noble or to the Church. On the corner of the edifice, on the fifth stone up, we see on either side the engraved letters 'SC', signifying the property of the convent of Ste-Catherine.

Walking up rue Payenne past the majestic Musée Carnavalet we arrive at square Georges-Cain. Entering by the little gate, we see on our right the vestiges of the former town hall burnt by the Communards in May 1871. The stones are still blackened from the soot of the flames.

The street leads us through the freshly renovated place de Thorigny into rue de Thorigny, which houses the most important collection of works by the greatest artist of our times, Pablo Picasso. The corner of the Hôtel Salé, at the intersection of rue des Coutures-St-Gervais, bears a very beautiful scar, another *cense*. The letters 'CFSG' are engraved around a cross, signifying the last building belonging to the convent Les Coutures des Filles St-Gervais.

You'll find some of the Marais's most beautiful hôtel particuliers *– and this striking synagogue – in* **rue Pavée***.*

Walking past the Musée Picasso gardens we come to rue Vieille-du-Temple. Back in the twelfth century, the Ordre des Templiers established its headquarters to the west of the swamps that later became the Marais. Linked to Jerusalem by their crusades, they made a fortune trading with the Middle East, and served as bankers to the pilgrims. Their eastern merchandise consisted of finely worked fabrics and other products requiring high craftsmanship. Jews came from the Holy Land to settle and to work in the Templiers' quarter, which lent its name to the rue du Temple and rue Vieille-du-Temple. Thus began the life and times of what is now known as the Jewish quarter.

Heading south to just short of the intersection with rue Ste-Croix-de-la-Bretonnerie, a street that wears the patina of time and weather with astonishing charm, we tumble suddenly into rue des Rosiers. We are in the heart, or rather the eye – or, better still, the blind spot – of the Jewish quarter. Everything here is *histoire*, implying both story and history. At the time of the Templiers, this street already bore the name 'of rose bushes', referring to a path running along the inside of the old Philippe-Auguste city wall that was surrounded by little gardens of rose bushes.

It is at this juncture that you must forget (you will anyway) all the guides and the advice of know-it-alls, and let yourself become lost in the flux of present time immersed in past time. Abandon all hope of trying to describe the flights of fancy provoked by the old doorways, the synagogues hidden up stairways, the glances, the ephemeral scenes of life, and little scraps of phrases thrown from one pavement to the other. Seize the moment, enjoy it and and keep it to yourself, as one

Cense *signifying the last building belonging to the convent Les Coutures des Filles St-Gervais.*

keeps to oneself a vivid dream. In the end, as you have known since earliest childhood, it is no use describing it: others will not be capable of understanding your excitement. Or (*mea culpa*) if you have a way with words, go ahead and write!

Give yourself over to your intuition, and let it carry you; do not hesitate to talk to the shopkeepers, or peek into a bookshop. Go and see Yvan Marihouani at No.22 on my behalf: he sells falafel and dispenses wisdom for free. Pass randomly by the Kosher Pizza shop directly opposite, and ask them to help you visit the synagogue upstairs at No.17. Carry on and you will find yourself at the intersection of rue des Rosiers and rue Ferdinand-Duval (known, a long, long time ago, as rue aux Juifs).

Here a fantastic restaurant holds pride of place. It is like a New York delicatessen, bearing the name of the Goldenberg family, where the patron Jo Goldenberg holds court. Go and say bonjour to him, with a friendly smile. He will welcome you; he has welcomed so many others already. You will see. The walls inside are lined with photographs of the famous folk who have left their mark on our times and who stopped by at Jo's.

History runs through the neighbourhood, through rue des Rosiers; it stopped by at Goldenberg's, too. In 1982 the restaurant was the target of a terrorist sniper attack, with seven deaths and many more injuries. Just like the cannonball embedded in the wall of the Hôtel de Sens in 1830, bullet-holes are still visible, at the back of the restaurant, and in the window…

Just opposite, tucked in between No.10 and No.14, is the gaping hole of a building site. Under the wreckage of the former building, the remains of the rose bush path at the foot of the Philippe-Auguste wall, dating from 1200, are said to have been unearthed – right here, now, at the dawn of the third millennium. At Nos.8 and 10 are the remains of a tower from the boundary wall.

At the foot of the street to the right, in rue Pavée (one of the first Paris streets to be paved, in 1450) a synagogue was erected in 1913 in a very modern style, with an entangled interior of wood and wrought iron. It was designed by Hector Guimard, creator of the Art

Nouveau Métro entrances. The wavy stone façade is designed to look like an open book, the Torah.

Before and parallel to that great arterial road, rue de Rivoli, you will find the peaceful and narrow rue du Roi-de-Sicile, which leads us to rue des Ecouffes. The first Jews who came with the Templiers created this neighbourhood, into which immigrants from the Diaspora drifted over the centuries. More recently, Jews have fled here from the pogroms in Russia, Poland and Hungary, just before and then just after World War II, and later still from events in North Africa.

Stop in at No.23, the book and newspaper shop run by Joseph Nachman. A bookshop opened here at the beginning of the century and took the name of Le Progrès in 1920, after World War I. The Préfecture pejoratively labelled it a '*gargote*' (third-rate eatery). The shop sold everything among its stacks of books and magazines: syrup served from brightly coloured tubes, sodas, cakes. The *gargote* was staffed by the owner's family, Jews from Odessa who had passed through Turkey and then settled in France, registered by the Préfecture as Jews from the Levant. Go and see old Nachman, buy a newspaper, a book or a postcard, and speak to him – humbly and without pushing it. He will tell you about the neighbourhood in the old days, the clients such as Trotsky and Chagall, who didn't even speak French. Above all, don't forget to talk to him about music, his records that carry tunes from afar, from beyond the mountains of time.

Returning via the rue des Ecouffes, pass by No.13 (with a very beautiful 15 marked for ever on the façade – the whole street has changed over time, numbers tumbling like dominoes). Let's lose ourselves in the village-like conviviality of the true Paris of yesteryear, the Paris of Jacques Prévert and of *la joie de vivre*. Enter the big grocery shop at No.16, head to the back, rummage around a bit. Then pass by the two butchers who sell the best pastrami, chicken sausages and pikel in this vicinity – and beyond.

Retracing your steps, we end up at the corner of rue de Rivoli, the intersection at

Rue des Rosiers – *the name refers to rose bushes that lined the path by the old city wall.*

PRODUCT OF ISRAEL
DEPUIS · SINCE 1882
CARMEL®
Rose of Carmel
IMPORTEUR MOISE TAIEB THIVOLET ROANNE FRANCE
ALC. 11% VOL.
750 ml
ADVOCAAT
z wysokiej jakości
naturalnych. Rozwarstwianie
stanowi wady. Przed rozlaniem
zawartość butelki wstrząsnąć.
POLSKA
5 900398 000055

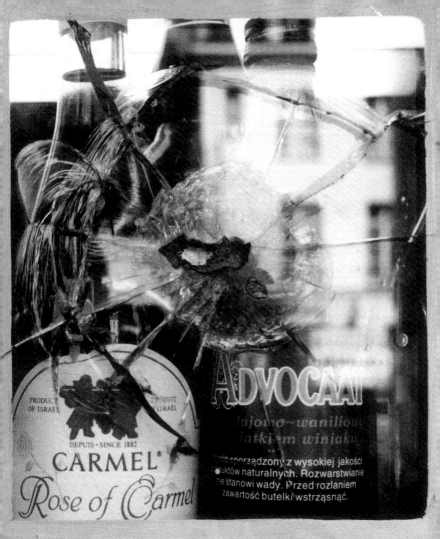

the heart of the city, bordered by a newsagent, a florist and, just to the left, a little café and wine bar called La Tartine.

To the north is the Jewish quarter and the Marais, with its little streets and hyperactive shops. To the east the road leads towards St-Paul, place des Vosges and, further on, Bastille. On the horizon looms the silhouette of the Opéra Bastille; above it hovers the winged Génie de la Bastille, suspended from the sky. South of us reverberates the slow beat of Paris's historical heart, under the patina of the Ile St-Louis and the Ile de la Cité. Imagine for a moment the unknown Celtic tribe that settled on the island, the Romans who did battle here before Jesus Christ, and the invading hordes of Huns who came from Asian hinterlands, lead by Attila. To the west this arterial road becomes more commercial, towards the Hôtel de Ville and where the great east-west axis (rue de Rivoli on to Concorde, the Champs-Elysées and La Défense) intersects the north-south artery, boulevard de Sébastopol. We can see the Tour St-Jacques in all its flamboyant Gothic beauty: it is all that remains of a sixteenth-century church, destroyed in 1797. At dusk, the sun sinks along the western axis behind the tower, causing it to sparkle with a thousand flames. Let's stay just where we are – it is from here that these nightly fireworks are the most spectacular.

Rue de Rivoli, over 3km long, was cut through old Paris between 1800 and 1835. The street was named in 1804 after Napoléon's 1797 victory at Rivoli. The thoroughfare was designed to be very elegant, with no artisans or food-stalls, and tight restrictions governed shop signs and much else. Today the street is largely lined with tacky souvenir shops, and McDonald's has succeeded in putting in not just a fast-food joint but street-side signs, just opposite the Louvre.

Reminder of a 1982 terrorist attack on **Jo Goldenberg's deli** *in rue des Rosiers when seven people were shot dead.*

We shall finish our journey at La Tartine, which has been here since 1900 and retains its original décor, and sample its excellent cheeses and wines. '*Plus de qualité que de profit*,' says Monsieur Jean Bouscarel, the elderly native of the Lot region who runs this outpost. He is there every morning, reading *Le Figaro*, in the corner behind the bar. 'Inside, everything is the same, outside, everything has changed,' he says. The biggest change for M Bouscarel has been the 'empty' streets. This part of town has lost three-quarters of its population since 1920, mostly due to renovation and real-estate developments, the disappearance of small workshops and the World War II deportations. There are no crowds in the street any more, he says, except for demonstrations occasionally passing by.

For the time being, our stroll ends here. I say 'for the time being', without knowing if that means for now, for a few centuries, or for an entire civilisation. Time is settling down and stratifying, like the stones in the buildings. While a historian can only delve into the past by approximations, the archaeologist uses stereotomy: the science of masonry and the assembly of stone. Each era has its own method of placing one stone on top of another, to fashion arcades, to create a thousand architectural inventions. At the bottom of it all remains the modest stonecutter, illiterate and brave, who carved the sign of the *tau* that we saw on the remains of Philippe-Auguste's wall in rue des Jardins-St-Paul, and the equally brave man who etched his revolutionary cry into history on the column of the St-Paul-St-Louis church. All those anonymous masses, who made history by marking a simple sign in stone. Go and see, if you have the chance, the concealed staircase that climbs up to the church bells inside St-Germain-des-Prés in the 6th arrondissement, one of Paris's oldest churches. The stairway is not well known, in fact it is unknown, and there is no public entrance, so one must manage by by oneself (but that's part of the game). The church's foundations date from the time of St-Germain, the Bishop of Paris between 555 and 576. On the first floor of the bell-tower, numerous stones are marked by a *tau*. The marks follow one another, climbing upwards, chasing each other like the notes in a symphony of infinite time.

May every journey through the past remain imbued with a little humility and respect for the mystery of time, and each visit be like a *tau* that we mark on our own stone, the stone that each of us is destined to become in the wall of human history.

Translated by Abigail Hansen.

Eating & drinking

L'As du Fallafel
34 rue des Rosiers, 4th (01.48.87.63.60). **Open** noon-midnight Mon-Thur, Sun; noon-5pm Fri; 8pm-midnight Sat. The best falafels on the street, and therefore in Paris.

Le Café des Nattes
22 rue des Rosiers, 4th (01.42.77.12.35). **Open** 11am-11pm Sun-Thur; 11am-sunset, Fri.

Café des Psaumes
14 rue des Rosiers, 4th (01.48.04.74.77). **Open** noon-3.30pm, 6.30-11.30pm, Mon-Thur; noon-2pm Fri; noon-11.30pm Sun. Build-your-own falafel plates and especially good cakes.

Jo Goldenberg
7 rue des Rosiers, 4th (01.48.87.20.16/ 01.48.87.70.39). **Open** noon-midnight daily. Worth a visit for the atmosphere, but perhaps wiser to stick to the *zakouski* platters for food.

Hammam Café
4 rue des Rosiers, 4th (01.42.78.04.45). **Open** noon-midnight Mon-Thur, Sun; noon-3pm Fri; 8pm-2am Sat. A kosher café in an Art Nouveau Turkish bath provides pleasant surroundings but plain food.

Kosher Pizza
11 rue des Rosiers, 4th (no phone). **Open** 12.30-3.30pm, 7.15-11.30pm, Mon-Fri; noon-midnight Sun.

mi-va-mi
23 rue des Rosiers, 4th (01.42.71.53.72). **Open** 10.30am-11.45pm Mon-Thur, Sun; 10.30am-sunset Fri. Fresh and generous fillings, serve-yourself sauces and a New York feel in this kosher addition to felafel row.

La Tartine
24 rue de Rivoli, 4th (01.42.72.76.85). **Open** 10am-10pm Mon, Thur-Sun; noon-10pm Wed.

Mansions & museums

Bibliothèque Historique de la Ville de Paris
Hôtel Lamoignon, 24 rue Pavée, 4th (01.44.59.29.40). **Open** 9.30am-6pm Mon-Sat.

Hôtel de Sens
1 rue du Figuier, 4th (01.42.78.14.60). **Open** *Forney Library* 1.30-8.30pm Tue-Fri; 10am-8.30pm Sat.

Musée Carnavalet
23 rue de Sévigné, 3rd (01.42.72.21.13). **Open** 10am-5.40pm Tue-Sun. **Admission** 27F; 14.50F concs.

Musée National Picasso
Hôtel Salé, 5 rue de Thorigny, 3rd (01.42.71.25.21). **Open** 9.30am-5.30pm Mon, Wed-Sun. **Admission** 30F; 20F concs.

Shopping

S Benchetrit
16 rue des Ecouffes, 4th (01.48.87.75.32). **Open** 8am-8pm daily.

Nachman's
23 rue du Roi-de-Sicile, 4th (no phone).

Other

Eglise St-Paul-St-Louis
99 rue St-Antoine, 4th (01.42.72.30.32). **Open** 7.30am-8pm Mon-Wed, Sat; 7.30am-10pm Thur; 9am-8pm Sun.

Hôtel de Ville
place de l'Hôtel-de-Ville, 4th (switchboard 01.42.76.40.40/reservations 01.42.76.50.49). **Open** *groups* make reservation 2 months in advance; *individuals* first Mon in every month following reservation made one month in advance.

St-Germain-des-Prés
place St-Germain-des-Prés, 6th (01.43.25.41.71). **Open** 8am-7pm daily. **Guided tour** 3pm third Sun of the month.

Synagogue
13 rue Pavée, 4th (no phone).

Tour St-Jacques
place du Châtelet, 4th. Closed to the public.

Rue de Rivoli, *named after Napoléon's 1797 victory at Rivoli, was designed to be very elegant – in some respects it still is.*

Plus ça change...

Geoff Dyer

Since the 11th is in a state of flux, just go with the flow.

Start: place de la Bastille, 11th
Finish: La Bague de Kenza, 11th
Time: 2-3 hours
Distance: 5km/3 miles
Getting there: lines 1, 5, or 8 to Mº Bastille
Getting back: short walk to Mº St-Maur (line 3)
Note: as the theme of the walk emphasises, this part of Paris is changing rapidly. Many of the venues mentioned, therefore, may change in name and nature.

In *Tristes Tropiques* Claude Lévi-Strauss recalls a time when São Paulo was developing so rapidly that maps became obsolete as soon as they were printed. The 11th arrondissement of Paris may not be changing as radically as that – the streets remain more or less in situ – but it is one of the fastest changing parts of the city. Not surprisingly, then, the goal of this walk is a bar that no longer exists. That much is certain. In addition, many of the places this itinerary advises you to visit may have followed it into non-existence by the time you retrace my steps (which, in their turn, retraced steps I took when I

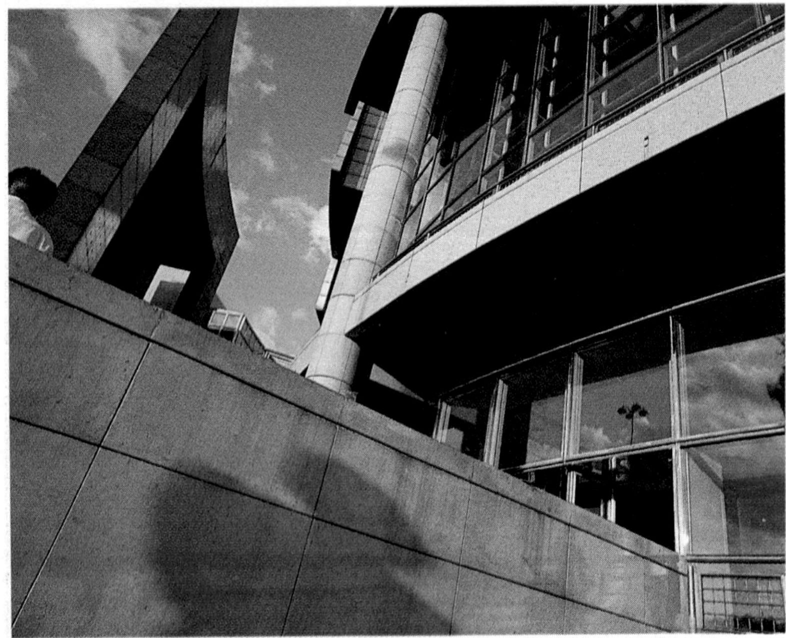

Opéra National de Paris Bastille – *now a resounding success after a chorus of concern.*

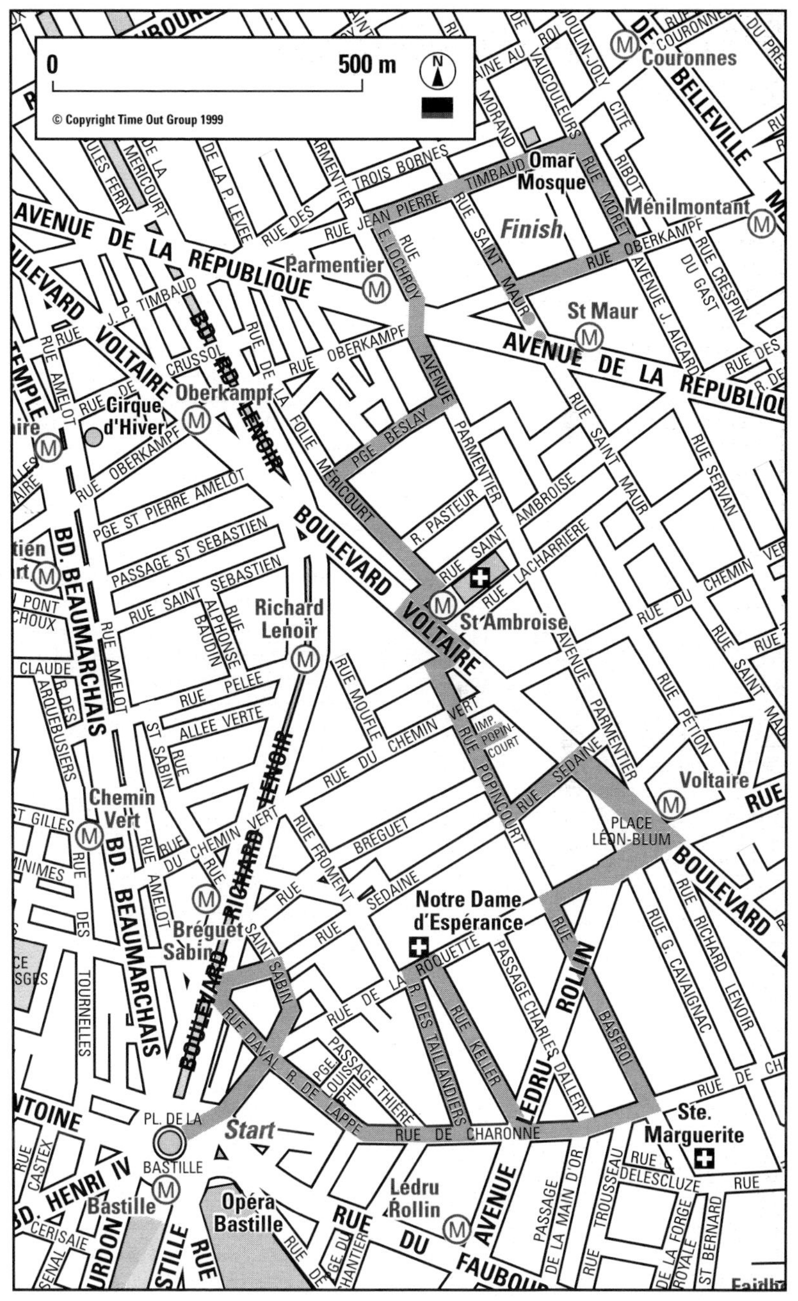
0
500 m
N
© Copyright Time Out Group 1999
Omar Mosque
Finish
Start
Couronnes
Ménilmontant
Parmentier
St Maur
Oberkampf
Cirque d'Hiver
St Ambroise
Richard Lenoir
Chemin Vert
Voltaire
Place Léon-Blum
Notre Dame d'Espérance
Bréguet Sabin
PL. DE LA BASTILLE
Bastille
Opéra Bastille
Ledru Rollin
Ste. Marguerite
AVENUE DE LA RÉPUBLIQUE
BOULEVARD VOLTAIRE
BD. RICHARD LENOIR
BOULEVARD RICHARD LENOIR
BD. BEAUMARCHAIS
BD. HENRI IV
AVENUE LEDRU ROLLIN
RUE DU FAUBOURG
BOULEVARD DE BELLEVILLE
RUE JEAN PIERRE TIMBAUD
RUE OBERKAMPF
RUE SAINT MAUR
RUE MORET
AVENUE PARMENTIER
RUE DE LA FOLIE MÉRICOURT
PGE BESLAY
RUE E. LOCHROY
RUE DES TROIS BORNES
AVENUE J. AICARD
RUE DU GAST
RUE CRESPIN
RUE SAINT AMBROISE
RUE LACHARRIERE
R. PASTEUR
RUE SERVAN
RUE DU CHEMIN VERT
RUE PÉTION
RUE SEDAINE
RUE POPINCOURT
IMP. POPINCOURT
RUE MOUFLE
RUE BREGUET
RUE FROMENT
RUE SAINT SABIN
RUE DE LA ROQUETTE
R. DES TAILLANDIERS
RUE KELLER
PASSAGE CHARLES DALLERY
RUE BASFROI
RUE G. CAVAIGNAC
RUE RICHARD LENOIR
RUE DE CHARONNE
RUE DAVAL
R. DE LAPPE
PASSAGE THIÈRE
PGE. LOUIS PHILIPPE
PASSAGE DE LA MAIN D'OR
RUE TROUSSEAU
RUE DE LA FORGE ROYALE
RUE ST BERNARD
RUE C. DELESCLUZE
RUE AMELOT
RUE DE CRUSSOL
J. P. TIMBAUD
PGE ST PIERRE AMELOT
PASSAGE ST SEBASTIEN
RUE SAINT SEBASTIEN
RUE ALPHONSE BAUDIN
RUE PELEE
ALLEE VERTE
ST SABIN
RUE DES TOURNELLES
RUE CASTEX
CERISAIE
RUE DE LA P. LEVEE
RUE MORAND
RUE VAUCOULEURS
CITE RIBOT
RUE DES ARQUEBUSIERS

lived in the 11th arrondissement in the early 1990s). On the positive side these gaps will almost certainly have been made good by places that have come into existence since this walk was devised. Take all this into account and the equation will, in Louis MacNeice's words, 'come out at last'. Especially if you remain absolutely faithful to the route described. And how do you do that? Why, by *deviating from it*, of course…

Start at the place de la Bastille. If you come out of the Métro, follow the signs for the rue de la Roquette exit – quite a walk in its own right. When you finally surface, the first thing you see is a classic Parisian café terrace, wicker chairs and tables fanning out. People sitting at these tables – of the café Le Bastille – will see you framed against a vast swathe of sky. Bear this in mind. Behind you traffic spins round the July column on the cobbled turntable of the place de la Bastille: wheels of steel, as it were. Lording it over the whole scene is the Opéra, one of those bold, defiant architectural enterprises at which Paris has always excelled. When it was opened in 1989 its sheer glass planes and harsh angles must have jarred with the surrounding area but, just as it now seems that there was a ready-made space (as opposed to a void created by a policy of ruthless architectural cleansing) in the middle of Rambuteau simply crying out for the Pompidou Centre, so the Bastille seems unimaginable without it. The Opéra kick-started the process of gentrification that has spread throughout the 11th, and rue de la Roquette has been the main artery of this process. When I first saw rue de la Roquette, in 1991, it seemed like the realisation of a dream of the perfect city street: a cross between Paris and New York. The best way to evoke it is by thinking of those classic American streets that, seen from a car or through a telephoto lens, are packed with neon possibilities that disperse when you are on foot. Rue de la Roquette is like that without the foreshortening illusion created by a car or lens. Not only can you live the dream, you can, so to speak, walk the drive.

From the Bastille you can see up Roquette only as far as the café La Rotonde where the first choice about your route has to be made. It's the best kind of choice in that there are no bad options. So walk past the café Iguana, a somewhat sterile bar, and turn left along rue Daval. On the right is the Lèche-Vin, a tiny bar – open only in the evenings, it is boarded up so thoroughly in the day as to make you wonder if it will ever reopen – whose toilet boasts such an impressive collage of sexually explicit photographs that you feel you are abusing the facilities if, of several possible -ates, you opt only to urin-. Turn right on to boulevard Richard-Lenoir, which on Sundays and Thursdays is home to one of the best produce markets in Paris. Take another right on rue Sedaine and you come to the Café de l'Industrie (closed, bizarrely, on Saturdays). Don't be deceived by the few tables that can be seen from the street; it's a Tardis of a place. Both the name and the brownish yellow walls suggest a century-long tradition of serving food to the oppressed sons and daughters of Zolaesque toil: an accurate image of its past, although in the early '90s its clientele more resembled idlers, bohos and yuppies. It may be a simulated environment but five minutes in there should be enough to have your clothes and hair reeking authentically of cigarette smoke. (I don't want to harp on this point, but assume that any café mentioned here, however lovingly described, is a smoke-filled pit in winter.) Turn left out of l'Industrie and walk down rue St-Sabin: on your left is the café La Rotonde again, on the right one of the best boulangeries in the *quartier* (the queue on Sundays is worthy of a nightclub). Having completed this little loop you can now cross over Roquette and

Notre-Dame d'Espérance *reflects the smartening-up of rue de la Roquette in its smooth, clean, ultra-modern look.*

Picture the scene at night on the normally quiet **rue de Lappe** *as clubbers fill the street.*

head along the cobbled rue de Lappe. Packed with bars and, well, more bars, on Friday and Saturday nights it's rammed with 'revellers' (ie drunks) but at other times of the week it is still very nice. About halfway down on the left, at No.27, there's a lovely little hotel and bar, the Sans-Culottes, and, further down, on the right at No.34, a sleek new juice bar, the Mix Café. Right at the end is Chez Paul, a restaurant serving meaty meat and earthy potatoes in an authentically cosy French atmosphere – so authentic that it is now full of German and English tourists.

Turn left at the end of rue de Lappe and then left again up rue des Taillandiers. but The main attraction on Taillandiers is Techno Import, an austere dance music shop and one of the best places in Paris to pick up flyers for clubs and parties. As you rejoin rue de la Roquette you can observe an interesting quirk of urban design. On the left-hand side of the street the protruding wall of a model shop forms a little triangle of pavement creating a backwater where the pedestrian traffic does not flow. In a river all sorts of flotsam accumulates at such places and a kind of scum usually develops. Something similar can be seen here in what is, effectively, a purpose-built trouble spot. I once witnessed a fight here that was remarkable less for its savagery than the way that one of the antagonists took off his shirt, folded it carefully and put it on the roof of a car before wading into his opponent. For watching fights I recommend a distance of five metres, ideally separated from the action by a parked car; that way your view is unobstructed but there is little chance of being obliged to make the transition from spectating to participating (ie you can run away).

Further up Roquette, on the corner of rue du Commandant-Lamy, a new secular-looking modern church has replaced the old one – God knows why – that inspired an absolute lack of devotion when I lived here. Just beyond this, also on the left, is one of the most pervasive sights in the 11th: a building site. The street is abruptly flooded with light because a whole apartment block has been razed to the ground. All you can see, to adapt Shakespeare's famous image, are blue and red cranes where late the sweet transistors sang.

Turn right on to rue Keller. Keller boasts galleries, a fine bookstore (Lady Long Solo), bars and restaurants including the Café Moderne at No.19, sister restaurant of Chez Omar, one of the great couscous eateries. At the end of Keller you meet rue de Charonne where you can pause at the Pause Café, a cross between new- and trad-style Parisian cafés. A poignant example of the pace of change is the Café de la Plage at No.59, which used to be a favourite hangout of mine but which is now all washed-up (only the wavy-beachy front remains). Rumours persist, however, that a revival is imminent.

Next door, at 61 rue de Charonne, behind an ugly, nondescript building, thrives one of the odder holdouts in this rapidly gentrifying neighbourhood. Poke your head into the entrance hall (which looks closed, but isn't) and you are suddenly in a boisterous ethnic food-fair on the ground floor of this foyer housing African workers. Young men crouch over makeshift braziers in the courtyard, hawking grilled ears of corn. Venture into the glassed-in area where a posse of entrepreneurial African mamas draped in bright *boubous* dish out generous plates of rice topped with ladlefuls of yassa, peanut sauce or other mysterious specialities swimming in battered cookpots. And the cost is 8.50F-10F, roughly half the price of a scrawny sandwich from a *boulangerie* – Europeans are welcome, but may be charged a little more than the regulars, maybe for the cutlery, which the latter often eschew.

In some respects Charonne has followed Roquette as a conduit of gentrification, the limits of which are symbolically expressed by the rues Basfroi and St-Bernard. On the corner of St-Bernard and Charonne is a house (No.78) that looks as if it has remained unpainted since the days of Atget. The walls appear to be made out of the residue of the glue of a hundred years of bill posting. In the window boxes of the upper floors, however, blooming geraniums lend a lovely lyrical touch – if any were needed – to the dereliction of the building. They are also flags, those geraniums, signalling to the world that the building, while it may have seen better days, still has some life in it, may yet outlast passingly fashionable cafés whose time is still to come. The building across the street, on the corner of Basfroi and Charonne, is even further gone. This place is not so much subsiding as sagging. Entrances have been bricked up, cracks are creeping up the walls in all directions. It has the look of a ruin that is somehow camouflaging itself as a building. The faded sign on the rue Basfroi wall – '*Antiquités*' – is nothing if not appropriate. Although there is no discernible point of entry, some upper windows are open, as if it has been squatted by ghosts. The building seems to compel decay, to accelerate decrepitude: even the neo-Bronx graffiti looks like it was done by a contemporary of Balzac. Still, it stands its ground, and the bottle of 1664 lager that I saw perched in its shade might well still be there 50 years from now.

Rue Basfroi itself is pretty uninteresting, so hurry along it until you are back on Roquette. From here, especially at twilight, you have a lovely view to the left down Roquette with all the signs – '*PRODUITS D'AUVERGNE*', '*TABAC*', '*BOUCHERIE*', the pulsing green crosses of pharmacies – of shops, bars and restaurants bunched up together in that pedestrian-telephoto effect mentioned earlier. In the other direction, place Léon-Blum is a site of immense and noisy convergence where the city's rival futures vie for space with each other. There is a boulangerie and the splendid Café Le Rey but, next to them, is a Barclays Bank (unobjectionable in England's homogenised, Swindonised towns, that corporate blue looks utterly hideous here) and – *quelle horreur!* – a McDonald's. If you continued up Roquette you would come, eventually, to Père Lachaise cemetery but, like Robert Frost, you have miles to go before you sleep. Specifically, you have to go along boulevard Voltaire for a few metres before turning left into Sedaine and right on rue Popincourt. Popincourt is an artery of the garment district where things are only sold wholesale (exaspérated signs declare that items are not for individual sale, '*Merci De Ne Pas Insister*'). A narrow street, Popincourt is always full of people loading and unloading vans, those mutually generating activities that have always seemed to me emblematic of all human activity: simultaneously necessary and – since loading implies subsequent unloading – utterly pointless. As a result it is also a perfect place to observe traffic jams with everyone honking pyrrhically at everyone else while the people blocking the road – not manning the barricades, simply loading and unloading clothes – carry on (and off) regardless. It also has its quieter corners – look down to the right and see through arched gateways such tranquil passageways as passage Lisa or impasse Popincourt.

The street leads you back on to boulevard Voltaire right by the church of St Ambroise. Recently spruced up, it's in such a composite of ecclesiastical styles as to give it – to atheist eyes at least – a pleasing lack of sincerity, of holiness. It was here that some 300 illegal immigrants – known as '*sans-papiers*' – most of them Africans, sought sanctuary in March 1996. The police, undeterred by the alleged sanctity of the edifice, finally stormed in and made their arrests. Thanks to public outcry over the incident and clever pressure tactics by the group's organisers, two years on some 90 per cent of the church's occupiers had been '*régulariés*' – granted resident status. Hundreds of thousands of other illegals still languish in daily fear of expulsion, many of them haunting back kitchens, sweat-shops and garment outlets dotting this patchwork neighbourhood.

Rue de la Folie-Méricourt brings you to passage Beslay, which I like because of the narrow catwalk of sky overhead. There was a time when the sky always seemed brightest round a tree; now it is brightest when squeezed like this between buildings. Beslay leads to avenue Parmentier and from here, looking north, you see what looks like a splendidly isolated tower. You look at it and you have only one thought in your mind, the one used by Roland Barthes as a caption for a photograph of a building in *Camera Lucida*: 'I want to live there.' In fact this lonely tower is the end of a terrace of buildings separating Parmentier from rue Eduoard-Lockroy, which is the road to take. Turn right at the end, on to rue Jean-Pierre-Timbaud.

L'Homme Bleu – open only in the evenings – specialises in Berber cuisine, but the street is littered with African restaurants from various parts of the continent. The further you go along Timbaud the more African and Arab it becomes. The three S's – sitting, staring and smoking– are the dominant activities here. TVs are turned up loud so that, by way of assimilation, the call to prayer seems to have given way to the call to compete on quiz shows, to get into a lather over soaps. Every conversation is an elaborately extended greeting, a lengthy prelude, not to beat about the bush, to saying goodbye. Just before rue Moret there is a kind of mini-park, a grassless rest area where a number of benches gather around a statue reminiscent of Rodin's *The Thinker*: a naked man resting his chin on hands that should, in turn, rest on a spade or – less probably – a shooting stick. There is no information about subject or sculptor, just a few soggy *baguettes*, pecked, perhaps even sucked, by pigeons. From here you can see three idyllic garrets, rearing like ships' prows from the top of a building separating

Lie down and look up so that the chiselled thinker finally finds his resting place on the garrets lining **rue Jean-Pierre-Timbaud**.

Timbaud from rue des Trois-Couronnes. Looking at them you feel certain that, if you lived there, a great novel would inevitably result – why, it would practically come with the lease! Stretch out on one of the benches and, Cartier-Bresson-style, the sculpture's chin and hands can be made to rest, gigantically, on one of these garrets. In the corner of the square, a bland blue building houses the mosque Omar where men seek spiritual refreshment.

Rue Moret, a little way up on the right, is the grail of our walk for this is where the Petit Centre – my favourite bar – used to be. If rue de la Roquette seemed the most perfect urban street, the Petit Centre seemed the most perfect bar imaginable: a neighbourhood bar in which you could meet people from all over the world. In contrast to over-stylised drinking environments like the Café Iguana, it seemed to have acquired its distinctive decorative character – part Charleston, part squat – almost accidentally, randomly. I can think of nowhere – neither pub nor bar – that resembles it in England. And now it's gone. In fact, the street has changed so much that it is difficult to tell exactly where the bar used to be. One thing is certain: the stretch of new developments makes the remaining buildings look even shabbier – ripe for demolition and redevelopment (ie ruination).

The disappearance of the Petit Centre is made bearable by the fact that a number of other bars, each with its own uniquely relaxed, ad hoc atmosphere have sprung up in the surrounding area, especially on rue Oberkampf. Running parallel to Timbaud, at the other end of rue Moret, Oberkampf, in terms of development, is now where Roquette was a decade ago. The Quincaillerie at No.100 and the nicely named Favela Chic at No.131 are among the best bars, but the biggest and most popular is still the Charbon at No.109. It's a little dark inside but, looking up from one of the pavement tables, you get an excellent view, across the street, of those wall-mounted rungs that are one of the unsung features of the Parisian skyline. The ones visible from the Charbon are particularly fine in that they are just rusty metal rods protruding from the side of a building, not even curved to form a hoop, crying out to be used in the climactic roof-top scene of the *policier* you would write if you lived in one of those garrets on Jean-Pierre-Timbaud. Less spectacularly, but more sweetly, your walk should climax with what are arguably the best Arab cakes in the whole of Paris, at La Bague de Kenza, 106 rue St-Maur, a few yards north of Oberkampf and St-Maur Métro. As I came out of the shop the sun pasted the shadow of a nimble cat on to the vertical wall of the building opposite. Do let me know if that is still there.

Eating & drinking

Le Bastille
8 place de la Bastille, 11th (01.43.07.79.95). **Open** 24 hours daily.

Café Charbon
109 rue Oberkampf, 11th (01.43.57.55.13). **Open** 9am-2am daily. Chic, trendy, popular, busy and not very relaxing.

Café Iguana
15 rue de la Roquette, 11th (01.40.21.39.99). **Open** 9am-4am Mon-Fri; 9am-5am Sat, Sun.

Café de l'Industrie
16 rue St-Sabin, 11th (01.47.00.13.53). **Open** 10am-2am Mon-Fri, Sun. Traditional salads and simple pastas.

Café Moderne
19 rue Keller, 11th (01.47.00.53.62). **Open** noon-2pm, 7-11pm, Tue-Fri; 7-11.30pm Mon, Sun. Delicious Maghreban dishes at reasonable prices.

Chez Paul
13 rue de Charonne, 11th (01.47.00.34.57). **Open** noon-2.30pm, 7pm-12.30am, daily. Reliable French favourites in a well-loved vintage bistro.

Favela Chic
131 rue Oberkampf, 11th (01.43.57.15.47). **Open** 7pm-2am daily. A brash Brazilian *cantina* with beautifully presented and tasty food.

Foyer Africain
61 rue de Charonne, 11th (no phone). **Open** 11am-6.30pm daily.

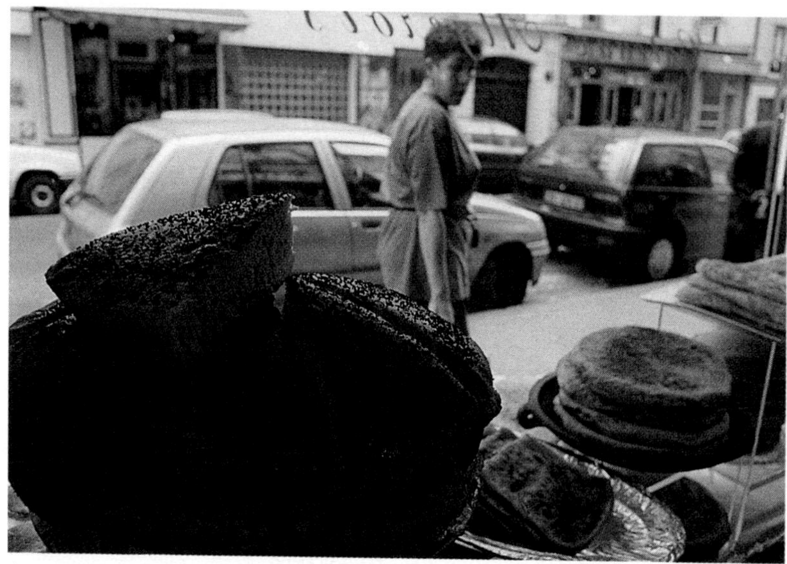

A sweet ending awaits in an Arab delicatessen – sugar and spice at **La Bague de Kenza**.

Le Lèche-Vin
13 rue Daval, 11th (01.43.55.98.91). **Open** 6pm-2am daily. Cheap drinks and low-maintenance chic.

Mix Café
34 rue de Lappe, 11th (01.40.21.34.05). **Open** noon-6pm Tue; noon-midnight Wed-Fri; noon-2am Sat. Fruit cocktails worth a taste, less so the food.

Pause Café
41 rue de Charonne, 11th (01.48.06.80.33). **Open** 8.30am-2am Mon-Sat; 8.30am-8.30pm Sun. Savoury *tourtes* are the speciality, but avoid at peak times.

Le Rey
130 rue de la Roquette, 11th (01.43.79.77.26). **Open** 11.30am-1.30am daily.

La Rotonde
17 rue de la Roquette, 11th (01.47.00.68.93). **Open** 7am-2am Mon-Sat; 8.30am-2am Sun.

Les Sans-Culottes
27 rue de Lappe, 11th (hotel 01.49.23.85.80/ bar 01.48.05.42.92). **Open** *bar* 7am-2am daily.

Shopping

La Bague de Kenza
106 rue St-Maur, 11th (01.43.14.93.15). **Open** 9am-10pm Mon-Thur; 9am-2pm, 3-10pm, Fri; 10.30am-10pm Sun.

Boulangerie Hubert
23 rue Daval, 11th (01.48.05.63.28). **Open** 7am-8.30pm Wed-Sun.

Lady Long Solo
38 rue Keller, 11th (01.53.36.02.01). **Open** 3.30-7.30pm Mon-Fri; 12.30-7.30pm Sat.

Techno Import
16 rue des Taillandiers, 11th (01.48.05.71.56). **Open** noon-8pm Mon-Sat.

Religion

Mosquée Omar
2 rue Morand, 11th (no phone).

Notre-Dame d'Espérance
47 rue de la Rochette, 11th (01.40.21.49.39). **Open** 8.30am-7.30pm daily.

St-Ambroise
2 rue St-Ambroise, 11th (01.43.55.56.18). **Open** ring for details.

Other

Opéra National de Paris Bastille
place de la Bastille, 12th (08.36.69.78.68). **Open** *box office* 130 rue de Lyon 11am-6.30pm Mon-Sat. *Guided visits (01.40.01.19.70).*

Walk like the man

Michael Palin

An Englishman trails an American in Paris.

Start: Mº Censier Daubenton, 5th
Finish: Mº Edgar Quinet, 14th
Time: 4-5 hours
Distance: 8km/5 miles
Getting there: line 7 to Mº Censier Daubenton
Getting back: Mº Edgar Quinet (line 6)
Note: the market on rue Mouffetard closes for a siesta.

I've a great fondness for the Paris Métro system – not just because it is efficient or because it smells of caramel or even because I've rarely been as moved by music as I was hearing a busking harpist play a slow, infinitely sad version of Pachelbel *Canon* in one of the pedestrian tunnels at Châtelet station, but because I've become obsessed by station names.

Which is why I make no apology for starting my Hemingway walk at the collectable Censier Daubenton station on line 7. Public information of all kinds is abundant in Paris and within moments of emerging from the station I learn from a street sign that rue Daubenton was named after a naturalist who lived from 1716 to 1800. Follow in the steps of the naturalist, left out of the station, until they meet the rue Mouffetard.

A copy of *A Moveable Feast*, a memoir of his Paris days written 30 years on, is obligatory for Hemingway pilgrims and you will find that it begins here in this 'wonderful narrow crowded market street'. Which is pretty much the way it still is. A working neighbourhood, not yet a tourist ghetto. To prolong the pleasures of the rue Mouffetard, I suggest you turn left first of all and begin at the bottom of the hill by the church of St-Médard, which has an unusual arrangement of fluted columns inside and was briefly associated with the activities of the *Convulsionnaires*, not Elvis Presley's backing group, but Protestant hysterics who believed miracles were effected here.

Opposite the church is an old house with a painted façade depicting country scenes. I don't know of another one quite like it anywhere in Paris.

Most mornings there is a street market in the rue Mouffetard and the smells of fresh-baked bread, cheese, coffee, crêpes, roasting chicken, almonds, herbs, sausages, shellfish and everything the French find so important in life induce a series of small olfactory orgasms as you start to climb the steeply sloping cobbles. A little way up the hill is a café called Le Mouffetard. It's modest and plain and family-run and a very good place to watch the ebb and flow of market life.

Follow the road up past a clutch of bars, clubs and inexpensive, often Greek, restaurants until it opens out into the place de la Contrescarpe. There was a Café des Amateurs here, which Hemingway described as 'the cesspool of the rue Mouffetard', and which even he avoided. Now it's reincarnated as the café La Chope, a cheerful, unselfconscious place popular with students from the local lycées. The day I was last in there a group of French girls was singing a terrific close-harmony version of 'Happy Birthday' into a mobile phone.

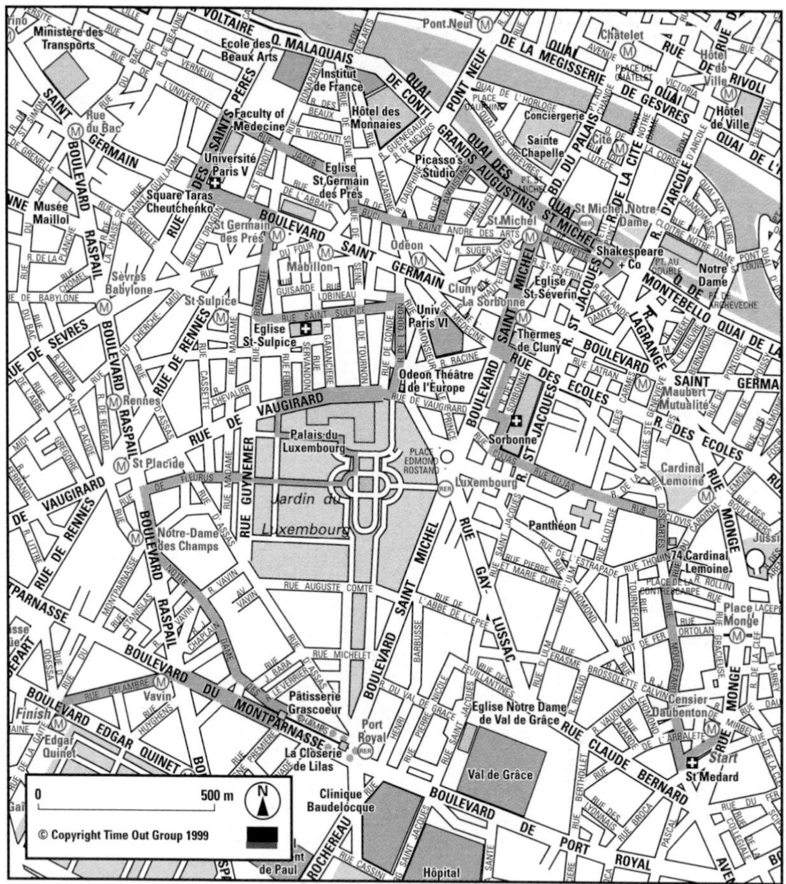

To the right as you look at the café is rue du Cardinal-Lemoine, and it's not far to No.74, where on the third floor the 22-year-old Hemingway and his wife Hadley found their first Paris apartment. He remembered it as having cold water and a squat toilet on the landing, the contents of which were pumped into a horse-drawn tank wagon at night. The toilet is inside the flat now, but that's about all that's changed, except that, at the time of writing, it was on the market for a million francs.

Though Hemingway initially came to Paris as a journalist for the *Toronto Star*, he was determined to become a proper writer and to this end he took a room in a hotel round the corner at 39 rue Descartes. He climbed to the top floor, taking with him twigs and bundles of wood to start a fire on cold winter days, and wrote about North Michigan.

He has been upstaged by Paul Verlaine, whose death in this same building in 1896 is commemorated by a large wall plaque, while Hemingway is inaccurately described on a sign squeezed in by the door as having lived here between 1921 and 1925.

In *A Moveable Feast*, he recalls writing

The old man and the beard – **Hemingway** *in 1952, two years before he won the Nobel Prize.*

George Whitman, current proprietor of **Shakespeare & Co**, *builds his premises on words.*

a story in 'a good café on the place St-Michel'. We can retrace his steps there.

Left off Descartes and along past the mighty Panthéon, where the remains of the Great and the Dead can be found, entombed in splendour. Perhaps the spirit of occupants such as Voltaire, Rousseau, Victor Hugo and Zola might have spurred Ernest on as he hurried across the windswept place du Panthéon clutching his notebook and pencils and the rabbit's foot he used to carry around for good luck.

To the right there is a first glimpse, down the side streets, of the river and the towers of Notre-Dame. University buildings and colleges proliferate. Take rue Cujas ('1520-1596, Jurisconsulte') past the back of the Faculty of Law and catch the political mood of the students from the fly-posters on the walls outside the union. When I last passed they read 'Non à l'Europe Socialiste. Oui à l'Europe des Etats', which was quite a shock to one brought up on the Red riots of 1968.

Take a right on rue Victor-Cousin ('1792-1867, Philosophe et Homme Politique'), noting the civilised Les Trois Collèges café on the corner. This will take you past the main gates of the famous Sorbonne, opened in 1253, and the site of the first printing press in France in 1470.

If you turn into place de la Sorbonne, then right down rue Champollion, you will be aware of one of the most important features of Parisian culture, along with books, jazz and clothes – the cinema. There are three of them in this narrow street alone, and between them an excellent cinema bookshop.

We've run out of ways of avoiding the main roads and must now face the noisy boulevard St-Michel. Turn right towards the Seine.

In place St-Michel you will search in vain for Hemingway's 'good café' where he sat and wrote, drank Rum St James – 'smooth as a kitten's chin' – caught the eye of a pretty girl and then ordered

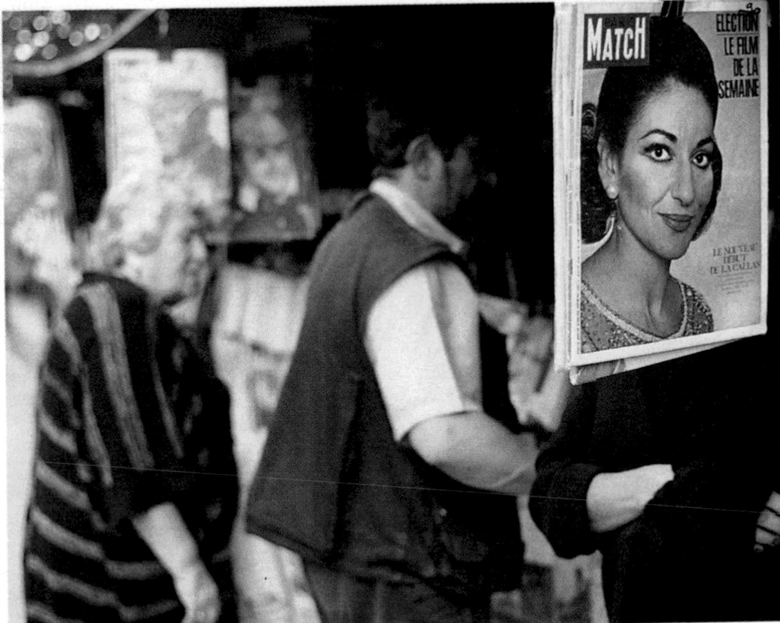

Hemingway liked to browse for reading material among the **bouquinistes** *along the quais.*

oysters and crisp white wine to celebrate finishing a story.

Today this is a place of high-volume eateries, bookstores and souvenir shops. Main north-south and east-west routes meet here at the river crossing. It's a concentration, a hub, a thrombosis and apart from an original set of Guimard Art Nouveau railings on the east-side Métro entrance, there is no reason to dawdle.

Instead, take the rue de la Huchette east off the place and follow it across rue du Petit Pont into rue de la Bûcherie. Here, sandwiched in a row of sixteenth-century houses, leaning at all angles, is Paris's most interesting foreign bookshop, Shakespeare & Company. Though it isn't the original shop run by Sylvia Beach throughout the 1920s and '30s at which Hemingway, Joyce, Henry Miller, Ezra Pound and others were regular visitors, it continues the tradition of personal and idiosyncratic service. George Whitman, the current owner, has surrounded himself with books, on shelves so precariously balanced you feel that if you took out the wrong volume it could bring the entire shop crashing about your ears. He has sleeping accommodation for visiting writers and serves tea on Sundays.

Walk across to the Seine and turn west along the quai des Grands Augustins. Hemingway liked to browse here among the *bouquinistes*, the second-hand booksellers whose dark green metal boxes are clamped to the stone walls of the embankment. Even on a quiet day, with less than a third of them open, I found their esoterica utterly beguiling – everything from ancient leather-bound treatises on medicine to magazines with names like *Fetish Girls*, back copies of the *Revue Naturiste*, old postcards, prints of tropical butterflies and even a copy of

The lively morning market on **rue Mouffetard** *was a feature of the street when Hemingway and Hadley moved to Paris.*

Hotspur comic for February 1946 – 'Trained by Tick-Tock Tacklers – A Dazzler Drake Story'.

You may well be entertained while browsing by a lone saxophonist playing moody jazz on the towpath below, the sound enclosed and amplified by the stone walls on either side, until the lights change and the next wave of traffic drowns him out.

When you get a chance, dive across the road and seek the quiet of rue des Grands Augustins, passing on the left No.7, a fine example of a Left Bank townhouse, or *hôtel* as they call them, complete with wide stone gates and an internal courtyard for horse and carriages. This was Picasso's studio for many years – it was where he painted *Guernica* – and where the Hemingways met up with him in 1946.

Central Paris must have the cleanest streets in the world. Water is sluiced down the gutters twice a day, garbage collected daily and at several points on the walk you will doubtless come across the green men of the Propreté de Paris, scrubbing streets and hosing rubbish bins with a thoroughness Lady Macbeth would be proud of. Which is why it's surprising that rue des Grands Augustins is so rich in graffiti. Maybe it merely emphasises that these are still working streets, full of shops, small businesses, laundromats, hair stylists and people going to and from their apartments.

Turn right on St-André-des-Arts, and cut through to rue Jacob, a long straight street full of elegantly displayed antiques. Keep your eyes peeled for an open doorway that might reveal some of the fast-disappearing old courtyards. At the junction with rue Bonaparte is the Café Pré aux Clercs, a Hemingway favourite, which is only a few doors down from the Hôtel d'Angleterre where he spent his first night in Paris, in Room 14 (still available for 1,000F a night), and opposite the bar/restaurant Aux Assassins with its resolute disdain for the 'that'll do nicely' approach: 'Pas de Réservations, Pas de Cartes de Crédit, Pas de Café, Pas de Téléphone.'

On a noisy junction at the end of rue Jacob is the Brasserie l'Escorailles, an establishment you might, quite justifiably, ignore, but which, in the 1920s, was the highly fashionable Michaud's, the restaurant where Hemingway pressed his nose to the window to watch James Joyce and his family eating – and all talking Italian – and where Scott Fitzgerald confided in Hemingway that he was worried about the size of his penis. Hemingway took him into the toilet, studied it and reassured him there was nothing to worry about. The only reason for spending any time here now is to visit what may well be the remains of the original loo – it has an Art Deco inlaid glass door, an old-fashioned squat toilet and graceful iron cistern. (But if someone claiming to be Scott Fitzgerald asks you to go in there and check the size of their willy, remember he died in 1940.)

Above and right: **La Sorbonne**, *the centre of learning in Paris since 1253.*

EN 1922.
DANS CETTE MAISON.
MELLE SYLVIA BEACH PUBLIA
"ULYSSES"
DE JAMES JOYCE.
J. J. S. S. F.

Sylvia Beach's *Shakespeare & Co was a focal point for Paris's anglophile literary scene.*

Up rue des Sts-Pères, passing on your left the Faculty of Medicine whose brutal neo-Fascistic façade seems to match the equally alienating swirl of smoke and noise as cars and bikes rev up the hill beside you. Boulevard St-Germain is equally busy, but wider and accommodates the traffic better. Along to the left are the well-visited cafés of Deux Magots and Flore. Though the roadside tables are the most popular, you must go inside for the period atmosphere and best-looking décor. The first floor of Café de Flore is especially recommended.

If you don't want to pay to enjoy the passing scene on the boulevard, there is a small waiterless haven on the corner of the rue des Sts-Pères called square Taras-Cheutchenko, which is a perfect place to meet, read or try and fold up your map.

Take a right on to rue Bonaparte, passing an imaginative piece of street sculpture that looks like a burst water main. Follow boutique-flanked rue Bonaparte up to St-Sulpice and then go left along rue St-Sulpice. This is an unusually arid stretch for refreshment of any kind, but relief is at hand if you can make it to the carrefour de l'Odéon. This is a popular gathering spot, and the Horse's Tavern has a quite un-Parisian bias towards beer, boasting twelve different brands on draught and 180 in bottle. Personally I would keep going up the attractive rue de l'Odéon until you come to the Bar Dix, a small, dark, friendly dive that serves jugs of sangria and is right next door to the original premises of Shakespeare & Company. Joyce's *Ulysses* was first published from here, Henry Miller borrowed books from here and never brought them back, and Hemingway smashed a vase of flowers here after reading a particularly bad review. It's now a Chinese import business.

At the end of the street is a superb fish restaurant, La Méditerranée, part of a small crescent of buildings that faces the elegant columned portals of the Odéon, Théâtre de l'Europe. The fact that there is a theatre in the centre of Paris committed to productions from all over the Continent, let alone one as prestigious as this, shows how natural and unselfconscious is the French relationship with Europe. And a stroll beneath the columns at the front of the theatre, looking back the way you've come, offers a wonderful tracking shot of St-Germain.

Take a right down rue de Vaugirard, past the *gendarmes* in their plastic boxes outside the Senate, and into a narrow lane called rue Férou. No.6 is an imposing building with stucco swags and medallions and a courtyard with gates guarded by a pair of sphinxes. This was Hemingway's last apartment in Paris and a greater contrast with the cold-water, outside-lavatory flatlet on Cardinal-Lemoine could hardly be imagined.

But by that time, Hemingway's bohemian days were over. After four years in Paris he had established himself with a hit novel – *The Sun Also Rises* – and a second and much richer wife, Pauline Pfeiffer.

Throughout the whole seven years he lived in Paris his favourite refuge was the incomparable Jardin du Luxembourg, a 60-acre park laid out in the early seventeenth century, which never intrudes upon or overwhelms the area around it. It is the city park par excellence, big enough to offer corners of peace and quiet, small enough to walk across in a matter of minutes. It connects what can loosely be called the Left Bank with Montparnasse.

As you walk in off the busy rue de Vaugirard you enter a serene and calming world created by a series of artfully constructed vistas. Immaculately trained avenues lead to low, dark, miniature forests of precision-planted limes and chestnuts reminiscent of the backgrounds of Bellini and Uccello

Sartre, Beckett and de Beauvoir also haunted **Les Deux Magots** *in place St-Germain.*

paintings in which awful things go on. These in turn give way to wide, open terraces looking out over the elegant pond and the Palais du Luxembourg. The gardens are dotted with nineteenth-century park furniture, little pavilions and shelters, all beautifully kept.

Hemingway talks often of the Jardin. He walked here with Hadley and their first son Jack, he loved to look at the Cézannes in the Musée de Luxembourg (now closed and the paintings moved to the Musée d'Orsay), and he came through here when he was very poor because 'you saw and smelled nothing to eat from the place de l'Observatoire to the rue de Vaugirard'. And, above all, he came through here on his way to visit his greatest single artistic influence in Paris, Gertrude Stein.

As the park has so little changed you can be pretty certain that if you make your way along the fresh-swept gravel paths, out of the middle gate on to rue Guynemer and across to rue de Fleurus you will be seeing pretty much what Hemingway saw as he made his way along to Stein's apartment at No.27.

'It was easy to get into the habit of stopping in at 27 rue de Fleurus for warmth and the great pictures and the conversation,' he wrote. Stein introduced him to writers and artists, and to new ideas about painting and writing. She and her friend Alice B Toklas served them liqueurs made from plums and raspberries. They fell out eventually and called each other names, but Hemingway did that with most people who helped him.

The apartment blocks on rue de Fleurus are big, bland, expensive and dull, and we should move rapidly to boulevard Raspail, left and then left again on to rue Notre-Dame-des-Champs. Ezra Pound, the poet, lived at No.70 and it was here he introduced Hemingway to one of his first publishers, Ernest Walsh. Hemingway, in turn, taught Pound to box. 'He has the general grace of the crayfish,' he wrote to a friend.

In 1924 Hemingway moved to an apartment at No.113, above a sawmill (which was why it was cheap). Nowadays the concrete-coated block is part of the Ecole Alsacienne. Much of the area is home to schools and colleges, and if you want to see the France of the future, turn up there about midday when the cafés are full of students and try to squeeze into the Avant-Scène bar.

Opposite Hemingway's apartment there was a bakery and Hemingway remembers going 'into the back door that fronted on to the boulevard Montparnasse and out through the good bread smells of the ovens and the shop to the street'. If you look carefully you'll find a short steep stairway that still leads to a boulangerie and pâtisserie and still smells so good that you may be tempted to buy one of their sensational filled baguettes, give up the walk and go back for a picnic in the Jardin du Luxembourg.

But we're almost there. The front door of the Pâtisserie Grascoeur opens on to the boulevard du Montparnasse and a final massed climax of Hemingway sites. Turn left for Librairie Abencerage at No.159, an upmarket travel bookshop that was once the Hôtel Venitia, where Hemingway carried on an adulterous affair with Pauline (who became the second Mrs Hemingway in 1927).

Carry on to the junction of rue de l'Observatoire where you will find La Closerie des Lilas, one of Hemingway's favourite writing, eating and drinking spots. He became disillusioned with it when it went upmarket in 1925. He was particularly appalled that the waiter was forced to shave off his moustache. The American Bar they opened then is still there and you can sit and have a cocktail named after him beside a brass plaque with his name on. Or sit at the front and look out past the statue of Marshal Ney flourishing his sword and see beyond it,

A second home – **La Closerie des Lilas** *served for a time as Hemingway's study, kitchen and, increasingly, drinks cabinet.*

La Closerie
RESTAURANT-BAR
des Lilas

Gertrude Stein *with Hemingway's son Jack.*

across the road, the sign of the Hôtel Beauvoir, where Hadley Hemingway and their young son stayed after Hemingway left her for Pauline, and Paris began to turn sour for all of them.

'Paris was never to be the same again, although it was always Paris and you changed as it changed,' he wrote of the break-up.

La Closerie des Lilas (with its own chapter in *A Moveable Feast*) is a convenient place to stop, but if you would like a cheaper restaurant and a more collectable Métro station at which to finish, then turn right out of the Closerie and follow the boulevard du Montparnasse to place Vavin. Here you have a choice of classic brasseries, all well known to Hemingway – La Rotonde, Le Dôme, La Coupole, Le Select. Pass them by for now and turn off the main road up rue Delambre, where you will find the site of the fabulously named Dingo Bar. It's now called the Auberge de Venise, and the cooking is Italian, but surely that's a small price to pay for eating on the spot where Hemingway first met Scott Fitzgerald and the two English aristocrats on whom he based the characters of Duff Twysden and Mike Guthrie in *The Sun Also Rises*, the book that made Hemingway, and Hemingway's Paris, famous.

We've covered the ground the way Hemingway liked to do it. On foot. I may be wrong but I can't remember him mentioning a single Métro station – even the one at the end of the rue Delambre and at the end of our walk – Edgar Quinet. 'Poète, Historien, Homme Politique 1803-1875.'

Eating & drinking

Auberge de Venise

10 rue Delambre, 14th (01.43.35.43.09). **Open** noon-2.30pm, 7-11.30pm, Tue-Sun. Cosy Italian restaurant with fine food.

Aux Assassins

40 rue Jacob, 6th (no phone). **Open** 7pm-midnight Mon-Sat. Closed Aug. A lively bistro for bawdy sing-song and trad fare.

L'Avant-Scène Café

53 rue Notre-Dames-des-Champs, 6th (01.45.48.91.10). **Open** 11am-2am Mon-Fri; 3pm-2am Sat.

Le Bar Dix

10 rue de l'Odéon, 6th (01.43.26.66.83). **Open** 6pm-2am daily. Trendy venue that was a hotbed of activity in the 1968 riots.

Brasserie l'Escorailles

29 rue des Sts-Pères, 6th (01.42.60.25.35). **Open** 6am-9pm Mon-Sat.

Café de Flore

172 boulevard St-Germain, 6th (01.45.48.55.26). **Open** 7am-1.30am daily. Expensive café that used to be a Surrealist haunt, and now hosts filmmakers and *café philosophique* sessions.

Café Pré aux Clercs

30 rue Bonaparte, 6th (01.43.54.41.73). **Open** 6.30am-2am daily.

La Chope

2-4 place de la Contrescarpe, 5th (01.43.26.51.26). **Open** 8am-2am daily. Basic salads and café fare.

La Closerie des Lilas
171 boulevard du Montparnasse, 6th (01.40.51.34.50). **Open** 11.30am-1am daily. Better value in the brasserie than the restaurant. Get a 'Hemingway' cocktail here.

La Coupole
102 boulevard du Montparnasse, 14th (01.43.20.14.20). **Open** 7.30am-2am daily. Reliable French food in this legendary art deco brasserie.

Les Deux Magots
6 place St-Germain-des-Prés, 6th (01.45.48.55.25). **Open** 7.30am-2am daily. Expensive and classy one-time haunt of Sartre, Beckett and de Beauvoir.

Le Dôme
108 boulevard du Montparnasse, 14th (01.43.35.25.81). **Open** noon-2.45pm, 7pm-12.30am, daily. Closed Mon and Sun in Aug. Legendary Montparnasse fish house, also an upmarket café-bar.

Horse's Tavern
16 carrefour de l'Odéon, 6th (01.43.54.96.91). **Open** 8am-2am Mon-Sat; 8am-1.30am Sun.

La Méditerranée
2 place de l'Odéon, 6th (01.43.26.02.30). **Open** noon-2.30pm, 7.30-11pm, daily. Stylish types enjoy excellent fish in beautifully renovated surroundings.

Le Mouffetard
116 rue Mouffetard, 5th (01.43.31.42.50). **Open** 7.30am-9pm Tue-Sat; 7.30am-8pm Sun. Closed July. Lively venue with fine brioches.

La Rotonde
105 boulevard du Montparnasse, 6th (01.43.26.68.84). **Open** 7am-2am daily. A classic café-brasserie offering oysters, and sandwiches

Le Select
99 boulevard du Montparnasse, 6th (01.42.22.65.27). **Open** 7am-3am Mon-Thur, Sun; 7am-4am Fri, Sat. Large, grand and historic self-styled 'American bar'.

Les Trois Collèges
16 rue Cujas, 5th (01.43.54.67.30). **Open** 10am-7.30pm Mon-Fri. Tearoom with fine selection of interesting teas and handmade pâtisseries.

Accommodation

Hôtel Beauvoir
43 avenue Georges-Bernanos, 5th (01.43.25.57.10).

Hôtel d'Angleterre
44 rue Jacob. 6th (01.42.60.34.72).

Hôtel des Trois Collèges
16 rue Cujas, 5th (01.43.54.67.30).

Churches

Eglise St-Médard
141 rue Mouffetard, 5th (01.44.08.87.00). **Open** 9am-noon, 2.30-7pm, Tue-Sat; 9am-noon Sun.

Eglise St-Sulpice
place St-Sulpice, 6th (01.46.33.21.78). **Open** 8am-7.30pm daily.

Literary information

Shakespeare & Co
37 rue de la Bûcherie, 5th (01.43.26.96.50). **Open** noon-midnight daily.

Ernest Hemingway's Paris books
A Moveable Feast, 1964
The Sun Also Rises (or **Fiesta**), 1926

Museums & buildings

Musée d'Orsay
62 rue de Lille, 7th (01.40.49.48.14/recorded information 01.45.49.11.11). **Open** 10am-6pm Tue, Wed, Fri, Sat; 10am-9.30pm Thur; 9am-6pm Sun. **Admission** 40F; 30F concs.

Le Panthéon
place du Panthéon, 5th (01.44.32.18.00). **Open** *Apr-Sept* 9.30am-6.30pm daily; *Oct-Mar* 10am-5.30pm daily. **Admission** 35F; 23F concs.

La Sorbonne
47 rue des Ecoles, 5th (01.40.46.20.15). **Open** *courtyards* 9am-4.30pm Mon-Fri.

Shopping

Marché Mouffetard
Open 9am-1pm, 4-7pm, Tue-Sat; 9am-1pm Sun.

Pâtisserie Grascoeur
151 bd du Montparnasse, 6th (01.43.26.38.88). **Open** *Apr-Sept* 7am-7.30pm Mon-Fri; *Oct-Easter* 7.30am-1.30pm.

Other

Faculté de Médecine
rue des Sts-Pères, 6th (01.43.289.78.79).

Jardin du Luxembourg
place Auguste-Comte, place Edmond-Rostand, rue de Vaugirard, 6th. **Open** *summer* 7.30am-9.30pm daily; *winter* 8am-5pm daily. *Children's playground* 10am-dusk daily. **Admission** *children's playground* 14F children; 7.50F adults.

Odéon, Théâtre de l'Europe
1 place de l'Odéon, 6th (01.44.41.36.36). **Open** *box office* 11am-6.30pm Mon-Sat; *telephone bookings* 11am-7pm Mon-Sat (Sun when plays are on).

The white ghosts of the Luxembourg

Marie Darrieussecq

Statues, ponds and lawns in the Jardin.

Start: place Edmond-Rostand entrance, Jardin du Luxembourg, 6th
Finish: rue de Vaugirard exit, Jardin du Luxembourg, 6th
Time: 1 hour
Distance: 1km/0.75 mile
Getting there: short walk from a number of Métro stations (see Michael Palin's map p129)
Getting back: short walk to a number of Métro stations
Note: the Jardin du Luxembourg has lawns, miniature sailboats on ponds, boules, chess, cards, tennis, ponies and a playground – so this is a good walk for children. It also has a café, but we have listed other venues within a few minutes' walk.

It's a curious idea, to visit the Jardin du Luxembourg for its statues. The statues in the Luxembourg are eyesores – and there are plenty of them: about 100[1] in all. But taken as a collection, these white silhouettes, lurking in the greenery or standing in the middle of lawns, are just as much a part of the beauty of the place as the trees and the green metal chairs; it's from a distance, gold-dusted by a ray of dappled sunlight, that they gain in grace, in bucolic lightness, set here and there in an artificially random but gracious way, like white pebbles fallen from the pocket of some giant Tom Thumb. However, seen up close, the statues in the Luxembourg are a kind of urban furniture[2], proliferating, solid, pitiful. Just as you find bus shelters, Decaux advertising hoardings and *chiraquettes* – urinal-bunkers that work with two-franc coins – on the boulevard St-Michel or on rue de Vaugirard, so in the same way, on the other side of the black and gold grilles, these century-old statues stand stubbornly, rustic and debonair, remnants from a time when people worshipped senators, poets with official posts, plump allegorical figures and huntress Dianas.

In fact, all of the statues in the Jardin du Luxembourg are allegorical. Not only the chunky stone women (such as *Painting*, on a façade of the Orangerie), who represent an art or an idea by their nourishing breasts and solid thighs; but also the fauns, official authors, '*d'après antique*' copies and naked ephebes. All these monuments embody a single idea: the self-assurance of established power, carved in stone by the sculptors of the regime. Bertaux, Forestier, Husson, Gatteaux – who remembers their names? Pompous, interchangeable artists, kow-towing equally to monarchical, imperial and then republican conformity, their lack of boldness, overcautious subjects,

1. More than 80 and less than 100, depending on what you consider to be a statue: do the large marble pots around the bassin du Sénat count as statues? Should the total include empty plinths? And do the pedal cars, practically national monuments, count as mobile statues, like machines by Tinguely?
2. 'Urban furniture' seems to me a typically French expression, a dream of street layout akin to the way one arranges the furniture in one's own living room.

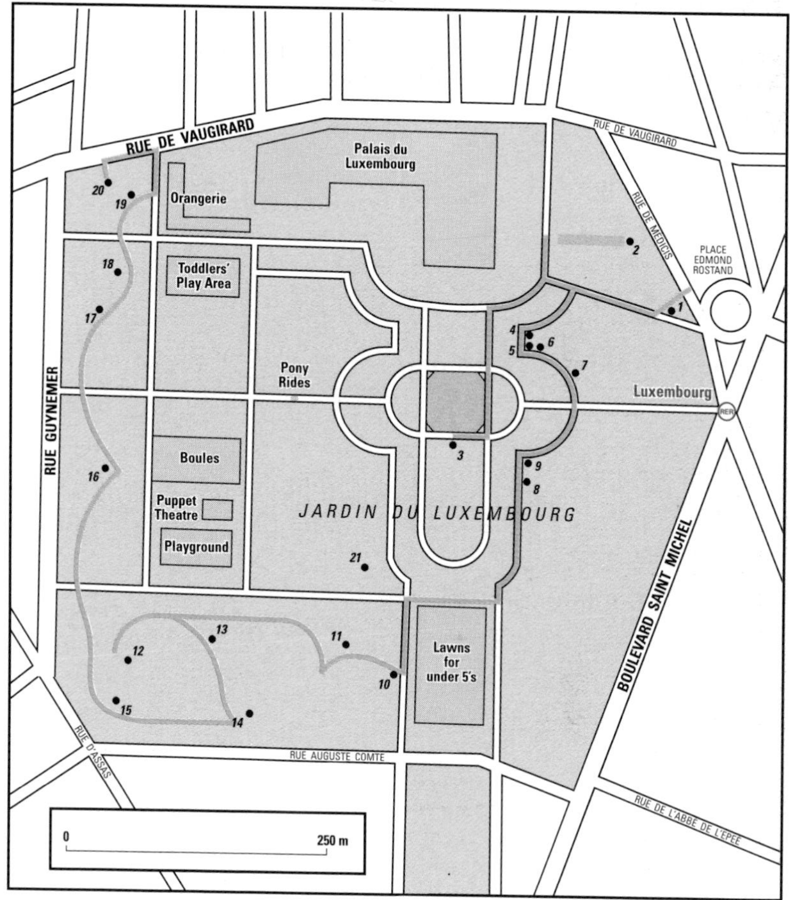

Jardin du Luxembourg

Marie Darrieussecq's walk

1. Faune Dansant - by Lequesne (1851)
2. La Fontaine Médicis - Ottin (1862)
3. Monument à Scheurer-Kestner, Senator (1833-99) - Dalou (1908)
4. Sainte Bathilde (680) - Thérasse (1848)
5. Berthe (783) - Oudiné (1848)
6. Mathilde (1083) - Elschoect (1850)
7. Sainte Geneviève (420-512) - Mercier (1845)
8. Madame de Montpensier (1627-93) - Demesmay (1848)
9. Clémence Isaure - Préault (1848)
10. Lion de Nubie - A. Cain (1870)
11. Harde de Cerfs - Le Duc (1885)
12. Les Joies de la Famille - Daillon
13. Watteau (1684-1721) - Gaudi (1912)
14. Baudelaire (1821-67) - Fix-Masseau (1939)
15. Sainte-Beuve (1804-69) - Puech (1898)
16. La Liberte - Bartholdi (1905)
17. Triomphe de Silène - Dalou (1897) - see also Maureen Freely's walk
18. La Frileuse (or L'Hiver) - Anon
19. L'Effort - Pierre Roche (1907)
20. Beethoven (1770-1827) - Bourdelle

Linda Lê's walk

21. Laure de Noves (1308-48) - Ottin (1850)

prematurely old-fashioned style and submissiveness set me free. Free to wander and daydream, free to feel indifferent to these minor works, free to overlook them; free not to go into raptures, free to look at the trees, people, children on ponies, flowers, lovers, fountains; free to see the space in which these marble landmarks act as punctuation, enhancement and boundary stones.

For these reasons, the statues in the Luxembourg make excellent garden statues (people say the same thing about gnomes). Of course, the Luxembourg is not a museum, but a place in which to stroll, flirt, relax, read, kiss, have a snack, study the effect of a new dress, etc. I grant you, museums – and above all open-air museums – can fill the same function[3]; but for that to be so, first you have to disregard the works, and control your acquired reflexes in front of Art: *a priori* respect, silence, a thoughtful expression, hesitant speech and shrinking timidity, all of which, in the presence of Art, condition our capacity for attention and momentarily paralyse the neurons. The sculptors presented in the Jardin du Luxembourg leave us in peace precisely because they so strenuously upheld that idea of Art, making themselves the senseless worshippers of compulsory forms and prêt-à-sculpter criteria. They sculpted immobility. Of their work, all that remains are cut blocks or cast bronze; no art, no liberty, no ideas; just peaceful landmarks – the décor for our stroll. So you can wander as you wish and not feel obliged to admire.

Usually, I enter from place Edmond-Rostand. As luck would have it, I immediately come face to face with a statue that's not too ugly (in other words, a statue I like): a *Dancing Faun*, a bronze by a certain Lesquesne[4] dating from 1851. Ethereal, joyful, athletic and slender, the faun is blowing into a cornet and dances smiling on one leg; he's also endowed with a delightful little tail. I've always found him extremely charming. He blesses the walk with a note of insolent and happy insouciance. By turning off to the right, just before getting to the Sénat (the former palace of Marie de Médicis), you come to the *La Fontaine Médicis*. It's something of a secret place, below the path, protected by tall plane trees[5] that screen out the noise from rue de Médicis. The fountain, decorated in 1861 in the spirit of Italianate grottoes with mosses, stalactites and rocks, shelters three figures, *Polyphemus Surprising Acis and Galatea*.

Acis and Galatea make a very lovely couple (illegitimate, unfortunately for them), the young and handsome Acis supporting the languorous, very sexy Galatea, with her taut breasts and soft belly; while Polyphemus[6], her cyclopean husband, stands above them, ready to spring. Polyphemus is enormous, not only sporting great muscles, but he's represented on a scale twice as large as that of the lovebirds; what's more, he's made of solid, sombre bronze, while they are made of very bright, finely lined marble. By this visual artifice alone, you realise that the scene is about to turn to drama, and that the couple don't have a chance. They occupy the central niche of the fountain, while the cyclops looks down on them from an artificial rock. The niche is a tunnel of love, a garden of Eden, a

Relax by **La Fontaine Médicis** *in the shade of 160-year-old plane trees that screen out the background noise from rue de Médicis.*

3. The Musée de la Sculpture de la Ville de Paris, on the banks of the Seine below the pont d'Austerlitz, may be a place to go on the pull, but it's first and foremost an authentic museum of contemporary art.
4. The fact that the sculptors of the Luxembourg are not held in the highest esteem frees me from having to exhaustively list their names and the dates and titles of their works, and allows me to select statues arbitrarily.
5. These plane trees were planted in 1840. A fact rare enough to be worth noting is that they are not pruned into awful stumps in the French fashion, but are allowed to branch out and so cast a very pleasant shade.
6. I've never been able to make out the single eye of Polyphemus, owing to the inclined position of the face half covered by hair, and because of the water being in the way; perhaps also owing to the reluctance of the sculptor to present such a monstrous face in such an idyllic setting.

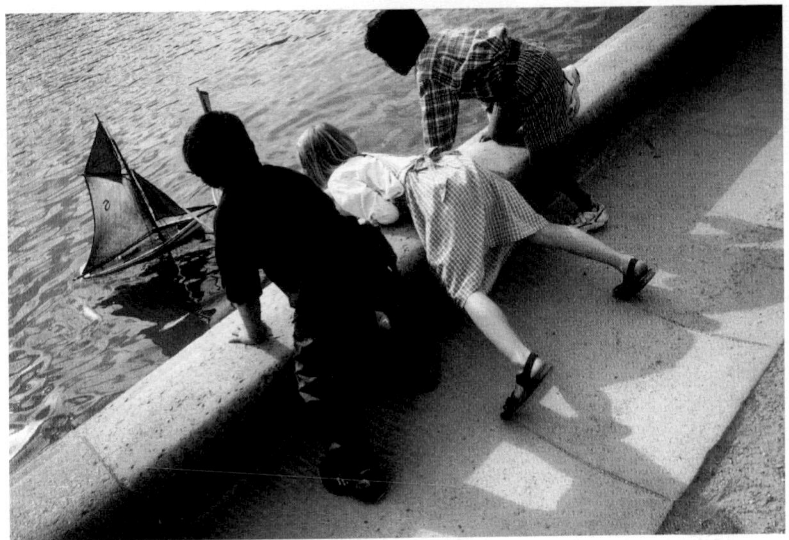

The **octagonal pond**, *in the middle of the Jardin, is a big hit with boat-minded children.*

hidden nest with menace hovering above. It's momentum frozen in matter, the pause before the climax, calm before the storm.

Witness this motionless tale on summer afternoons, when the light turns gloomy beneath the plane trees: the sky between the broad leaves is so deep it turns violet; the heat has built up, so you look for a little coolness at the water's edge, in front of the sleeping ducks and the fish cooking beneath the water lilies; the grotto has widened to the dimensions of the plane trees, the vault of the foliage is going, for another instant, to withstand the storm's large raindrops. And when the first lightning streaks across the Paris sky, you would think that Polyphemus is bearing down in his rage, and that Acis is going to release Galatea, and that the rain is going to make ripples in a fountain full of blood.

It's pleasant to read beside the fountain. A few senators, between sessions, peruse *Le Monde* or *Le Figaro*, or dream of one day having their own statue, like Scheurer-Kestner. You can make out his monument from here, facing the Sénat from the other side of the octagonal pool where children sail their miniature boats. It's an idiotic obelisk, surrounded by female allegorical figures – naked Truth on one side, Justice on the other with her sword and scales half hidden in the folds of her toga. It's exactly 100 years since Scheurer-Kestner's death: nine years after it, in 1908, Dalou sculpted this Egyptian nonsense in his honour. The senator deserved better: he defended Dreyfus, in other words the idea of impartial justice, and, like Zola, he embodies the fight against racist and anti-Semitic prejudice.

Surrounding this figure of the republican ideal, on each side of the esplanade, 20 white queens line up in the shadow of the chestnut trees. These ladies of a bygone age, these *neiges d'antan* straight out of Villon, were sculpted between 1846 and 1850, each by different artists, who all applied themselves to respect a perfectly uniform style. The queens are upright, tall, draped in marble as in virtue. Queens of France, *régentes*, saints or illustrious ladies, dignified and severe, they are a part of the legend that built France – and if their historical reality is contested, they testify above all to a Middle Ages mythology as dreamed

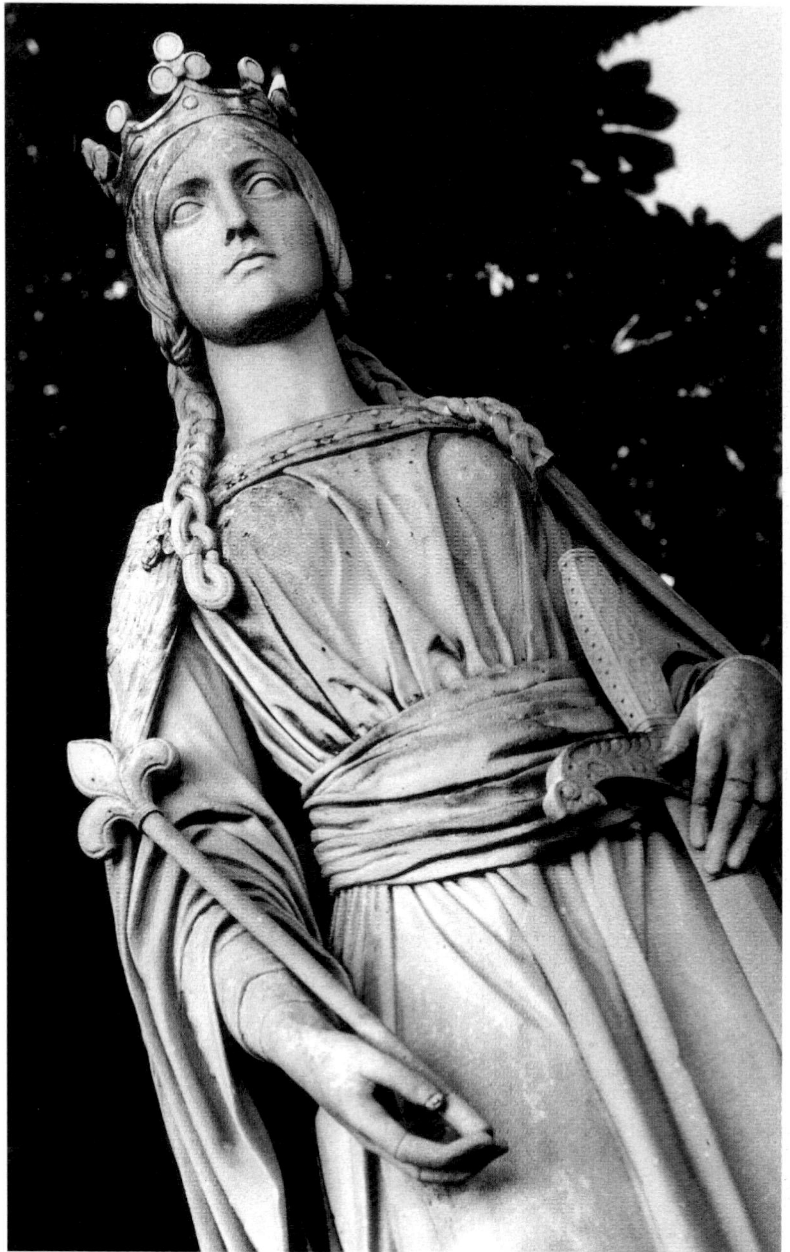

Mathilde – *one of 20 white queens lining the esplanade, sculpted between 1846 and 1850.*

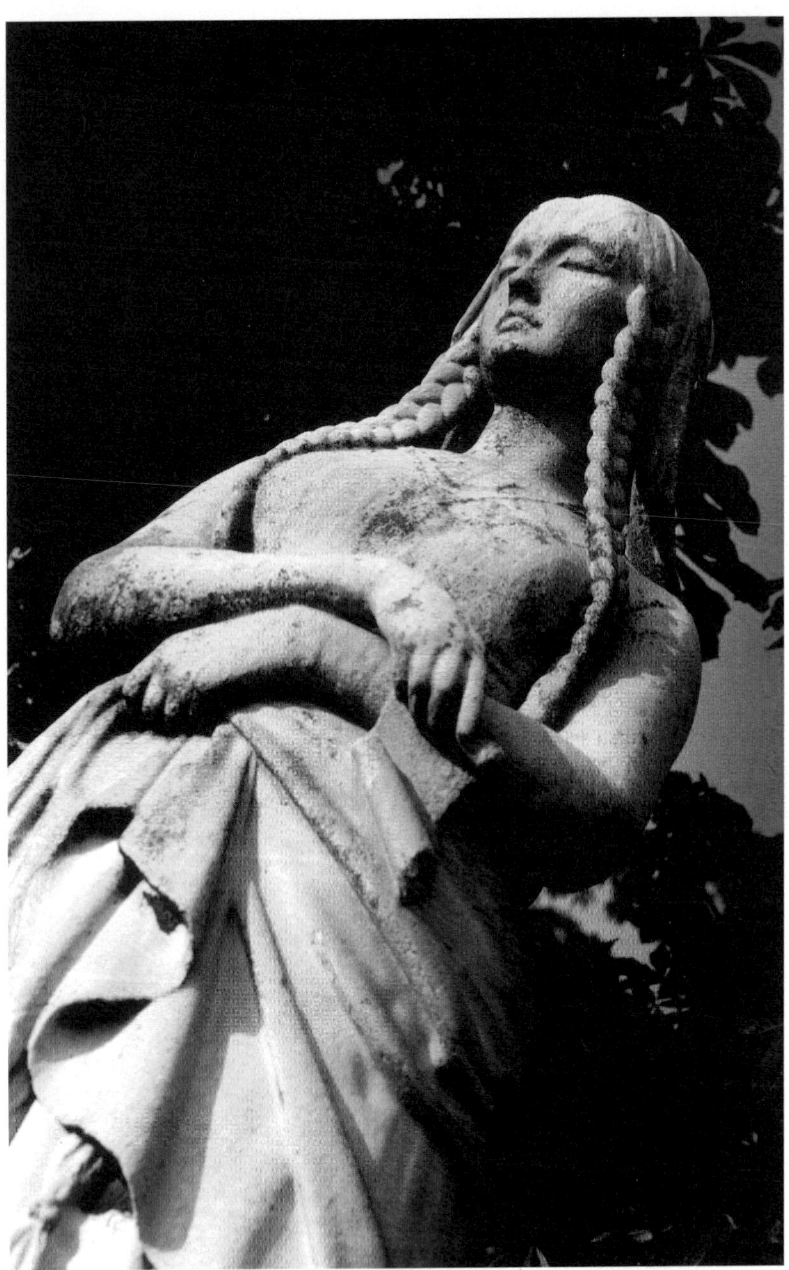

Ste-Geneviève, *patron saint of Paris – in the fifth century, she held the Vikings at bay.*

of by 1840s romanticism. Veils, ermine muffs, bonnets or crowns, ruffs or collarets, the marble follows medieval fashion. After *Bathilde*, *Berthe* and *Mathilde*, on your left starting from the fountain, stands the beautiful *Ste-Geneviève*, patron saint of Paris. Magnificent tresses accentuate her figure and flow down to her thighs. Geneviève is the most ancient of all the figures represented – in the fifth century, through force of character alone, she pushed back the Viking Drakkars invading the Seine. The most recent of these figures is *Mademoiselle de Montpensier*, first cousin of Louis XIV, otherwise known as 'La Grande Demoiselle'. She stands at the top of the steps, opposite the obelisk. This restless, amorous and warlike woman, who had the cannon fired against the King's troops, then, at 42, secretly married an adventurer, was, on my last visit, veiled in plastic sheeting. No doubt she was being cleaned of moss and lichen, unless the pigeons, which habitually perch among the ribbons in these worthy *demoiselles'* hair, had shown a baleful preference for her; yet all one could see was her impassive head, and she seemed to be taking a bath behind a screen. Her immediate neighbour, on the other side of the steps, is *Clémence Isaure*. Her name alone is a splendour, a condensation of time past; this legendary native of Toulouse, saint or courtesan – or both at once – is superbly hip-swaying, her belly encircled, very low down, with a fine chain, her breasts moulded so close by the folds of her clothing that the stone seems to be a mere veil over palpitating flesh.

I like these grand stone ladies, these white phantoms from another age. Adolescents and small girls scrutinise them, fascinated; the former study their curves without fearing a rebuff, the latter dream of giant Barbie dolls, dressed as princesses or fairies. But when one contemplates these statues as an adult, what kind of nostalgia is at play? It's a sentiment as evanescent as the stone is solid, an impression of ruin and disaster in front of these solitary bodies mummified in the strollers' midst, exiled from life by a spell, the sleeping beauties in a cemetery of desires.

Let's go on to the end of the esplanade, passing in front of the rectangles of lawn reserved for children. On the right, under the large trees that mark the beginning of what I call 'the English garden' (curved borders laid out to appear random), a magnificent bronze lion, the smaller cousin of the one that lords it over place Denfert-Rochereau, has just pulled down a wretched ostrich. At the end of the path, an equally superb stag nobly protects his startled fawn and doe. On the rue Guynemer side, *Les Joies de la Famille* are the human equivalent of this ideological scene: this group, arguably one of the ugliest in the Jardin, presents a dominant male encircling the shoulders of a well-endowed female, who is playing with her little one. Fortunately, a few steps away, the bust of the charming *Watteau*, freshened with roses by a creature ready to set off for Cythère, presents a less strictly reproductive vision of love. This very *décolletée* young woman, who offers herself, with roses, to the libertine painter, is perched on a small wall; her tiny feet swinging in the empty air, her swelling skirt, her little round face, her penetrating gaze, are a breath of the eighteenth century in these overly raked pathways.

I love to daydream along these artificial paths, in this serpentine, calm, shady part of the garden, populated during break times by pupils from the lycée opposite, and at all times of the day by eternal readers with heads down and legs in the sun. But nineteenth-century convictions also assert themselves on the literary front. By following rue Auguste-Comte, one meets a small bust of *Baudelaire*, frowning in the sunlight: in this unfrequented corner, it's as though he's banished from the trees, excluded from damp shadow, even from the garden. In winter, the rain and the grey sky weigh directly on his head. Not far away, at the end of the path, near the rue d'Assas gate, his contemporary, *Sainte-Beuve*, a perfunctory, round-bellied critic, has been honoured by his 'admirers and friends at the Académie Française' with a full-length statue twice as large. He looks very pleased with it. His immortal *Causeries* hang beneath his chin, threaded together with laurels. He seems to be ready to return to his petty declamations in the gilded salons of a century reassured by his conformist ideas[7]. It's the perfect, timeless allegory of Criticism. I take great pleasure in sticking my tongue out at him.

By following rue Guynemer, you get a surprise: that raised arm, that flame, that crowned head… This is the smallest of the models that Bartholdi used for his *Statue of Liberty.* The Atlantic, here, is the lawn; the benches are the liners. The flame illuminates the beds of petunias, lovers' kisses, footballs and pushchairs. No one pays any attention to this little black statue. The classic, imperious gesture becomes a pitiful appeal: like the travelling acrobats whose art lies in standing motionless, who disguise themselves as Statues of Liberty and stand frozen, ignored by the crowds, at the ends of bridges or in Métro tunnels. In the centre of the next flowerbed, Dalou's 1897 *Triumph of Silenus* is the paradoxical companion piece, bawdy and saturated, to austere *Liberty*. There are eight heads in this teeming group: Silenus, emulator of Bacchus, whose enormous bare belly is like an obscene ninth head in the centre of the swarm; two fauns and two bacchantes, who are trying to haul the fat sybarite on to the back of a stamping donkey; a small boy and a laughing baby, the childhood of Silenus. Baskets of fruit, tambourines, ropes and overturned baskets add to the orgy of flesh. Two steps away, like a mediocre and offended reminder of the *Statue of Liberty*, the *Frileuse*, otherwise called *Winter*, turns her back on these antics. Muffled by heavy veils with indeterminate folds, she warms herself over a small brazier, as if, harassed, she had just put down her torch. A comical crown of anti-pigeon spikes completes the resemblance, and gives the impression of a sulky and worn-out Liberty[8].

Approaching the rue de Vaugirard kiosk, near the exit towards the Eglise St-Sulpice, you pass *Effort* by Pierre Roche. This sculptor with a doubly appropriate name picks up the expressive heritage of Rodin, at a period when the garden offers nothing but copies of ancient statues, or lacklustre realist whimsy. The masculine allegorical figure of effort is a contorted athlete, holding up a heavy stone on which shrubs have since grown. The position is astonishing, the body twisted, bunched up and muscular. Like the neighbouring bust, Bourdelle's *Beethoven*, this work lifts the Jardin from its idiotic idyll, from a golden age of mental laziness when sculpting seems to have been an activity hardly different from sleeping, when sculptors were careful to disturb neither accepted forms, nor the public. *Effort* and *Beethoven* disturb the stroll, jostle daydreams… It's time to set free one's gaze, and to wander the pathways in a dream, or follow a game of boules, draughts or tennis, or go and watch Punch and Judy, or take lessons in

Mademoiselle de Montpensier, or **'La Grande Demoiselle'** *– a restless, amorous and warlike woman.*

7. Flaubert, Stendhal and Verlaine have finally, like Baudelaire, been honoured with a statue in the garden. Stendhal has only a small medallion, but it's by Rodin, on the right near the St-Michel entrance. Flaubert, opposite, is strangely perched on the high back of a stone bench. Verlaine's severe, expressive bust can be found on the rue Guynemer side. An amusing game is to check the following hypothesis in the garden: the more insignificant the writer (Sainte-Beuve, Fabre, Murger or even Banville), the more imposing his statue (and vice versa); and the shorter the time elapsed between the date of his death and his statuary consecration.

8. I've no idea why this *frileuse* has been so privileged as to receive pigeon protection. Most statues in the Luxembourg, however proud, are topped with birds and their droppings. The visual effect encourages a certain sense of derision in Parisians at an early age.

The smallest of the models that Bartholdi used for his **Statue of Liberty** *never draws a crowd.*

beekeeping, or hire a pony, or fraudulently pick a pear from the orchard… Outside, Paris is a murmur. We are 20 minutes' walk from the Louvre.

Translated by Simon Cropper.

Eating & drinking

Buvette des Marionnettes
Jardin du Luxembourg, 6th. **Open** *Sept-May* 8.30am-6.30pm daily; *June-Aug* 8.30am-7.30pm daily.

Flowers Café
5 rue Soufflot, 5th (01.43.54.75.36). **Open** 6am-midnight daily. Fine view of the Panthéon out front.

Les Fontaines
9 rue Soufflot, 5th (01.43.26.42.80). **Open** noon-3pm, 7-11pm, Mon-Sat. Authentic French cuisine.

La Gueuze
19 rue Soufflot, 5th (01.43.54.63.00). **Open** noon-2am daily. Belgian beers and Flemish food.

Japotori
41 rue Monsieur-le-Prince, 6th (01.43.29.00.54). **Open** 11am-3pm, 6-11.45pm, daily. Popular, busy and very good-value Japanese venue.

La Méditerranée
2 place de l'Odéon, 6th (01.43.26.02.30). **Open** noon-2.30pm, 7.30-11pm, daily. Left Bank types enjoy excellent fish in beautifully renovated surroundings.

Chez Maître Paul
12 rue Monsieur-le-Prince, 6th (01.43.54.74.59). **Open** 12.15-2.30pm, 7.15-10.30pm, daily. Closed Sun & Mon lunch in July & Aug. Rich, consoling cuisine from the eastern French region.

Les Papilles
30 rue Gay-Lussac, 5th (01.43.25.20.79). **Open** 9.30am-8.30pm Mon, Wed, Fri, Sat; 9.30am-11pm Tue, Thur. A knowledgeable wine bar with a Provence theme.

Au Petit Suisse
16 rue de Vaugirard, 6th (01.43.26.03.81). **Open** 7am-8pm Mon-Fri. Simple snacks and student-watching opposite the Jardin.

Polidor
41 rue Monsieur-le-Prince, 6th (01.43.26.95.34). **Open** noon-2.30pm, 7pm-12.30am, Mon-Sat; noon-2.30pm, 7-11pm, Sun. Authentic respectable *cuisine bourgeoise* in elbow-to-elbow seating.

Information

Jardin du Luxembourg
place Auguste-Comte, place Edmond-Rostand, rue de Vaugirard, 6th. **Open** *summer* 7.30am-9.30pm daily; *winter* 8am-5pm daily. *Children's playground* 10am-dusk daily. **Admission** *children's playground* 14F children; 7.50F adults.

Imperious, haughty, magnificent – the **bronze lion** *is a smaller cousin of the one on the loose in place Denfert-Rochereau.*

Sleeping with the enemy

Philippe Alexandre

The Republic sleeps in the monarchy's bed.

Start: Assemblée Nationale (Palais-Bourbon), 7th
Finish: Palais de Justice, 1st
Time: 3-4 hours
Distance: 7km/4.5 miles
Getting there: line 12 to Mº Assemblée Nationale
Getting back: short walk to Mº Cité (line 4)
Note: many of the state buildings are not open to the public, except for one Saturday in September known as the Journées du Patrimoine (see listings). This walk also contains long stretches between locations (see map).

For many years French politics had just one, flamboyant centre: the Palais-Bourbon, which now houses the Assemblée Nationale. Attracted no doubt by its name, the Republic took it over after a century of revolution, the Napoleonic Empire, a badly restored monarchy and, finally, a military disaster that saw the Prussians nearly arriving at the gates. What's more, the building faces the place de la Concorde, which ought to inspire peace among its occupants. The Palais-Bourbon harbours a *buvette*, a bar, which used to be this political cathedral's holy of holies. Members of Parliament were among themselves there, shielded from the gaze of journalists. After insulting and cursing one another throughout the session, they would get together over an *apéritif*, preferably the speciality of their electoral district. One day, as two Deputies from opposing parties clinked glasses after having exchanged particularly virulent words, Clemenceau replied to a puzzled colleague, 'What stands between them? Their ideas? Surely you must agree with me that that is very little indeed…'

Over the past 120 years, the Palais-Bourbon has grown ever more beautiful. For their own quarters, the Deputies have spared no expense and the Assemblée Nationale (known 60 years ago as the Chamber of Deputies, which sounded more intimate) boasts one of the only budgets under the Republic never to have run a deficit. The Palais-Bourbon adjoins another palace inherited from the Ancien Régime, the Hôtel de Lassay, residence of the National Assembly President: such a lovely dwelling that it is bitterly coveted. Its principal asset is a cellar harbouring grand and old vintages, a leftover from the 1960s when Bordeaux Mayor Jacques Chaban-Delmas was the master of the house. This great sportsman was also a famous connoisseur of his territory's fine wines: his nostrils poised over a glass, Chaban-Delmas was capable of reciting the name and the year of the wine, whose colour he admired with a gaze worthy of Don Juan eyeing a young bride.

The Palais-Bourbon and the Hôtel de Lassay are connected by a large corridor decorated with Gobelins tapestries. When the President goes to the Assembly, he doesn't get his feet wet: he is preceded by a platoon of Gardes Républicains sporting sabres and gilt epaulettes, marching to the sound of a drum roll.

Deputies and journalists rub shoulders

The **Assemblée Nationale***, formerly the Chamber of Deputies, is housed in the beautiful Palais-Bourbon.*

ASSEM
NATIONAL

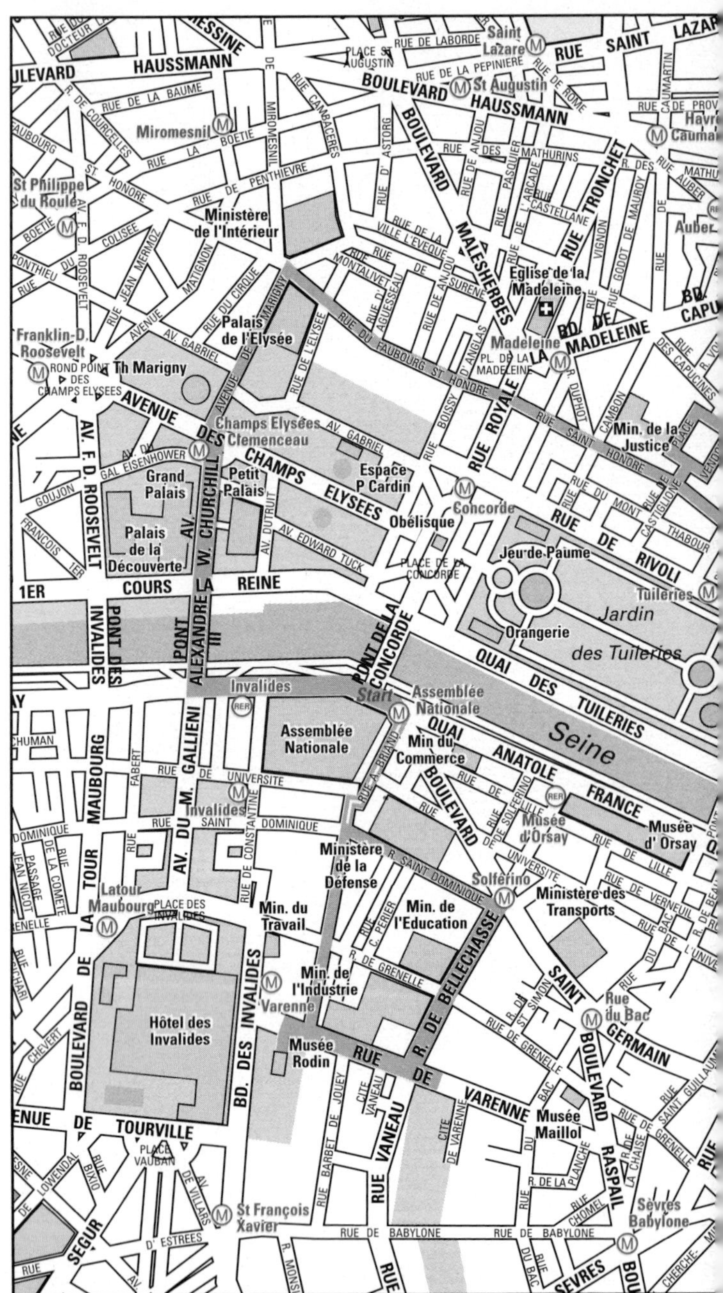

Miromesnil
St Philippe du Roule
Ministère de l'Intérieur
Palais de l'Elysée
Franklin-D. Roosevelt
Th Marigny
Champs Elysées Clemenceau
Grand Palais
Petit Palais
Palais de la Découverte
Espace P Cardin
Obélisque
Concorde
Eglise de la Madeleine
Madeleine
Saint Lazare
St Augustin
Min. de la Justice
Jeu de Paume
Tuileries
Jardin des Tuileries
Orangerie
Seine
Invalides
Start
Assemblée Nationale
Min du Commerce
Musée d'Orsay
Ministère de la Défense
Solférino
Ministère des Transports
Min. de l'Education
Min. du Travail
Min. de l'Industrie
Latour Maubourg
Varenne
Hôtel des Invalides
Musée Rodin
Musée Maillol
Rue du Bac
St François Xavier
Sèvres Babylone

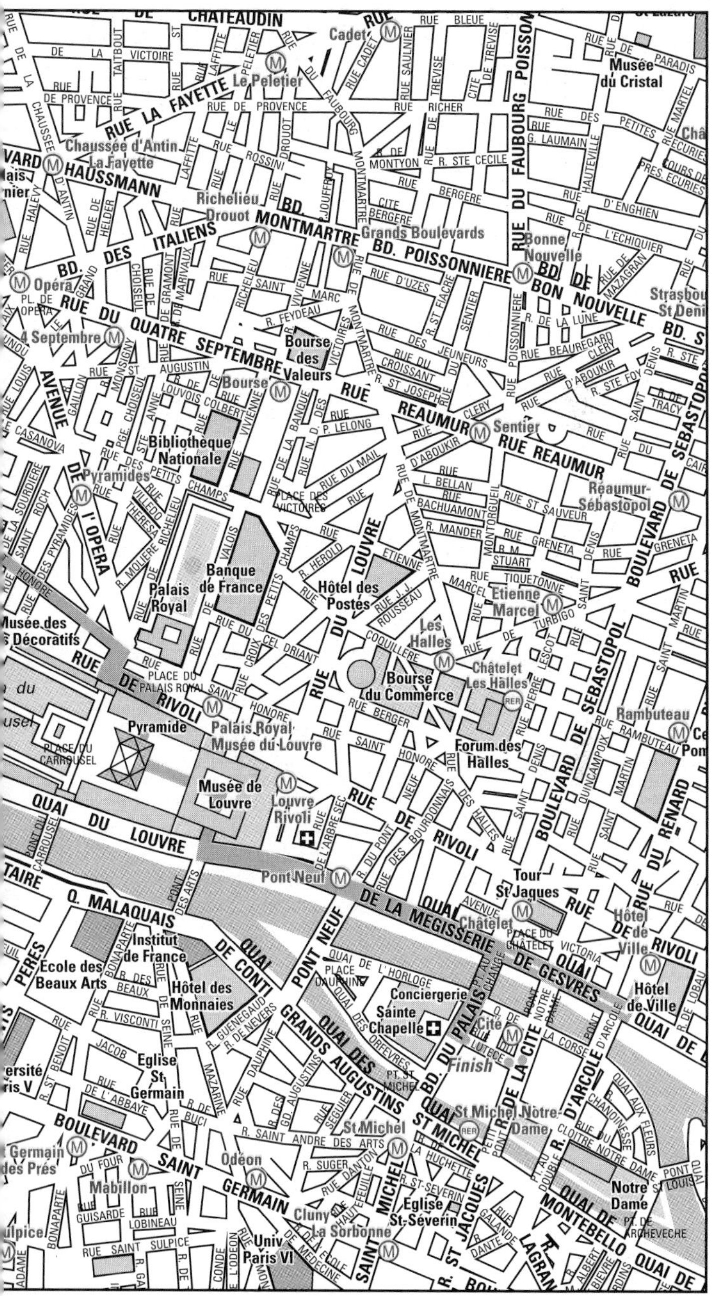
CHATEAUDIN
Cadet
Le Peletier
Musée du Cristal
RUE LA FAYETTE
RUE DE PROVENCE
RUE RICHER
RUE DE PARADIS
Chaussée d'Antin La Fayette
HAUSSMANN
Richelieu Drouot
BD. MONTMARTRE
Grands Boulevards
BD. POISSONNIERE
Bonne Nouvelle
BD. DE BON NOUVELLE
BD. DES ITALIENS
RUE DU FAUBOURG POISSONNIERE
Opéra
RUE DU QUATRE SEPTEMBRE
4 Septembre
Bourse
Bourse des Valeurs
RUE REAUMUR
Sentier
Strasbourg St Denis
Bibliothèque Nationale
Pyramides
AVENUE DE l'OPERA
Réaumur-Sébastopol
BOULEVARD DE SEBASTOPOL
PLACE DES VICTOIRES
Banque de France
Palais Royal
Hôtel des Postes
RUE DU LOUVRE
Etienne Marcel
Les Halles
Musée des Décoratifs
Bourse du Commerce
Châtelet Les Halles
RUE DE RIVOLI
Palais Royal Musée du Louvre
Pyramide
PLACE DU CARROUSEL
Forum des Halles
Rambuteau
Musée de Louvre
Louvre Rivoli
QUAI DU LOUVRE
Pont Neuf
Tour St Jaques
Châtelet
QUAI DE LA MEGISSERIE
Hôtel de Ville
Q. MALAQUAIS
Institut de France
QUAI DE CONTI
PONT NEUF
Ecole des Beaux Arts
Hôtel des Monnaies
Conciergerie
Sainte Chapelle
QUAI DE GESVRES
Cité
Finish
GRANDS QUAI DES AUGUSTINS
Eglise St Germain
BOULEVARD SAINT GERMAIN
St Michel
St Michel Notre-Dame
QUAI ST MICHEL
St Germain des Prés
Mabillon
Odéon
Cluny La Sorbonne
Eglise St-Séverin
Notre Dame
QUAI DE MONTEBELLO
Univ Paris VI
RUE ST JACQUES
QUAI DE

and congregate in the two large halls, one called the Salon des Colonnes, which overlooks a bit of French garden. In the old days, governments were made and unmade here, upon the large, four-sided red velvet settee so well suited to whisperings. The carefully vetted audience, guests of the Deputies, can observe sessions from the galleries above *l'hémicycle*, as the semicircular chamber is known. All they can see of their representatives is the tops of their often bald heads, nodding in after-lunch torpor. Former Prime Minister Raymond Barre became famous for his catnaps, and he refused to attend any afternoon sessions.

Many of the government ministries reside near here, south of Palais-Bourbon. Leave place du Palais-Bourbon via rue St-Dominique, and past the Ministry of Defence on your left. Take rue de Bellechasse to the right, and as you head towards rue de Varenne, its name recalling Louis XVI's ill-fated flight from the clutches of the Revolution, you pass the Ministry of Education on the junction with rue de Grenelle. Further on, the rue de Varenne is home to the Prime Minister's residence, the Hôtel Matignon, and to another ministry, Agriculture and Fisheries. Throughout this area, the Republic has made itself at home amid the plush furnishings and wood panellings, taking the place of the aristocrats it condemned to exile. Each one of these seventeenth- or eighteenth-century mansions is fiercely coveted as soon as a new government is formed. Each mansion has its own garden, lawn and flowerbeds, and the Mobilier National has more than enough pieces to furnish them and to avoid any manner of aesthetic *faux-pas*. Each mansion also boasts its own dining room and porcelain tableware bearing the arms of the Republic, for in France matters of politics, large or small, are decided at table, over bites and sips savoured with an air of feigned indifference. Further west along rue de Varenne lies the pretty Musée Rodin, another eighteenth-century mansion set in gardens filled with the sculptor's works. In the background the gilded dome of Les Invalides peeks above the trees.

As you wander back towards the Palais-Bourbon, consider how the hierarchy of power is respected in the kitchens. Whatever the vicissitudes of politics, and the political hue of those in power, the best table is at the Elysée. De Gaulle's chef, a master-cook from the Navy, was kept on by Pompidou. But when Giscard d'Estaing became President he appointed his own chef and the Gaullists immediately saw in this an obvious treason. Another remarkable table is that of the President of the National Assembly, at the Hôtel de Lassay: current President Laurent Fabius invites Leftist supporters in droves. He is said to have invented '*le socialisme hôtelier*' – caterers' Socialism – a charge he doesn't deny. Fabius is the figurehead of the new ideological movement dubbed '*la gauche caviar*'. As for politicians bereft of ministerial headquarters, they fall back on the restaurants you can reach on foot from the Palais-Bourbon or the Hôtel Matignon. Years ago, parliamentarians liked to be seen at the Brasserie Lipp, in St-Germain-des-Prés, as much reputed for its faïence walls as for its cooking. But these days, a sign of the times, politicians favour upmarket restaurants distinguished by Michelin stars: L'Arpège, a classy, expensive *haute cuisine* restaurant; Le Divellec, on the Esplanade des Invalides opposite the Foreign Ministry; and, a little further along, the fish restaurant Paul Minchelli, which allows politicians to mind their waistlines in preparation for television appearances. On Wednesdays, the day when Deputies have meeting upon meeting, they pop in for a quick bite amid the brouhaha of lingering debates, at Chez Françoise, the restaurant in the

This way for the **Musée Rodin**, *on rue de Varenne, and its gardens filled with the sculptor's works.*

Les Invalides, *which houses the Musée de l'Armée, as seen from Pont Alexandre III.*

airport-coach station, the Aérogare des Invalides. Only the lowliest Members, obscure and provincial, still stoop to take their lunch at the National Assembly dining room, whose cellars just barely make the grade.

But in our day and age, the Palais-Bourbon is no longer the place where politics happens. Since de Gaulle was elected President of the Republic in December 1958, the National Assembly's status has been downgraded, the Deputies reduced to commentaries and quarrels. Power set up its nerve-centre across the Seine, on the Right Bank. From the quai d'Orsay, walk across the Pont Alexandre III, which the capital wears like a bracelet of pearls set in fine gold, and past the glass-domed Grand Palais and Petit Palais, built for the 1900 Exposition Universelle. As you pass towards place Clemenceau, note the successive statues of Churchill and Clemenceau, both bearing walking sticks, but only Churchill in need of its support. Cross over the Champs-Elysées (peering right and left for the spectacular vistas), and its gardens to reach the Elysée Palace in place Beauvau.

De Gaulle hated this palace, heavy as it was with the dubious scent of the Belle Epoque (President Félix Faure died there, victim of his mistress's voluptuous charms). De Gaulle called the Palace 'the box of sorrows', and dreamed of moving to the Château de Vincennes, a military fortress from the Middle Ages, at the eastern end of the capital, close to the routes that led French soldiers off to war. But, baulking at the expense, the General finally lived more than ten years in this palace through which, just once a year, the curious are allowed to tip-toe (during September's Journées du Patrimoine).

Two or three times a year, de Gaulle put on a theatrical press conference in the Elysée's Salle des Fêtes, under a ceiling adorned with nymphs and angels, amid the shimmer of gold and of crimson velvet. But the crown jewel of the Elysée is its basement kitchen, a veritable basilica populated with copper saucepans and gigantic cooking pots. All of the Presidents of the Republic, up to and including Chirac, have been gourmets and made it a point of honour to serve their guests meals worthy of France, with a pronounced taste for lush, rural fare – what Pompidou described with relish as '*les plats canailles*' (riffraff food). On 14 July, the President of the Republic hosts a garden party in the Parc de l'Elysée, the largest private garden in Paris, which sprawls over the hillside to the Champs-Elysées. A joyous throng jostles around the buffets, military uniforms mingling with the ladies' preferably low-cut dresses. One day, during Giscard d'Estaing's tenure, a general was seen, in the proximity of the petits-fours, crushing under his heel the foot of a poor woman who let out a horrible cry of pain. The Elysée is an ivory tower: crowds, demonstrations and political debates sound here only as a distant echo. A veritable court of *fonctionnaires* filters the populace's demands. At the Elysée, silence and boredom reign. François Mitterrand, Paris's most famous pedestrian, liked to go on foot, followed at a reasonable distance by a few policemen, from his quarters on the Rive Gauche, to where intelligence, intrigue, fashion and above all politics are concentrated, between the Palais-Bourbon and St-Germain-des-Prés. He would often drop in on the bookshops such as La Hune on boulevard St-Germain, before joining politicos in Brasserie Lipp.

From the Elysée, we have a long walk to Paris's other centre of power, the Hôtel de Ville. Before heading east, look back at the Ministry of Interior, whose chief is dubbed 'France's top policeman', and which is located just opposite the Elysée, as if the chief of state wanted to keep an eye and an ear on the warring factions of the police. Follow the map along rue du Faubourg St-Honoré to place Vendôme, passing behind the British and American embassies (hidden from view), and in front of l'Eglise de la Madeleine, the church begun in 1764 but only finally consecrated in 1845. The colonnades on the façade mirror those on the Assemblée Nationale across the Seine. Place Vendôme boasts another *hôtel particulier* built in the seventeenth century, and is now home to the Ministry of Justice, the Ritz and a number of luxury jewellers. At the end of rue St-Honoré another ministry holds court in a royal palace. The Palais-Royal, with its beautiful enclosed garden, was left to Louis XIII by Richelieu, and now houses the Ministry of Culture (and the constitutional body, the Conseil d'Etat). Opposite is the largest palace of them all, the Louvre.

Not long ago, the Ministry of Finance – fortress of the formidable French administration, the State within the State – occupied half of the Palais du Louvre. The Minister's office overlooked the Cour d'Honneur, the windows opened on to memories of the monarchy. Then Mitterrand decided to return the Louvre to Art: he had a brand-new ministry built, on the banks of the Seine, but at quai de Bercy in the 12th arrondissement in the eastern end of the city, from which the Palais-Bourbon or the Elysée can be reached in a fast, and very noisy, motorboat. The Minister at the time was a Socialist: he gracefully agreed to vacate the Louvre. But then there were new elections, and a rightist government: the new Minister of Finance, Edouard Balladur, put on aristocratic airs. *Le Monde* depicted him being carried by litter and wearing a powdered wig. He demanded to return to the Louvre. The new move was very costly. In the end a Socialist replaced Balladur and the Louvre was wholly and permanently given over to its vocation as a museum: Ministers now fight over the honour of inaugurating the new halls that reopen regularly.

Continue on towards the Hôtel de Ville. Follow through the arches, past the huge windows that allow a view into the sculpture galleries of the Louvre, past Pei's glass Pyramid in the Cour Napoléon, and out on to quai du Louvre. Follow the river's edge east, past Châtelet and the Gothic splendour of the Tour St-Jacques that rises on rue de Rivoli to your north. This explosion of gargoyles is the bell-tower, all that remains of St-Jacques-la-Boucherie church, built for the butchers' guild in the sixteenth century. Soon after is the majestic place de l'Hôtel-de-Ville.

Tourists, as they sail through Paris aboard one of the numerous Bateaux-Mouches, cannot help but be intrigued by the gigantic palace on the Rive Droite, in the garish neo-Gothic style that was all the rage in France in the nineteenth century, as it was in England: it is the Hôtel de Ville, Paris's town hall. With its caryatids, statuary and double-spiralled stairways, it thumbs its nose at the Elysée Palace, just a mile away. In days gone by, Parisians had no right to elect a mayor: the Monarchy, the Empire and the Republic feared that sooner or later their power would be threatened by the representative of the eternally rebellious and insolent inhabitants of Paris.

In 1976, however, President Giscard d'Estaing thought he would curry favour with Parisians by granting them a popularly elected mayor. He especially sought to please one of his closest friends, the Comte d'Ornano, who bore the name of the Napoléonic marshal, commemorated by one of the boulevards ringing the capital. Alas! The chief of state's protégé was defeated by a young man whose ambition and appetite were already legendary, and whose name was Jacques Chirac. He came from the Corrèze region, in the south of the Auvergne, but this detail didn't bother Paris, where four-fifths of the residents hail from the provinces, and where nine cafés out of ten are run by Auvergnats. In his palace, the stairs of which he leapt up four at a time, Jacques Chirac set up a grand apartment with pastel walls, vast enough to house display cases for his collection of Chinese antiquities. The Chiracs lived there for over 18 years, entertaining with royal pomp all the celebrities from the world over who passed through Paris. The mayor commanded a workforce of 30,000 *fonctionnaires* and managed a budget equal to that of a developing country; his opponents hinted at dark deeds with the financing of his presidential campaigns in 1981, '88 and '95. When he left the Hôtel de Ville in 1995 to move into the Elysée, there was talk of magistrates looking into the way money was spent. But once he had become the chief of state, Chirac was above any kind of judicial or other scrutiny. It is to him that Paris's Hôtel de Ville owes its reputation as the maker of Presidents.

In fact, on the other side of the Seine, the Hôtel de Ville looks out upon the Palais de Justice, which has become, in the last 12 or so years, one of the most feared places in politics. To get there take the Pont au Change, so called because an earlier bridge drew money changers and goldsmiths to its houses to trade.

How many careers and hopes have been buried inside this palace, one of the only ones in the city not to have cleaned up its walls, as if the blackness of its towers and façades illustrated the extreme severity of the law? Many politicians frequent the Palais de Justice, some as the accused, some as plaintiffs (generally for libel), some as witnesses and one or two as solicitors. When they climb the stairs of the Palais de Justice, via the main entrance on the eastern side, or by the more discreet western entrance, politicians abandon all pomp and seem eager to keep their heads down. Scandals implicating political figures in corruption, influence-peddling and misuse of funds have proliferated since 1987/88. New laws have been instituted to prevent certain confusions between state money and personal enrichment. Arriving at the Elysée, Mitterrand condemned, with Socialist vigour, money that corrupts, money that dirties, money that rots… But a few years later, little was done when misdeeds were carried out in his shadow, by his own friends. Junior magistrates endeavoured to restore public morality.

Look out for statues of **Churchill** *and Clemenceau as you approach the Champs-Elysées.*

And at once politicians began to fear a Republic of magistrates, the first step towards a totalitarian regime.

Across from the Palais de Justice are cafés with pavement tables and waiters in white aprons. Sometimes, in the late afternoon, you can see politicians there, having a drink with their solicitors to wash away a long afternoon of questions, shame and suffering.

Translated by Karen Albrecht.

Eating & drinking

L'Arpège

84 rue de Varenne, 7th (01.45.51.47.33). **Open** noon-2pm, 7.30-10.30pm, Mon-Fri. As the name suggests, meals build through subtle dishes to a crescendo of *haute cuisine* and *haute, haute* prices.

Brasserie Lipp

151 boulevard St-Germain, 6th (01.45.48.53.91). **Open** 11.30am-1am daily. Reliable cuisine and reasonable prices given its distinguished past.

Café-Bar Le Nemours

2 place Colette, 1st (01.42.61.34.14). **Open** 7am-1am Mon-Fri; 8am-1am Sat; 9am-9.30pm Sun. Decent *croques* and light snacks in an ideal setting.

Café Marly

93 rue de Rivoli, cour Napoléon du Louvre, 1st (01.49.26.06.60). **Open** 8am-2am daily. Modish spins on brasserie fare, overlooking Pei's Pyramid.

Chez Françoise

Aérogare des Invalides, 7th (01.47.05.49.03). **Open** noon-2.30pm, 7pm-midnight, daily.

Le Dauphin

167 rue St-Honoré, 1st (01.42.60.40.11). **Open** noon-3pm, 7-11pm, daily. Mixed results, low prices.

Le Divellec

107 rue de l'Université, 7th (01.45.51.91.96). **Open** noon-2pm, 8-10pm, Mon-Sat. Excellent fish dishes.

Hemingway Bar

Hôtel Ritz, 15 place Vendôme, 1st (01.43.16.30.30). **Open** 6.30pm-1am Tue-Sat. Closed 25 July-25 Aug. Hemingway claims that he 'liberated' the Ritz in August 1944. Be prepared to liberate your wallet.

Paul Minchelli

54 boulevard de la Tour-Maubourg, 7th (01.47.05.89.86). **Open** noon-2.30pm, 8-10.30pm, Tue-Sat. Closed Aug, 25 Dec-2 Jan. Stunning interior.

Government buildings

Assemblée Nationale

33 quai d'Orsay, 7th (01.40.63.60.00). **Open** guided tours 10am, 2pm, 3pm, Sat when Chamber not in session; ID required; arrive early.

Conseil d'Etat
1 place Palais-Royal, 1st (01.40.20.80.00).

Hôtel de Ville
place de l'Hôtel-de-Ville, 4th (switchboard 01.42.76.40.40; reservations 01.42.76.50.49). **Open** *groups* make reservation 2 months in advance; *individuals* first Mon in every month following reservation made one month in advance.

Hôtel Matignon
rue de Varenne, 7th.

Ministère de l'Agriculture et de la Pêche
78 rue Varenne, 7th (01.49.55.57.46).

Ministère de Culture
3 rue de Valois, 1st (01.40.15.80.00).

Ministère de la Défense
14 rue St-Dominique, 7th (01.42.19.30.11).

Ministère de l'Education
101 rue de Grenelle, 7th (01.55.55.10.10).

Ministère des Finances
12 quai de la Rapée, 12th (01.40.04.04.04).

Ministère de l'Intérieur
6 rue Cambacérès, 8th (01.47.42.08.69).

Ministère de la Justice
13 place Vendôme, 1st (01.44.77.60.60).

Palais de l'Elysée
55-57 rue du Faubourg-St-Honoré, 8th.

Museums & churches

Grand Palais
avenue Winston-Churchill, avenue du General-Eisenhower, 8th (01.44.13.17.17./01.44.13.17.30).

Les Invalides
esplanade des Invalides, 7th (01.44.42.54.52/Musée de l'Armée 01.44.42.37.67). **Open** *Apr-Sept* 10am-6pm daily; *Oct-Mar* 10am-5pm daily. **Admission** 37F; 27F concs.

Le Louvre
entrance through Pyramid, cour Napoléon, 1st (01.40.20.50.50/recorded information 01.40.20.51.51/advance booking 01.49.87.54.54). **Open** 9am-6pm Mon, Thur-Sun; 9am-9.45pm Wed; *temporary exhibitions, Medieval Louvre, bookshop* 10am-9.45pm Mon, Wed-Sun. Closed Tue. **Admission** 45F (until 3pm); 26F (after 3pm and Sun) concs.

Musée Rodin
Hôtel Biron, 77 rue de Varenne, 7th (01.44.18.61.10). **Open** *Apr-Sept* 9.30am-5.45pm Tue-Sun; *Oct-Mar* 9.30am-4.45pm Tue-Sun. **Admission** 28F; 18F concs. *Gardens only* 5F.

Palais de la Découverte
Grand Palais, avenue Franklin-D-Roosevelt, 8th (01.40.74.80.00/01.40.74.81.73). **Open** 9.30am-6pm Tue-Sat; 10am-7pm Sun. Closed 1 Jan, 1 May, 14 July, 15 Aug, 25 Dec. **Admission** 27F; 17F.

Petit Palais
avenue Winston-Churchill, 8th (01.42.65.12.73). **Open** 10am-5.40pm Tue-Sun. **Admission** 45F; 35F concs.

Ste-Chapelle & Palais de Justice
4 boulevard du Palais, 1st (01.53.73.78.50). **Open** *Apr-Sept* 9.30am-6.30pm daily; *Oct-Mar* 10am-5pm daily. **Admission** 35F; 23F concs; 50F combined ticket with Conciergerie.

Ste-Marie-Madeleine
place de la Madeleine, 8th (01.44.51.69.00). **Open** 7.30am-7pm Mon-Sat; 9am-1pm, 3.30-7pm, Sun.

Tour St-Jacques
place du Châtelet, 4th. Closed to the public.

Accommodation

Hôtel Ritz
15 place Vendôme, 1st (01.43.16.30.30).

Bookshops

La Hune
170 boulevard St-Germain, 6th (01.45.48.35.85). **Open** 10am-11.45pm Mon-Sat.

Information

Bateaux-Mouches
pont de l'Alma, Rive droite, 8th (reservations 01.42.25.96.10/recorded information 01.40.76.99.99). **Departs** *summer* every 30 min 10am-11pm daily; *winter* approx every hour from 11am-9pm daily; lasts one hour. **Tickets** 40F; 20F concs.

British Embassy
35 rue du Faubourg-St-Honoré, 8th (01.44.51.31.00). **Open** 9.30am-1pm, 2.30-6pm, Mon-Fri.

Journées du Patrimoine
mid-Sept. Detailed information can be found in *Le Monde*, *Le Parisien* and from the *Hôtel de Sully, 62 rue St-Antoine, 4th (01.44.61.20.00).*

US Embassy
2 avenue Gabriel, 8th (01.43.12.22.22). **Open** 9am-6pm Mon-Fri, by appointment.

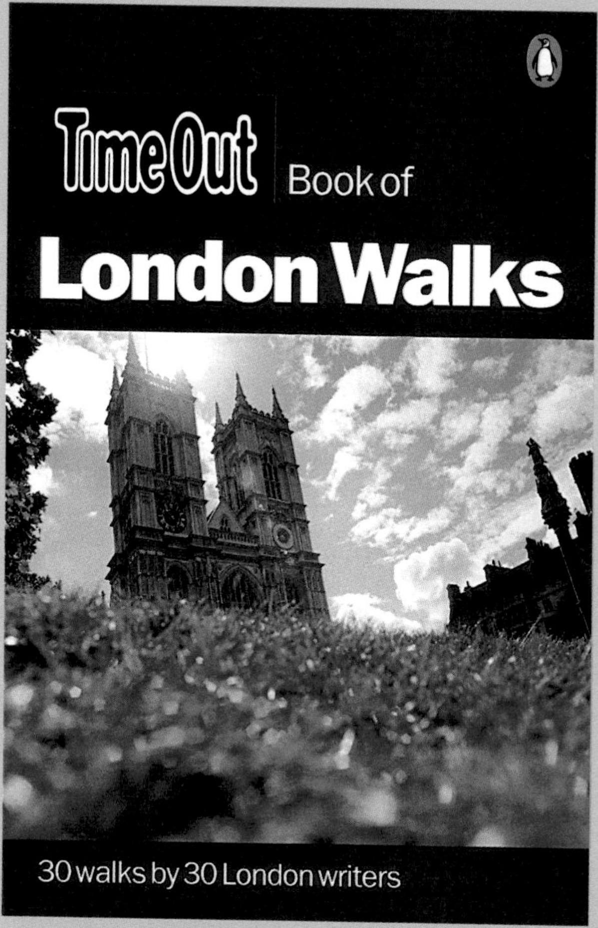

Saints and sinners

Alan Furst

Attila the Hun, the Occupation, Ste Geneviève and the sweet taste of Berthillon.

Start: rue du Roi-de-Sicile, 4th
Finish: Eglise St Etienne-du-Mont, 5th
Time: 1-2 hours
Distance: 3km/2 miles
Getting there: short walk from Mº St-Paul (line 1)
Getting back: short walk to Mº Cardinal Lemoine (line 10) or Luxembourg (RER line B)
Note: the odd opening times of the Adam Mickiewicz library (see listings).

I lived in Paris for a long time and my favourite walk began in a bakery and ended in a church – two highlights of the Paris life, if not life itself. The bakery is in the heart of the Marais, on the corner of rue du Roi-de-Sicile and rue Ferdinand-Duval. Here you are a block south of the rue des Rosiers, a street associated with the Jewish community of Paris, on and off, since the Middle Ages.

And that is very much to the point, because the bakery looks and smells like the usual Parisian *boulangerie* but it is actually a combination of a Jewish and a French bakery. So to taste the result of combining two of the world's great and serious dessert cultures, I can recommend the *craqueline au chocolat*, a large, hand-held pastry, though your hand isn't going to be holding it all that long.

Roi-de-Sicile is an in-between street, with the burly rue St-Antoine to the south and the rue des Rosiers to the north. It's narrow, with slightly strange little shops – second-hand fashion for women, dried flowers (a bit west of where you are now) and, on the corner of rue Pavée, my wife once found an excellent hair-cutter installed in the back of his wife's dress shop.

Fine summer weather brings the sunbathers out on to the quais of the **Ile St-Louis**.

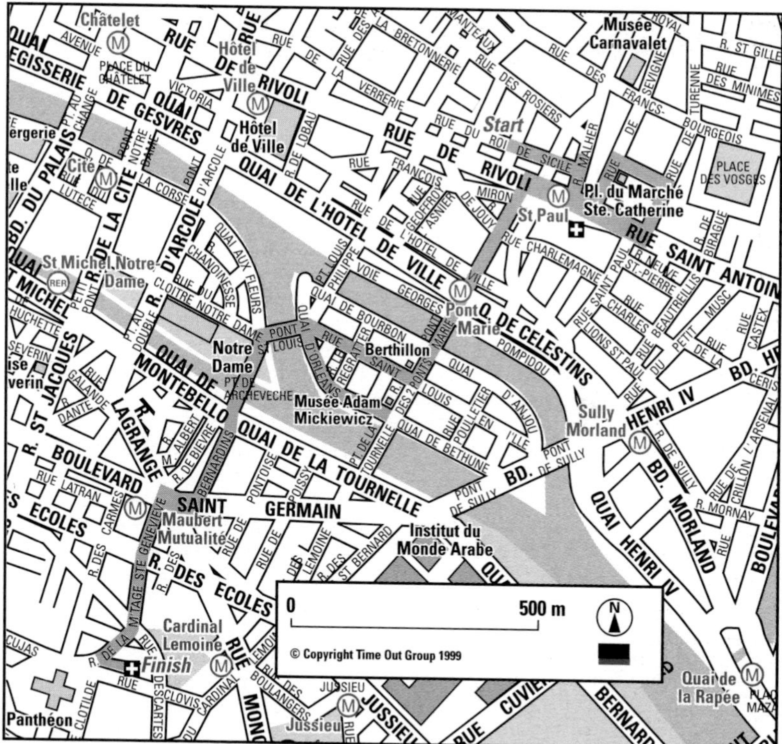

Go past rue Pavée to rue Malher, and detour about half-way up the block for one of Paris's most fashionable shops, Sisso's. This is a small treasure – gloves made of cotton, very chic, in all kinds of colours, alongside handmade hats and jewellery. This is simply the show-room of a woman who has a fashion instinct that is miles ahead of any magazine.

Continue east – by now you've run out of rue du Roi-de-Sicile and must dip a little south, to rue St-Antoine, to get to your next left, rue de Sévigné. Just up rue de Sévigné turn right on to rue de Jarente and just after a trellised *trompe l'oeil* you will find the place du Marché-St-Catherine opening out to your right. This is an odd little square, drawing travellers with backpacks, and harbouring a good, inexpensive pizza restaurant. At the top of the square is rue Caron, where at one time stood the Hôtel Caron. This was home, in the late 1930s and early '40s, to Abraham Rajemann, a professional forger who made passports and identity cards for Leopold Trepper, leader of the Red Orchestra, one of the most aggressive and successful Soviet spy networks of the period. Rajemann is said to have been arrested at the Hôtel Caron around 1942, and his arrest led in turn to Trepper's arrest at the office of his dentist (a very bad day). Curiously, both Trepper and Rajemann survived Gestapo custody and in fact survived the war.

There are a few well-known Résistance sites in Paris – a spy network was run from the convent of the sisters of Ste-Agonie, and the ossuary (The Catacombs) by the Denfert-Rochereau Métro stop in the 14th arrondissement was supposedly a Resistance headquarters – but historians of the period point out that Paris wasn't extensively used. The British Special Operations Executive, for instance, didn't care for the capital as a base for secret operations: too many German police, field police, Gestapo, all sorts, were drawn here to protect important Germans who came to the city. The spy networks (including the Red Orchestra) tended to be run from anonymous villas in the suburbs. For their part, the Nazis ran Paris from the Hôtel de Crillon on place de la Concorde and Hôtel Meurice on rue de Rivoli.

In the north-west corner of the square is a Jewish restaurant called the Pitchi Poi serving up blintzes, kreplach, matzoh ball soup and the like. One night I asked the proprietor what the restaurant's name meant, and he said it was a game played by Jewish children who'd been rounded up and imprisoned in the unfinished housing project the French police used as a holding area out in Drancy, before deportation to the camps.

From the square go south to rue St-Antoine, which ranges from frantic to busy and offers some of the most real-life shopping you'll find in the city.

King Henry II used to practise jousting here with a certain Montgomery, the Scottish Captain of his bodyguard, until the Scot's splintered lance caught the King's throat and pierced his eye. He died ten days later in July 1559. In 1556 the seer Nostradamus had written:

> The young lion shall overcome the old,
> The warlike field in single fight:
> In a cage of gold he will pierce his eyes,
> Two wounds one, then die a cruel death.
> (*Nostradamus* by James Laver, Penguin, 1942.)

Such a prediction gave the seer some credibility, especially when he also foresaw Montgomery's subsequent death on the orders of Henry II's widow some 15 years later.

Head a little west just past the St-Paul Métro stop. Here you will find rue de Fourcy, which turns into rue des Nonnains-d'Hyères, and you can just about make out the opening of the Pont Marie, named after the contractor, Christophe Marie, who built it in 1635. I love this bridge – it affords world-class idling and Seine-staring – casting views east to a curve in the river, and west to the Pont Louis-Philippe.

The Pont Marie also shows off the façades of the beautiful and expensive houses on Ile St-Louis to fine effect – one of them, the Hôtel Lambert, at 2 rue St-Louis-en-l'Ile, was built in 1642 by Jean-Baptiste Lambert, or Lambert-the-Rich. If I'd been Lambert-the-Rich, this is pretty much where I would have chosen to do my riching.

The Ile St-Louis looks so sexy on the map that everyone goes there. On the other hand, as you proceed along the rue des Deux-Ponts you'll discover that some of the crowd are indigenous and on a very specific mission. On the corner of rue des Deux-Ponts and rue St-Louis-en-l'Ile is a store called Berthillon. Here the French come in droves for ice-cream and sorbet. You can get some of the best ice-cream in the world here (you've walked off your *craqueline*, right?), exceptionally intense and extraordinary tastes of pear, lemon, strawberry – whatever they've got. In the Christmas/New Year season the queue is particularly long, contradicting my contention that standing in line is the one Anglo-Saxon perversion that the French really don't like. What they're after here at Christmas time is the Marron Glacé (glazed chestnut) ice-cream. I once actually tried to describe this stuff, but it's too good for that. Note that there are several other Berthillon outlets dotted around this crossroads. If it's lunchtime, you might try Nos Ancêtres les Gaulois, which is all refectory tables and waiters in Gallic costumes. No, don't say that – some very sophisticated Parisians come here to eat, and to indulge an unanticipated

Rest awhile in the shade or dip into the cafés and restaurants in the cobbled square **place du Marché-St-Catherine**.

PLACE
DU MARCHÉ
SALON DE THE
01 42 77 16 26
ARIRA

The shops, too, are small, tidy and coiffured on **rue St-Louis-en-l'Ile**, *the island's main street.*

streak of silliness in the Gallic character. On the other hand, I will say you have to be in the mood.

Go along rue St-Louis-en-l'Ile to the western end of the island. There's almost nothing down here, which is terrific in a city crowded with people and history. This end of Ile St-Louis has lovers, people having a picnic or reading books, only steps away from a very active streetlife. Swing round the corner on to quai d'Orléans, where you can visit one of my favourite little places in Paris. I like the Musée de la Chasse in the Marais, and I am a fan of small monuments. At 6 quai d'Orléans is the Adam Mickiewicz library. Mickiewicz is one of the most revered poets of Poland, and this library/museum is a fine place to visit – nice people work here, the manuscripts and books are interesting, and you get a taste of Paris as the chosen place of exile for Polish intellectuals, which it has been (read your Balzac) for at least 200 years. It also has the advantage of a lovely view across to the Latin quarter and of getting you inside one of these handsome buildings.

Now, retrace your steps a few hundred yards to the bridge that goes to the eastern end of the Ile de la Cité. (You can descend some iron steps opposite the library for a brief walk along the river's edge, past sunbathers, re-emerging up a ramp at the Pont St-Louis.) Cross to the foot of the Ile de la Cité. Looking up, you see Notre-Dame. I believe that right here, from the south-east corner, is the best angle on the cathedral. The most dramatic I ever saw it was one autumn when a great blanket of mist lay on the Seine, and the cathedral floated in the air like a fourteenth-century ghost ship. It has always had a vast magnetic energy for the population here. When I was writing for the *International Herald Tribune*, a man I met begged me to go to see an extraordinary phenomenon. On a certain day of the year, two beams of sunlight touch on the edge of a column, forming an ovoid shape. 'An egg!' he cried. His eyes glittered. 'An egg!'

You are passing through the gardens of

Peek through the grand doorway of **51 rue St-Louis-en-l'Ile**, *if you dare, to catch a glimpse of a hidden courtyard.*

square Jean XXIII here, a little on the municipal side, often changed by the City of Paris parks people and Mother Nature, but not to much effect either way.

Cross the Pont de l'Archevêché to the rue des Bernardins. This is the former neighbourhood of a monastery, and there is a strange medieval gloom that hangs over the place. Somewhere here – on your left – is the residence of a religious order. It's very closed, resolutely unadvertised, and a little forbidding. Head up to the place Maubert, where you'll find a busy market life two days a week, and oriental food shops that have everything from wonton wrappers to Bok Choy cabbage. Cross the square (it may take 20 minutes, but so what – there's a lot going on here) and find the street on the south side of Maubert called rue de la Montagne-Ste-Geneviève and go up. Up! They're not kidding about the *montagne* part of this, but it's an interesting climb. This is a student district, where people actually go to college and have been since the twelfth century. Some have since graduated. The street is lined with little restaurants, some with cellars where you can drink wine, and it curves restlessly like a real medieval street ought to.

At the top you will find two grand edifices. The Panthéon, a monument to those in France who have been officially declared Great Men. Ignore it. Spend your time instead in the sumptuous Eglise St-Etienne-du-Mont, one of the loveliest churches in Paris. They are prodigious with organ recitals here – the organ is said to have 90 stops – and they have the only rood-screen in Paris, as well as the shrine to Ste Geneviève.

Ste Geneviève is one of the great women in the history of a country with a history of great women. In the fifth century, confronted by the advancing barbarian armies of Attila the Hun, she convinced the Parisians not to flee the city. If they remained, repented of their sins and prayed with her, she proclaimed, Paris would not be sacked. It was not, and Ste Geneviève became venerated as the patron saint of Paris. Which is a profoundly echoic event in a city that many people have wanted to destroy but that seems always somehow to save itself at the last minute. The bridges you cross on this walk, for instance, have been prepared for detonation at least twice this century – 1914 and 1944 – but they still stand today.

By her shrine there is also a plaque in commemoration of Father François Basset, deported in 1943 for working for the Résistance. He died in Mathausen. For you I can't say, but I visited this church quite often when I lived in Paris and I never left without lighting a candle.

Eating & drinking

Anahuacalli

30 rue des Bernadins, 5th (01.43.26.10.20). **Open** 7.30-11pm Tue, Sat; noon-2pm, 7.30-11pm, Wed-Fri, Sun. Closed two weeks in Aug. Diverse regional cuisines of Mexico.

Auberge de Jarente

7 rue de Jarente, 4th (01.43.77.49.35). **Open** noon-2.30pm, 7.30-10.30pm, Tue-Sat. Closed two weeks in Aug. Pays Basque menu specialising in fish fare.

Berthillon

31 rue St-Louis-en-l'Ile, 4th (01.43.54.31.61). **Open** 10am-8pm Wed-Sun. Closed school holidays.

L'Escapade

10 rue de la Montagne-Ste-Geneviève, 5th (01.46.33.23.85). **Open** 7pm-1am daily. Three hearty courses and limitless wine for 105F.

L'Ilot Vache

35 rue St-Louis-en-l'Ile, 4th (01.46.33.55.16). **Open** 7pm-midnight Mon; noon-3pm, 7pm-midnight, Tue-Sun. Steaks abound, but so do fine fish dishes in this bistro.

Isami

4 quai d'Orléans, 4th (01.40.46.06.97). **Open** noon-2pm, 7-10.30pm, Tue-Sat; 7-10.30pm Sun. Closed two weeks in Aug. Tiny Japanese restaurant with above-average sushi and fish dishes.

Kim Lien

33 place Maubert, 5th (01.43.54.68.13). **Open** noon-3pm, 7.30-11pm, Mon-Sat. Closed one week in Aug. Well-loved Vietnamese restaurant – go à la carte.

Nos Ancêtres les Gaulois

39 rue St-Louis-en-l'Ile, 4th (01.46.33.66.07). **Open** 7pm-midnight Mon-Sat; noon-3pm Sun. All-you-can-eat courses that require a legionnaire's courage.

Cathédrale Notre-Dame de Paris *towers over the Ile de la Cité – and over passing boats.*

Pitchi Poi
7 place du Marché-Ste-Catherine, 4th (01.42.77.46.15). **Open** noon-2.30pm, 7.30-11pm, daily. Modern central European restaurant offers reliable and good-value Jewish fare.

Le Violon Dingue
46 rue de la Montagne-Ste-Geneviève, 5th (01.43.25.79.93). **Open** 6pm-1.30am daily. American-style bar serving cocktails attracting English speakers and consequent vultures.

Shopping

Le Mezel
1 rue Ferdinand-Duval, 4th (01.42.78.25.01). **Open** 7.30am-8pm daily.

Sisso's
20 rue Malher, 4th (01.44.61.99.50). **Open** 10am-7pm Mon-Sat.

Museums

Musée Adam Mickiewicz
6 quai d'Orléans, 4th (01.43.54.35.61). **Open** 2-6pm Thur, or by appointment.

Musée de la Chasse et de la Nature
Hôtel Guénégaud, 60 rue des Archives, 3rd (01.53.01.92.40). **Open** 11am-6pm Tue-Sun. **Admission** 30F; 15F concs.

Le Panthéon
place du Panthéon, 5th (01.44.32.18.00). **Open** *Apr-Sept* 9.30am-6.30pm daily; *Oct-Mar* 10am-5.30pm daily. **Admission** 35F; 23F concs.

Churches

Cathédrale Notre-Dame de Paris
place du Parvis-Notre-Dame, 4th (01.42.34.56.10). **Open** 8am-6.45pm daily. **Admission** free. *Towers* (01.44.32.16.70) entrance at foot of north tower. **Open** 10am-4.30pm daily. **Admission** 35F; 25F concs.

St-Etienne-du-Mont
place Ste-Geneviève, 5th (01.43.54.11.79). **Open** 8am-noon, 2-7.15pm, Tue-Sat; 9am-noon, 2.30-6.30pm, Sun.

Other

Hôtel de Crillon
10 place de la Concorde, 8th (01.44.71.15.00).

Hôtel Lambert
2 rue St-Louis-en-l'Ile, 4th (no phone).

Hôtel Meurice
228 rue de Rivoli, 1st (01.44.58.10.10). Currently undergoing renovation.

Square Jean XXIII
Ile de la Cité, 4th. **Open** 8.30am-9.30pm daily.

The path to modernity

Natasha Edwards

If you don't know your Art Nouveau from your Art Deco, take a stroll through the 16th.

Start: Bar Antoine, 16th
Finish: Maison Prunier, 16th
Time: 3-4 hours
Distance: 7km/4.5 miles
Getting there: short walk from Avenue du Président-Kennedy/ Maison de Radio France (RER line C)
Finish: short walk to Mº Charles de Gaulle Etoile (lines 1, 2, 6 & RER line A)
Note: check opening times of the various museums, especially La Fondation Le Corbusier (see listings).

It's all too easy to write off the 16th arrondissement as boring and bourgeois, pearls and poodles, but it was in this part of Paris at the beginning of the twentieth century, as the former villages of Passy and Auteuil were developed, that there was space to build and adventurous patrons with the money to commission avant-garde architects. This area is less conventional than it first seems, witness to the paradox of innovative architects who often dreamed of housing for the masses and yet built for the elite.

This walk spans roughly 7km and some 30 years that take us from one architectural era to another, from the ornate Beaux Arts style that had

The **Castel Béranger** *at 14 rue La Fontaine – Guimard's exotic masterpiece built 1895-8.*

Rue Agar – *and more Hector Guimard. This time he even designed the street sign.*

dominated the late nineteenth century via Art Nouveau to the structural and aesthetic experimentation of the Modern Movement that set so many models for the twentieth century, despite sometimes contradictory aesthetics as functionalism and mass production met the luxe of Art Deco. The walk takes in mainly private houses (including a couple that can be visited), rather than monuments, with exclusive villas – streets of individual houses of varying degrees of privacy – unusual artists' studios, the bistros and cafés so important to a *vie de quartier*, and a few curiosities.

The walk starts with Hector Guimard, Paris's best-known Art Nouveau architect, if only because of his leafy green Métro entrances dotted all over town. It was in the 16th arrondissement that he had his fief and where over half the buildings he designed are situated. First fortify yourself with a coffee at the Bar Antoine at 17 rue La Fontaine, opened in 1911: the façade was designed by Guimard. Inside is a more conventional view of the time, but still delicious with its mahogany bar, roses on the tiles, chipped glass ceiling and idyllic pastoral scenes. The old *patronne* who looked as if she had been there since it opened is no longer around, but the new owners have carefully preserved, yet not over-restored, the interior. On Tuesday and Friday mornings, it overlooks a small but classy street market, a sign that there is life in the area after all.

Across the street, at 14 rue La Fontaine, is the Castel Béranger, Guimard's masterpiece built 1895-8. Influenced by the Arts and Crafts movement in Great Britain and Belgian Art Nouveau, Guimard sought not just a new aesthetic, in rejection of the historical eclecticism of the nineteenth century, but also explored new materials. Here you can see all his ideas of design: his love of brick and wrought iron rather than stone, asymmetry, the inspiration of the vegetal and the renunciation of harsh angles not found in nature. Along with the whiplash motifs characteristic of Art Nouveau, there are still signs of Guimard's taste for fantasy and the medieval consistent with a disciple of Gothic revivalist Viollet-le-

Porte Dauphine
Place du Maréchal de Lattre de Tassigny
Avenue Foch
Avenue Foch
Avenue de la Grande Armée
Place Charles de Gaulle
Arc de Triomphe
Charles de Gaulle
Maison Prunier
Avenue Victor Hugo
Finish
Kléber
Avenue Kléber
Avenue d'Iéna
Victor Hugo
Place Victor Hugo
Avenue Foch
Boissière
Cité de l'Argentine
Marché
Av. Raymond Poincaré
Lycée Janson de Sailly
Avenue Victor Hugo
Avenue Henri Martin
Henri Martin
Rue de la Pompe
Av. Georges Mandel
Trocadéro
Pl. du Trocadéro et du 11 Novembre
Cimetière de Passy
Palais de Chaillot
Musée Guimet
Iéna
Avenue du Président
Avenue de New
Avenue des Nations Unies
Pont d'Iéna
Tour Eiffel
Seine
Avenue Paul Doumer
La Muette
Ch. de la Muette
Rue de Passy
Petite Ceinture (old railway line)
Av. Ingres
Villa Beauséjour
Avenue Mozart
Boulainvilliers
Pl. de Costa Rica
Musée du Vin
Passy
Bd Delessert
Av. des
Av. du Président Kennedy
Musée Balzac
Kennedy-Radio France
Champ de Mars Tour Eiffel
Quai Branly
Pont de Bir-Hakeim
Av. du Bir-Hakeim
Bir Hakeim
Boulevard de Grenelle
Quai de Grenelle
Musée Bouchard
Jasmin
Orphelins Apprentis d'Auteuil
Castel Béranger
Maison de la Radio
Start
Bar Antoine
Av. du Pres. Kennedy
Foundation Le Corbusier
Avenue Mozart
R. la Fontaine
M. Ange Auteuil
Église d'Auteuil
Mirabeau
Avenue de Versailles
Quai Louis-Blériot
Quai André Citroën
Javel
Avenue Émile Zola
Avenue Émile Zola
Charles Michels
0
500 m
N
© Copyright Time Out Group 1999

Duc, until a visit to Victor Horta in Brussels in 1895 that changed the course of his career. Green sea horses climb up the façade, while the faces on the balconies are supposedly Guimard's self-portrait, inspired by Japanese figures intended to ward off evil spirits. Last time I came here it was being cleaned and renovated, but it was still possible to see through the wrought iron and glass doorway into the entrance hall. Wander up Hameau-Béranger to get a glimpse of the courtyard with its massive gatepost and the peculiar blue-grey tiles in the form of a sea monster over one window. Guimard had his architecture studio here and neo-Impressionist painter Paul Signac was an early tenant. Guimard designed all the interiors, too, from door handles and keyholes to fireplaces and fitted kitchens. On the stairway he used glass blocks, soon to become a fetish material with architects, notably at Pierre Chareau's iconic Maison de Verre.

Return to Bar Antoine – Guimard designed the whole block (43 rue Gros, 17, 19, 21 rue La Fontaine, 8, 10 rue Agar), and, although it's much simpler than the Castel Béranger, take a look at the chunky apartment buildings opposite from roughly the same period, and you can see how clever Guimard was, not just with metal and ornament but with structure. The stone becomes almost fluid as it wraps round the street corners, and in the vegetal growth of the doorways; he even designed the lettering for the street sign for rue Agar.

A few doors up, as you pause perhaps to buy tiny chocolate or coffee macaroons at Maison Piechowski (as with much of Paris it's hard not to do this walk without getting hungry and *pâtisseries* seem to be particularly abundant here), Art Nouveau details begin to leap out at you all over the place – there's another rather sombre building by Guimard, with a tall doorway, in the side-street at 11 rue François-Millet.

Opposite at 40 rue La Fontaine stands the curious Orphelins Apprentis d'Auteuil. A charitable institution (a bit like Dr Barnardo's) founded in 1866 to train abandoned orphans for a craft or profession, it now has 30 centres around France that educate problem children and aim to reintegrate them into society. Two former pupils run a Crêperie d'Insertion in the grounds; the rose garden on the corner is usually full of small children and elderly ladies. Enough of philanthropy: the Aston Martin garage beyond is rather more typical of the area's style.

At No.60 is the Hôtel Mezzara (1910), a three-storey house built by Guimard in 1910-11 for a fabric manufacturer. Despite its turret-like staircase on the left, romantic bay window and finely wrought balcony, it looks a little gloomy and dilapidated, probably because it's now an annexe of the Ministry of Education, but the tendril-like iron railings climbing along the street still inspire Sleeping Beauty fantasies.

There are some serious but classy 1930s buildings along here. Look at the fan-shaped, Cubist-influenced Art Deco motifs of the iron and glass doorways of Nos.49-51, and the starker No.82 opposite. The road narrows at an unassuming junction with rue George-Sand, giving little sign of what lies beyond the kink. First pay homage to *A la recherche du temps perdu* as a small plaque at No.96 announces that this is where Marcel Proust was born in 1871.

The Studio Building at No.65 (1926-8) was designed by Henri Sauvage, who is consistently interesting, but not one of France's most famous architects, perhaps because he was too eclectic and too original to fit neatly into any one category. He was one of the first architects to use stepped-back terraces as a way of getting light and air into the different storeys (conceived in part as a health measure against tuberculosis) in the tiled building at 6 rue Vavin in the 6th arrondissement in 1912. As a forerunner of the Modern Movement dichotomy, he designed luxury dwellings and La Samaritaine department

The Cubist-influenced Art Deco **Nos.49-51 rue La Fontaine**, *taken from the starker No.82.*

store as well as the public housing and swimming pool at rue des Amiraux in the 18th. The Studio Building (50 duplex flats each with an artist's studio) is Sauvage at his most colourful. The best view is from behind as you descend the rue des Perchamps (if you arrive from Métro Michel-Ange Auteuil you may have already come by here). Great big bay studio windows alternate with inset ones; square, brown glazed tiles at the base, pale grey above and stripy, almost garish details around the bays. It has been described as postmodern before its time, but ultimately its bravura and clever details, like the small golden-brown tiles that punctuate the window surround, are very daring when you see the far more conventional 1930s block next door on rue du Général-Landon.

Turn right at the junction with avenue Mozart. A wide thoroughfare cut through in the 1860s, today it has several antique shops, lots of food shops and an inordinate number of estate agents. In 1911 Guimard built the *hôtel particulier* at No.122 for himself and his American artist wife, Adeline Oppenheim, who had her *atelier* at the top; his office was at the bottom. Most striking is the tall doorway and the corner soaring outwards from the base so that the upper floors overhang. On the side in villa Flore (another street sign by Guimard), a rusty plaque forbids cars foreign to the street from parking there. That's the downside of the area – the feeling that sometimes you're intruding on the private.

Continue up the street: more estate agents and a *brocante* selling vintage garden furniture. Two imposing 1904 apartment blocks near Métro Jasmin show what was going on at same time: on the one hand avant-garde buildings for artists and enlightened patrons; on the other the last flourishing of the grandiose Beaux Arts style by the since-forgotten J Broussard. In a sort of neo-Renaissance cacophany, two pairs of big busty ladies sit on rocaille cornucopias on either side of the doorway; it's easy to sneer, but peer through the glass into the entrance and there's an amazing mosaic floor and skirting with dogs, cupids and classical shepherds. Broussard designed the less-ostentatious building next door at 6 rue Jasmin, too: note the sphinxes peeking out of the balconies.

Turn right up rue Henri-Heine (where there's a late, 1926, block of flats by Guimard at No.18; fallen from fashion, he had abandoned most of his Art Nouveau extravagance for a more geometrical style), then left into rue du Dr-Blanche – comfortable, self-contained residential Paris. At No.55, though, the unimposing square du Dr-Blanche draws architectural pilgrims from the world over. The attraction is two villas side by side by Charles-Edouard Jeanneret, alias Le Corbusier, perhaps the most influential – and most controversial – architect of the twentieth century: the Villa La Roche built for wealthy Swiss banker and art collector Raoul La Roche, as much to show off an art collection at chic dinner parties as to live in, and the Villa Jeanneret built for Le Corbusier's brother, violinist Albert Jeanneret. It was here that Le Corbusier could first try out some of his radical ideas, putting into practice the principles of the 'machine for living' later enunciated in the article *'Cinq points d'une architecture nouvelle'*: pilotis or stilts, free façade, strips of windows with metal frames, a free floor plan thanks to the use of a concrete frame rather than load-bearing walls, and roof terraces. Today both belong to the Fondation Le Corbusier – Jeanneret houses the library and archives, and La Roche is open to the public. However much the exterior seems the epitome of the 'villa blanche' (white house), with its pilotis and curved white end wall, the inside – hung with Le Corbusier's paintings and furnished with his and Charlotte Perriand's furniture designs – may surprise you with its original colour scheme: black tiles, sludge pinks, blues, greens and browns, which played out Le Corbusier's idea of the structural role of colour. The curved room with a ramp mounting up one side was the gallery where La Roche hung his Picassos, Braques and Légers, and the highly sculptural staircase leads to a series of different spaces and roof terraces. Le Corbusier envisaged it as a

The ***Studio Building*** *at No.65 rue La Fontaine – no, not Guimard this time, but Sauvage.*

The **Fondation Le Corbusier** *– one of the twentieth century's most influential buildings.*

form of architectural promenade: 'The architectural show unrolls as one looks: one follows a route and perspectives develop in great variety; one plays with the influx of light, lighting up the walls or creating shadows. Bays open up the perspectives out to the exterior, where one rediscovers the architectural unity.'

At the same time Le Corbusier was also developing his ideas of urbanisation and housing for the masses. In Paris, ideas for multiple habitation can be seen on a moderate scale at the Refuge de l'Armée du Salut (Salvation Army hostel, 12 rue Cantagrel, 13th) of 1929-33 and the Pavillon Suisse, student lodgings at the Cité Universitaire (14th), of 1930-3. In *La Ville radieuse*, published in 1935, he analysed the chaotic modern city and conceived the idea of 'zoning' in a draconian model for an organised city. Part Utopian, part totalitarian social engineering, mixing, like his built work, the pragmatic and practical, it became the foundation of the Charter of Athens published by the CIAM (Congrès Internationaux d'Architecture Moderne) in 1943.

Whatever Le Corbusier's influence on mass housing after the war – often debased versions of the Unités d'Habitation he constructed at Marseilles, Nantes and Firminy – here at a luxury level, when built for a private individual, the result is stunning. The entrance hall is particularly wonderful when you look down from the first floor and appreciate the multiple viewpoints, the fluidity of interior space and play of light from different windows and balconies.

Turn back up rue du Dr-Blanche. If you're here at the right time for its rather peculiar opening hours, take a detour along rue de l'Yvette. At No.25 sits the Musée Bouchard, the *atelier* of prolific sculptor Henri Bouchard, who moved here from Montparnasse in 1924 and bought the house with a vacant plot next door to construct his studio. Crammed top-to-toe with sculptures, casts and moulds, sketchbooks and tools, it gives an idea of the official art of the time. Bouchard moved around between 1907 and 1909 from the realism of the late nineteenth century to a more stylised, pared-back, often linear modern style, whether in his reliefs for the Eglise St-Jean de Chaillot (sculpted against the naily wooden board) or his monumental Apollo for the Palais de Chaillot. Not a great artist, but not such a bad one either.

Return to rue du Dr-Blanche. From afar you can see the white geometric forms of rue Mallet-Stevens, six houses grouped together designed by Robert Mallet-Stevens in 1926-7. By far the most glamorous figure of the Modern Movement and unrivalled for his elegance, Mallet-Stevens moved in a *mondaine* circle of artists, designers, film directors and aristrocratic patrons. There are no foibles about social housing here. No.10, built for two brothers who were sculptors, is particularly impressive with its staircase culminating in a round turret, and its series of balconies and roof terraces, although a couple of storeys have been added and it was probably more pure and minimalist without the abundance of greenery and pot plants there is today. On the corner, the studio with its big windows still has 'Joël et Jan Martel sculpteurs' engraved on the door. No.4 has a stairwell with Cubist stained glass, typical of the architect's collaboration with high-quality craftsmen. Mallet-Stevens, whose own house and office were at No.12, was criticised by some as being a mere 'decorator', but this is one of my favourite streets in Paris. When Mallet-Stevens was not building this street, a luxury villa for the Vicomte Charles de Noailles at Hyères or the casino at St-Jean-de-Luz, he was designing sets for film director Marcel L'Herbier, whose mysterious Frankenstein-esque *L'Inhumaine* (1924) was the ultimate style film. Despite its daft plot (the femme fatale who is killed by one lover and brought back to life by another) it was a sort of showcase for the artistic avant-garde of the day, including sets by Mallet-Stevens and Fernand Léger, costumes by Paul Poiret and music by Darius Milhaud.

Opposite at 12 rue du Dr-Blanche, a large school building (accommodation for

Inside the **Musée Bouchard** *at No.25 rue du Dr-Blanche,* atelier *of prolific sculptor Henri.*

Brother sculptors Joël and Jan Martel moved into **No.10 rue Mallet-Stevens** *in 1927.*

lycéennes) is a reminder that the 1930s also saw a vast programme of public housing and school construction in the outer arrondissements, generally adopting the new modern style. No.5 with black mosaics sprinkled round the door was designed as artists' studios in 1928 by Pierre Patout, famed for the Art Deco interiors of the luxury cruise liners *L'Ile de France* and *La Normandie*. The result of the vertical stack of big studio windows is rather odd, although each level is stepped back slightly to let in light.

Turn right down rue de l'Assomption, past the chunky church of Notre-Dame de l'Assomption de Passy, back to avenue Mozart. Keep walking up the hill, then turn left up rue du Ranelagh and right along avenue Vion-Whitcomb, a private crescent lined with smart apartments. The 1930s building at No.5 by Jean Ginsberg (a pupil of Le Corbusier) and François Heep shows how the Modernist style had quickly filtered – at least in part – through to the mainstream, with its long, banded horizontal windows, a Modern Movement fave. At the end, you can see the overgrown greenery of the disused Petite Ceinture, the railway line that once encircled Paris, and the platforms of the former Passy-La Muette station, now converted into the fashionable La Gare restaurant.

Turn right. Everything is not what it seems. Head through the left-hand gate of the exclusive Villa de Beauséjour. At the end, among the quiet houses and gardens, is a foreign curiosity, a slice of Zagorsk transposed – three carved wooden dachas built by carpenters from St Petersburg for the Exposition Universelle of 1867 on the Champs-de-Mars, and then reconstructed here; No.6 is the most ornate, with fancy carved gables – strange but perhaps only appropriate as numerous Russian immigrants later settled in the area after the Russian Revolution.

Past Métro La Muette. From here you could go down rue de Boulainvilliers and rue des Vignes, named in memory of the vineyards that used to grow here, but take the chaussée de la Muette, once the lands of the Château de la Muette, a royal hunting lodge (demolished in 1920) where

Madame de Pompadour once resided, leading into rue de Passy. The former high street of Passy, before the village became part of Paris in 1860, it still has something of a villagey feel, even if now it is mainly a destination for *fringues* (clothes). Either turn down rue Duban past the covered market and rue Singer, or into place de Passy and along partly pedestrianised rue de l'Annonciation, busy with delis, food shops and cafés, past the parish church of Notre-Dame de Grâce de Passy into rue Raynouard for another important mover in the Modern Movement.

Today the 1930s apartment building at 51-55 rue Raynouard may not look very revolutionary, but Auguste Perret, who ran a construction firm with his brother and was builder as well as architect, was a pioneer in the use of reinforced concrete. A visible frame and walls entirely in concrete illustrate his belief in 'truth to structure', while above the door an inscription pays tribute to Perret 'who as early as 1903 gave to reinforced concrete the nobility of ancient materials'. Le Corbusier came to study with Perret in 1908 and was influenced by his structural innovation, if not by his aesthetic. Perret lived here from 1932 until his death in 1954 and had his offices in the pavilion at the end. As with the Théâtre des Champs-Elysées and the Conseil Economique et Social at place d'Iéna, here Perret remained within a broadly classical aesthetic and coloured the concrete yellow to match Paris stone (why don't more people do that now?). It's certainly nothing like some of the social solutions that he, like Le Corbusier, wished to impose on Paris (a notorious Maison-Tours skyscraper scheme devised in 1922 to replace the Champs-Elysées) or his post-war reconstruction in Amiens.

A more ancient Passy is apparent next door at 47 rue Raynouard. The Maison de Balzac takes up the whole building where Balzac had an apartment from 1840 to his death in 1860, and where he wrote many of the novels of *La Comédie Humaine*. The museum is a rather dry presentation of his work and life, but the garden is pretty and it gives an idea of the sort of country villas that lined this street when Passy was famed for mineral springs, where a fashionable clientele took cures for anaemia.

Retrace your steps beyond Perret's home to the steep staircase at the side and descend into rue Berton. This offers a view from below of Perret's building, with the glass-curtain strip of studios along the side. Follow picturesquely cobbled rue Berton with its old lamp-posts. Narrow walls back on to the garden of the Turkish embassy (hence the strong police presence), while No.24 was the lower gateway of Balzac's house (the double access was apparently a big attraction so he could escape from creditors). Continue into rue Marcel-Proust, where you see the backs of the grand 1930s apartments on rue Raynouard, and on into rue Charles-Dickens. Amid the private houses of square Charles-Dickens, at No.5 is the

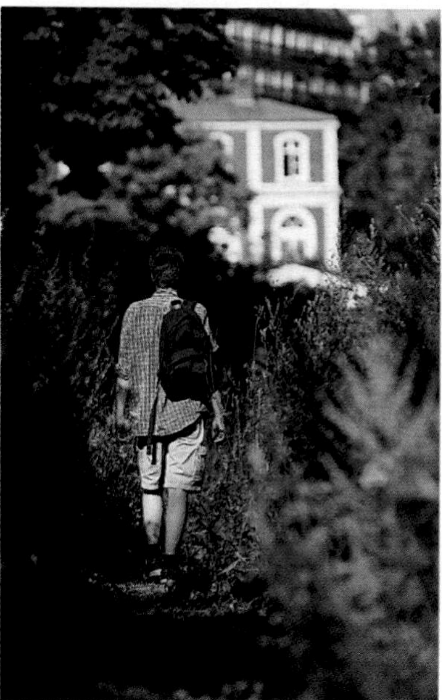

The architecture-free **Petite Ceinture.**

Musée du Vin, depicting wine production, housed in the vaulted cellars of the Abbaye des Minimes de Passy, a wine-producing monastery destroyed in the Revolution. Then climb up the passage des Eaux – the street where one of the mineral springs that made Passy's reputation as a health spa was discovered in the seventeenth century – back on to rue Raynouard.

At place du Costa-Rica, Art Nouveau freaks can take a small detour back up rue de Passy to rue Claude-Chahu. On the corner with rue Eugène-Manuel is a whacky Art Nouveau building dating from 1903, and signed by the architect Charles Klein and the ceramicist Emile Müller. Its amazing green and pink thistles around the doorway and on the façade, and the glazed entrance hall, show the decorative if not structural influence of Guimard.

Cross place du Costa-Rica, one of several circular junctions that ventilate the district, into rue Benjamin-Franklin (another former local resident). Forget the po-mo excrescence at No.15. Take a glance at the apartment building at No.17 – concrete again – designed in 1928 by Marcel Hennequet. It alternates small and large bay windows, and is topped with a crown, as it rounds the corner into rue Scheffer, that is reminiscent of the Statue of Liberty. Then inspect more Perret at 25 bis. It was built in 1904 and is a true indication of how revolutionary Perret was. Its reinforced concrete structure allowed new freedom for the floor plan, with a U-shaped façade that gave everyone Seine views. But far from Adolph Loos's maxim 'ornament is crime', Perret stuck to the decorative ethos of the time, covering the façade in a forest of leaves and berries in moulded ceramic tile. The ground floor now contains the trendy APC casualwear boutique.

Cross the street and enter the Jardins du Trocadéro by the little gate on the right for an unfamiliar side perspective of the huge Palais de Chaillot designed by Azéma, Boileau and Carlu for the Exposition Universelle of 1937. This is 1930s architecture in its official form, part of the revival of classicism that took place

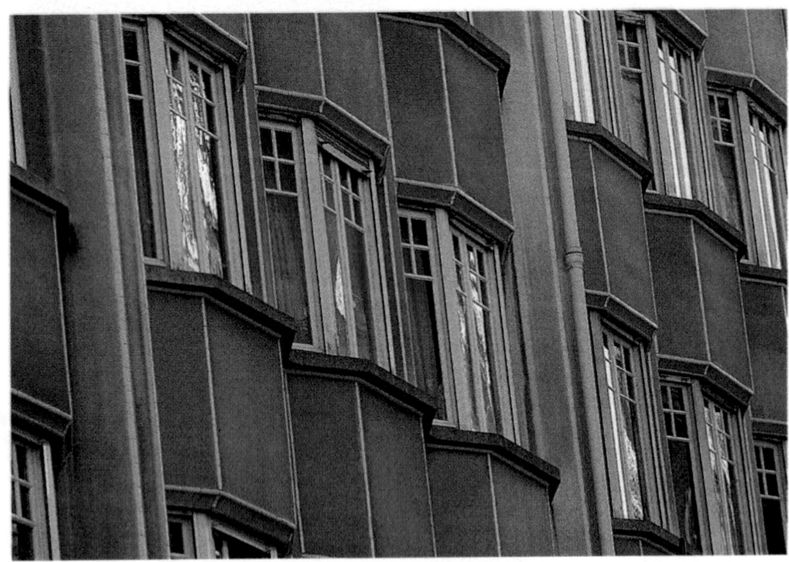

Contrast the bay windows of **Marcel Hennequet***'s No.17 rue Benjamin-Franklin...*

... with ***Auguste Perret****'s joyous, but somewhat unfashionable, façade at No.25.*

at the same time as Le Corbusier's experiments and projects for mass housing. It's often accused of being a totalitarian building and the sheer scale of the colonnaded façade and marble foyers are certainly daunting. However, while it was certainly an expression of state prestige, such an accusation is probably an anachronistic reading of the 1930s classical revival (at the same fair the Soviet and German pavilions were notoriously built facing each other, similar versions of totalitarian classical architecture, one Communist and the other Fascist). The building is adorned with sculpted bas-reliefs and inscriptions by Paul Valéry, while at the end of the two central pavilions stand giant bronzes of Apollo by Henri Bouchard (east wing) and Hercules by Albert Pommier (west wing). Today the Palais contains the Musée de l'Homme, Musée de la Marine, the Cinémathèque repertory cinema and film archive, the huge Théâtre National de Chaillot and the former Musée des Monuments Historiques (due to reopen in 2001 as the Centre pour le Patrimoine Monumental et Urbain devoted to French architectural heritage).

Ideally you would descend the picturesque paths and grottoes of the Trocadéro gardens and then climb up between the two wings through the central portico to appreciate the perspective across the river to the Champs de Mars and the Eiffel Tower. Unfortunately the parvis is in danger of collapsing, either due to failures of modern construction techniques or to the fact that the Palais was put up in a rush on the foundations of the Palais de Trocadéro, built for a former World Fair in 1878. As a result it has been barricaded off until at least 2001, so you will either have to retrace your steps or walk round the entire building to the front on place du Trocadéro.

You could stop here, but to take in a couple more key buildings, cross the place and walk up avenue d'Eylau. Behind you is a perfect view of the Eiffel Tower held between the symmetry of the two wings of Chaillot, with grand apartments on either side. At place de México, turn right along rue des Sablons. Look up above the tiled doorway of No.11, where two storeys of artists' studios, with red and white patterned bricks and wood façades, have been massacred by the Mercedes garage

Palais de Chaillot – *designed by Azéma, Boileau and Carlu for the Exposition Universelle.*

below. In rue St-Didier, the remains of a covered market, its nineteenth-century cast iron structure now rather oddly filled in with brick, competes against an ugly modern shopping centre. The rue Mesnil façade shows the old market must have once been rather pretty.

Continue up the street, where alleys of houses can be spotted through some of the doorways. The fire station at No.8 was designed by Mallet-Stevens in 1936. It is less luxurious than his villas, but still a play of geometrical shapes. With its porthole windows and horizontal bars topped by a vertical turret like a steamship funnel, you can see why Modernist architecture was often referred to at the time as '*le style paquebot*'.

Almost opposite, Le Petit Rétro bistro is a nostalgic survivor from the turn of the century, with a lovely floral-tiled interior. At place Victor-Hugo, turn left along avenue Victor-Hugo (already called this when the writer lived here at the end of his life). At No.111, sticking out against the stone-faced Haussmannian apartments and clothes shops of the busy commercial street, is another example of Sauvage's ever-experimental eclecticism, the strangely neglected Galerie Commerciale Argentine, a glazed shopping arcade and apartment block built in red brick and green cast iron (1904). The Au Nez Rouge fancy dress supplier, an antiquarian bookshop, estate agents, dry cleaners and a dog-grooming parlour suggest its commercial heyday is past, although there are some signs of renovation work, and you can climb up the stairs and look down from the balconies.

To finish your walk in true Art Deco style, double back up avenue Victor-Hugo. Ahead you can see a corner of the Arc de Triomphe, built 1806-36 in honour of Napoléon's military prowess. At No.16, shortly before L'Etoile, glints the turquoise mosaic façade of the absurdly glamorous (and very expensive) fish restaurant Maison Prunier, a perfect example of the pure decorative style of *les années folles*, and with not a hint of Modernist functionalism or social planning. Inside is a feast of marble, onyx,

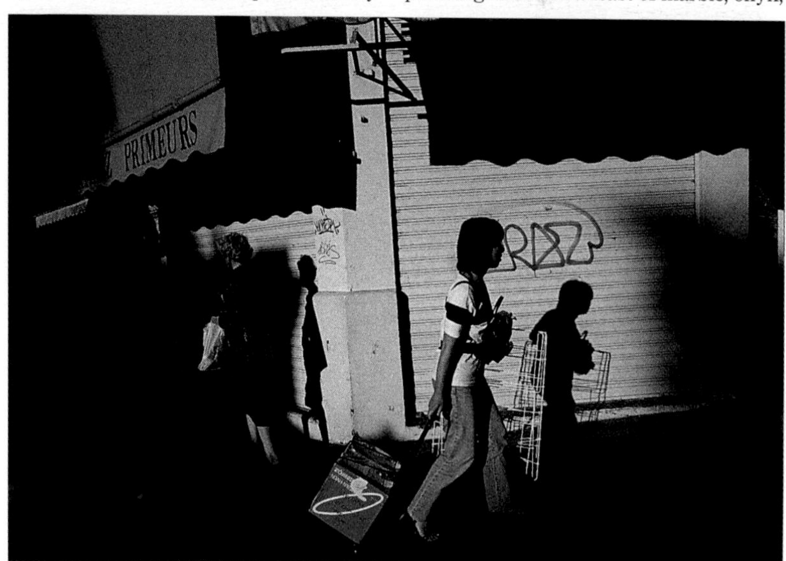

Rue St-Didier *is an architectural mish-mash. But you can always do some shopping here.*

mosaic and etched glass, and you can stop off all day at the bar for oysters and French caviar from the Gironde, just like when it opened in 1925.

Eating & drinking

Bar Antoine
17 rue La Fontaine, 16th (01.40.50.14.30). **Open** 7.30am-11pm Mon-Sat. Delightful, if pricey, steaks.

La Gare
19 chaussée de la Muette, 16th (01.42.15.15.31). **Open** noon-3pm, 7pm-midnight, daily. Fashionable fare in a converted railway station.

Le Totem
Musée de l'Homme, 17 place du Trocadéro, 16th (01.47.27.28.29). **Open** noon-2am daily. Contemporary French food and snacks, grander fare in the evenings.

Maison Prunier
16 avenue Victor-Hugo, 16th (01.44.17.35.85). **Open** 7.30-11pm Mon; noon-3pm, 7.30-11pm, Tue-Sat. Closed mid-July to mid-Aug. Spectacular setting and prices, but less reliable for the food.

Le Petit Rétro
5 rue Mesnil, 16th (01.44.05.06.05). **Open** noon-2.30pm, 7.45-10.30pm, Mon-Fri; 7.45-10.30pm Sat. Closed two weeks in Aug. Well-rendered bistro fare with a twist.

Restaurant des Chauffeurs
8 chaussée de la Muette, 16th (01.42.88.50.05). **Open** noon-2.30pm, 7-10pm, daily. Closed two weeks in Aug. Quintessential Parisian bistro fare at reasonable prices.

Museums

Arc de Triomphe
place Charles-de-Gaulle (access via underground passage), 8th (01.43.80.31.31). **Open** *Apr-Oct* 9.30am-11pm daily. *Nov-Mar* 10am-10.30pm daily. Closed public holidays. **Admission** 40F; 32F concs.

Atelier-Musée Henri Bouchard
25 rue de l'Yvette, 16th (01.46.47.63.46). **Open** 2-7pm Wed, Sat. Closed last two weeks of Mar, June, Sept, Dec. **Admission** 25F; 15F concs.

Fondation Le Corbusier
Villa La Roche, 10 square du Dr-Blanche, 16th (01.42.88.41.53). **Open** 10am-12.30pm, 1.30-6pm, Mon-Thur; 10am-12.30pm, 1.30-5pm, Fri. *Library* 1.30-6pm). Closed Aug. **Admission** 15F; 10F concs.

Maison de Balzac
47 rue Raynouard, 16th (01.42.24.56.38). **Open** 10am-5.40pm Tue-Sun. Closed public holidays. **Admission** 17.50F; 9F concs.

Musée de la Marine
Palais de Chaillot, place du Trocadéro, 16th (01.45.53.31.70). **Open** 10am-6pm Mon, Wed-Sun. **Admission** 38F; 25F concs.

Musée de l'Homme
Palais de Chaillot, pl du Trocadéro, 16th (01.44.05.72.72). **Open** 9.45am-5.15pm Mon, Wed-Sun. Closed public holidays. **Admission** 30F; 20F concs.

Musée du Vin
rue des Eaux, 5 square Charles-Dickens, 16th (01.45.25.63.26). **Open** 10am-6pm Tue-Sun. Closed 25 Dec-1 Jan. **Admission** 35F; 29F concs.

Film & theatre

La Cinémathèque Française
Palais de Chaillot, 7 avenue Albert-1er-de-Monaco, 16th (01.56.26.01.01). **Admission** 29F.

Théâtre des Champs-Elysées
15 avenue Montaigne, 8th (01.49.52.50.50). **Open** *box office* 11am-7pm Mon-Sat; *telephone bookings* 10am-noon, 2-6pm, Mon-Fri. **Tickets** 50F-690F.

Théâtre National de Chaillot
Palais de Chaillot, place du Trocadéro, 16th (01.53.65.30.00). **Open** *box office* 11am-7pm Mon-Sat; 11am-5pm Sun. *Telephone bookings* 9am-7pm Mon-Sat; 11am-6pm Sun. **Tickets** 160F; 120F concs.

Shopping

APC
25 bis rue Benjamin-Franklin, 16th (01.45.53.28.28). **Open** 10.30am-7pm Mon-Sat.

Au Nez Rouge
Galerie Commerciale Argentine, 111 avenue Victor-Hugo, 16th (01.47.55.05.40). **Open** 10.15am-6.30pm Tue-Sat.

Maison Piechowski
29 bis rue La Fontaine, 16th (01.42.24.86.13). **Open** 7.30am-1.30pm, 3-7.30pm, Tue-Sun.

Others

Notre-Dame de l'Assomption de Passy
88 rue de l'Assomption, 16th (01.42.24.41.50). **Open** 9am-noon, 2-7pm, Mon-Sat; 10am-noon, 6.30-8pm, Sun.

Orphelins Apprentis d'Auteuil
40 rue La Fontaine, 16th (01.44.14.75.75).

The **Arc de Triomphe** *– built 1806-36 in honour of Napoléon's military prowess – not a bad place to end a walk.*

LILLE
HONDSCHOOTTE
WATTIGNIES
ARLON
COURTRAI
TOURCOING
WEISSEMBOURG
MAESTRICHT
ALDENHOVEN
LANDAU
NEUWIED
RASTADT
ETLINGEN

Island in the stream

Olivier Morel (Relom)

You can't escape the past on the Ile de la Cité.

Eating & drinking

Le Vieux Bistro

14 rue du Cloître-Notre-Dame, 4th (01.43.54.18.95). **Open** noon-2pm, 7.30-11pm, daily. Perfect renditions of classic French cuisine.

Museums

Cathédrale Notre Dame de Paris

place du Parvis-Notre-Dame, 4th (01.42.34.56.10). **Open** 8am-6.45 daily. **Admission** free. *Towers* (01.44.32.16.70) entrance at foot of north tower. **Open** 10am-4.30pm daily. **Admission** 35F; 25F concs.

La Conciergerie

1 quai de l'Horloge, 1st (01.53.73.78.50). **Open** *Apr-Oct* 9.30am-6.30pm daily; *Nov-Mar* 10am-5pm daily. **Admission** 35F; 23F concs; 50F combined ticket with Ste Chapelle.

Sainte-Chapelle & Palais de Justice

4 boulevard du Palais, 1st (01.53.73.78.50). **Open** *Apr-Sept* 9.30am-6.30pm daily; *Oct-Mar* 10am-5pm

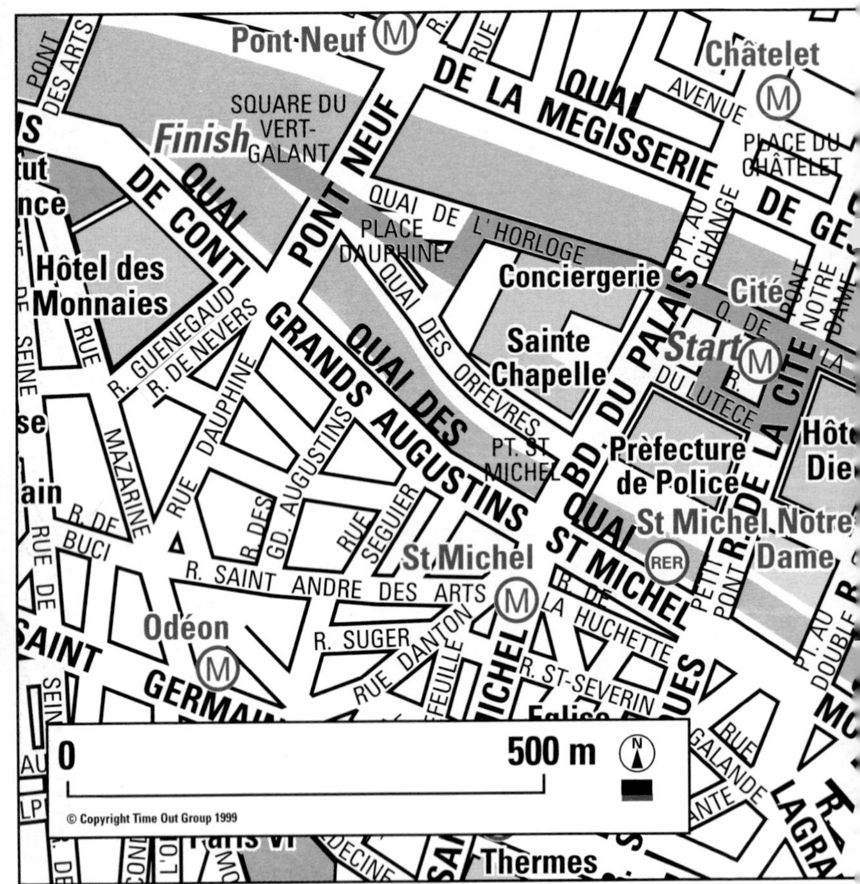

daily. **Admission** 35F; 23F concs; 50F combined ticket with Conciergerie.

Mémorial de la Déportation

square de l'Ile de France, 4th (no phone). **Open** 10am-noon, 2-5pm, daily.

Hôtel de Ville

place de l'Hôtel de Ville, 4th (switchboard 01.42.76.40.40/reservations 01.42.76.50.49). **Open** groups make reservation 2 months in advance; individuals first Mon in every month following reservation made one month in advance.

Other

Flower Market

place Louis Lépine, 4th (no phone). **Open** 9.30am-6.30pm Mon-Sat.

Start: Mº Cité, 4th
Finish: square du Vert-Galant, 1st
Time: 45 minutes
Distance: 2km/1 mile
Getting there: line 4 to Mº Cité
Getting back: short walk to Mº Pont Neuf (line 7)
Note: further details about (and listings relating to) the Ile de la Cité are included in walks by Chantal Barbe and Maureen Freely.

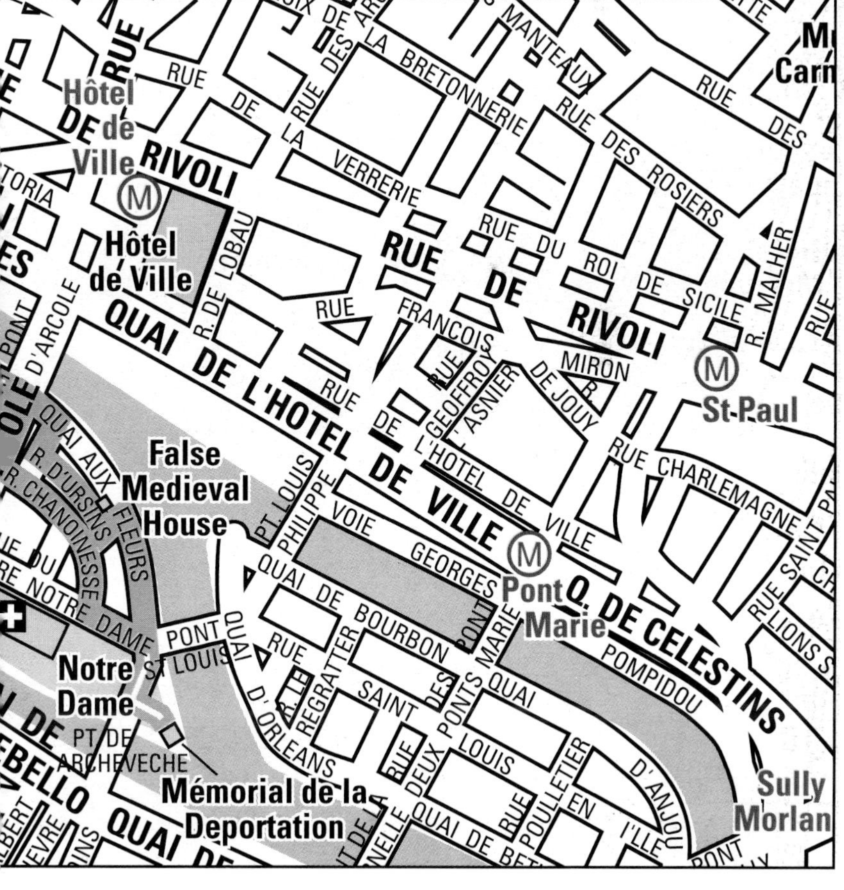

ISLAND IN THE STREAM
LEAVE THE MÉTRO AT CITÉ, NOTING THE PRETTY SIGN BY GUIMARD AND THE ABUNDANCE OF FLOWER SELLERS. YOU'RE IN RUE DE LUTÈCE. TWO THOUSAND YEARS AGO, THIS IS WHERE THE PARISII TRIBE LIVED. THE ISLAND HAS GONE THROUGH SOME CHANGES SINCE THEN.
MÉTROPOLITAIN
AT ONE END OF RUE DE LUTÈCE YOU'VE GOT LA SAINTE-CHAPELLE HEMMED IN BY THE WALLS OF THE PALAIS DE JUSTICE. AT THE OTHER END OF THE STREET YOU'LL SEE THE HÔTEL DIEU, AN ENORMOUS HOSPITAL WHERE THE EMERGENCY SERVICES WOULD DRIVE GEORGE CLOONEY WILD WITH ENVY. HEAD TOWARDS THE HÔTEL DIEU AND TURN LEFT ON TO RUE DE LA CITÉ.
NEXT, HEAD RIGHT ALONG QUAI DE LA CORSE. ON THE OPPOSITE BANK YOU CAN SEE THE HÔTEL DE VILLE, THE RESIDENCE OF THE MAYOR OF PARIS. IT'S VERY IMPRESSIVE, ITS OCCUPANTS OFTEN LESS SO. TURN RIGHT INTO RUE D'ARCOLE.
TAKE THE FIRST LEFT, RUE CHANOINESSE. NO.14 IS A CHARMING HOUSE, ITS PORCH DECORATED WITH FREESTONES.
RUE CHANOINESSE

RUE CHANOINESSE COMES OUT INTO RUE DU CLOÎTRE NOTRE-DAME WITH ITS UNIMPEDED VIEWS OF THE CATHEDRAL'S GARGOYLES.

FOLLOW RUE DU CLOÎTRE NOTRE DAME TO THE LEFT AS FAR AS SQUARE DE L'ILE DE FRANCE, HOME TO THE STARK CONCRETE MEMORIAL FOR THE 200,000 (MAINLY) JEWS SENT TO THE NAZI CAMPS BY THE AUTHORITIES. IF YOU'RE LUCKY, IN SUMMER IT'S ALSO HOME TO YOUNG WOMEN SOAKING UP THE SUN.
GOOD JOB I BROUGHT MY CAMERA.
AUX DEUX CENT MILLE MORTS DANS LES CAMPS
MARTYRS FRANCAIS DE LA DEPORTATION
1945

NOW FOR SOME ROMANTICISM. LEAVING THE SQUARE, WANDER DOWN THE QUAI AUX FLEURS AS FAR AS NO.9, WHICH WAS HOME TO HÉLOÏSE AND ABÉLARD. IN THE TWELFTH CENTURY, ABÉLARD WAS A TEACHER. A CANON AT NOTRE-DAME BY THE NAME OF FULBERT ENTRUSTED TO HIM THE EDUCATION OF HIS NIECE, HÉLOÏSE. ABÉLARD AND HÉLOÏSE FELL IN LOVE AND DISAPPEARED OFF TO BRETAGNE TO START A FAMILY. ON THEIR RETURN TO PARIS, FULBERT, MAD WITH RAGE, SENT HIS HIRED MEN TO CASTRATE ABÉLARD. HENCEFORTH, THE POOR DEVIL DEVOTED HIMSELF TO SPIRITUAL MATTERS, NOT THAT HE HAD MUCH CHOICE. HÉLOÏSE AND ABÉLARD NOW LIE TOGETHER IN PERE-LACHAISE.

TAKE THE FIRST LEFT, WHERE ON THE CORNER OF RUE DES CHANTRES AND RUE D'URSINS THERE'S A 'FALSE MEDIEVAL HOUSE' RESTORED ROOM BY ROOM IN 1958 BY THE ARCHITECT FERNAND POUILLON.

TAKE THE NARROW RUE D'URSINS TO RUE DE LA COLOMBE, WHERE YOU SHOULD TAKE A RIGHT, THEN TURN LEFT ON TO THE QUAIS.

AS YOU WANDER DOWN THE QUAIS YOU'LL NOTICE FOUR BIG TOWERS. THEY BELONG TO THE CONCIERGERIE...
...PARIS'S FIRST PRISON. RAVAILLAC (HENRI IV'S ASSASSIN) STAYED HERE A WHILE BEFORE GOING OFF TO BE QUARTERED. DURING THE REVOLUTION, LOTS OF CHARACTERS CAME HERE TO TWIDDLE THEIR THUMBS BEFORE BEING DECAPITATED. MARIE-ANTOINETTE ALSO AWAITED EXECUTION HERE.

FOLLOW THE MAP TO PLACE DAUPHINE, A PEACEFUL, SHADED TRIANGLE COMMISSIONED BY HENRI IV IN HONOUR OF HIS SON, THE DAUPHIN, LATER LOUIS XIII.

CROSS PLACE DAUPHINE AND YOU'LL COME FACE TO FACE WITH A STATUE OF HENRI IV... MUCH APPRECIATED BY THE PIGEONS. IF HENRI IV WERE TO COME BACK TO LIFE, TOP OF HIS LIST WOULD BE TO TAKE A SHIT ON A PIGEON.

FINISH OFF BY STROLLING THROUGH SQUARE DU VERT-GALANT AND ENJOYING ITS FLORAL BORDERS. BONNE PROMENADE!
RELOM 99

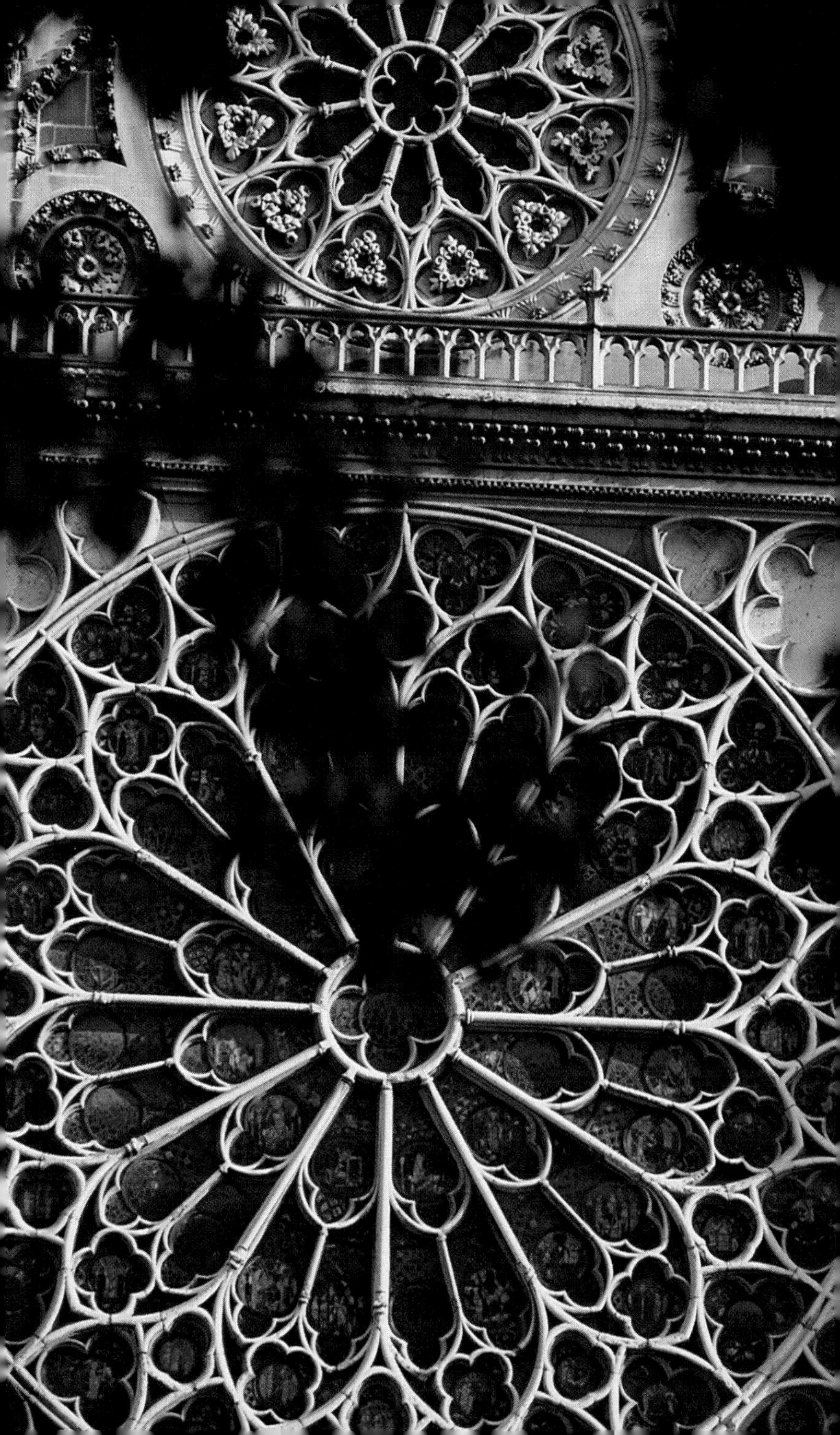

In search of Simone

Maureen Freely

'Women, you owe her everything!' Take a day to follow in the footsteps of Simone de Beauvoir.

Start: Le Select, 6th
Finish: La Coupole, 14th
Time: 6-7 hours
Distance: 12km/7.5 miles
Getting there: line 4 to Vavin followed by very short walk
Getting back: very short walk to Vavin (line 4)
Note: this is a very long (circular) walk. It is strongly recommended that you set off early enough in the day in order to reach the Cimetière du Montparnasse at the end of the walk before it closes (see listings for opening and closing times).

When I was in my early twenties and struggling to write the novel that would cancel out all other novels, but never quite managing to get beyond the first line, I spent some time in Montparnasse. Well, I would, wouldn't I? This was where Ernest and Gertrude and Zelda and Scott and Ezra and Henry and Arthur and Anaïs and June and so many other members of the Lost Generation found themselves between the two world wars. These were my idols. I wanted to eat like them, sleep like them, drink like them, and write like them, while also turning out work so original that it would have caused even them to tremble. But I was doomed from the start, as I did not have a trust fund, could not even look at a drink without getting a hangover, and had nothing to say.

The harder I tried to follow in my idols' footsteps, the more I grew to resent them. My relations with the living patrons of the Montparnasse bars and cafés were just as tormented. I was madly, deeply impressed with the fragments of conversation that wafted my way. I would have given anything, anything, to know where they found the money to pay for their daring clothes, or how they managed to keep their minds on things intellectual even after the sixth cognac and soda. And who had taught them to purse their lips like that when they exhaled? But at the same time I hated them for looking down their noses at me – better to suspect them of that than to see that they didn't see me at all – and so I made sure that whenever they looked in my direction, I was gazing disdainfully at a point above their heads.

One of the people I might have noticed had I not been so busy wrapping myself up in fake poses is Simone de Beauvoir. She spent most of her life in Montparnasse. During the mid-1970s, when I was there, she lived fewer than five minutes away from the Select, the café I used as my base. Her favourite place for Sunday lunch was La Coupole, just opposite the Select. She edited Sartre's masterwork, *Being and Nothingness*, at a table in the Dôme, the café-restaurant a few hundreds yards to the left. The church just a little way down to the right, Notre-Dame-des-Champs, was her family's parish church. La Rotonde, the café to the left, was where she and her sister would hide as teenagers when they were playing hookey from school.

Simone de Beauvoir is almost overwhelmed by the crowds at the funeral of **Jean-Paul Sartre** *in April 1980.*

I knew none of this during my brief stay in Montparnasse. I doubt that I would have wanted to know. Of all the writers and thinkers who overshadowed me in those days, she was the one who overshadowed me the most. She continues to do so. Whenever I come up with an idea I think to be original, it's only a matter of time before I find out that she thought of it first. But now I'm old enough to understand how hard it is to be original. I can imagine how lonely it must have been for her to hold ideas that were so far ahead of their time. And, thanks to the recent run of biographies, I don't even have to imagine what it was like to be almost-but-not-quite married to almost-always-philandering Jean-Paul Sartre.

It was only when I read the Deirdre Bair biography that I found out that the walk we'll be taking today – the walk I took so often when I was trying to settle in Montparnasse, and still take, every single time I come back to Paris – is a walk Simone had already been taking for decades and decades before I was even born. All these years I've been following in her footsteps, literally, without even knowing it. But today I'm hoping to make up for lost time.

So, let's begin at the beginning. If we leave the ´café S´lect, and turn left to walk along the boulevard du Montparnasse, we soon come to the intersection with boulevard Raspail. It is in one of these grand apartment buildings that Simone de Beauvoir spent the first 11 years of her life. Her earliest memories are of standing on a wrought iron balcony, looking down at the people and the traffic below. Simone was born into the *haute haute bourgeoisie*, but her family's situation was precarious. Her maternal grandfather went bankrupt just after her parents married, and before he was able to pay his daughter's dowry. The de Beauvoirs were able to keep up a front during the years leading up to World War I, but by 1919 they were ruined.

If we turned left here and carried on down the gracious, tree-lined boulevard

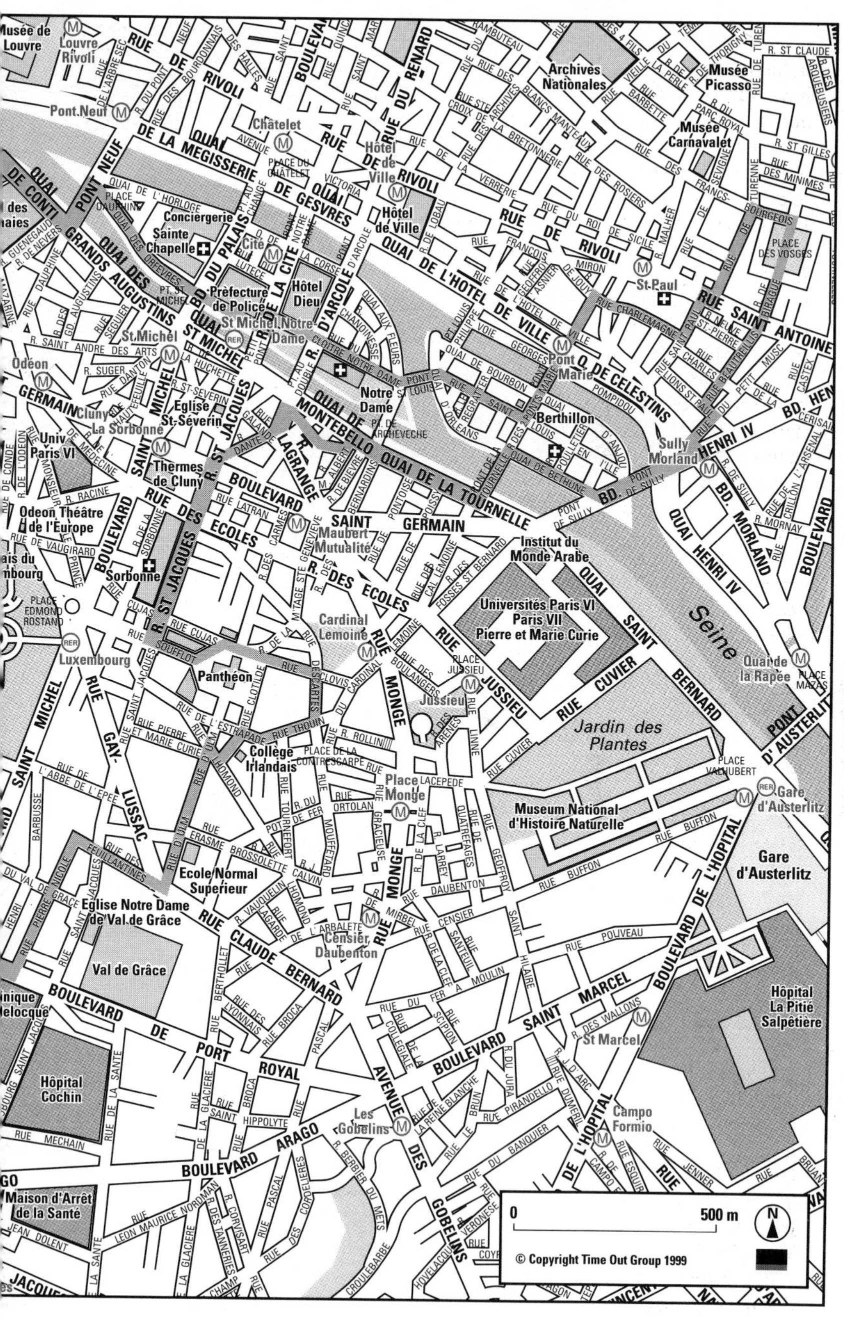
Musée de Louvre
Louvre Rivoli
Pont Neuf
Châtelet
Place du Châtelet
Hôtel de Ville
Archives Nationales
Musée Picasso
Musée Carnavalet
Place des Vosges
St Paul
Conciergerie
Sainte Chapelle
Cité
Hôtel Dieu
Préfecture de Police
St Michel Notre-Dame
St Michel
Notre Dame
Pont Marie
Berthillon
Sully Morland
Odéon
Cluny La Sorbonne
Eglise St-Severin
Thermes de Cluny
Univ. Paris VI
Odeon Théâtre de l'Europe
Sorbonne
Maubert Mutualité
Institut du Monde Arabe
Universités Paris VI Paris VII Pierre et Marie Curie
Seine
Quai de la Rapée
Place Edmond Rostand
Luxembourg
Panthéon
Cardinal Lemoine
Jussieu
Place Jussieu
Jardin des Plantes
Place Valhubert
Gare d'Austerlitz
Collège Irlandais
Place de la Contrescarpe
Place Monge
Museum National d'Histoire Naturelle
Ecole Normal Superieur
Eglise Notre Dame de Val de Grâce
Val de Grâce
Censier Daubenton
Hôpital La Pitié Salpêtière
St Marcel
Campo Formio
Les Gobelins
Hôpital Cochin
Maison d'Arrêt de la Santé
Rue de Rivoli
Quai de la Megisserie
Quai de Gesvres
Quai de l'Hotel de Ville
Quai de Conti
Quai des Grands Augustins
Quai St Michel
Quai de Montebello
Quai de la Tournelle
Quai de Celestins
Quai Henri IV
Quai Saint Bernard
Rue Saint Antoine
Boulevard Henri IV
Boulevard Saint Germain
Boulevard Saint Michel
Boulevard du Palais
Rue des Ecoles
Rue St Jacques
Rue Cuvier
Rue Jussieu
Rue Monge
Rue Gay-Lussac
Rue Claude Bernard
Boulevard de Port Royal
Boulevard Saint Marcel
Boulevard de l'Hopital
Boulevard Arago
Avenue des Gobelins
Pont d'Austerlitz
0
500 m
N
© Copyright Time Out Group 1999

Jean-Paul runs through the plot of Being and Nothingness *for the fourth time that afternoon.*

Raspail, and then turned right on to the workaday rue de Rennes, we would eventually reach No.71, the 'cramped, dark and gloomy' apartment to which Simone's family decamped after that disaster. But we won't go that far today. Instead we'll leave the boulevard Raspail to turn right on to rue de Fleurus and follow this quiet street to the point where it intersects with rue Guynemer and leads into the wide paths, concentric circles and precise lawns of the Jardin du Luxembourg.

When Simone came to this park with her mother and her younger sister, she was not allowed to speak to any other child unless her mother had taken the calling card of that child's mother and paid her a visit to make sure the child came from the right sort of family. The park still has an ordered grandeur that harks back to that time, but (to the Anglo-Saxon eye) there are details that don't fit. Take the bronze statue we see on our left as we make our way along the path that runs parallel with rue Guynemer in the direction of rue de Vaugirard. It features a scantily clad Bacchus with friends. An image comes to mind: Simone and her sister Hélène standing on this patch of grass wearing perfectly starched white dresses, holding their hoops in just the right way, while behind them there is this writhing mass of pagan green representing all that *la mission civilisatrice* will never tame.

It occurs to me that I've never stopped to notice how often these two worlds collide in Paris, and how beautifully they collude with each other. As we make our way through the park and out on to the city streets we can see mementoes of their monumental struggle everywhere. There is the *orangerie* to our right as we head for rue de Vaugirard, lined with palm trees. In front of it, the tiny patch of lawn reserved for children under six years, who can only use the space when accompanied. It comes with a built-in sandbox and its own small and sublime statue. As we leave the Jardin, turning left and then crossing the street, we find a similar containment of opposing styles in the allée du Séminaire, the pathway running alongside rue Bonaparte. Halfway along is a lovely little fountain that suggests a foreshortened obelisk. One side is dedicated to arts and sciences, the three others to those strange bedfellows, agriculture, commerce and peace. Even here, it was never a stable alliance. A plaque on the building where we rejoin rue Bonaparte commemorates those who died on the battlefields or in front of firing squads, as well as the thousands of French and Belgian refugees who found shelter inside its walls during World War II.

In those days, this building was the seminary for St-Sulplice. Now it has been modernised and upgraded to become the Hôtel des Finances. It still fits in nicely with the arches, towers and colonnades of the church it once served, and also with the fountain that stands in the middle of the church courtyard. Statues of four very important and fully dressed priests sit in its recesses. None is sterner than 'l'Evêque de Nîmes' as he stares over at the naked cherubs standing proud on the walls of the building opposite.

Continuing down rue Bonaparte past boutique after boutique of priceless clothes, and crossing rue du Four, one of the few streets in the *faubourg* still to carry the same name it did in the fifteenth century, we finally come into the neighbourhood where Simone de Beauvoir and Jean-Paul Sartre ruled for so many years as the two leading apostles of Existentialism. It is only a ten-minute walk from the neighbourhoods of Simone's childhood but what a distance she had to travel to get there. Her early attempts at independence were fiercely blocked by her mother. The only reason she was able to get an education was because her father could not give them dowries and so assumed them to be unmarriageable. Simone's sister trained to become an artist, while Simone, who had 'the brain of a man', chose philosophy and fought her way into the Sorbonne. This is where she linked up with Sartre. In the final exams, he came in first, and she second. It was a ranking that persisted in their minds and most particularly in her mind, for the rest of their lives. He was the creative genius; she had been placed on this earth to explain *Being and Nothingness* to the world. But during her St-Germain years she clocked up quite a few honours of her own, most notably, the book that gave birth to the contemporary feminist movement, *The Second Sex*.

Her association with St-Germain dates back to the late 1930s, when she was still a celebrity-watcher rather than a celebrity – except, perhaps, for her pupils at the Lycée Molière in the 16th arrondissement. The bolder ones often followed her to St-Germain, where a few had the good or bad fortune of meeting and then falling under the spell of Sartre. Even during their early years together, Sartre and de Beauvoir had an open relationship, but at the same time they were far from casual about their obligations to each other and to the many other lovers and friends they called their 'chosen family'.

The café they used as their base during the 1940s and '50s was the Café de Flore. It's still there, on the northern side of the boulevard St-Germain, just left of the Deux Magots and right across the street from the Brasserie Lipp. It can no longer boast to be the centre of intellectual Paris, but it's as packed as ever, and still favoured by people who have gone to great lengths to look as if they are entertaining deep and mysterious thoughts – just possibly about what must continue to be the ultimate challenge for any true artist – how to pay the bill.

The art deco interior is much the same as it was in de Beauvoir's day, but for the stove that made it one of the warmest places in Paris during the Nazi Occupation. De Beauvoir was in the habit of arriving just after it opened at eight, so that she could claim one of the tables right next to it. She wrote two philosophical essays, a novel and a play at this table during the war years. She was such a regular that when there were air raids, the manager allowed her to hide out in the upstairs salon, which was closed to the public throughout the war, instead of forcing her to take refuge in the Métro St-Germain like everyone else.

The café was considered out of bounds by many French intellectuals, on account of it being the favourite meeting place of the German propaganda staff. After the war, de Beauvoir's enemies took her to task for placing herself so close to them. But (as she said in 1982 to Deirdre Bair), 'People who were not there cannot understand how all pervasive the Germans were. They were everywhere. There may have been one or two little *zincs* on the outskirts, but I had never gone to these places, they were difficult to get to even if one could find them, and why would I put myself to so much trouble when I was tired and hungry all the time?'

Indeed, it is hard to look beyond the prosperous surfaces of today's St-Germain and imagine what these cafés were like during and just after the war. Many of the people who used them as their sitting rooms did so out of necessity: like Simone, they lived in small, spartan, badly heated hotel rooms. The hours and hours they spent at these tables may have been full of intrigue and intellectual stimulation, but the strains of being 'on show' took their toll. De Beauvoir, who was famous for her drinking capacity on most days, was also famous for cracking on the very bad days, and launching into crying jags that lasted hours.

These would drive Sartre to distraction – did he realise that his (officially condoned) infidelities were often the cause? Apparently, he was the only one who knew just how to pull her out of the trough of despondency, with a proposal, or a promise, or a wicked joke that made her laugh. Once they were over, she would powder her face, straighten her clothes and return to the conversation as if nothing had happened.

So let us leave her there, holding forth at that table in the corner. Let's cast one last look inside and see her in the electric-blue dress that she wore on the day she won the Prix Goncourt for her 1954 novel, *The Mandarins*, and that she continued to wear, for years, until the seams gave out. To her right is her friend, colleague and occasional lover, Bost. Beyond him is Camus, the Other Existentialist. He doesn't look very happy today. He is about to have a serious rift with Sartre, which is why de Beauvoir is giving him withering looks. To her left is Olga, who was Sartre's lover until she married Bost; and Michelle Vian, who is still Sartre's lover even though she is married to the writer Boris Vian; and Claude Lanzmann, who will be famous one day for his film *Shoah*, but who is still mostly famous at this point for being de Beauvoir's youngest ever lover. And there, next to him, is the skittish Wanda, who is Olga's sister, and another former lover of Sartre's. She has already appeared in a number of his plays under the name of Marie Ollivier, but she is most famous for her temper. This is why no one will be surprised when, in 1958, she expresses her views on de Beauvoir's first autobiography, *Memoirs of a Dutiful Daughter*, by chopping it into little pieces with a butcher's knife.

De Beauvoir was known for her sharp tongue and her lack of tact. But even the most refined of bourgeois hostesses would have had a hard time keeping the peace with that lot. Her troubles don't end there, because the Café de Flore is slowly being infiltrated by the men who are already negating everything Sartre stands for. There they are now, in the other corner – Lacan, and Barthes, and Derrida, and can that be Foucault? It is clear from their snide and self-satisfied smiles that they are thinking about the rabbits in their hats. The days of Existentialism are numbered. So let us hope they are making the most of them, and move on.

As we turn left into place St-Germain-des-Prés – the abbey to our right, and assorted temples to *haute couture* on our left – we can see right ahead of us the Café Bonaparte. The apartments above it belong to 42 rue Bonaparte. Sartre lived here with his mother during the 1950s and early '60s. They left for safer havens when Sartre and de Beauvoir became targets of

From about 1970, de Beauvoir became a dutiful figurehead for the **women's movement**.

the national front because of their opposition to French colonialism in Algeria. The bomb campaign against them went on for a year. Although they spent most of it in hiding, there were a number of near misses. A plastic bomb went off in the foyer of No.42, but apparently it caused little damage.

If we continued right along the rue de l'Abbaye, we would soon reach the Hôtel Louisiane, where de Beauvoir lived for a few years after the war. But today we're turning left, and then right on to rue St-Benoît, and past the Muniche and the pretty tile walls of Le Petit Zinc, to turn left on to rue Jacob. Now we are following the same path Simone herself took almost daily during those post-war years. She would take the rue Jacob and then its continuation, the rue de l'Université, which probably was not wall-to-wall antique stores in those days, and then left on to the tiny rue Sébastian-Bottin, to the offices of Gallimard, which also housed *Les Temps Modernes*, the periodical that Sartre and de Beauvoir founded in 1945. Having done her work here, she would proceed out to the rue du Bac and the basement bar at the Hôtel Pont-Royal (now undergoing massive renovation), which became the alternative meeting place for de Beauvoir and Sartre when fame overtook them and spending time at the Flore, the Deux Magots and the Lipp was no longer quite as much fun.

The décor at this bar was pretty basic. The tables were wooden kegs. But it was here that de Beauvoir carried on her lukewarm flirtation with Koestler. ('One night I got so drunk I let him come home with me. We slept together. It wasn't any good.') And it was here that Truman Capote got the ammunition that allowed him to get even with de Beauvoir and Sartre for calling him an 'existentialist fairy'. Noting the bar in *Answered Prayers*, he recalled seeing 'wall-eyed, pipesucking, pasty-hued Sartre sitting with his spinsterish moll, de Beauvoir, propped in the corner like an abandoned pair of ventriloquist's dolls'.

De Beauvoir was a great walker. I can imagine that when the Left Bank gossip got too much to take, she had the same urge I have sometimes, to leave it all behind. I can see her striding off in the direction of the Seine, muttering, '*Oh la la! Mais c'est insupportable! J'en ai marre!*'

If we follow her footsteps down the rue du Bac, we come to Pont-Royal. If we crossed it, we would walk straight into the Jardin des Tuileries. From there we would only be one right turn away from the Pyramide de Napoléon and the Louvre. If we stayed on the Left Bank and turned left, we would come to the Musée d'Orsay, which was a train station in de Beauvoir's day and now hosts one of the city's finest collections of Impressionist art. But I must confess that I'm not a museum person, especially not in Paris. It seems to me that the things going on in the streets are far more interesting than these lifeless exhibits.

So today I propose that we forget the museums and continue with our ghosts along the quai Voltaire. This stretch of the Seine is full of them. Voltaire lived and died at No.27, Ingres at No.13. Baudelaire wrote *Les Fleurs du mal* at No.19. Wagner, Sibelius and Wilde all lived for a time at the same address. Beyond the quai Voltaire, on the quai Malaquais, we can see the outer walls of the Ecole des Beaux-Arts. Once we have passed along these, we come to a beautiful edifice with an oval cupola and a semicircular façade. This is the Institut de France. Built in the late seventeenth century, originally known as the Collège Mazarin, it now houses five academies, the most famous of which is the Academie Française. There is no greater honour for a writer in France than to be elected to its ranks. Its 40 members are known as *'les immortels'*. Note the gender. In de Beauvoir's time, the idea of *'une immortelle'* would have been unthinkable. It wasn't until 1980 that the writer Marguerite Yourcenar became the first female academician.

Next to the institute is L'Hôtel des Monnaies, the old mint. Just beyond it is the rue Dauphine, the site of the most miserable hotel de Beauvoir ever lived in. She was here at a time when she was making almost daily visits to the Bibliothèque Nationale (then housed on the right bank, in a building just north of the Louvre and the Palais-Royal). I can imagine her pausing halfway across the Pont Neuf to look at the impenetrable façades of the mint and the Institute on the one side of the Seine, and the high walls of the Louvre on the other. I can imagine that it was after she made a mental count of the doors that were forever closed to the likes of her, that she first entertained the thought that women might be the second sex.

Approached from the Pont Neuf – despite its name, the oldest bridge on the Seine – the Ile de la Cité looks like a huge stone boat. At the westernmost tip is the square du Vert-Galant, with a statue of its namesake, Henri IV. Looming over the place Dauphine to our right is the forbidding Palais de Justice. Inside it you can find one of the most beautiful churches in the world – the Ste-Chapelle, with its soaring arches and stained-glass windows – and one of its most infamous prisons. It was in the Conciergerie that the Terror began in September 1792, with the massacre of 350 enemies of the people. It was here that Marie Antoinette awaited the guillotine. Later on, Charolotte Corday, Danton and Robespierre all met the same fate. Also within these walls is the Chambre Correctionelle, where Flaubert was put on trial for *Madame Bovary* in 1857. Later on that same summer, Baudelaire stood trial here for *Les Fleurs du mal.*

As we move beyond this fortress along the quai des Orfèvres, we come to the Préfecture de Police, where Simenon's Maigret worked for so many long and fictitious years. Passing this, we have our first good view of Notre-Dame, the cathedral that gave birth to Gothic architecture. Henry VI of England was crowned King of France here in 1431. Napoléon I chose it as the place to have himself crowned Emperor. De Gaulle used it for his thanksgiving service upon his return to Paris in 1944. But its most powerful associations in most people's minds are with Quasimodo, the hunchback hero of the Victor Hugo novel, *Notre-Dame de Paris*. It was the great success of this same novel that prompted a revival of interest in all things Gothic, and that led to the restoration of Notre-Dame in 1844. It was not long afterwards that much of the rest of the Ile de la Cité was destroyed.

The first settlements on the Ile de la Cité date back to Roman times. The crossroads between two natural routes across northern France, it was the fortified capital of the Parisii tribe and went by the name Lutétia. Later it became the site of Frankish Paris. Although the city soon spread to both riverbanks, the island continued to be the royal, legal and ecclesiastical centre of Paris throughout the Middle Ages. Even today, the bronze marker in front of Notre-Dame is still known as 'Kilomètre Zéro'. In the mid-nineteenth century, it was still pretty much as the Capetian Kings had built it in the thirteenth century.

Then along came Baron Haussmann. He did not like the narrow, twisting, foul-smelling streets of old Paris. He had seen how well they had lent themselves to the building of barricades in 1830 and 1848. He saw them as breeding grounds for sedition and disease and so decided that the time had come to clear them. To make room for his improvements, he evicted 25,000 people from the island and razed 20 of its churches.

He did not destroy every last bit of it. Turn left on to the rue de la Cité, and then turn right in front of the Hôtel Dieu, a hospital that was founded in 660 and rebuilt by Haussman in 1868. Underneath the Parvis de Notre-Dame, the open space just in front of the cathedral, is the Crypte Archéologique. Here you can see the old city foundations that construction workers unearthed in 1965 while making an underground car park.

Stop for a quiet drink on the **Ile St-Louis**.

The history of the other island, the Ile St-Louis, which we reach by walking under the shadow of the northern walls of Notre-Dame along the rue du Cloître-Notre-Dame and then leaving the Cité by a small footbridge, is shorter and sweeter. Until the seventeenth century, it was made up of two islands, divided by a canal, and inhabited by grazing animals. Then a developer named Christophe Marie persuaded Louis XIII to fill in the canal and let him build streets and houses. After he went bankrupt, an architect named La Vau took over the project. Many of the island's most beautiful mansions are his. Even today, its streets have a restrained and comforting neighbourhood feel to them. There is no Métro, and there is not one shop that is not in very, very good taste. If we make our way past the busy Brasserie de l'Ile and Berthillon, the equally busy ice-cream parlour, and walk down rue St-Louis-en-l'Ile, the city noises fade away and it is soon very hard to believe we are in the epicentre of Paris.

If we continued to the far end of the rue St-Louis-en-l'Ile, we would pass two of the island's best-known mansions – the Hôtel Chenizot at No.51 and the Hôtel Lambert at No.2. But we'll be turning left on to the rue des Deux-Ponts. At the quai d'Anjou on our left, more ghosts lie in wait. The artist Honoré Daumier lived at No.9, Baudelaire and Théophile Gautier lived at No.7, and Ford Madox Ford published the *Transatlantic Review* out of No.22.

Crossing over to the Right Bank on the Pont Marie, we walk straight on down the rue des Nonnains-d'Hyères, past the fortress-like Hôtel de Sens (which was not very well restored not long ago, and resembles a medieval castle out of Disney). Then we turn right on to the cool, narrow, shady, authentically medieval rue Charlemagne. Now we are in the heart of the Marais. Until the thirteenth century it was, as its name suggests, a marsh. Then the Knights Templar and other religious houses arrived and turned it into arable land. Charles V moved the court here from the Cité in the mid-fourteenth century. Courtiers followed and until the Faubourg St-Germain took precedence in the early eighteenth century, it was the most fashionable place in Paris. Following the Revolution, all the nobles fled. The state confiscated their property and sold it on to craftsmen and merchants. The grand buildings fell into neglect. The Jewish quarter (to the north, centred around the rue des Rosiers) has been through just as many changes. The original community was expelled in the thirteenth century. Although some were reinstated later on, it remained fairly small until about a century ago, when many refugees from the pogroms in eastern Europe settled here. Many of these were deported (with the help of French authorities) to German concentration camps in 1942. Today a good number of the residents are Sephardic Jews from North Africa.

But the Marais is no longer a poor neighbourhood. Even its backstreets are packed with expensive shops. For example, the village St-Paul, the large courtyard just to our right as we continue along rue Charlemagne, is now the place to go for antiques. The area owes much of its chic new veneer to the gay community, who have bought up and developed a lot of the property over the past two decades. The improvements still go on – every third building seems to be covered with scaffolding – but as we turn left on to rue St-Paul, and cross over the busy rue St-Antoine to rue de Turenne, we can see that the neighbourhood is still very mixed, and still very lively.

If we turned left at rue des Francs-Bourgeois, we would soon arrive at the Musée Carnavalet, famous for the interiors its curators have reconstructed from eighteenth-century mansions demolished by our friend Haussmann. But let's turn right instead to visit my favourite square in Paris, the place des Vosges. This was the site of the Palais des Tournelles. The Duke of Bedford, the English regent of France in the late fifteenth century, lived here. And in 1559, Henri II died here after being pierced in the eye during a jousting tournament. His widow, Catherine de Médicis, had the palace demolished afterwards. Other opportunists turned the open space into a horse market. It was Henri IV who decided to turn it into the almost perfect Renaissance square we see today. Except for the Queen's Pavilion to the north, and the King's Pavilion to the south, its buildings are identical, with brick, stone and stucco façades, simple dormers and arcaded ground floors.

During the reign of the Sun King, Louis XIV, the place Royale, as it was then known, was *the* fashionable address. It was the centre of the *Nouvelles Précieuses*, satirised by Molière. In the Revolution, the name was changed to place de l'Indivisibilité. It became the place des

Originally place Royale, renamed place de l'Indivisibilité, now called **place des Vosges** *– beautiful square, beautiful people.*

Vosges in 1799, when the Vosges became the first departement to discharge its revolutionary war debts.

When I first came here as a teenager, the square's 39 houses had a uniformly dusty and neglected look, and the park was empty. Now every window looks freshly washed, and the carefully manicured park is full of well-dressed adults and their beautifully behaved children. Plaques on the walls remind us of its earlier inhabitants. No.6, the house in the south-western corner, is now the Victor Hugo museum, best known for its pen and wash drawings and its superlative top-floor view. The square's Hugo associations mean a lot less to me now. As I sit in the middle of the park, on the bench next to a statue of Henri XIII on yet another horse, I can only vaguely remember the literary dramas that played themselves out here. As I struggle to remember which writers were Hugo's contemporaries, and what literary school it was that he helped found, I am struck by how much the literary wars of the twentieth century have in common with the ones that Hugo and his friends and enemies waged in the nineteenth. All the drinking in cafés. All those manifestoes and fiery speeches as one school topples to make room for another. How strange, then, that after the revolution is over, they all end up in the same cafés.

These are my thoughts as I head under the arch and down rue de Birague, but as I make my way, I see so many things that don't fit into my shallow theory. Everywhere I look I see monuments to the ideas that were put into action with some violence, and that did change things, not just this city, but the world over. There, on my left, as I cross rue St-Antoine, I can see the golden-winged figure at the top of the Colonne de Juillet on the place de la Bastille. This is where the French Revolution began, although the column was put up to commemorate those killed in the uprising of 1830. Today it is the destination for the 150,000 men and women marching on the annual Gay Pride Parade. We'll get a better view of it after we take the rue Beautreillis to the rue des Lions-St-Paul, turn right and follow the rue du Petit Musc to the place H Galli.

Now we are back on the banks of the Seine. The parade is still coming over the Pont de Sully. The politicians have long since passed this point, as have most of the tranvestites wearing bridal gowns and the delegations representing gays and lesbians of Tunisian, Brazilian and Jewish origin. But we are not too late to receive a leaflet of solidarity from Groupe Claaaaaash (Collectif Libertaire Anticapitaliste Antifasciste Antiraciste Antimilitariste Antiréligieux Antirévisioniste Antisexiste et AntiHomophobe) de Paris Bastille. Behind them are floats from what must be every gay and lesbian disco in the city. All of the spectators are applauding their wild gyrations. Does this mean that it is no longer possible to shock the *bourgeoisie* – and no need to worry about being persecuted? The answer is in today's *Libération*, a newspaper that Sartre and de Beauvoir helped found. Included in its report on the parade are photographs of the anti-gay parade of the previous January. Its banner of choice was *'Les pédés au bûcher'* ('death to gays').

The banners of choice today are: *'A bas l'ordre moral!'* and *'L'Orientation sexuel est un droit humain'* and *'Homophobie n'est pas gai'*. All are direct descendants of the pronouncements Sartre and de Beauvoir made when they became involved in the human rights movement and liberation politics in the 1950s and '60s. They travelled all over the world together during these decades. There is hardly a revolutionary leader they didn't meet. But they were not quite the same couple when they got back to Paris. As time went on, both became more and more involved with their other significant others.

And so to another landmark. Let's cross the first half of the Pont de Sully and turn right on to the quai de Béthune, which runs along the south side of the Ile St-Louis. If we turn left on to the Pont de la Tournelle, and right on to the quai de la Tournelle, and walk along the Seine until we're almost level with the buttresses of Notre-Dame, we come to the rue des Grands-Degrés on our left. This takes us to rue de la Bûcherie, which is where Simone de Beauvoir rented her first ever flat in 1948. She did so because she was about to receive a visit from the greatest (physical) passion of her life, the American author, Nelson Algren. 'This will be our place,' she wrote to him that October. 'No man but you will ever sleep here.' He was not able to take much comfort from her assurances. Although he was at first a great hit with 'the Family', he grew to resent the fact that Sartre and his needs always but always came first. Even the flat's beautiful view of Notre-Dame cannot have given him much pleasure. After all, one of Beauvoir's media nicknames was 'Notre-Dame de Sartre'.

The address (as confirmed by her stationery) was No.11. Today it is nowhere to be seen. Only two notables are commemorated on this quiet street. One was an anatomist, the other a writer named Nicholas Edner, who died in 1806 after writing *Paysan pervert* and *Nuits de Paris.* It is not very hard to draw lines between his exemplary career and the sights awaiting us after we've turned left on to rue Lagrange, right on to rue Dante, and arrived at the intersection with boulevard St-Germain to see the tail end of the Gay Pride Parade. The dancers from Banana Café, the last float in the parade, have now taken off their little outfits and have begun to simulate sex. Meanwhile, the boys in the back are pouring a wave of foam on to the street – and in front of the battalion of trucks that are patiently waiting to clear up the mountains of rubbish in the gutters.

As I cross over and make my way down rue St-Jacques, I recall why Haussmann invented the boulevard in the wake of the 1848 uprising. He hoped to be able to shoot cannon down them should something like that ever happen again. How he must have been turning in his grave when the students and the workers united to march down these same streets in May 1968.

If we continue along rue St-Jacques to its intersection with rue des Ecoles, we can see on our right the epicentre of that short-lived revolution of the late 1960s, the Sorbonne. Both Sartre and de Beauvoir came here to give speeches of solidarity that May. The experience changed both their lives. The links Sartre formed with the Maoist students continued until his death. And it was here that de Beauvoir made the speeches that made the women in the audience discover *The Second Sex*. During the 20 years between the time de Beauvoir wrote this book and the time when its ideas took root, de Beauvoir herself wrote little about the 'woman question'. But between the beginning of the movement proper in 1970 and her death in 1986, she was a very dutiful figurehead – particularly in the campaigns for contraception and abortion.

Here are some of the graffiti that she would have seen on these buildings when she visited them in 1968: *'Je suis venu, j'ai vu, j'ai cru.' 'Sous les pavés, la plage.' 'Etre libre en 1968, c'est participer.' 'La barricade ferme la rue mais ouvre la voie.' 'Interdit d'interdire.' 'Nous sommes tous des indésirables!' 'Je suis Marxiste tendance groucho.' 'Jeunes femmes rouges toujours plus belles.'* And the most existential of them all: *'Sisyphe!'* They were washed away soon afterwards, but the grimy building looks as if it has not been washed since. Sartre's old school, Lycée Louis-le-Grand, on our left as we carry on, looks better. So does the Faculté de Droit, also on our left.

Arriving on rue Soufflot, we can see the Eiffel Tower in the distance on the right, but we'll leave that for another day and another walk and instead turn left. If we snake around the north side of the Panthéon on to rue Clovis, and turn right on rue Descartes, we come to the place de la Contrescarpe. The cafés here will be packed come the evening, but they are quiet and empty now. So let's stop for a coffee before making the final leg of our pilgrimage.

We leave by turning right on to rue Blainville, which takes us out on to rue de l'Estrapade. We then turn left on to rue des Irlandais, home of the Collège des Irlandais, which can trace its origin back to 1578. It was the most important of the continental colleges educating Irishmen who could not receive an education at home. It moved to these premises in 1769. During the Terror, its students were shipped home and its teachers kept prisoner inside their own buildings. Things got easier after Napoléon turned the college into a trust in 1805. Now it provides lodging for Irish students and scholars and serves as a cultural centre. Beyond its tall iron doors, a beautiful courtyard beckons, but it is dangerous to follow your every whim in this part of the city.

There are so many unusual buildings with unusual histories that we could get lost here for days. So let's turn right on to rue Lhomond, and then left on to rue d'Ulm, quickly passing the also probably fascinating Maronite church on the left and the Institut Curie on the right, until we come to the Ecole Normale Supérieure.

There's a little detail here that's worth a pause. Written over the main door is the foundation date according to the Revolutionary Calendar: the 9th of Brumaire, Year 3. This new calendar began from 21 September 1792, from which Year 1 commenced; months were renamed according to the season – Brumaire (Foggy month) was October, Germinal (Budding month – March/April) in the spring. It was finally abandoned by Napoléon on 1 January 1806. When Sartre was a student here in the 1920s, he and his friends were in the habit of throwing water bombs from the roof, as they chanted, 'So pissed Zarathustra!'

But it's sad to think about such pranks at this late stage in our walk, now that we are just to the north of the Hôpital Cochin, where Simone de Beauvoir died. We're not going to go that far today. Instead we'll turn right and take rue des Feuillantines across rue St-Jacques, and follow rue P Nicole out to the boulevard de Port-Royal. Here we turn right, pass the gazebo RER station of Port-Royal, and cross boulevard St-Michel, where it intersects with avenue de l'Observatoire.

If we look right here we can see all the way down to the Jardin du Luxembourg. If we look left, we can see the Observatory. Straight ahead of us is the Closerie des Lilas, the bar and restaurant where the Surrealists drank (and staged a riot) during the 1920s, and where Hemingway has a drink named after him. But let's leave their ghosts in peace and turn left down rue Boissonade, then left on boulevard Raspail, and cross over to take a right on to rue Schoelcher.

The namesake of this street was the author of the decree that abolished slavery in the French colonies. For the last 29 years of her life, de Beauvoir lived at No.11 bis. It was a bright and airy artist's studio on the ground floor, right across the street from the same open space Sartre could contemplate from his own last apartment on rue Edgar-Quinet. That open space is the Cimetière du Montparnasse, where they are now buried, both in the same grave.

That's where we're going next. First we turn right on rue Froidevaux, then right again on rue Emile-Richard. Just on our left is the side entrance to the cemetery.

Opened in 1824, this cemetery covers 19 hectares and now contains 34,000 graves. Step on the path in any direction, and you'll see a name you know. In the eastern section behind us are the graves of

La Coupole – *a haunt of Sartre and de Beauvoir. Even after he had begun having strokes, Sartre continued to lunch there.*

La Coupol
OUPOLE

Mauriac, Maupassant, Dreyfus, Brancusi and Citroën. On our right as we proceed to the cenotaph inside the circle in the centre is Poincaré, on the right are Beckett, Brassai and Gainsbourg. Beyond the cenotaph are Tristan Tzara, Man Ray, Durkheim and Baudelaire. As we turn right to pass the cenotaph and carry on in the direction of the Edgar Quinet entrance, we pass Belmondo, Seberg, Duras and Général Raspail.

The grave de Beauvoir shares with Sartre is just to the left of the Edgar Quinet entrance, right against the wall. He died first, in April 1980 – at his funeral she was so distraught and so numb from whisky and Valium that she could not stand. Her friends brought her a collapsible metal chair so that she could sit next to the open grave. At one point the crowd lunged forward and she was nearly knocked into it. Some fifty thousand people attended the funeral – Lanzmann called it the 'last of the '68 demonstrations'. But there was a repeat when de Beauvoir was buried here six years later.

Four former ministers of the Mitterrand government were among the friends and family members who followed the hearse from Hôpital Cochin to the Cimetière du Montparnasse. Hanging from the door of the hearse was a huge wreath from *Libération*. Following the cortège were scholars and feminists from all over the world. But there were many more ordinary working people, quite a few of whom had brought with them mothers and grandmothers who were de Beauvoir's contemporaries. Many young fathers had brought very little children to the funeral so that one day they could say they had paid their respects to 'one of France's greatest women'.

A taxi driver who had stepped outside to complain about the procession was so upset when he found out whose funeral it was that he parked his taxi and joined the other mourners. As they filed past the grave, some reacted in anger at the sight of her name sitting under that of her beloved Sartre. Others echoed what the writer and feminist Elisabeth Badinter had said earlier: 'Women, you owe her everything!'

For weeks after the funeral, the mountain of flowers was so high that you could not even see the grave. Today there are two separate roses, and a scattering of pebbles. Underneath some of these are Métro tickets. On the back of one there are a few words in Italian: 'You are always in our memories.'

Standing here in front of the grave, it reads like a statement of fact – to me, the line between life and death has never seemed thinner. It becomes thinner still as we leave the cemetery, turn left on rue Edgar-Quinet, and make the sharp right on to rue Delambre. Now we are back to my old haunts – the Hôtel des Bains, my old home base in this neighbourhood, and the Rosebud, the bar where we used to go after the Select. As we walk slowly in the direction of the boulevard du Montparnasse, I think of my friend Claire and my friend James, and all the other friends from those days who are dead now, and soon I am carrying so many memories that I can hardly put one foot in front of the other.

But there's one more thing we need to do. We have to turn left on the boulevard, walk past the Dôme and have a drink at La Coupole. It might seem a strange thing to do, when you consider that (like a few of my own departed friends) both Sartre and de Beauvoir died of cirrhosis. But they never regretted the way they lived their lives. They believed in making choices and then facing the consequences with courage. When Sartre found out that his many bad habits had caught up with him, he told de Beauvoir, 'I've run through my store of health, I won't live past 70.' He took a stoical view of it all, saying, 'It's natural to come to pieces, little by little.' Even after he began to have strokes, and lost the use of parts of his face, he continued to come to La Coupole for lunch.

And so the circle is completed. **La Rotonde** *was where de Beauvoir went to play truant.*

So let's imagine they're over there, sitting under that beautiful painted pillar. Sartre and his adopted daughter Arlette are on one banquette, de Beauvoir and the companion of her later years, Sylvie le Bon, are on the other. As always, there is tension just under the surface, because Sylvie and Arlette do not like each other, and Simone is secretly jealous of Arlette's place in Sartre's affections, and all three women are worried that Sartre might not be able to chew that steak he's ordered, but they still manage to smile and lift their glasses and propose a toast.

If they were here today, wouldn't they want us to do the same?

Eating & drinking

L'Ambroisie

9 place des Vosges, 4th (01.42.78.51.45). **Open** noon-1.30pm, 8-9.30pm, Tue-Sat. Closed two weeks in Feb/Mar, three weeks in Aug. Luxury dishes in sumptuous surroundings, but the bill is somehow more memorable.

Auberge de Venise

10 rue Delambre, 14th (01.43.35.43.09). **Open** noon-2.30pm, 7-11.30pm, Tue-Sun. Cosy Italian restaurant with fine food.

Banana Café

13 rue de la Ferronnerie, 1st (01.42.33.35.31). **Open** 4.30pm-dawn daily.

Berthillon

31 rue St-Louis-en-l'Ile, 4th (01.43.54.31.61). **Open** 10am-8pm Wed-Sun. Closed school holidays.

Le Bonaparte

42 rue Bonaparte, 6th (01.43.26.42.81). **Open** 8am-2am daily.

La Brasserie de l'Ile St-Louis

55 quai de Bourbon, 4th (01.43.54.02.59). **Open** 11.30am-1am Mon, Tue, Fri-Sun; 5pm-1am Thur. Solid, sturdy and generous portions in this Alsatian brasserie.

Brasserie Lipp

151 boulevard St-Germain, 6th (01.45.48.53.91). **Open** 11.30am-1am daily. Reliable cuisine and reasonable prices given its distinguished past and present patrons.

Buvette des Marionnettes

Jardin du Luxembourg, 6th. **Open** *Sept-May* 8.30am-6.30pm daily; *June-Aug* 8.30am-7.30pm daily.

Café de Flore

172 boulevard St-Germain, 6th (01.45.48.55.26). **Open** 7am-1.30am daily. Expensive café that used to be a Surrealist haunt, and now hosts filmmakers and *café philosophique* sessions.

La Chope
2-4 place de la Contrescarpe, 5th (01.43.26.51.26). **Open** 8am-2am daily. Basic salads and café fare.

La Closerie des Lilas
171 boulevard du Montparnasse, 6th (01.40.51.34.50). **Open** 11.30am-1am daily. Restored to its former glory, this institution gives especially good value in the brasserie rather than the restaurant. Get a 'Hemingway' cocktail here.

La Coupole
102 boulevard du Montparnasse, 14th (01.43.20.14.20). **Open** 7.30am-2am daily. Art Deco brasserie serving reliable French food.

Les Deux Magots
6 place St-Germain-des-Prés, 6th (01.45.48.55.25). **Open** 7.30am-2am daily. Expensive and classy one-time haunt of Beckett, Sartre and de Beauvoir.

Le Dôme
108 boulevard du Montparnasse, 14th (01.43.35.25.81). **Open** noon-2.45pm, 7pm-12.30am, daily. Closed Mon and Sun in Aug. Legendary Montparnasse fish house, also an upmarket café-bar.

Le Muniche
7 rue St-Benoît, 6th (01.42.61.12.70). **Open** noon-1am daily.

Le Petit Zinc
11 rue St-Benoît, 6th (01.42.61.20.60). **Open** noon-4pm, 7.30pm-2am, daily.

Le Rosebud
11 bis rue Delambre, 14th (01.43.35.38.54). **Open** 7pm-2am daily. Closed Aug. A dimly lit cocktail haunt with fair food.

La Rotonde
105 boulevard du Montparnasse, 6th (01.43.26.68.84). **Open** 7am-2am daily. Another classic Montparnasse café-brasserie, offering oysters, sandwiches and traffic-watching.

Le Select
99 boulevard du Montparnasse, 6th (01.42.22.65.27). **Open** 7am-3am Mon-Thur, Sun; 7am-4am Fri, Sat. Hot food served 11am-closing time. Large, grand and historic self-styled 'American bar'.

Thanksgiving
20 rue St-Paul, 4th (01.42.77.68.28). **Open** noon-2.30pm, 7.30-10.30pm, Tue-Fri; noon-4pm, 7.30-11pm, Sat; 11am-4pm Sun. Closed three weeks in Aug, one week in Jan. May be the best American restaurant in Paris, showcasing regional cuisine, especially Cajun.

La Tour d'Argent
15-17 quai de la Tournelle, 5th (01.43.54.23.31). **Open** noon-1pm, 7.30-9pm, Tue-Sun. Haute cuisine with stunning views of Notre-Dame. Book in advance.

Le Vieux Bistro
14 rue du Cloître-Notre-Dame, 4th (01.43.54.18.95). **Open** noon-2pm, 7.30-11pm, daily. Perfect renditions of classic French cuisine.

Accommodation

Collège des Irlandais
5 rue des Irlandais, 5th (01.45.35.59.79).

Hôtel des Bains
33 rue Delambre, 14 (01.43.20.85.27).

Hôtel La Louisiane
60 rue de Seine, 6th (01.44.32.17.17).

Hôtel Pont-Royal
5-7 rue Montalembert, 7th (01.42.84.70.00).

Churches

Eglise St-Sulpice
place St-Sulpice, 6th (01.46.33.21.78). **Open** 8am-7.30pm daily.

Maronite church
17 rue d'Ulm, 5th (01.43.29.47.60). **Open** 9am-1pm, 2-8pm, daily.

Notre-Dame-des-Champs
91 boulevard du Montparnasse, 6th (01.40.64.19.64). **Open** noon-6pm daily.

St-Germain-des-Prés
place St-Germain-des-Prés, 6th (01.43.25.41.71). **Open** 8am-7pm daily. **Guided tour** 3pm third Sunday of the month.

Educational establishments

Ecole Nationale Supérieure des Beaux-Arts
13 quai Malaquais, 6th (01.47.03.52.15). **Open** *Courtyard* 8.30am-8pm Mon-Fri; *exhibitions* 1-7pm Tue-Sun. School visits Mon, by appointment. **Admission** *Exhibitions* 20F.

Ecole Normale Supérieure
45 rue d'Ulm, 5th (01.44.32.30.25).

Institut de France
23 quai de Conti, 6th (01.44.41.44.41). **Guided tours** 9am, 2pm, Sat, Sun (call ahead). **Admission** 20F.

La Sorbonne
47 rue des Ecoles, 5th (01.40.46.20.15). **Open** *Courtyards* 9am-4.30pm Mon-Fri.

The grave de Beauvoir shares with Sartre in the **Cimetière de Montparnasse** *is just to the left of the Edgar Quinet entrance.*

SARTRE
– 1980
DE BEAUVOIR
908 – 1986

Parks & cemeteries

Cimetière du Montparnasse

3 boulevard Edgar-Quinet, 14th (01.44.10.86.50). **Open** *16 Mar-5 Nov* 9am-6pm daily; *6 Nov-15 Mar* 9am-5.30pm daily.

Jardin du Luxembourg

place Auguste-Comte, pl Edmond-Rostand, rue de Vaugirard, 6th. **Open** *summer* 7.30am-9.30pm daily; *winter* 8am-5pm daily. *Children's playground* 10am-dusk daily. **Admission** *children's playground* 14F children; 7.50F adults.

Hôtels & mansions

Hôtel Chenizot

51 rue St-Louis-en-l'Ile, 4th.

Hôtel de Sens

1 rue du Figuier, 4th (01.42.78.14.60). **Open** *Forney Library* 1.30-8.30pm Tue-Fri; 10am-8.30pm Sat.

Hôtel Lambert

2 rue St-Louis-en-l'Ile, 4th.

Museums

Cathédrale Notre-Dame de Paris

place du Parvis-Notre-Dame, 4th (01.42.34.56.10). **Open** 8am-6.45pm daily. **Admission** free. *Towers* (01.44.32.16.70) entrance at foot of north tower. **Open** 10am-4.30pm daily. **Admission** 35F; 25F concs.

La Conciergerie

1 quai de l'Horloge, 1st (01.53.73.78.50). **Open** *Apr-Oct* 9.30am-6.30pm daily; *Nov-Mar* 10am-5pm daily. **Admission** 35F; 23F concs; 50F combined ticket with Ste Chapelle.

La Crypte Archéologique

place du Parvis-Notre-Dame, 4th (01.43.29.83.51). **Open** *Apr-Oct* 10am-5.30pm daily; *Nov-Mar* 10am-4.30pm daily. **Admission** 32F; 21F concs.

Le Louvre

entrance through Pyramid, cour Napoléon, 1st (01.40.20.50.50/recorded information 01.40.20.51.51/advance booking 01.49.87.54.54). **Open** 9am-6pm Mon, Thur-Sun; 9am-9.45pm Wed; *temporary exhibitions, Medieval Louvre, bookshop* 10am-9.45pm Mon, Wed-Sun. **Admission** 45F (until 3pm); 26F (after 3pm and Sun) concs.

Musée Carnavalet

23 rue de Sévigné, 3rd (01.42.72.21.13). **Open** 10am-5.40pm Tue-Sun. **Admission** 27F; 14.50F concs.

Maison de Victor Hugo

Hôtel de Rohan-Guéménée, 6 place des Vosges, 4th (01.42.72.10.16). **Open** 10am-5.40pm Tue-Sun. **Admission** 17.50F; 9F concs.

Musée de la Monnaie de Paris

11 quai de Conti, 6th (01.40.46.55.35). **Open** 11am-5.30pm Tue-Fri; noon-5.30pm Sat, Sun. *Guided tours* (in French) 2.15pm Wed, Fri. **Admission** 20F; 15F concs.

Musée d'Orsay

62 rue de Lille, 7th (01.40.49.48.14/recorded information 01.45.49.11.11). **Open** 10am-6pm Tue, Wed, Fri, Sat; 10am-9.30pm Thur; 9am-6pm Sun. **Admission** 40F; 30F concs.

Observatoire de Paris

61 avenue de l'Observatoire, 14th (01.40.51.22.21). **Open** by appointment only, first Sat of the month.

Le Panthéon

place du Panthéon, 5th (01.44.32.18.00). **Open** *Apr-Sept* 9.30am-6.30pm daily; *Oct-Mar* 10am-5.30pm daily. **Admission** 35F; 23F 12-25s; free under 12s.

Ste-Chapelle & Palais de Justice

4 boulevard du Palais, 1st (01.53.73.78.50). **Open** *Apr-Sept* 9.30am-6.30pm daily; *Oct-Mar* 10am-5pm daily. **Admission** 35F; 23F concs; 50F combined ticket with Conciergerie.

Publishing

Editions Gallimard

5 rue Sébastien-Bottin, 7th (01.49.54.42.00). **Open** 9am-7pm Mon-Fri.

Libération

11 rue Béranger, 3rd (01.42.76.17.89).

Books & films

Simone de Beauvoir: A Biography Deirdre Bair (Touchstone Press, US)
The Second Sex Simone de Beauvoir 1949 (Vintage)
The Mandarins Simone de Beauvoir 1954 (WW Norton, US)
Memoirs of a Dutiful Daughter Simone de Beauvoir 1954 (Penguin)
Answered Prayers (unfinished) Truman Capote (Penguin)
Notre-Dame de Paris Victor Hugo 1831 (Oxford)
Being and Nothingness Jean-Paul Sartre 1943 (Routledge)
Shoah (Claude Lanzmann, 1985, Fr) 566 min.

Information

Gay Pride Parade

At the end of June. **Information** *Centre Gai et Lesbien (01.43.57.21.47).*

Hôpital Cochin

27 rue du Faubourg-St-Jacques, 14th (01.42.34.12.12).

Institut Curie

8 rue Louis-Thuillier, 5th (01.44.32.40.00).

An opera of phantoms

Stephen Mudge

Time for a little Chopin in the *Grands Boulevards* and covered *passages*.

Start: Opéra Garnier, 9th
Finish: Parc Monceau, 8th
Time: 3 hours
Distance: 6km/3.5 miles
Getting there: lines 3, 7 or 8 to Mº Opéra, or line A to RER Auber
Getting back: Mº Monceau (line 2)
Note: set off early enough to catch the museums at the end of the walk before they close.

For a musician, a walk in a European city often begins at the opera house – not only is it the musical centre of the city, but it also tends to be the focal point of most Western capitals. Only the English, with their knack for individual gesture, could have constructed Covent Garden in the middle of a vegetable market. Paris made no such error, and if the Parisian Right Bank has a pulse point then it is here. Haussmann's spectacular plan for the *Grands Boulevards* is centred on the Opéra, built to be the biggest and grandest in the world. He achieved his aim and Garnier's opera house remains the world's largest theatre. Garlanded in sculptures and surrounded by the names of great composers, this huge building towers in marbled splendour over its surroundings. Currently, the building is wrapped like a Christo sculpture while undergoing a facelift.

Some of the composers' commemorative plaques now raise an eyebrow; works by Cherubini and Auber rarely grace the programme these days. Even the magnificent sculptures were at the time of the house's inauguration as controversial as the Chagall ceiling is today, covering as it does the decorative original by Elie Delaunay that still lurks underneath. The most famous of the sculptures, *La Danse* by Carpeaux, has been transferred for safekeeping to the Louvre, replaced with a copy by Paul Belmondo, father of actor Jean-Paul. At the time of the opening, the original was described by a contemporary critic in the following terms: 'These Maenads with flaccid, flabby, worn-out flesh, whose legs seem to sink under their tired bodies, are not these Maenads drunk? They smell of vice and stink of wine…' – proving perhaps that time will be the ultimate judge of the Chagall. The Opéra is built astride a natural lake, which still swills around under the building. 'The phantom of the opera rows nightly and can be met by appointment…' Maybe not, but the chandelier did crash down on the audience during a performance of *Faust* in 1896.

If you get a chance, take a look in the museum, which houses the complete collection of scores performed in the theatre since the original was built in 1669, Massenet and Spontini's pianos, as well as Renoir's portrait of Wagner, for which the great man provided only a minimum of sittings. For ballet buffs there is a mass of Diaghelev memorabilia, as well as souvenirs of the dancers Pavlova and Nijinsky.

Outside, we find ourselves in an area that in the 1800s was dominated by High Society and great cafés, often of English inspiration. In front of the Opéra is the only survivor, the Café de la Paix, which reflects something of the nineteenth-century life of the *boulevardier*, a witty,

Opéra National de Paris Garnier – *the legend of the Phantom of the Opera started here.*

intellectual stroller, now probably found in a different form sipping cocktails near the Bastille. Turn left into the boulevard des Capucines. We now enter the heart of the *Grands Boulevards*. Behind a gnarled doorway at No.8 a plaque identifies the home of Jacques Offenbach, whose output never aspired to the hallowed walls of the Opéra, but who was very much a *boulevardier*. His operettas introduced a world of frivolous, sexy political satire, very French and almost impossible to translate into another culture. Neither as prissily Victorian as Gilbert and Sullivan, nor as saccharine as German operetta, it is delicate comedy written to crackling music; he deserved Wagner's nickname as 'the Mozart of the Champs-Elysées'. His final masterpiece was *Les Contes d'Hoffmann*, a fully blown Grand Opera on the subject of a love-deprived wastrel; like so many comics he craved recognition for a serious work. Unfortunately, he lay dying in this apartment as rehearsals went on at the Opéra Comique, and he never lived to see the success of the work, giving rise to the musicologist's nightmare of identifying just what the composer intended as the final version.

As you pass down the rows of tourist restaurants that line the boulevard des Italiens you will notice a sad decline from the heyday of the area, where at No.13 was the fashionable Café Anglais, the scene of Balzacian trysts and scandals exchanged over a cup of tea. At No.27 was the famous Bains Chinois, a luxury sauna where the publicity of the time boasted 'a pretty woman comes out beautiful, a beautiful woman comes out ravishing'. Now, the saunas have gone underground and pizzas are the order of the day.

On the right is the Crédit Lyonnais, built between 1876 and 1913, a building of pompous fiscal grandeur. A few years back, in the midst of a massive mismanagement scandal, it was the site of one of the capital's most spectacular fires. Worried safe-holders lined the pavement as the possibility of their valuables going up in smoke clouded the city. Turn right down the rue de Marivaux, which skirts the Opéra Comique. You will notice that the theatre has virtually no backstage area – this has proved its downfall as a venue for twentieth-century opera productions, where the ability to install at the very least a motorway and spectacular revolving stage seem to have become de rigueur. The present theatre was built between 1894 and 1896 on the site of the eighteenth-century château de Choiseul. It is a jewel of an auditorium and has seen the première of a good deal of the staple repertoire of French opera, including *Carmen*, *Pelléas*, *Manon* and, of course, *Les Contes d'Hoffmann*. Originally, it was destined to be the home of the Théâtre Italien, which explains the name of the boulevard. Place Boïeldieu in front of the theatre recalls another name all but forgotten nowadays, but his *Dame Blanche*, premiered in 1825, was one of the great hits of its time. The French assiduously surround their famous buildings with street names that pay homage to a relevant profession or activity of an area – here the adjoining street is rue Grétry, named after another fine, and too often ignored, composer of Opéras Comiques.

Pass down the rue Favart on the other side of the opera house. The brightly illuminated sign of the bistro Les Noces de Jeannette quaintly boasts, 'Salons, Restaurants, Soupers'; we're told the food

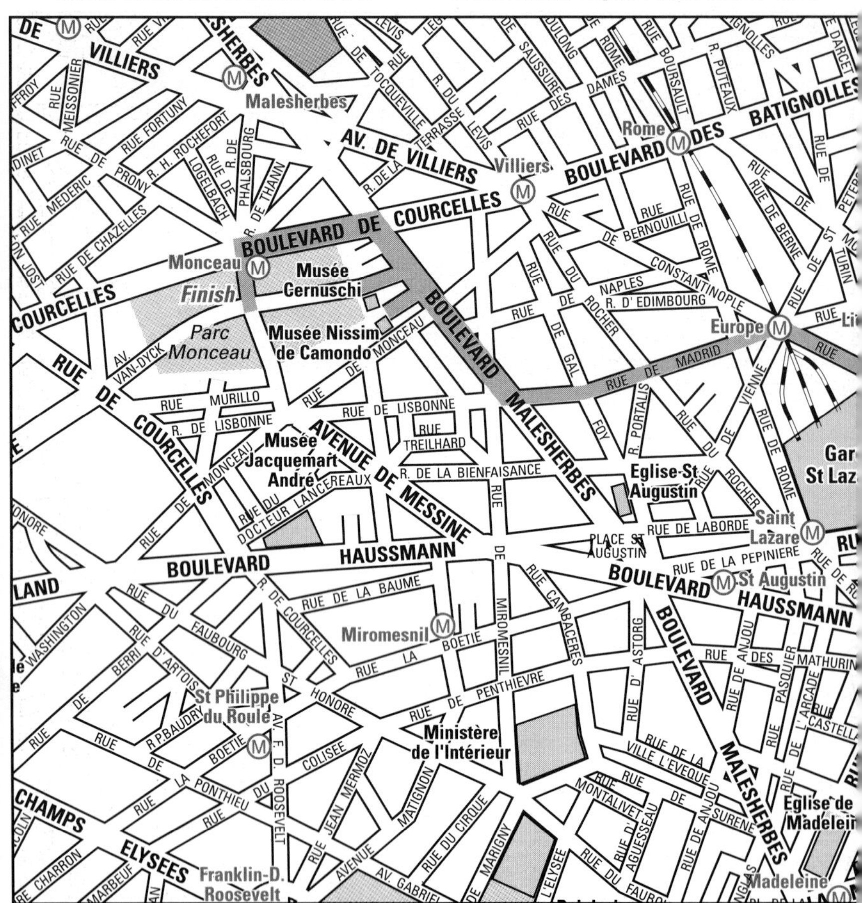

does not live up to this *vieille France* introduction. Continue down the boulevard des Italiens and just before it becomes the boulevard Montmartre you will see the remains of the Poccardi restaurant, once the finest Italian restaurant in Paris, now unceremoniously taken over by the Bistro Romain chain. On the same side of the boulevard is the passage des Princes, which has suffered a heavy-handed mall-style restoration. From here you can glimpse the Sacré-Coeur to the north, its undistinguished architecture looking at its best from this distance.

A little further down the boulevard Montmartre, two of Paris's prettiest theatres face each other, the Théâtre des Variétés and the Théâtre Grévin. The former saw the premières of many of Offenbach's most celebrated operettas, including *La Belle Hélène*, *La Périchole* and *La Grande Duchesse*. To see the interior you now have to sit through the Parisian equivalent of a West End hit – not something to be undertaken lightly. Just beside the theatre is the passage des Panoramas, which was the first to benefit from gaslights in 1817. It is worth taking a look at the printers Stern, which has retained its original shop frontage and

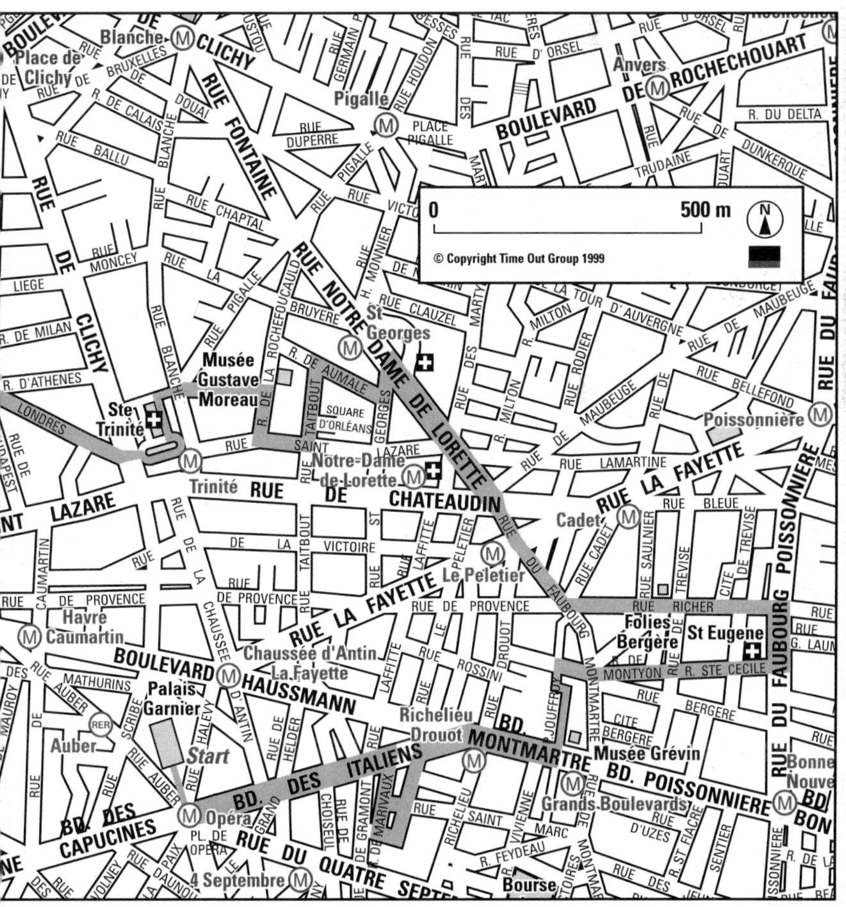

Hidden away in passage Jouffroy, **Hôtel Chopin***'s connection to the composer is unclear.*

remains the choicest place to get your visiting cards printed. These passages or arcades are very much part of Right Bank Paris – secret and deserted in contrast to out-of-town superstores, they retain a singular, melancholic air.

Opposite the passage des Panoramas is the passage Jouffroy and the Théâtre Grévin, which is home to a popular concert series and boasts an interestingly painted stage curtain by Chéret, a picture of which can be seen in the foyer. Here you will also find the Musée Grévin, founded by the caricaturist Grévin in 1882. Personally, wax works have always posed me a problem. Even as a child I was aware that the models neither looked like the personalities in question nor evoked their presence. Perhaps they were exciting before the media showed us graphic representations of the intimate habits of even the moderately famous. Far more fun is Monsieur Segas's shop selling canes and walking sticks, not necessarily for the infirm but to give you that essential nineteenth-century swagger.

By the kink in the passage there is a hint of our destination to come, the Hôtel Chopin. Its connection with Chopin may be obscure, but this has to be one of the hotels that most evoke quintessential France, shabby but intriguingly Gallic. Leaving the passage behind you, take a right turn, which leads you down the rue de la Grange-Batelière, cross into the rue de Montyon, which in turn becomes the rue Ste-Cécile, the patron saint of music – a hint that we are on our way to the former music conservatoire, which is, naturally, on the corner of rue du Conservatoire. This was the original music academy of Paris, numbering Auber and Ambroise Thomas among its directors. Now it is used as a drama school, but if you get a chance, try to visit the *salle de concerts*, one of the most charming venues in Paris, where the 27-year-old Berlioz saw the first performance of his *Symphonie Fantastique*. It must have been quite a cramped affair, room for the orchestra and maybe the megalomaniac composer himself. 'Sure of his genius but uncertain of his talent,' as one French critic put it.

Opposite the conservatoire is the Gothic Revival church of St-Eugène, which is one of the last bastions of Latin mass in the capital, and importantly manages to do this without Lefebvrite right-wing implications. Facing you at the end of the street is the Hôtel Benoît-de-Ste-Paulle, a beautiful eighteenth-century *hôtel particulier*, home of, among others, one Louise O'Murphy, mistress of Louis XV, a name that lends an unexpected Celtic accent to the area.

Turn left up the rue du Faubourg-Poissonière, where fish swept into Paris directly from the North Sea to the market at Les Halles, past No.34, which was the home of Sully Prudhomme, one of the Parnassian poets, who inspired Fauré to set many of his texts to music. When you turn left into rue Richer, Paris throws up one of its surprises; without warning, you are in a street of delicatessens and kosher restaurants. A street away in either direction and you could not buy pork-free sausage for love nor money. On the right is the cité de Trévise, with a charming fountain – a copy of the statue *The Virtues* by Germain Pilon (the original can be seen in the Louvre). Amid all the culinary delights is the Folies Bergère, ironically nicknamed at its inauguration '*La salle des sommiers élastiques*' (the bouncy mattress theatre). After a dodgy start in 1869, the theatre took off with the patronage of the young ladies from the adjoining Lorette area. In the nineteenth century, this *quartier* became home to a group of kept girls. Balzac said of them: 'Lorette is a decent word used to express the condition of a girl who is difficult to give a name to, and who, by modesty, the Académie Française has neglected to define, given the advanced age of its 40 members.'

On the corner of rue du Faubourg-Montmartre is the perfectly preserved 1761 sweetshop A la Mère de Famille, a haven of *bonbons* and elaborately packaged boxes of mysterious specialities. Going up past the Pianos Schillio, on the right is a hidden passageway of humble artisan dwellings, the passage des Deux-Soeurs. Carry on across the big junction up rue de Notre-Dame-de-Lorette, past the back of the richly decorated nineteenth-century church of the same name.

We now arrive at the place St-Georges and the heart of a district previously known as La Nouvelle Athènes, not just because of the classical style of the

Place St Georges *is at the heart of a district previously known as La Nouvelle Athènes.*

architecture, but also because it became the intellectual mecca of Paris. A centre where artists, writers and musicians lived, but less well known than the later Montparnasse or St-Germain colonies, or in our own time the Bastille.

The place St-Georges is particularly charming, crowned by a fountain depicting the painter Gavarni, an artist who lived in the area, but not as famous as one of his nearby neighbours, Delacroix, who had his apartment further up the hill at No.58. The nineteenth-century pastiche of a Renaissance palace on one side of the square was the home of the Marquise Païva, famous as a society hostess, adventuress and spy. Later she moved to even more sumptuous premises on the Champs-Elysées, now home to the exclusive Travellers Club. Opposite her home is the Bibliothèque Thiers, saved from destruction after the Commune by the intervention of the painter Courbet. Should you be here at a mealtime there is a favourite bistro just a little further up the hill, La Table de la Fontaine, on rue Henri-Monnier. Otherwise take a sharp turn down rue St-Georges, past the theatre of the same name, built on the site of a former mansion. The rue St-Georges might now seem unassuming, but it was the home of, among others, painters Renoir and Suzanne Valadon, mother of Utrillo, and the composer Auber; salons were attended by Hugo, Balzac and Lamartine.

Turn right up rue d'Aumale, where Wagner lived at No.3 (no plaque but it seems nonetheless true), then turn left down rue Taitbout. On the left you will find the square d'Orléans, designed in the nineteenth century by the English architect Cresy, where Chopin and Georges Sand lived out their love story. Chopin lived at No.9, while Sand lived on the other side of the square at No.5; the possibilities for message-sending must have been irresistible. After her break-up with Chopin, Georges Sand retreated from the square to her château in Nohant. The place must have buzzed with activity, as it was also the home of the great nineteenth-century diva Pauline Viardot and the writer Alexandre Dumas to name but two.

Turning right along rue St-Lazare, we pass an official building, which now houses the dreaded tax collector, but previously was the home of another great society hostess, Marie Dorval. Now we turn right up rue de la Rochefoucauld to the Musée Gustave Moreau, one of the most atmospheric museums in the city, with a real feeling of the artist at work, clearly displaying his mystical Symbolist view of the world. Here we turn left down rue de la Tour-des-Dames. Three of the most attractive villas were homes to great actors of the Comédie Française, including Talma, who reformed the theatre of his time. Previously, actors wore their own glamorous clothes to portray a character, but Talma insisted on wearing appropriate costumes for his roles. It created a sensation from which we have never looked back. The other two actors, Mlles Mars and Duchesnois, were next-door neighbours living at Nos.1 and 3 respectively – apparently, things did not go smoothly. Hopefully, no such problems exist for another glamorous lady, Inès de la Fressange, who has her offices at No.7.

At the far end of the street, turn left down rue de Cheverus, which follows the walls of the church of the Trinité. This rather pompous structure is notable for being the church where Messiaën was organist for many years from 1931. At the end of each mass there was the mouthwatering prospect of the great man launching into an improvisation, which made Sundays a must for extra-liturgical reasons. In front of the church, turn up rue de Londres. No.2 was known at the turn of the century as the most celebrated brothel in Paris, where the great beauty Casque d'Or spent some time. Simone Signoret portrayed her in Jacques Becker's 1952 film of the same name; apparently,

Chopin *and Georges Sand lived out their love story on opposite sides of the Cresy-designed square d'Orléans in the 9th arrondissement.*

Messiaën was organist at **Eglise de la Trinité**.

however, Casque d'Or in the flesh was rather more delicate and fragile than the comely form of the great French actress.

On the left is La Cité de Londres, a rather grim affair, which fails to do justice to its splendid name. Far more amusing is the Société des Eaux Minérales (No.30), a delightfully kitsch, tiled building.

At the top of the street you arrive at the place de l'Europe with a spectacular view over the Gare St-Lazare. The scene was often painted by the Impressionists, in particular Monet, who was thrilled by this picture of modern life and the play of light on steel, smoke and glass, that the new station afforded. Even now this is a view to provoke childish 'engine driver' fantasies. Around this area all the streets have names of tempting European destinations to match the technological wonder that was the Gare St-Lazare. We are going to take rue de Madrid, past the pretty Art Nouveau Guimard Métro station, Europe, and across rue de Rome, which, like rue Richer earlier, has a theme: music shops. Should you need to unearth an ancient score or get your Strad violin authenticated, this is the place to stop. The reason for this emphasis on music is to be found a little further down rue de Madrid, where stands the dull and lifeless building that was the former music conservatoire before the institution was transferred to the spectacular Cité de la Musique at La Villette. It cannot really be regretted – even the street itself has an academic gloom that one is anxious to escape.

Towards the end of rue de Madrid, which changes country and becomes rue de Lisbonne, you can catch a glimpse of the church of St-Augustin, an audacious cast iron structure clad in bricks by the architect Baltard, whose most famous Parisian landmark was the former Halles. At the end of the street you arrive at the boulevard Malesherbes.

On the far side of the boulevard skirting the Parc Monceau are two of Paris's most underrated museums. The Musée Nissim de Camondo has a turn-of-the-century collection of palatial eighteenth-century furniture and paintings, and a great view over the park. Further up on the left, beyond the gilded gates, is the Musée Cernuschi with its unjustly neglected collection of oriental pottery and artefacts.

At the top of the boulevard, turn left past the house of the great *melodie* writer Ernest Chausson, a disciple of Wagner and César Franck (his early death in a bicycle accident is a warning to all would-be geniuses on the dangers of pedalling around Paris). Turn left into the Parc Monceau beside the rotunda, built as a smuggling control point by Ledoux. The park itself was created by the Duc de Chartres, and was known as the Folie de Chartres, nearly double the size of the park we see today. From the original gardens there remain various follies, the most amusing of which is the eighteenth-century miniature pyramid. It was the site

The spectacular perspective on the Gare St Lazare from **place de l'Europe** *has attracted many admirers – and artists – over the years.*

in 1797 of the first parachute landing. Later, under Napoléon III, the park took on its present form, designed by Alphand in the English style that was so popular then. It is a busy park with nature playing second fiddle to the architectural elements, including a fine sculpture of Chopin by Mercié. Nestling in the nature you will find other statues of great French musical figures Charles Gounod and Ambroise Thomas… phantoms of the Opéra indeed.

Eating & drinking

Bar des Variétés
12 passage des Panoramas, 2nd (01.42.36.98.09). **Open** 8.30am-2am Mon-Fri. Bistro-bar hidden down the covered passage.

Bistro Romain
9 boulevard des Italiens, 2nd (01.42.97.49.55). **Open** 11.30am-1am daily.

Café de la Paix
12 boulevard des Capucines, 9th (01.40.07.30.20). **Open** 10am-1.30am daily. A huge showcase Parisian café, with a Garnier interior, and extortionate prices.

Café Runtz
16 rue Favart, 2nd (01.42.36.10.96). **Open** 11.45am-2.30pm, 6.30-11.30pm, Mon-Fri. Closed one week in May, three in Aug. A pleasant and reliable Alsatian café – sample a dessert.

Le Café Zéphyr
12 boulevard Montmartre, 9th (01.47.70.80.14). **Open** 8am-2am Mon-Sat; 8am-10pm Sun. North African-inspired décor; dishes from the Auvergne.

Le Convivial
47 rue St-Georges, 9th (01.42.85.22.35). **Open** noon-2.30pm, 7.30-10.30pm, Mon-Fri; 7.30-10.30pm Sat. Classic and creative French cuisine with a Provençal slant.

Les Noces de Jeannette
angle 14, rue Favart/9 rue d'Amboise, 2nd (01.42.96.36.89). **Open** noon-2pm, 7-10pm, daily.

Restaurant Opéra
5 place de l'Opéra, 9th (01.40.07.30.10). **Open** noon-2pm, 7.30-10.30pm, Mon-Fri. Closed mid-July-end Aug, one week at Christmas, one week in Feb. Some interesting contemporary dishes alongside a roster of classics, and stunning interior décor.

La Table de la Fontaine
5 rue Henri-Monnier, 9th (01.45.26.26.30). **Open** noon-2.30pm, 7.30-11.45pm, Mon-Fri. Closed two weeks in Aug. Charming bistro offering French classics with a modern twist.

La Taverne
24 boulevard des Italiens, 9th (01.55.33.10.00). **Open** 11.30am-2am daily. A flashy, festive brasserie that focuses on seafood platters; various choucroutes.

Shopping

A la Mère de Famille
35 rue du Faubourg-Montmartre, 9th (01.47.70.83.69). **Open** 8.30am-1.30pm, 3-7pm, Tue-Sat. Closed Aug.

Pianos Schillio
41 rue du Faubourg-Montmartre, 9th (01.48.24.62.79). **Open** 10am-6pm Tue-Sat.

M&G Segas, Cannes de Collection Antiquités
Galerie 34, passage Jouffroy, 9th (01.47.70.89.64). **Open** 11.30am-6.30pm Mon-Sat.

Stern Graveur
47 passage des Panoramas, 2nd (no phone). **Open** 9.30am-12.30pm, 1.30-5.30pm, Mon-Fri, Sun.

Museums

Cité de la Musique
Grande Halle de la Villette, 211-219 avenue Jean-Jaurès, 19th (01.44.84.45.00/01.40.03.75.03). **Open** 10am-6pm Mon, Wed-Sat, Sun. **Admission** 50F; 35F concs.

Musée Cernuschi
7 avenue Velasquez, 8th (01.45.63.50.75). **Open** 10am-5.40pm Tue-Sun. **Admission** 17.50F; 9F concs.

Musée de l'Opéra
Palais Garnier, 1 place de l'Opéra, 9th (01.40.01.24.93). **Open** 10am-4.30pm daily. **Admission** 30F; 20F concs.

Musée Grévin
10 boulevard Montmartre, 9th (01.47.70.85.05). **Open** *term-time* 1-6.30pm daily; *school holidays* 10am-7pm daily. **Admission** 55F; 44F concs.

Musée Gustave Moreau
14 rue de la Rochefoucauld, 9th (01.48.74.38.50). **Open** 11am-5.15pm Mon, Wed; 10am-12.45pm, 2-5.15pm, Thur-Sun. **Admission** 22F; 15F concs.

Musée Nissim de Camondo
63 rue de Monceau, 8th (01.53.89.06.40). **Open** 10am-5pm Wed-Sun. **Admission** 30F; 20F concs.

Opéra Comique/Salle Favart
place Boïeldieu, 2nd (01.42.44.45.40/reservations 01.42.44.45.46). **Box office** 14 rue Favart 11am-7pm Mon-Sat; *telephone bookings* 11am-6pm Mon-Sat. **Tickets** 50F-610F.

Le Pont de l'Europe – Gare St Lazare à Paris – *Claude Monet's 1877 impression of the view.*

Opéra National de Paris Garnier
place de l'Opéra, 9th (08.36.69.78.68). **Box office** 11am-6.30pm Mon-Sat. **Tickets** 60F-650F; *concerts* 45F-245F.

Churches

Eglise de la Trinité
place d'Estienne-d'Orves, 9th (01.48.74.12.77). **Open** 7.15am-7.30pm Mon-Sat; 8.30am-1pm, 5-8pm, Sun.

Eglise Notre-Dame-de-Lorette
8 rue Notre-Dame-de-Lorette, 9th (01.48.78.92.72). **Open** 4.30-6.30pm daily.

Eglise St-Augustin
46 boulevard Malesherbes, 8th (01.45.22.23.12). **Open** 8.30am-6.45pm Mon-Fri; 8.30am-1pm, 2.30-6.45pm, Sat, Sun.

Eglise St-Eugène
4 rue du Conservatoire, 9th (01.48.24.70.25). **Open** 10am-12.30pm, 4-7pm, daily.

Sacré-Coeur
35 rue du Chevalier-de-la-Barre, 18th (01.53.41.89.00). **Open** *Crypt/dome Oct-Mar* 9am-6pm daily; *Apr-Sept* 9am-7pm daily. **Admission** *Crypt* 15F; *dome* 15F; *crypt/dome* 23F.

Theatres

Folies Bergère
32 rue Richer, 9th (01.44.79.98.98.). **Open** 9-11.30pm Tue-Sun.

Théâtre des Variétés
7 boulevard Montmartre, 2nd (01.42.33.11.41).

Théâtre St-Georges
51 rue St-Georges, 9th (01.48.78.74.37).

Others

Bibliothèque Thiers
27 place St-Georges, 9th (01.40.16.94.18). **Open** noon-6pm Thur, Fri.

Hôtel Chopin
46 passage Jouffroy/10 boulevard Montmartre, 9th (01.47.70.58.10).

Parc Monceau
boulevard de Courcelles, 8th. **Open** *1 Nov-31 Mar* 7am-8pm daily; *1 Apr-31 Oct* 7am-10pm daily.

My Latin Quarter

Jean Paul Dollé

On the Rive Gauche, everything begins and ends with the love of words.

Start: La Closerie des Lilas, 6th
Finish: Editions Gallimard, 7th
Time: 2-3 hours
Distance: 4km/2.5 miles
Getting there: RER line B to Port-Royal
Getting back: short walk to Mº Rue du Bac (line 12)
Note: some of the cafés, clubs and bars mentioned in this walk are either closed, or not actually on the route – it is therefore worthwhile having a larger map than the one provided if you wish to track down some of the sites.

My Latin Quarter never changes, yet it is never quite the same. It's a question of light. Paris is subject to infinite atmospheric variations. The weather is not the same in the Jardin du Luxembourg, in rue de Fürstemburg, in rue St-Benoît or in rue Mouffetard. Meteorologists insist otherwise, but not all of them are poets. They don't necessarily understand that heat varies according to the intensity of emotion and the power of memory. Not all streets and places have the same ability to warm the heart.

Littérature oblige, I begin my walk at the Closerie des Lilas. This bar-restaurant, located at the intersection of the Latin Quarter and Montparnasse, boasts an extraordinary past. Within its walls and on its terrace met all the great minds of the twentieth century. Here various artistic and literary movements locked horns, political factions forged alliances, revolutionaries hatched plots. It's impossible to cite all the names: encyclopaedias, dictionaries and social registers would hardly suffice.

Among a thousand noteworthy events, I will choose that which, it seems to me, best illustrates the spirit of freedom and revolt that inhabits this spot. The Surrealists, headed by André Breton, Louis Aragon and St-Paul Roux, organised a banquet during which they knowingly derided France's chauvinism and arrogance after its victory over Germany in 1918, shouting, 'Down with the French army! Long live Germany!' The brasserie's customers showered them with blows, the policemen called to the rescue beat them up: the Surrealists redoubled their insults against France and its arrogant stupidity.

Certain traces of this act of insubordination, this persistent refusal to bend to the majority opinion, this courage in the affirmation of their convictions whatever the price, are still to be found in many parts of what, between the two wars, journalists and intellectuals termed the Rive Gauche, in contrast to the Rive Droite, the side of power and of money.

From the Closerie, cross through the Jardin du Luxembourg. Consider as you go the area to your east, around place de la Contrescarpe. There also lies the path of marginality, that of contesting accepted doctrine, established institutions and public order. In the surrounding cafés, conspirators have plotted a new world, before attempting to do away with the old.

Anarchists of all stripes, libertarians of all nationalities have always favoured this neighbourhood, the printers'

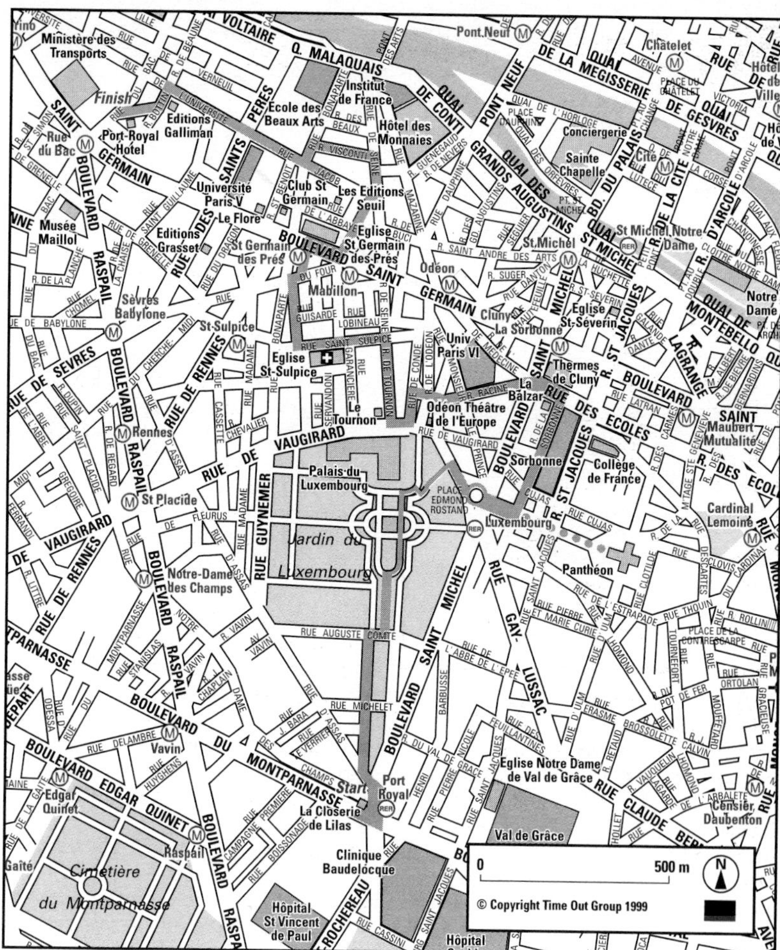

workshops in the back courtyards of the rues Lhomond or Gassendi, the discreet dens that welcomed clandestine meetings, for example Les Quatre Sergents, whose name harks back to the four young Republican soldiers who died for their ideals, condemned by King Louis-Philippe. It was here, near the Ecole Polytechnique, that stood one of the last barricades of the Commune de Paris.

In May 1968 the student Commune, reprising in a more playful mode the illustrious example of 1871, also held its last barricade near the Ecole Normale Supérieure in rue d'Ulm, after the barricades erected in rue Gay-Lussac had been taken by the police.

But we will take a more literary path. Leave the Luxembourg for rue de Médicis, where the Café Rostand offers a haven for the weary walker. Next door is a bookshop, the Librairie Corti, which published Breton and Julien Gracq; its owner never bowed to the dictates of marketing and remained faithful to his

The **Jardin du Luxembourg** – *subject to its very own meteorological conditions.*

literary ethic. The shop is still there, the pride of French literature.

The Latin Quarter, which we are now entering, has two major axes at its heart. The first is the rue St-Jacques, the path of pilgrims setting off for Santiago de Compostela, path of heavenly salvation. The second is the rue des Ecoles, path of earthly accomplishments, of humanism, which we can reach by wandering north down rue Victor-Cousin. Here tower two monuments to thought, the two secular sanctuaries of knowledge, the venerable Sorbonne and the glorious Collège de France, where all the greatest minds of the kingdom, and later of the French Republic, carry out their research in total freedom and share with all, without discrimination, the fruits of their research. Sometimes, the most fortunate among them are declared 'immortals' by a Republic grateful to its *grands hommes*. They then rest until the end of time in the Panthéon, just nearby. I dream that one day, perhaps, those that I was lucky enough to hear speak in the crowded amphitheatres – for their contemporaries considered them masters – the philosopher Gilles Deleuze at the Sorbonne, Michel Foucault at the Collège de France and the psychoanalyst Jacques Lacan at the Ecole Normale Supérieure in rue d'Ulm, will in their turn be visited by tourists interested in ideas and who will bow before their tombs in this august temple to great men.

Paris has its 'mountains': Montmartre, Montparnasse. It also has its inspired hilltop: Ste-Geneviève, the mystical heart of the Latin Quarter. But mere mortals cannot linger for ever in this Olympus, tarrying indefinitely at the Hôtel des Grands Hommes, place du Panthéon. They need to come back down to earth.

Great men are none the less human. They need to eat, and sometimes they do so with pleasure. Brasserie Balzar is to earthly food what the Sorbonne is to intellectual fodder: an institution. This brasserie, located near the principal entrance to the Sorbonne, is practically an annexe of the university. Many professors come here after their classes for a meal, or for a *rendez-vous* with their colleagues.

One also runs into members of the media, the publishing establishment and the world of politics. President Mitterrand was also a regular.

Continue west along rue Racine. At the bottom of rue Monsieur-le-Prince, which we cross, all the greats of 'the sound' – which was not yet called 'salsa' – turned up in a club known by all of Paris's Latin-American community. My friend Pierre Goldman – a young and revolutionary student, fascinated by metaphysics, ardent admirer of the Resistance and more particularly of the Warsaw ghetto uprising, an atheist Jew hungry for heroism and revolution, transfixed by the *guerilleros* and the austere figure of Che Guevara – and I often went there to let our souls get drunk on the heart-rending cries of lost love, exile and the injustice of tyrants. We danced until we fell into the unconsciousness of a trance, until we fell out of time. The club no longer exists. But salsa has flourished in Paris since 1978, when Ray Baretto, Azukita and a few other percussionists along with Pierre Goldman, back from his Venezuelan adventures, opened, in Les Halles's rue des Lombards, the first Parisian temple to salsa: La Chapelle des Lombards. Alongside all the disillusioned souls and those nostalgic for May 1968, I warmed myself to 'the sound', forgetting for a moment the chill of hard times.

This music spread, and its nerve centre migrated toward the Bastille, rue de Lappe, birthplace of the *valse-musette*, that symbol of Parisian working-class music, a mixture of the Auvergne region's *bourrée* and of Piedmontese melodies brought by labourers who emigrated to France in search of work. When I now go to the Lombards in the rue de Lappe to listen to 'the sauce', I don't feel that I'm betraying my youth and my chosen *quartier*, for my neighbourhood is not so much a strictly delimited topographical space as a region of the mind, where past, present and future join together in the same purpose and the same quest for emancipation and brotherhood. Latin, for me, will forever remain the best adjective to describe this memory and this hope.

Mitterrand was a regular at the **Brasserie Balzar**, *practically an annexe of the Sorbonne.*

At the end of rue Racine we emerge in place de l'Odéon. The Théâtre de l'Europe, built in neo-Hellenic style and a key spot in the Paris theatre world, has hosted countless memorable shows. Jean Genet's *Les Paravents*, performed by Jean-Louis Barrault's company, provoked violent demonstrations by army parachutists and far-right militants who were incensed that France's army and colonial empire should be thus insulted, with the blessing of the Minister of Culture, the ex-revolutionary André Malraux. Performances had to be given under the protection of armed guards. A homosexual poet and radical subversive, protected by the official police of the Republic! The situation was not lacking in humour.

In the uprising of May 1968, the theatre was occupied. For more than four weeks a permanent 'happening' allowed thousands of anonymous orators to be heard and to believe, for just one minute, that they were famous.

Pass alongside the theatre to reach the street that begins at the Palais du Luxembourg, home of the Sénat, under the name of rue de Tournon and ends up at the river as the rue de Seine. This street has had considerable significance over the course of the century, as successive waves of various immigrants all washed up here. First, after Hitler's rise to power, came the wave of German and Austrian writers and artists. Joseph Roth, Walter Benjamin, Hannah Arendt and their friends often came to the café Le Tournon, just opposite the Sénat, to sit and forget their troubles and fears in the heat of alcohol and conversation.

Follow down rue de Tournon, and turn left to arrive in place St-Sulpice. Here you are suddenly in Rome, in front of one of Paris's truly Baroque churches. In summer, when the weather is warm, on the terrace of the Café de la Mairie and in rue des Canettes, where there is an excellent Italian restaurant (Santa Lucia), Paris becomes a southern city and remembers that it is Latin. It was in Paris that 'ethnic' music, Rumba and Cha-cha-cha, came into their own in the 1960s. The Tango had paved the way in the '20s.

A monument to thought and a sanctuary of knowledge – the venerable **Sorbonne**.

Continue down to boulevard St-Germain. At the end of my adolescence I, too, found refuge in this quarter, where ever since François Villon poets have rubbed shoulders with bad boys and where youthful students often imagine barricades to be the logical extension of philosophical arguments, political analyses and economic controversies.

At the time I knew nothing of life save for what my favourite poets, Baudelaire, Rimbaud, Apollinaire, or my prestigious elders Malraux, Sartre and Camus, had given me to dream about it. The only way not to resemble the boring and tyrannical adults I endured at school or frequented in my *petit-bourgeois* suburb of Vincennes, was to rise to the prestigious status of an intellectual.

Although totally ignorant of politics, I gathered, via well-circulated rumours, that the intellectual was necessarily '*de gauche*', that is to say indignantly opposed to 'the bastards', and against the '*bourgeois*'. That suited me. In reading Sartre's *La Nausée* and *Les Chemins de la liberté*, I had noted that the heroes had neither family nor home. They all lived in hotels, took their meals in restaurants, drank in bars, listened to jazz and danced in clubs. I had to follow this programme to the letter. Write, get published in Sartre's review *Les Temps modernes*, haunt the cafés, those new temples of learning: Le Bonaparte on the place St-Germain-des-Prés, in the building where Sartre lived with his mother; the Café de Flore, where on the first floor, in the afternoon, the silence was as sacred as in any library; Le Mabillon, between Odéon and St-Germain, and at *l'heure de l'apéritif*, Le Bar du Pont-Royal, where Sartre and Simone de Beauvoir met with other writers, as the place served as the de-facto annexe of Editions Gallimard.

For the moment, the bar is undergoing renovation, but one can still spot Philippe Sollers around here conversing with Americans, Italians, South Americans, and sometimes Czechs and Russians.

In the evening, after having dined at the Petit St-Benoît, or if the financial conjuncture was favourable, at the Montana or the Brasserie Lipp, we were spoilt for choice: drink Cuban cocktails or Caribbean punch at La Rhumerie, listen to cool jazz or be-bop at the Caméléon in rue St-André-des-Arts, chat up the prettiest girls in Paris at Club Castel in rue Princesse, dance at Le Tabou in rue Dauphine or at the Caveau de la Huchette.

After World War II and the Liberation of Paris, many American GIs who had participated in the action decided to stay on in the city. Among them were black writers who found the air of the Left Bank to their taste, because it was the air of freedom and, for a time, they were not the butt of racist humiliation and

Bebop oh la la! **Thelonious Monk** *was drawn to the Café de Seine as to the jazz clubs.*

persecution. In rue de Seine one finds traces of the anti-fascist writers, in contact with the new generation of French-speaking African poets such as Aimé Césaire and Léopold Senghor, and in the company of Sartre, who admired their direct style. All this little crowd did some serious drinking at the Café de Seine, now defunct, just at the intersection of boulevard St-Germain and the rue de Seine.

Before a concert, musicians would sometimes stop in at the Café de Seine for a drink. I remember seeing the most fabulous among them spend long hours in meditation – massive, silent, thinking. Thelonious Monk, the genius, in the flesh. Every time I am in the rue de Seine he is there, still there.

When it comes down to it, old Thelonious, the metaphysician of jazz, came to the right place. This magical island: Mabillon, rue de Seine, rue de Buci. A hotel of myth: La Louisiane. All the big names of jazz stayed here. Oscar Peterson, Miles Davis, Bud Powell, Max Roach, Dizzy Gillespie, Art Blakey… The clubs are close by: the Club St-Germain, the most famous, in rue St-Benoît, a little further along the Montana, Le Chat qui Pêche in rue St-Séverin, the Caveau de la Huchette in rue de la Huchette.

Continue down the rue de Seine. Alas, as Baudelaire remarked in *Les Fleurs du mal*, 'the form of a city changes faster than the heart of a mortal'. Today, as Juliette Gréco sings, '*Il n'y a plus d'après à St-Germain-des-Prés*' – there's no afterwards. Many of the bars have vanished, replaced by pizzerias; many bookshops, including the legendary Divan, have given way to luxury boutiques. The neighbourhood has become more snobbish. But the streets remain, sinuous and mysterious: find rue de l'Echaudé, which joins on the left, and then rue Visconti, a narrow vessel reminiscent of some dark Venetian alley where murderers may lurk.

Pressing further on towards rue du Bac, return south to rue Jacob. We have arrived at the central bank of intelligence and of the culture industry: '*Les Grandes Maisons*', the major publishing houses. Les Editions du Seuil (meaning 'threshold' – on the threshold of what, of truth, of fortune?) is to the left on rue Jacob. Continuing west towards rue de l'Université; Editions Grasset is further south in rue des Sts-Pères (strange name, the 'holy fathers': what a wonderful subject for Doctor Lacan, who held a still-famous conference on the Name of the Father). And Editions Gallimard, at the outermost reaches of the *quartier* in rue Sébastien-Bottin. On the Rive Gauche, everything starts and ends with the love of words. Often an empty promise, but sometimes, when anger grumbles and revolt begins to stir, an awesome power.

I love this neighbourhood because, even today, words, for the moment sleeping, tomorrow may awaken.

Translated by Abigail Hansen.

Eating & drinking

Le Bonaparte

42 rue Bonaparte, 6th (01.43.26.42.81). **Open** 8am-2am daily.

Brasserie Balzar

49 rue des Ecoles, 5th (01.43.54.13.67). **Open** 8am-midnight daily.

Brasserie Lipp

151 boulevard St-Germain, 6th (01.45.48.53.91). **Open** 11.30am-1am daily. Reliable cuisine and reasonable prices given its distinguished past.

Buvette des Marionnettes

Jardin du Luxembourg, 6th. **Open** *Sept-May* 8.30am-6.30pm daily; *June-Aug* 8.30am-7.30pm daily.

Café de Flore

172 boulevard St-Germain, 6th (01.45.48.55.26). **Open** 7am-1.30am daily. Expensive café, formerly a Surrealist haunt.

Rue Visconti – *'a narrow vessel reminiscent of some dark Venetian alley where murderers may lurk'.*

Café de la Mairie
8 place St-Sulpice, 6th (01.43.26.67.82). **Open** 7am-1am Mon-Sat.

Café Mabillon
164 boulevard St-Germain, 6th (01.43.26.62.93). **Open** 7am-6am daily. Cocktails and snacks while watching streetlife.

La Closerie des Lilas
171 boulevard du Montparnasse, 6th (01.40.51.34.50). **Open** 11.30am-1am daily. Restored to its former glory, this institution gives better value in the brasserie than in the restaurant. Try a 'Hemingway' cocktail.

Le Petit St-Benoît
4 rue St-Benoît, 6th (01.42.60.27.92). **Open** noon-2.30pm, 7-10.30pm, Mon-Sat. Closed Aug. Flavoursome food in traditional surroundings.

Le Rostand
6 place Edmond-Rostand, 6th (01.43.54.61.58). **Open** 8am-2am daily.

La Rhumerie
166 boulevard St-Germain, 6th (01.43.54.28.94). **Open** 9am-2am daily.

Santa Lucia
22 rue des Canettes, 6th (01.43.26.42.68). **Open** noon-2.30pm, 7pm-midnight, Mon, Wed-Sun. Excellent pizzas, possibly the best in Paris.

Le Tournon
16 rue de Tournon, 6th (no phone). **Open** 7am-8pm Mon-Fri.

Accommodation

Hôtel La Louisiane
60 rue de Seine, 6th (01.44.32.17.17).

Hôtel Le Montana
28 rue St-Benoit, 6th (0144.39.71.00). The club is now closed.

Hôtel du Pont-Royal
5-7 rue Montalembert, 7th (01.42.84.70.00). Due to open after renovation Sept 1999.

Clubs

Caveau de la Huchette
5 rue de la Huchette, 5th (01.43.26.65.05). **Open** 9.30pm-2.30am Mon-Thur, Sun; 9.30pm-3.30am Fri, Sat. **Admission** 60F Mon-Thur, Sun; 70F Fri, Sat; 55F students Mon-Thur, Sun.

La Chapelle des Lombards
19 rue de Lappe, 11th (01.43.57.24.24). **Open** 10.30pm-dawn Thur-Sat; *concerts* 8pm Thur (70F). **Admission** 100F Thur (women free before midnight); 120F Fri, Sat with drink.

Le Chat qui Pêche
10 rue Huchette, 5th (01.43.54.98.89). **Open** 3.30pm-midnight Mon-Fri; 11am-midnight Sat, Sun.

Club Castel
15 rue Princesse, 6th (01.40.51.52.80). **Open** 9pm-dawn Tue-Sat. **Admission** members only.

Club St-Germain
13 rue St-Benoît, 6th (01.42.22.51.09). **Open** ring for details.

Literature

Editions Bernard Grasset
61 rue des Sts-Pères, 6th (01.44.39.22.00). **Open** 9am-1pm, 2-5pm, Mon-Fri.

Editions du Seuil
27 rue Jacob, 6th (01.40.46.50.50). **Open** not open to the public.

Editions Gallimard
5 rue Sébastien-Bottin, 7th (01.49.54.42.00). **Open** 9am-7pm Mon-Fri.

Librairie José Corti
11 rue de Médicis, 6th (01.43.26.63.00). **Open** 9am-6pm Mon-Fri. Closed mid-July to mid-Aug.

Buildings & gardens

Collège de France
11 place Marcelin-Berthelot, 5th (01.44.27.12.11). **Open** lectures are open to the public.

Eglise St-Sulpice
place St-Sulpice, 6th (01.46.33.21.78). **Open** 8am-7.30pm daily.

Jardin du Luxembourg
place Auguste-Comte, place Edmond-Rostand, rue de Vaugirard, 6th. **Open** *summer* 7.30am-9.30pm daily; *winter* 8am-5pm daily. *Children's playground* 10am-dusk daily. **Admission** *children's playground* 14F children; 7.50F adults.

Odéon, Théâtre de l'Europe
1 place de l'Odéon, 6th (01.44.41.36.36). **Open** *box office* 11am-6.30pm Mon-Sat; *telephone bookings* 11am-7pm Mon-Sat (Sun when plays are on).

Le Panthéon
place du Panthéon, 5th (01.44.32.18.00). **Open** *Apr-Sept* 9.30am-6.30pm daily; *Oct-Mar* 10am-5.30pm daily. **Admission** 35F; 23F 12-25s; free under-12s.

La Sorbonne
47 rue des Ecoles, 5th (01.40.46.20.15). **Open** *courtyards* 9am-4.30pm Mon-Fri.

City of light

Elisabeth Quin

From movie-set Montmartre to those doomed lovers of the Pont Neuf.

Start: Mº Pigalle, 18th
Finish: quai des Orfèvres, 1st
Time: 2-3 hours
Distance: 5.5km/3.5 miles
Getting there: lines 2 or 12 to Mº Pigalle
Getting back: short walk to Mº Cité (line 4)
Note: this walk includes a brief Métro journey just before the end. For a detailed map of the Cimetière de Montmartre, see Jeanloup Sieff's walk. Where applicable, a film's English title is included in the listings.

There are so many places in Paris associated with the cinema and enshrined on the world's screens that suggesting a film-themed walk across Paris is a dangerous or almost impossible business.

The nickname 'city of light' (*ville-lumière*) is clearly not an empty phrase, but a pun both apt and playful, since it was here that Louis Lumière patented the *cinématographe* in 1895. At a private industrial meeting on 22 March 1895, the Lumière brothers presented their first ever screening. (The first public screening took place on 28 December the same year at the Grand Café on the boulevard des Capucines.) One hundred and four years

Jean-Pierre Melville, who would go on to make Le Samurai, *directed* **Bob le flambeur** *in 1956.*

Jean Renoir lived in **avenue Frochot** *from 1937-69. Valérie Lemercier lives here today.*

later, going by the city's 343 screens and 69,000 cinema seats, you can conclude that the light shines as brightly as ever…

Confronted with so much material, we will try to spare you a saunter through the timeless Parisian clichés: Jean Seberg and her *Herald Tribunes* on the Champs-Elysées from *A Bout de souffle*, Fabrice Luchini at the Café de la Mairie on place St-Sulpice, Brando and his dairy butter at Passy in *Last Tango in Paris*, or even Woody Allen at the Ritz in *Everyone Says I Love You*… All marvellous clichés that feed the legend, but that show a different Paris to the one we have chosen for our walk, which is the rougher, less glamorous, less playful, rather more marginal Paris of the '*Messieurs les hommes*' of the underworld.

For the hoodlums or bosses who were known in the 1940s and '50s as *gonzes poilus* (hairy geezers), the Paris underworld had its lodgings not under the city but on raised ground to the north – a paradox that only *caves* (outsiders, or honest folk) find surprising. We suggest you discover the underworld and its geographical, aesthetic and social reality for yourself – the 9th and 18th arrondissements, shabby streets, populous *faubourgs* well suited to clandestine activity, the protective Butte Montmartre – in short, just so many unsettling or picturesque settings for the most typical post-war French gangster films.

Incidentally, *Milieu*, the French name for the criminal underworld, appeared in popular literature in the 1930s (long before the cinema adopted it), thanks to Francis Carco, author of the novel *Pigalle*, who heard it from the *poissons*, the pimps of the time.

It's time to step into the world of likely lads togged out like lords, with their flashy suits and flashier rings.

If you leave Pigalle Métro as rosy-fingered dawn is gently caressing the crossroads, say around 6.45am, you will be able to salute the memory of gambler Bob, hero of Jean-Pierre Melville's film *Bob le flambeur*, which opens at the end of a long, hard night. Robert Duchêne, alias Bob, walks around place Pigalle, passes a few weary bar hostesses and a few leery

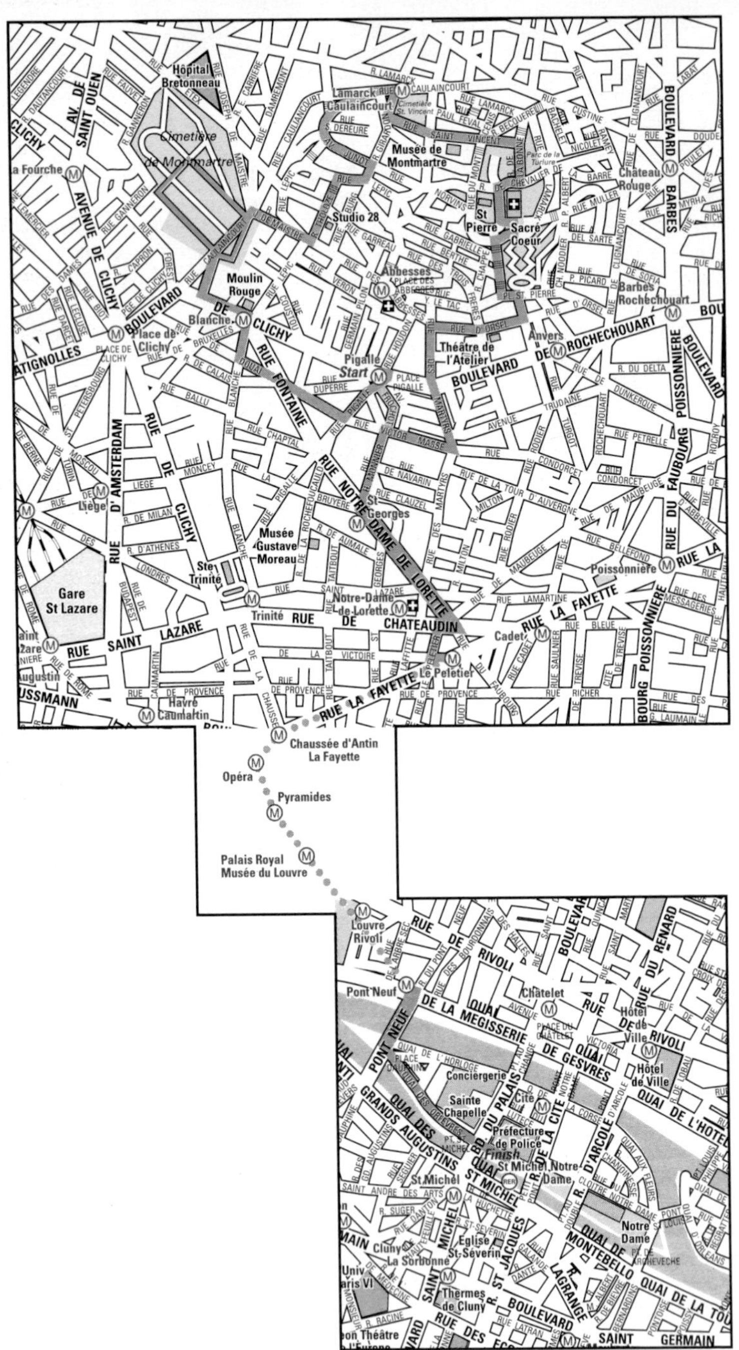
Start
Finish
Pigalle
Moulin Rouge
Blanche
Cimetière de Montmartre
Hôpital Bretonneau
Lamarck Caulaincourt
Musée de Montmartre
Studio 28
Abbesses
St Pierre
Sacré Coeur
Château Rouge
Barbès Rochechouart
Anvers
Théâtre de l'Atelier
Place de Clichy
Liège
Gare St Lazare
Ste Trinité
Trinité
Musée Gustave Moreau
St Georges
Notre-Dame de Lorette
Le Peletier
Cadet
Poissonnière
Havre Caumartin
Chaussée d'Antin La Fayette
Opéra
Pyramides
Palais Royal Musée du Louvre
Louvre Rivoli
Pont Neuf
Châtelet
Hôtel de Ville
Conciergerie
Sainte Chapelle
Cité
Préfecture de Police
St Michel
St Michel Notre Dame
Notre Dame
Cluny La Sorbonne
Eglise St-Séverin
Thermes de Cluny
BOULEVARD DE CLICHY
BOULEVARD DE ROCHECHOUART
RUE FONTAINE
RUE NOTRE DAME DE LORETTE
RUE DE CHATEAUDUN
RUE LA FAYETTE
RUE SAINT LAZARE
RUE D'AMSTERDAM
RUE DE CLICHY
RUE DE RIVOLI
QUAI DE LA MEGISSERIE
QUAI DE GESVRES
QUAI DES GRANDS AUGUSTINS
QUAI ST MICHEL
BD. DU PALAIS
BOULEVARD SAINT GERMAIN

GIs, then contemplates his reflection in a shop window and murmurs, 'A fine rogue's face…' His is the inhuman and precarious condition of the criminal, but he wouldn't have it any other way…

Like urban ethnologists documenting the reality of the *quartier*, Auguste le Breton, Albert Simonin and Georges Simenon – among others – have done more for Pigalle than any tourist office. A fistful of films put the finishing touches to the shady legend: *Razzia sur la schnouf* (1953), *Du Rififi chez les hommes* (1955), *Bob le flambeur* (1956), or *Touchez pas au grisbi* (1954).

Max (Jean Gabin) and Riton, 'the hedgehog', holders of a large amount of *grisbi* (loot), were regular customers of Le Mistific, at 24 rue Frochot. In this cabaret that overlooked place Pigalle, the two gentlemen's *poules* (girlfriends) – Jeanne Moreau and Dora Doll – would perform disguised as mermaids, with starfish in their hair – all in the best possible taste. At the start of the film, Max gets mildly ticked off by the Mistific's *patronne*: 'Perhaps I should thank you for ruffling the feathers of my flock!' Max's rascally elegance calms her down. But how can he shift his loot?

Opposite, at 18 boulevard de Clichy, there was a safe haven called Les Pierrots, frequented by Henri Charrière – aka Papillon – an escapee from Cayenne prison. Right next door, at No.20, the defunct Iris Bar was an unlucky address for him: on 26 March 1930, the day after the murder that earned him hard labour, 'the butterfly' claimed to have spent the night at the Iris Bar; but the owner, who had a grudge against him, blew his cover. The rest is history.

After a quick *petit noir* at the Chào-Bà-Café, quite an improvement on the Iris, take rue Pigalle and walk as far as No.66. Here you can mourn another defunct watering hole, in this case Le Monico, where gangster Antoine La Rocca – alias *La Scoumoune* (*The Hit Man*) – was gunned down on 2 September 1947. The episode was religiously reprised in two films by Jean Becker and José Giovanni, who both gave the role of the unfortunate Marseillais to Jean-Paul Belmondo. Le Monico very nearly witnessed another bloody incident in 1911; Fréhel was arrested there in possession of a knife that she planned to try out on Maurice Chevalier, her lover, who was cheating on her with Mistinguett…

Take rue de Douai, the territory of Tony le Stéphanois, hero of *Du Rififi chez les hommes* by Jules Dassin. You can't help but admire the dazzling on-screen osmosis between the director, just off the boat from America (a refugee from Macarthyism), and the stamping ground of Tony, Mario, Jo and Milano César, played by Dassin himself. With his zombie-like appearance and waxen face that borrows as much from Buster Keaton as Droopy, Jean Servais *is* Pigalle, a seedy Pigalle at the end of its tether, already on the decline but capable of panache and grandeur when need be – like Tony, who gives his life at the end of the film to return a child to its mother. It all started on rue de Douai and rue Fontaine, thanks to Mado, who could not wait for Tony to come out of the slammer to team up with the unscrupulous boss of the L'Age d'or café. Because of César, who has a thing for Viviana, a bright young thing who jigged about at the L'Age d'or and who sings the Rififi song:

It ain't no ordinary word –
you won't find it in
the dictionary –
Rififi!
like nothing you have heard
when push comes to shove –
Rififi!
when rough stuff's what's inferred
by real men, it's
Rififi…

Then comes a breathtaking robbery at the Mappin & Webb jeweller's – 20 minutes without a single word or a note of music – carried out by four gangsters as precise as clockmakers and slinky as cats in their Repetto slippers (still available at the shop).

Pass rue Fontaine, and take rue Blanche on the right in the direction of the square of the same name.

In front of you stands the Moulin Rouge, filmed by Jean Renoir and wept over by Fréhel in a film full of uprooted gangsters, *Pépé le Moko*.

Where is my moulin
on place Blanche
my tabac
my corner bistro
every day
for me was like Sunday…

… yelled Fréhel in the heart of the Algiers casbah! The Moulin Rouge still stands, but these days it's a tourist trap that doubles up as conference space and a location for video shoots. Duvivier and Renoir must be turning in their graves!

By turning right on to the boulevard de Clichy – if you feel like making a few saucy purchases, now's your chance – you get to avenue Rachel, the main access to Montmartre cemetery. Ten and something hectares, the third largest Parisian cemetery is a pleasant place in which to dawdle and muse, far from the hordes who flock to Père Lachaise. Here lies François Truffaut, who shot the scene with the adulterous kiss from *Les 400 coups* nearby, on place de Clichy; here also lie Louis Jouvet and Henri-Georges Clouzot, who immortalised nearby avenue Junot in a witty police fantasy, *L'Assassin habite au 21*.

Start climbing up towards Montmartre by rue Caulaincourt and rue Joseph-de-Maistre. If you feel a sudden need for sweet refreshment, the terrace of Le Terrass Hôtel offers a panoramic view over Paris and refined snacks, all of which make a change from the crowded or fake-trendy eateries nearby. Carry on along rue Tholozé: this narrow alley is famous among cinephiles for its Studio 28, situated at No.10, a gem, which proudly displays the words *'La salle d'art et d'essai de Montmartre'* on its façade. Take a peek into its hall, designed by Alexandre Trauner (set designer on *Hôtel du Nord*), and at the fantastic lamps hanging in the auditorium. Studio 28's fairy godmothers were Jean Cocteau and Abel Gance, and it is proud to have been the site of a veritable *'bataille d'Hernani'* in 1930: during the screening of Buñuel's *L'Age d'or*, rotten eggs and bottles were thrown at the screen along with cries of 'Scandal! Pornography! Heresy!' Tuesday evening advance screenings and oldie-but-goodie revivals are much more peaceful these days.

At the top of rue Tholozé, pass in front of the Moulin de la Galette and walk up on the left towards avenue Junot. You will have crossed rue Lepic which, further down, is filled with shimmering fruit and vegetable stalls: in *Le Rouge est mis,* Gilles Grangier had given Jean Gabin and Marcel Bozzufi, 'good sons but bad boys both', a fruit and veg merchant for a mother. Jules Dassin, who did the location scouting for *Rififi* himself, also chose rue Lepic as the setting for the sequence where *le Stéphanois* sets off to put the good fellows of the *quartier* in the picture regarding the imminent settling of the score. These days, the street feeds and waters the thirtysomething boho-chic-arty population of Montmartre.

Avenue Junot, Montmartre's smartest residential thoroughfare, curves gently towards the rear of the *butte*; at No.1, Claude Lelouch, the director of *Un Homme et une femme*, set up a tiny cinema, the Ciné-théâtre 13. No.13, on the left, is doubly evocative: in *Les Noces sanglantes*, the tenth *Fantômas* episode dating from 1913, it was the last hideout of the vampires. The current building is decorated with a mosaic of Poulbot, who lived at this address, by way of a tribute to the creator of the dewy-eyed brat who has become the symbol of Montmartre.

A little further on, on the same side, you won't find No.21 – the numbering inexplicably peters out between Nos.15 and 23. No.21 was the address of the Pension des Mimosas, the home of the mysterious Monsieur Durand, serial killer before the term had been coined in Clouzot's film *L'Assassin habite au 21*. Madame Point, the virago mistress of the house, shouts at Pierre Fresnay (disguised as a priest for the sake of the investigation), 'There are more tarts than priests in Montmartre!' A handy, all-in-one summary of a certain sociological reality in the area. A clearing where people play *pétanque* in summer now occupies the site of No.21. At No.39, on the other hand, Truffaut fans will be pleased to find the building the director used as the Hôtel Alsina in *Baisers volés*, where Antoine Doinel had a melancholy job as nightwatchman; unfortunately, the naïve lad allowed up a bailiff and a jealous husband who both witnessed adultery on the third floor. 'The lady from 24 was with the man from 19… – Fired!!!' The final exchange with the boss was brief, as was Antoine's time at the Alsina.

The very peaceful avenue Junot joins rue Lucien-Gaulard, which in turn leads to the St-Vincent cemetery. This is the final resting place of Marcel Carné, who was so fond of the *faubourgs* with their particular atmosphere, from Barbès (*Les Portes de la nuit*) to the boulevard du Crime (*Les Enfants du paradis*). Adjoining the cemetery and running beside the capital's most famous vineyard (which every year produces a few litres of undrinkable plonk), the rue St-Vincent wriggles up towards Sacré-Coeur. With a 20-year interval, Julien Duvivier made the street the setting for two films: on the second floor of No.35, in a small residential

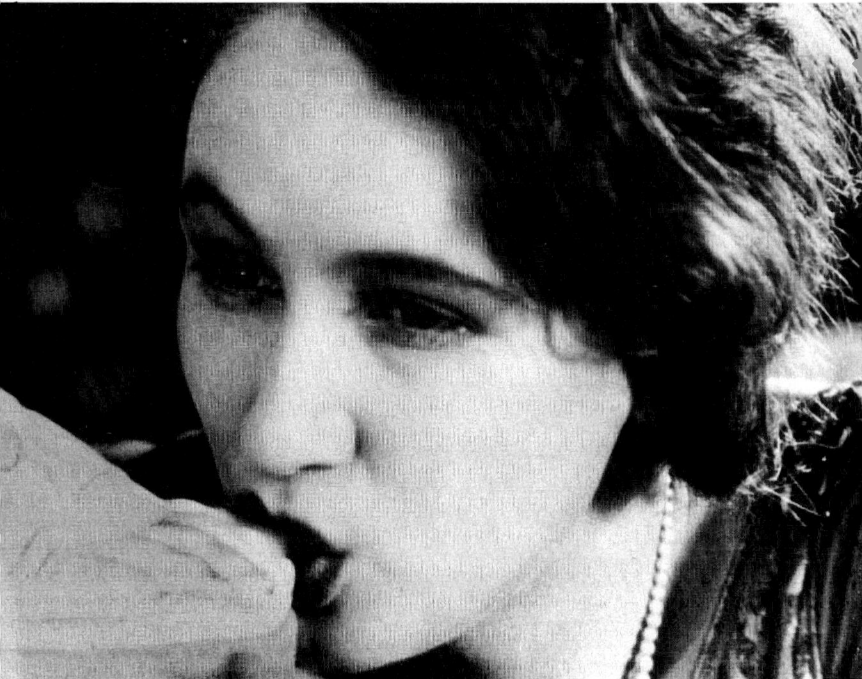

Rotten eggs and other missiles greeted a screening of Luis Buñuel's **L'Age d'or** *in 1930.*

building, a lady of easy virtue and occasional chorister at the Théâtre du Châtelet was murdered a few hours before Fernandel came to visit her in *L'Homme à l'imperméable*. A blackmailer who witnessed the crime made the poor lover's life a misery. In *La Bandera*, the hero Pierre Gilieth commits a crime at dusk in the same street. He flees to Morocco, pursued by a stubborn cop, and distinguishes himself in Franco's army – which in these politically correct times seems either dubious or deliberately provocative.

At the end of rue St-Vincent, turn right and take rue de la Bonne, heading towards the Basilica: you'll cut across rue du Chevalier-de-la-Barre, in which the cameraman Henri Alekan has dreamed up a 'pathway of lights'. By night, this staircase leading up to the Sacré-Coeur is transformed into a starry sky, thanks to a sophisticated network of fibre optics buried beneath the stones. The magician of *La Belle et la Bête* has left nothing to chance, since the constellations mirror the skies of Paris. In a less poetic vein, super-independent satirist Jean-Pierre Mocky, the most iconoclastic, couldn't-care-less French director of his generation, used the Sacré-Coeur for *Un Drôle de paroissien*, a sensational film about a true scoundrel. Bourvil played its anti-hero Monsieur Georges, who gleefully pillaged the Basilica's collection boxes to feed his family: the irreverent fellow worked methodically onwards and upwards, pinching 60 francs from St-Hippolyte's church (a poor taking) before finishing with the jackpot – 460 francs from St-Joseph's, 'the boss's stepfather'. Mocky, a model of self-sufficiency since being cold-shouldered by the decision-makers of French cinema, bought himself a cinema in which he screens his own films (*bien sûr*) as well as alternating programmes of revivals and porn.

Truffaut *lies in the* **Cimetière de Montmartre**.

Come back down towards boulevard de Rochechouart by the stairway that runs beside the Montmartre funicular railway, which, unlike the one in Vienna, hasn't had the good fortune to inspire filmmakers.

Follow the map to rue d'Orsel, which takes you to the Théâtre de l'Atelier, dozing under chestnut trees on place Charles-Dullin. In *Le Dernier Métro*, François Truffaut told of the dark days its director lived through under the Occupation. Carry on towards rue des Martyrs, immortalised in a song by the Garçons Bouchers, a famous 1980s alternative rock group. This part of the street between boulevard de Clichy and rue de la Vieuville was also a wilderness for pathetic transvestites and affectionate drop-outs in Karim Dridi's film *Pigalle*. Through his description of the local wildlife, he confirmed the disappearance of the *Milieu* and of its neo-Melvillian portrayal. Before him, in Juliet Berto's film *Neige*, snow fell on the same pavements in a story about decline that was as gloomy as you could wish for.

Cross the boulevard and, further down on the left, take rue Victor-Massé, which was the territory of Alphonse Allais, an aphorist in the line of Oscar Wilde – but without the snobbery. He held court at the Chat Noir cabaret at No.12. 'Why put off until tomorrow what you can do the day after?' Don't listen to his advice, but if you speak French, amuse yourself with his seriously nonsensical thoughts. Nothing to do with cinema, but tremendous fun.

Just before turning into rue Henri-Monnier, you'll notice a private passageway on the right blocked by a heavy gate that is impervious to sweet talk: this is avenue Frochot, where Jean Renoir lived from 1937 to 1969. As a tribute to the director, Truffaut filmed a scene from *Les 400 coups* in the avenue. The humorous young filmmaker/actress/stylist/singer Valérie Lemercier lives here and even edited her last film, *Le Derrière*, here. To the left of the gate, a low building intrigues passers-by and makes me very jealous of its tenants: with its fabulous stained-glass window that mixes memories of the fashionable *japonaiseries* from the early part of the century and Klimt's paintings, the former *billard* academy of the Boulevards is a good example of Nouvelle Athènes architecture. This portion of the 9th saw gentrification in the mid-nineteenth century.

From rue Henri-Monnier, make for place St-Georges. You're in Truffaut territory once more, since the Théâtre St-Georges was used to stand in for the Théâtre de l'Atelier in *Le Dernier Métro*. At this point on the walk you're coming dangerously close to the best restaurant in the *quartier*, La Casa Olympe, on rue St-Georges (on the left going down), very well frequented by local producers, scriptwriters and actors; I remember a wonderful *thon au lard* with polenta. Booking is essential, owing to the Casa's modest dimensions. At this point on the walk you will also have noticed that you are moving away from the *butte* and its environs, but that's because you're heading for the logical terminus of this walk through criminal territory, a terminus that all villains cordially loathe. Walk down rue Notre-Dame-de-Lorette as far as the start of rue du Faubourg-Montmartre, close your eyes and listen to the song of suffering souls as was hummed in a film by Raymond Bernard, *Faubourg Montmartre*, in 1931:

> *There are kids/like ghosts*
> *who stroll/on the pavements*
> *at dusk/and whose hope is so*
> *stubborn/that nothing can weaken*
> *their faith in a beautiful love…*

Can you feel it, can you hear the *faubourg* rustle, so full of hope, so short on promise? The Paris *faubourg* that so enriched French cinema in the 1940s and '50s?

Take the Métro at Le Peletier and get out five stops later at Pont Neuf. While crossing the first part of the bridge you will remember two damned, destitute and magnificent young lovers from Léos Carax's *Les Amants du Pont Neuf* whom Marcel Carné could have taken under his wing. Turn left and go to 36 quai des Orfèvres, headquarters of the PJ, the Police Judiciaire. Clouzot's *Quai des Orfèvres* is the obvious reference here, with its hilarious interrogations lead by super-smooth inspector Louis Jouvet; its final line is spoken by Jouvet to a lesbian, a rare character type in popular cinema of the day: 'I like you. You're my kind of fellow, you'll never have any luck with women!' The film's dialogue was written by another kind of *orfèvre* – or master craftsman – Henri Jeanson.

But the final shot of quai des Orfèvres, to finish, an unforgettable image lingering on the retina, is thanks to Jean-Pierre Melville.

In full sunlight stands Jeff Costello (Alain Delon), aka *le Samourai*; the most dapper, the most impenetrable of killers, a character teetering on the brink of abstraction, a stuffed suit, a principle.

His release from custody, filmed by Melville, is like the opening of a cage: eyes

Les 400 coups *(1959) – François Truffaut's début feature – was shot in and around the 18th.*

Antoine Doinel (Jean-Pierre Léaud) and date in Montmartre-set **Baisers volés** *(Truffaut, 1968).*

dazzled, but a happy ending seems too much to hope for. This is a release from custody that feels more like a reprieve than an acquittal.

Jeff Costello, who carries out his deadly contracts and missions like a sleepwalker, with precision and indifference; Jeff Costello, who has sounded the death knell of 'old gent' villains, comes out of the Police Judiciaire. Pale trenchcoat, brooding stare.

Free, Jeff. And alive.

At least for the time being.

Translated by Simon Cropper.

Eating & drinking

Chào-Bà-Café
22 boulevard de Clichy 18th (01 46 06 72 90). **Open** 9am-2am Mon-Wed; 9am-4am Thur; 8.30am-2am Sun. French Indochina theme in décor and menu – quiet in the day, busy at night.

La Casa Olympe
48 rue St-Georges, 9th (01 42 85 26 01). **Open** noon-2pm, 8-11pm, Mon-Fri.

La Fourmi
74 rue des Martyrs, 18th (01.42.64.70.35). **Open** 8.30am-2am Mon-Sat; 10.30am-2am Sun. Salads and sandwiches in this arty bar.

Le Moulin de la Galette
83 rue Lepic, 18th (01.46.06.84.77). **Open** noon-3pm, 8pm-midnight, daily.

La Table de la Fontaine
5 rue Henri-Monnier, 9th (01.45.26.26.30). **Open** noon-2.30pm, 7.30-11.45pm, Mon-Fri. Closed two weeks in Aug. Charming bistro offering French classics with a modern twist.

Le Trèfle
68 rue Lepic, 18th (01.42.54.44.11). **Open** noon-3pm, 7pm-12.30am, daily. Short but succulent menu of North African cuisine.

Au Virage Lepic
61 rue Lepic, 18th (01.42.52.46.79). **Open** noon-3pm, 6pm-2am, daily. Good-value, low-key meal after an evening walk in Montmartre.

Accommodation

Hôtel Ritz

15 place Vendôme, 1st (01.43.16.30.30).

Terrass Hôtel

12-14 rue Joseph-de-Maistre, 18th (01.46.06.72.85).

Cemeteries

Cimetière de Montmartre

20 avenue Rachel, access by stairs from rue Caulaincourt, 18th (01.43.87.64.24). **Open** *summer* 9am-5.45pm daily; *winter* 9am-5.15pm daily.

Cimetière St-Vincent

6 rue Lucien Gaulard, 18th (01.46.06.29.78). **Open** *16 Mar-5 Nov* 8am-6pm Mon-Fri; 8.30am-6pm Sat; 9am-6pm Sun; *6 Nov-15 Mar* 8am-5.30pm Mon-Fri; 8.30am-5.30pm Sat; 9am-5.30pm Sun;

Cinemas

Cine-Théâtre 13

1 avenue Junot 18th (01 42 51 13 79).

Studio 28

10 rue Tholozé, 18th (01.46.06.36.07).

Theatres

Moulin Rouge

82 boulevard de Clichy, 18th (01.46.06.00.19). **Dinner** 7pm daily. **Shows** 9pm,11pm, daily. **Admission** *with dinner* 750F, 790F, 880F; *with drink* 350F (at bar), 510F (9pm), 450F (11pm).

Théâtre de l'Atelier

place Charles Dullin, 18th (01.46.06.49.24).

Théâtre St-Georges

51 rue St George, 9th (01.48.78.74.37).

Films

A Bout de Souffle (*Breathless*)
(Jean-Luc Godard, 1959, Fr)
L'Age d'or
(Luis Buñuel, 1930, Fr)
Les Amants du Pont Neuf
(Léos Carax, 1991, Fr)
L'Assassin habite au 21
(Henri-Georges Clouzot, 1942, Fr)
Baisers volés (*Stolen Kisses*)
(François Truffaut, 1968, Fr)
La Bandera
(Julien Duvivier, 1935, Fr)
La Belle et La Bête (*Beauty and the Beast*)
(Jean Cocteau, 1946, Fr)

Théâtre St-Georges was used to stand in for the Théâtre de l'Atelier in **Le Dernier Métro**.

Michèle (Juliette Binoche) and Alex (Denis Lavant) in **Les Amants du Pont Neuf** *(1991).*

Bob le flambeur (*Bob the Gambler*)
(Jean-Pierre Melville, 1956, Fr)
Le Dernier Métro (*The Last Métro*)
(François Truffaut, 1980, Fr)
Le Derrière
(Valérie Lemercier, 1999, Fr)
Un drôle de paroissien
(Jean-Pierre Mocky, 1963, Fr)
Du Rififi chez les hommes (*Rififi*)
(Jules Dassin, 1955, Fr)
Les Enfants du Paradis (*Children of Paradise*)
(Marcel Carné, 1945, Fr)
Everyone Says I Love you
(Woody Allen, 1996, US)
Faubourg Montmartre
(Raymond Bernard, 1931, Fr)
L'Homme à l'imperméable
(Julien Duvivier, 1956, Fr)
Hôtel du Nord
(Marcel Carné, 1938, Fr)
Last Tango in Paris
(Bernardo Bertolucci, 1972, It/Fr)
Neige
(Juliet Berto, 1981, Fr)
Les Noces sanglantes from **Fantômas**
(Louis Feuillade, 1913, Fr)
Papillon
(Franklin J Schaffner, 1973, US)
Pépé le Moko
(Julien Duvivier, 1937, Fr)
Pigalle
(Karim Dridi, 1994, Fr)
Les Portes de la nuit (*Gates of the Night*)
(Marcel Carné, 1946, Fr)
Quai des Orfèvres
(Henri-Georges Clouzot, 1947, Fr)
Les 400 coups (*The 400 Blows*)
(François Truffaut, 1959, Fr)
Razzia sur la schnouf
(Henri Decoin, 1955, Fr)
Du Rififi chez les hommes
(Jules Dassin, 1955, Fr)
Le Rouge est mis
(Gilles Grangier, 1957, Fr)
Le Samourai (*The Samurai*)
(Jean-Pierre Melville, 1967, Fr)
La Scoumoune (*The Hit Man*)
(Jose Giovanni, 1972, Fr)
Touchez pas au grisbi (*Honour among Theives*)
(Jacques Becker, 1953, Fr)
Un homme et une femme
(Claude Lelouch, 1966, Fr)

Others

Sacré-Coeur

35 rue du Chevalier-de-la-Barre, 18th (01.53.41.89.00). **Open** *crypt/dome Oct-Mar* 9am-6pm daily; *Apr-Sept* 9am-7pm daily. **Admission** *crypt* 15F; *dome* 15F; *crypt/dome* 23F.

Fit for a king

Chantal Barbe

A walk inspired by the rulers of Paris – but it doesn't go in a straight line.

Start: place de la Concorde, 8th
Finish: place de la Bastille, 4th
Time: 3-4 hours
Distance: 6.5km/4 miles
Getting there: lines 1, 8 or 12 to Mº Concorde
Getting back: Mº Bastille (lines 1, 5, 8)
Note: for a more contemporary political walk, see Philippe Alexandre's.

A king in his kingdom is the centre of activity. When Paris, on its island in the middle of the Seine, grew into a fishing village of some substance, the Kings of France came to live in it, on the appropriately named Ile de la Cité. And when Paris, making the most of its strategic position, grew into a major trading centre on the Right Bank where docks could easily be dug and warehouses built, its rulers walled in the new development with fortresses to the east and west. Eventually, they moved into it, often residing in the Marais in the shadow of the Bastille, then in the Louvre.

Paris lost its king – but remained the capital – when Louis XIV, the Sun King, declared that the court was to be beyond the city walls, at Versailles. Even so, the kings saw to it that they continued to be adequately honoured in stone or in bronze. After the Revolution, their successors, royal or imperial, graced the same part of Paris – where you are going to take your Royal Walk.

Situated on the Right Bank but close to the Left Bank, at the crossroads of two of the most impressive views of Paris, the place de la Concorde is a truly royal vantage point. The French are perspective addicts: they seem to believe that only straight lines and symmetry will create beauty and lead to perfection.

Dodge the traffic and reach the centre of the square where the obelisk rises, proudly wearing its newly restored golden 'pyramidion'. The obelisk is often said to be the oldest monument in Paris. Indeed, it used to stand with its twin at the gate of Rameses' temple in Luxor. Both obelisks were given to France by Mehmet Ali, the Egyptian Pacha. The transportation of one obelisk and its erection in place de la Concorde in 1836 in the presence of King Louis-Philippe proved such a highly difficult technical feat that the second obelisk was left in Luxor. The French government only recently told Egypt that they were dropping their claim to it. Walk around the obelisk, where its erection is depicted in gold on the pedestal. Every year, for the 14 July military parade, the modern-day monarch, Le Président, stands under the obelisk facing the Champs-Elysées while he reviews his troops.

The square, built in honour of Louis XV at the end of the eighteenth century, was designed by Jacques Ange Gabriel, who also built the Petit Trianon at Versailles. The square bridged the gap between two elegant spaces: the Tuileries gardens and the Champs-Elysées. It has kept its original shape but King Louis-Philippe asked architect Jacques Hittorf to embellish the square: ornate lamp-posts

The obelisk from Rameses' temple in Luxor, now standing in ***place de la Concorde****, surrounded by a roaring wall of traffic.*

EN PRESENCE DU ROI
LOUIS PHILIPPE Ier

and two fountains were added in 1840, celebrating Navigation on Rivers and Seas. Gabriel's pavilions were topped with statues representing the main French cities. The Seine borders the square to the south and you can see the Eiffel Tower and the glimmering dome of Les Invalides. On the north side, Gabriel built two symmetrical classical buildings: one, to the east, houses the Ministry of the Navy, while the other, to the west, is shared by the Automobile Club and the prestigious Crillon hotel. Between the two buildings, the rue Royale leads to the Madeleine church, echoing the Palais-Bourbon on the Left Bank, where members of the Assemblée Nationale sit. Both resemble Greek temples.

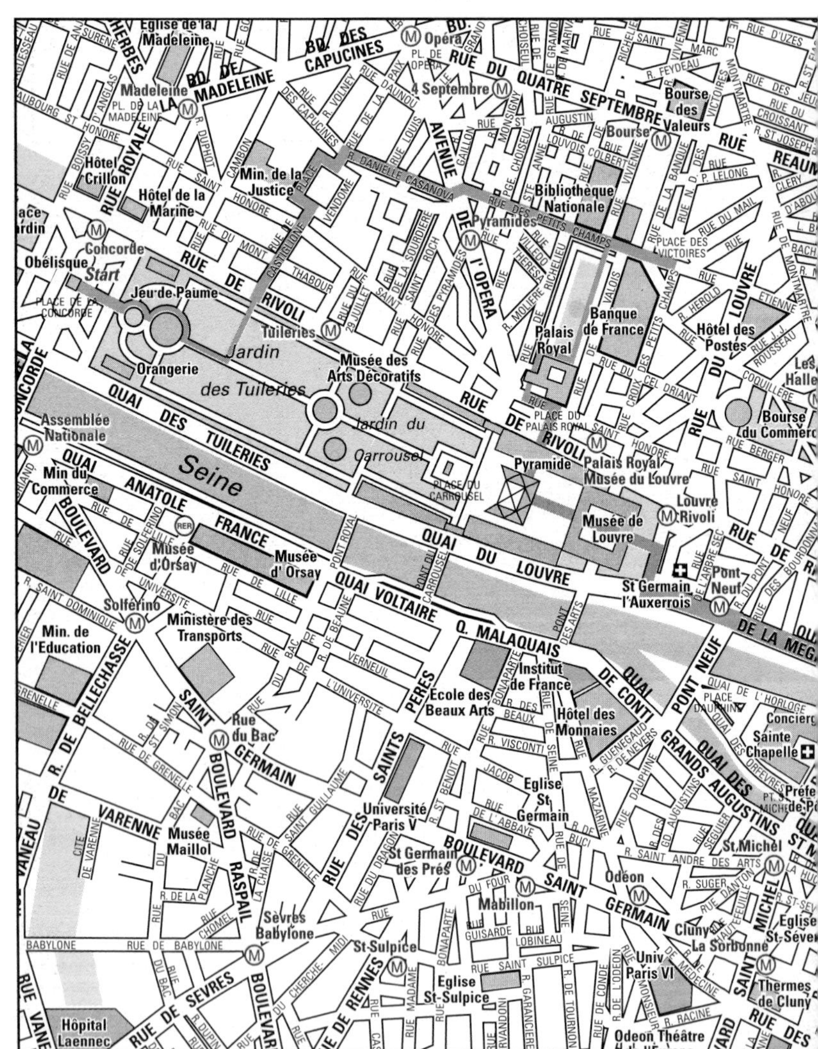

Now look at the east-west perspective, the longest by far in Paris: the Champs-Elysées opens between copies of equestrian statues saved from the Royal Park at Marly; the originals can be seen in the Louvre, protected from pollution. The Arc de Triomphe and, further on, the futuristic Grande Arche de la Défense, an arch-shaped building stuffed with offices – including the Ministry of the Environment – stand in line, the latter visible through the former's arch.

Walk now from the obelisk to the gilded gates of the Tuileries gardens. You will tread on the site where the guillotine stood during the Revolutionary Terror. Many heads fell here, including those of the King and Queen. The square,

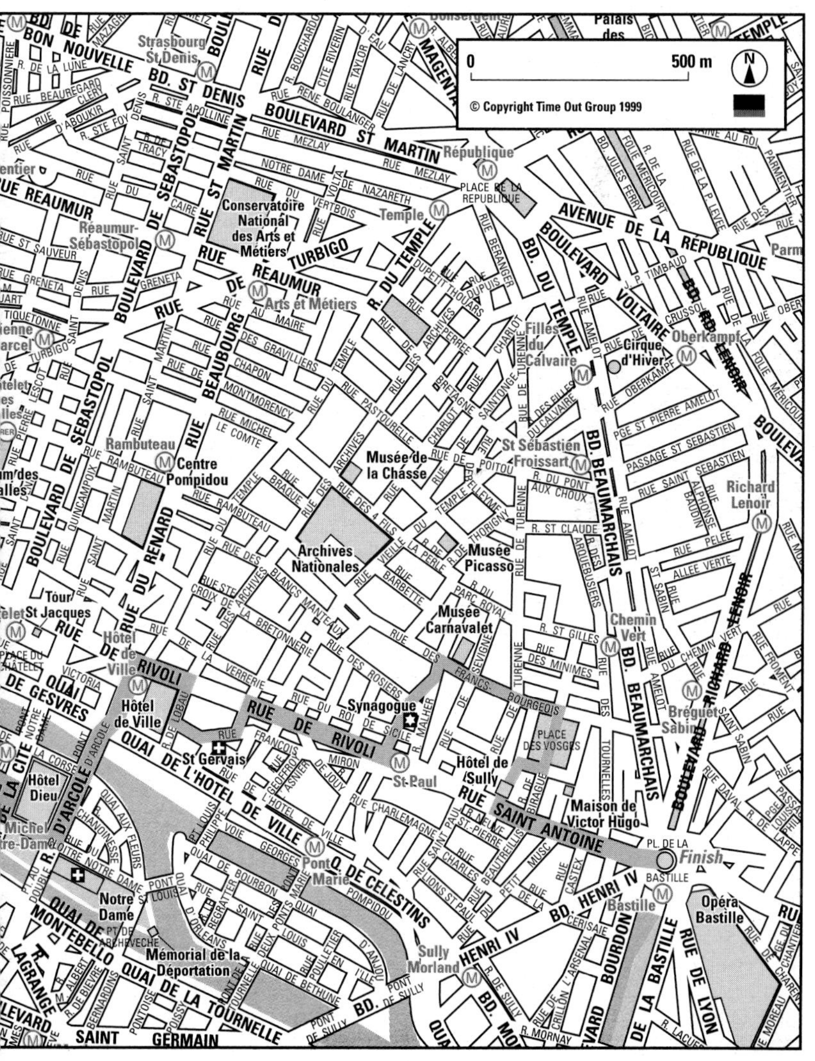

originally called place Louis XV, with an equestrian statue of the Beloved King in its middle, was then declared place de la Révolution, but was eventually renamed place de la Concorde in public tribute to the reconciliation of the French.

On either side of the entrance to the Tuileries, copies of Coysevox's winged allegories of Fame and Mercury and two elegant pavilions welcome you. On the Seine side, the Orangerie Museum is world famous for its two underground rooms displaying Monet's *Nympheas,* while the Jeu de Paume hosts temporary exhibits of modern and contemporary art. As you walk through the Tuileries, spare a thought for Louis XIV's gardener, André Le Nôtre, who designed both the Jardin des Tuileries and the Champs-Elysées as a continuation of the gardens. The *jardins à la Française* show once again the French need for order and symmetry: every flowerbed, every stone vase must have its symmetrical counterpart. The garden could ideally be folded into two. Over the last decade, efforts have been made to bring the gardens back to their original state.

Walk on the left-hand side of the octagonal pond, continue straight ahead in the shade of the horse chestnut trees until, on the left, you see a green column rising in the distance. Walk towards it, and after climbing a few steps, leave the gardens. Cross rue de Rivoli and follow rue Castiglione, passing the British and American Pharmacy on your right, until you reach place Vendôme. Behind this majestic square's elegant façades can be found the Ministry of Justice, a number of famous jewellers and the Ritz hotel. Opened by César Ritz in 1898, the hotel is now owned by Mohammed Al Fayed, and was the starting point for Dodi and Di's ill-fated journey in 1997. The square was part of a seventeenth century urban development project and was devoted to the glory of the Sun King, who was represented riding the then highest statue ever produced in France. Napoléon had the royal statue replaced in 1806 by a symbolic monument recounting his own military exploits, cast in the bronze of the cannons taken from his many enemies. In 1871 the revolutionaries of the Commune tore this column down – only for a replica to be erected three years later. Napoléon stands at the top as if he were Emperor Trajan, whose column in Rome this one so slavishly imitates. Are the French not addicted to Roman culture?

Walk on across place Vendôme and turn right into rue Danielle Casanova, which will lead you to the avenue de l'Opéra. Cross it and continue as the street becomes rue des Petits-Champs – quite a stretch allowing you to see on your left the Bibliothèque Nationale and three of the covered passages that became so popular in the first half of the nineteenth century, most notably Galerie Vivienne. Eventually, you'll reach rue de la Feuillade, leading into place des Victoires. La Feuillade was one of Louis XIV's sycophantic courtiers, who built himself the mansion that now houses the Banque de France.

The Baroque place de la Victoire was designed in 1685 by Hardouin-Mansart to commemorate Louis XIV's victories over Holland. In the middle stood an impressive statue of the Sun King; torches burnt night and day at each corner; the chained enemies decorating the pedestal are now kept in the Louvre. The original statue was melted down during the Revolution; this one's a copy erected in 1822.

Retrace your steps and turn left into rue Vivienne. Through the passage du Perron in front of you, enter a haven of peace in the heart of Paris: the Jardin du Palais-Royal. Harmonious classical arcades dating from the 1750s run around the rectangular space, which has always been a meeting place for collectors, politicians and artists. The blue and white flowerbeds, the sound of water, and the lime trees create a refreshing atmosphere. The Ministry of Culture is housed in the building at the further end, and the garden has become an open-air museum of contemporary sculpture. Temporary exhibitions of French or foreign sculptors are organised and two compositions are on permanent display: under the portico, two fountains house Pol Bury's 1970 aquamobile metallic spheres, and in the open space, formerly a car park, Daniel Buren erected, in the 1980s, his controversial black and white striped columns of varying heights. They have been adopted by children to sit, jump or stand on, while some use magnets to try and catch the coins thrown into the underground stream by visitors.

The Palais-Royal was built by Louis XIII's Chief Minister, Cardinal Richelieu, as his own luxurious residence and was originally known as Palais-Cardinal. Its garden, the largest in Paris at the time, was irrigated by the waters of the Seine. Richelieu cannily donated his property to the future Sun King, then a young child who lived in it for while with his Regent mother before they moved nearby to the safer Louvre. It then took the name of Palais-Royal and was later the residence of Henriette-Maria, the French widow of King Charles I of England and aunt to the young king.

As you leave the garden into place Colette, on your right is the stage-door of the Comédie Française, France's oldest theatre company, founded in 1680 out of Molière's wandering troupe. Turn left into place du Palais-Royal, a favourite haunt of street mimes and acrobats on rollerskates but surrounded with imposing buildings: the Conseil d'Etat, in the Palais-Royal, facing the north wing of the Louvre and, left and right, two Hausmann buildings: the Louvre des Antiquaires and the Grand Hôtel du Louvre.

Cross rue de Rivoli: the passage Richelieu leads through one wing of the Louvre to the Pyramid courtyard. Take a few minutes to peep through the huge windows into the museum. On the right-hand side, you see the two winged steeds

The **Conciergerie** *on the Ile de la Cité, 1st.*

and the two Marly horses of the place de la Concorde; on the left-hand side, the bronze vanquished enemies that used to adorn the pedestal of the statue in place des Victoires. Then walk into the courtyard of the Louvre, with its wonderful view of IM Pei's 1988 glass pyramids. Every time I visit the Louvre, I bless these pyramids and their vast subterranean lobby, which have so greatly improved the museum. (Incidentally, although the French are said to be chauvinistic, note that the majority of the architects to whom the *Grands Travaux* were entrusted by the late President Mitterrand are not French: a Sino-American for the five Louvre glass pyramids, a Canadian for the Bastille Opéra, a Dane for the Grande Arche de la Défense, an Italian for the interior design of the Musée d'Orsay and, before Mitterrand, English and Italian architects worked on the Centre Pompidou.)

Stand with your back to the Pyramid entrance, in front of the bronze cast of a Bernini statue of Louis XIV. Look at the perspective framed by the Carrousel arch, which was ordered by Napoléon to celebrate his victory at Austerlitz – the Tuileries gardens, the obelisk in the place de la Concorde, the Champs-Elysées, the Arc and the Arche stretch away from you. In front, bushes in the middle of the roundabout hide the base of the inverted Pyramid, which brings light to the underground 'Carrousel du Louvre', a shopping precinct and food-court. Looking around, you realise that the

Louvre has a U-shape. It used to be rectangular, with the court closed by the Tuileries Palace. The latter, built in the Renaissance for Catherine de Médicis, the Queen Mother, was burnt down at the same time as the Hôtel de Ville and the Audit Chamber (where the Musée d'Orsay now stands) during the riots of the Commune in 1871. The Tuileries Gardens were first designed for the Queen Mother and later extended by Le Nôtre.

Now might be the perfect time to sip a glass of chilled Chablis on the terrace of Café Marly while watching the waterworks of the seven triangular fountains splashing on the polished slabs of black Brittany marble.

Before leaving for the Crusades with Richard the Lionheart, in about 1200, King Philippe-Auguste built a wall to protect his capital city, which was just starting to develop on the Right Bank: the wall was semicircular, starting and ending on the Seine. Both ends of the Right Bank wall were fortified. On the west side the fortress of the Louvre rose. On the east side the river was guarded by the Bastille fortress. A century later, Charles V built a new wall further out around the still-expanding Right Bank, so that the Louvre and the Bastille were no longer fortresses facing potential enemies, but now stood within the city limits. Charles V had his architect transform Philippe-Auguste's Louvre into a royal residence. Later, the Renaissance King, François I, decided to settle in the Louvre. Used to living in the Loire Valley's pleasant Italianate residences, he did not fancy living in a medieval fortress, so ordered its destruction. He meant to build a Renaissance château on the medieval foundations, but died too soon. His son, Henri II, took up the project but decided to quadruple its size. Nothing of the earlier Louvre can be seen from outside, but extensive archeological digs done at the time of the building of the Pyramid unearthed the medieval foundations: the underground medieval Louvre is really worth a visit (approach through the Pyramid entrance).

As you emerge from the Pyramid court, walk towards the Renaissance façade, right behind the Pyramid. Make your way through the passage and enter the Cour Carrée, the heart of the Louvre. Leave by the St-Germain-l'Auxerrois gate in front of you. When out, turn round to face the eastern façade, once the entrance to the palace and a superb classical colonnade built for Louis XIV. Bernini had been invited to Paris to design it but the extremely classical and symmetrical ideas of Perrault were preferred to Bernini's heavy Baroque. By the time the colonnade was completed, Louis XIV had lost interest in the Louvre and was busy extending Versailles. The palace was then inhabited by artists under royal patronage. Louis XVI was forced by the revolutionaries to return to the Louvre before his arrest and execution; Napoléon I and the restored Kings afterwards lived in the Louvre, including Napoléon III. If most of his predecessors made additions and alterations, the Louvre, as we see it today, owes a lot to Napoléon III, who added the Cour Napoléon.

Although Louis XV and Louis XVI considered opening a museum within the palace, it was the revolutionaries who finally opened the museum in 1793. In time, the royal collections were enlarged by purchase and, lawfully but not always legitimately, by confiscation and conquest. Now the Louvre proudly exhibits the best of its more than 30,000 works of art in seven departments, covering the whole history of art from ancient times to 1848. The more modern works are to be seen at the Musée d'Orsay just across the river, and at the Centre Pompidou just east of here.

You are standing in place du Louvre, designed in 1853 so that the colonnade would stand out. Opposite the Louvre, two buildings look very similar. On the river side, the Gothic St-Germain-l'Auxerrois church used to be the parish

Hector Guimard's art nouveau **Métro Cité**.

church of the Royal Palace where the kings attended mass. Many of the artists who lived in the Louvre are buried inside. The porch is a fine example of flamboyant gothic. In the nineteenth century Baron Haussmann, the prefect of Paris, asked the architect Hittorf to build the town hall for the first arrondissement in a style similar to that of St-Germain. A belfry was added later at the junction of the two buidings. Parisians call the whole structure 'the oil and vinegar cruet'.

Walk towards the Seine, turning left along quai du Louvre. Look at the western extremity of the Ile de la Cité across the river. It honours the memory of Henri IV, the 'Vert Galant', whose love for women has become a myth. His equestrian statue faces place Dauphine, built of white stones and red bricks similar to those in place des Vosges, which we'll come to later. Further on, between Pont Neuf and Pont au Change, the Palais de Justice was built on the site of the first residence of the Kings of France. The three medieval towers remind us of the Conciergerie, once the entrance to the palace, later a prison where Queen Marie Antoinette was separated from her family and held before her execution.

Continue along quai de la Mégisserie, one of the oldest quais in Paris. Gardening has recently become a Parisian passion. The shops along the quai sell everything you need to transform your window sill, tiny balcony or luxury terrace into a green paradise. Next, gaze at the *bouquinistes* across the street. They are a tradition dating from the seventeenth century. The city authorities regulate their number as well as the shape, colour and location of the boxes. On Sunday afternoons, the road you can see below by the side of the river is closed to car traffic, alowing cyclists or rollerbladers a Sunday treat. Bicycles are available for hire near the place du Châtelet.

As you reach the Pont au Change, named after the bankers who traded on it, have a look at place du Châtelet to your left. Its name derives from a small defensive fortress that protected the routes on to the island. The column in the middle celebrates Napoléon I's victories: the palm-tree shape of the column and the sphinxes spitting out water remind us of Bonaparte's Egyptian odyssey. East and west of the square, facing each other, two theatres were built at the time of Napoléon III. On the left, Châtelet, Théâtre Musical de Paris, has made a powerful comeback in recent years. Opposite, the Théâtre de la Ville is more important as a contemporary dance venue. It used to be named after Sarah Bernhardt, one of its famous managers when it was devoted to drama. The splendid Gothic Tour St-Jacques rises behind.

Leaving the Right Bank, walk across the river and set foot on the Ile de la Cité. The cradle of Paris, once called Lutétia, was the seat of the two powers, lay and spiritual: the Royal Palace, where the kings lived until they moved into the Louvre; and Notre-Dame. Baron

Despite appearances, you may actually visit the **Palais de Justice**, *the city's law courts.*

Haussmann, asked by Napoléon III to modernise Paris, razed the bulk of the medieval buildings on the island, except the cathedral and what was left of the Palace, the Conciergerie, Ste-Chapelle, and some small streets at the north-eastern end.

The first building you come to is the Conciergerie. It boasts the largest gothic civilian hall in Europe and several moving mementoes of the victims of the Revolutionary Terror. The entrance is from the quai de l'Horloge.

Behind the glorious classical railings along the boulevard du Palais lies the Palais de Justice – the Law Courts. Once in the courtyard, members of the public are free to climb the majestic steps and enter a courtroom to watch the proceedings. Do not mistake the *gendarmes* for policemen. The *gendarmes* are accountable to the Ministry of Defence and are soldiers, responsible for law and order over all French territory except where a national or municipal police force is operating. In Paris, where there is a national police force, they are in charge of the protection of state and government offices.They can be recognised by their *képi* (a hat with a horizontal peak).

The highlight of your walk, however, is likely to be Ste-Chapelle. This Gothic marvel was built in the thirteenth century as a shrine for the relics (mainly Christ's Crown of Thorns) bought by Louis IX, known as St-Louis. This is why it can bear the title of 'Ste-Chapelle'. The Crown of Thorns is now kept in the Treasury of Notre-Dame. The Ste-Chapelle is also a 'palatine' chapel, a chapel within a royal palace, which means that it has two levels – one for the royals and their closer associates and another below for the rest of the court.

Climb the 33-step spiral staircase and have your breath taken away: the light coming through the windows will transport you into Heavenly Jerusalem. The paintings were heavily restored in the nineteenth century but they are a reminder that churches and chapels used to be lavishly painted. The twelfth-century windows, mainly blue and red with small figures on a geometric pattern, depict Biblical tales and are very different from the fourteenth-century flaming rose window over the entrance, where green and grey dominate.

Leaving Ste-Chapelle, walk across the street, into the square to the left that hosts a flower market and an original art nouveau Métro entrance by Guimard. On your right is the Préfecture de Police; the policemen are the responsibility of the Ministry of the Interior and they wear a flat *casquette* (cap). On the wall, just before you turn to the right, there's a plaque in memory of a victim of the Liberation of Paris in August 1944. Many such plaques can be seen all over Paris.

As we walk towards Notre-Dame, the lines on the ground of the large parvis in front of the cathedral show the medieval streetplan, which can be seen in the Crypte Archéologique below. Also on the ground there's a brass star marking Kilomètre Zéro for all distances between Paris and other cities. If you wish to come back to Paris, rub it with your left foot...

The powerful gothic façade of the cathedral should be read carefully: it tells many stories. The central tympanum depicts the Last Judgement – look up at Michael, the Archangel, weighing up your deeds before sending you to Paradise or Hell. The right tympanum tells the life of the Virgin Mary and the left one her coronation. Let your eyes drift upwards, reaching the gallery of the Kings of Judaea, ancestors of the Virgin Mary and Christ. The statues were beheaded by the revolutionary mobs, who mistook them for Kings of France, although the heads were later found during archaeological digs on the Right Bank and can be seen in the Musée Cluny. Higher up still, the Virgin Mary stands in the centre of the rose window, and beyond rise the towers and their nineteenth-century gargoyles. You can climb the towers – look out for Quasimodo or Esmeralda up there...

Since the completion of Notre-Dame in 1345, many royal ceremonies have taken place there – weddings, funerals and coronations. During the Revolution, the cathedral was used as a temple of reason and a wine warehouse, and only returned to its traditional role for Napoléon's self-coronation as Emperor in 1804.

Less well known is the Mémorial de Déportation at the eastern end of the island, behind the chevet of Notre-Dame. This poignant and highly symbolic memorial has been built in remembrance of all the French who died in the concentration camps during World War II.

Leave the island by Pont d'Arcole from where you can see the brightly coloured pipes of the Centre Pompidou. You are back on the Right Bank. Use the pedestrian subway to reach place de l'Hôtel-de-Ville. In vote-catching mode, the authorities seem happy to lay on a load of free activities here, the most popular being ice-skating in the winter.

As mentioned earlier, the Hôtel de Ville was burnt down by the Commune in 1870 and then rebuilt in a similar style but on a larger scale. Each of the 20 arrondissements of Paris has a *mairie*, (town hall), but this is the one Hôtel de Ville of Paris. The position of Mayor of Paris is now sought by many politicians, ever since Jacques Chirac made it a stepping stone to the presidency. Walk to the right round the Hôtel de Ville, passing the statue of Etienne Marcel, a famous medieval *prévôt* (a forerunner to mayor) who led a rebellion against Charles V in the fourteenth century.

You'll reach place St-Gervais below the classical façade of St-Gervais-St-Protais church. You are entering the St-Paul neighbourhood, part of the Marais district. An elm tree has always stood in front of the church, as St-Gervais was known to have heard cases and decided them under an elm. It became a meeting place for Parisians, especially lenders and borrowers who wanted to settle their accounts. The present tree was planted in 1914.

Before continuing on the left side of the

church along rue François-Miron, note, on the right of the church, the house of the *Compagnons du devoir*, who continue the tradition of a medieval guild of cathedral builders and devote themselves to the training of young craftsmen.

Cross place Baudoyer diagonally past the 4th arrondissement *mairie* to rue de Rivoli. Turn right and walk until you reach the St-Paul Métro station, then turn left into rue Pavée. You will soon pass, on your right, the façade of an art nouveau synagogue by Guimard (whose wife was an American Jew). Continue until you reach rue des Francs-Bourgeois, the high street of the Marais.

A strong movement for the restoration of the Marais started in the 1970s. Now the Marais has recovered its unique and multifaceted charm. Narrow streets run through different neighbourhoods: antique-dealers' shops, jewellers' boutiques, kosher stores, gay bars, trendy boutiques, cosy tearooms, art galleries. Every corner holds a surprise.

Many lavish and elegant mansions were built in the seventeenth and eighteenth centuries in this area, most of them with secluded courtyards and gardens. The majority are privately owned, but some have become museums. The fascinating Musée Carnavalet at the corner of rue Pavée and rue des Francs-Bourgeois is devoted to the history of Paris. Others include the Musée National Picasso, the Musée Cognaq-Jay – with a collection of French and English eighteenth-century art – and the newly opened Musée d'Arts et d'Histoire du Judaïsme.

The rue des Francs-Bourgeois leads to elegant, symmetrical place des Vosges, with its pink bricks, white limestone and dark blue slate roofs. Sit down on a bench near the fountains in the shade of the plane trees and examine the scene. The harmonious square owes its existence to a sad event. Here stood the Hôtel des Tournelles where the court used to stay. In June 1559, Henri II and his court were celebrating the betrothal of the King's sister. The King took part in a tournament and was wounded in the eye; he died after ten days of agony. His wife, Catherine de Médicis, decided to demolish the royal residence completely and replace it with something more Italian. The square was inaugurated in 1612 by Henri IV and the statue in the middle is that of his son, Louis XIII. The area became fashionable and many mansions were built until Louis XIV withdrew to Versailles with his court. During the Revolution, the royal statue disappeared, and in 1800 First Consul Bonaparte renamed the square place des Vosges in tribute to the citizens of the *département* of Vosges who were the first to pay their income tax.

If you have some energy left, visit the Maison de Victor Hugo in the south-east corner and look at the square from the second-floor windows.

Leave the square by a passage in the south-west corner in order to enjoy fully a perfect example of a Marais mansion, the Hôtel de Sully. Walk through the garden to the elegantly carved front yard. Today the mansion houses the National Foundation for Historic Buildings, with its 'Librairie du Patrimoine'.

On leaving Hôtel de Sully, you find yourself back in rue de Rivoli. Turn left towards Bastille Métro in place de la Bastille. Here are the new Bastille Opéra and a noble column commemorating yet another Revolution (1830) with its lovely gilded '*génie*' at the top. The lines of stone on the ground mark the walls of the medieval fortress that was stormed by the revolutionaries on July 1789, releasing prisoners, but more importantly providing gunpowder for the rebels.

On 14 July 1789, the symbolic start of the Revolution, Louis XVI entered only one word in his diary: 'Nothing' – something to ponder at the end of this Royal Walk.

During the Revolution, **Notre-Dame** *was used as a wine warehouse; now it's business as usual (with added tourists).*

Rioters burned down the **Hôtel de Ville** in 1870, but it came back even bigger than before.

Eating & drinking

L'Ambroisie

9 place des Vosges, 4th (01.42.78.51.45). **Open** noon-1.30pm, 8-9.30pm, Tue-Sat. Closed two weeks in Feb, Mar, three weeks in Aug. Luxury dishes in sumptuous surroundings, but the bill is somehow more memorable.

Aux Bons Crus

7 rue des Petits-Champs, 1st (01.42.60.06.45). **Open** 11am-5pm Mon; 11am-10pm Tue-Sat. Closed three weeks in Aug. Amiable little bar with indifferent food.

Café Marly

93 rue de Rivoli, cour Napoléon du Louvre, 1st (01.49.26.06.60). **Open** 8am-2am daily. Modish spins on brasserie fare, overlooking the Louvre's Pyramid.

Café de Vendôme

1 place Vendôme, 1st (01.55.04.55.55). **Open** noon-3pm, 7.30-11pm, daily. Thought and creativity given to classic French cooking.

Café Very

Jardins des Tuileries, 1st (01.47.03.94.84). **Open** noon-10.30pm daily. Decent food, stylish interior and a unique location.

Ma Bourgogne

19 place des Vosges, 4th (01.42.78.44.64). **Open** noon-1am daily. Closed Feb. Of course, it's a tourist trap, but it has an enviable location and some enjoyable but basic bistro fare.

Macéo

15 rue des Petits-Champs, 1st (01.42.96.98.89). **Open** noon-2.30pm, 7-11pm, Mon-Sat. Fine contemporary cuisine, overlooking the Palais-Royal.

Miravile

72 quai de l'Hôtel-de-Ville, 4th (01.42.74.72.22). **Open** noon-2.30pm, 7.30-10.30pm, Tue-Fri; 7.30-10.30pm Mon, Sat. Closed ten days in Aug. A contemporary slant to French cuisine.

Le Trumilou

84 quai de l'Hôtel-de-Ville, 4th (01.42.77.63.98). **Open** noon-3pm, 7-11pm, Mon-Sat; noon-3pm, 7-10.30pm, Sun. Popular with anglophone expats.

Le Vieux Bistro

14 rue du Cloître-Notre-Dame, 4th (01.43.54.18.95). **Open** noon-2pm, 7.30-11pm, daily. Perfect renditions of classic French cuisine.

Accommodation

Hôtel de Crillon

10 place de la Concorde, 8th (01.44.71.15.00).

Hôtel Ritz

15 place Vendôme, 1st (01.43.16.30.30).

Museums & monuments

Arc de Triomphe

place Charles-de-Gaulle (access via underground passage), 8th (01.43.80.31.31). **Open** *Apr-Oct*

9.30am-11pm daily; *Nov-Mar* 10am-10.30pm daily. Closed public holidays. **Admission** 40F; 32F concs.

Cathédrale Notre-Dame de Paris
place du Parvis-Notre-Dame, 4th (01.42.34.56.10). **Open** 8am-6.45 daily. **Admission** free. *Towers* (01.44.32.16.70) entrance at foot of north tower. **Open** 10am-4.30pm daily. **Admission** 35F; 25F concs.

Centre Pompidou
rue Beaubourg, 4th (01.44.78.12.33). **Open** noon-10pm Mon, Wed-Fri; 10am-10pm Sat, Sun. **Admission** temporary exhibitions fee varies.

La Conciergerie
1 quai de l'Horloge, 1st (01.53.73.78.50). **Open** *Apr-Oct* 9.30am-6.30pm daily; *Nov-Mar* 10am-5pm daily. **Admission** 35F; 23F concs; 50F combined ticket with Ste-Chapelle.

La Crypte Archéologique
place du Parvis-Notre-Dame, 4th (01.43.29.83.51). **Open** *Apr-Oct* 10am-5.30pm daily; *Nov-Mar* 10am-4.30pm daily. **Admission** 32F; 21F concs.

Hôtel de Sully
62 rue St-Antoine, 4th (01.44.61.20.00). **Open** *courtyards* 8am-6.30pm daily.

Hôtel de Ville
place de l'Hôtel-de-Ville, 4th (switchboard 01.42.76.40.40; reservations 01.42.76.50.49). **Open** *groups* make reservation 2 months in advance; *individuals* first Mon in every month following reservation made one month in advance.

Les Invalides
esplanade des Invalides, 7th (01.44.42.54.52/Musée de l'Armée 01.44.42.37.67). **Open** *Apr-Sept* 10am-6pm daily; *Oct-Mar* 10am-5pm daily. **Admission** 37F; 27F concs.

Jardins du Palais-Royal
main entrance to palace place du Palais-Royal, 1st. **Open** *Gardens only* dawn-dusk daily.

Jeu de Paume
1 place de la Concorde, 1st (01.47.03.12.50). **Open** noon-9.30pm Tue; noon-7pm Wed-Fri; 10am-7pm Sat, Sun. **Admission** 38F; 28F concs.

Le Louvre
entrance through Pyramid, cour Napoléon, 1st (01.40.20.50.50/recorded information 01.40.20.51.51/ advance booking 01.49.87.54.54). **Open** 9am-6pm Mon, Thur-Sun; 9am-9.45pm Wed; *temporary exhibitions, Medieval Louvre, bookshop* 10am-9.45pm Mon, Wed-Sun. **Admission** 45F (until 3pm); 26F (after 3pm and Sun) concs.

Maison de Victor Hugo
Hôtel de Rohan-Guéménée, 6 place des Vosges, 4th (01.42.72.10.16). **Open** 10am-5.40pm Tue-Sun. **Admission** 17.50F; 9F concs.

Mémorial de la Déportation
square de l'Ile-de-France, 4th (no phone). **Open** 10am-noon, 2-5pm, daily.

Musée Carnavalet
23 rue de Sévigné, 3rd (01.42.72.21.13). **Open** 10am-5.40pm Tue-Sun. **Admission** 27F; 14.50F concs.

Musée Cognac-Jay
Hôtel Donon, 8 rue Elzévir, 3rd (01.40.27.07.21). **Open** 10am-5.40pm Tue-Sun. **Admission** 17.50F; 9F concs.

Musée d'Arts et d'Histoire du Judaïsme
Hôtel de St-Aignan, 71 rue du Temple, 3rd (01.53.01.86.53). **Open** 11am-6pm Mon-Fri; 10am-6pm Sun. Closed Jewish holidays.

Musée National Picasso
Hôtel Salé, 5 rue de Thorigny, 3rd (01.42.71.25.21). **Open** 9.30am-5.30pm Mon, Wed-Sun. **Admission** 30F; 20F concs.

Musée de l'Orangerie
Jardins des Tuileries, 1st (01.42.97.48.16). **Open** *May-Aug* 9.45am-5.15pm Mon, Wed-Sun. **Admission** 30F; 20F concs. Closed until end 2001.

Musée d'Orsay
62 rue de Lille, 7th (01.40.49.48.14/recorded information 01.45.49.11.11). **Open** 10am-6pm Tue, Wed, Fri, Sat; 10am-9.30pm Thur; 9am-6pm Sun. **Admission** 40F; 30F concs.

Ste-Chapelle & Palais de Justice
4 boulevard du Palais, 1st (01.53.73.78.50). **Open** *Apr-Sept* 9.30am-6.30pm daily; *Oct-Mar* 10am-5pm daily. **Admission** 35F; 23F concs; 50F combined ticket with Conciergerie.

Château de Versailles
20km from Paris by A13 or D10. RER C to Versailles-Rive Gauche. Further information (01.30.84.74.00).

Other

Bibliothèque Nationale Richelieu
58 rue de Richelieu, 2nd (01.47.03.81.26). **Open** *Galerie Mansart/Mazarine* 10am-7pm Tue-Sun. *Cabinet des Médailles* 1-5pm Mon-Sat; noon-6pm Sun. **Admission** *Galerie Mansart/Mazarine* 35F; 24F concs. *Cabinet des Médailles* 22F; 15F concs.

Flower Market
place Louis Lépine, 4th (no phone). **Open** 9.30am-6.30pm Mon-Sat.

Tour St-Jacques
place du Châtelet, 4th. Closed to the public.

Politics

Assemblée Nationale

33 quai d'Orsay, 7th (01.40.63.60.00). **Open** *guided tours* 10am, 2pm, 3pm, Sat when Chamber not in session; ID required; arrive early.

Conseil d'Etat

1 place Palais-Royal, 1st (01.40.20.80.00).

Ministère de la Culture

3 rue de Valois, 1st (01.40.15.80.00).

Ministère de la Justice

13 place Vendôme, 1st (01.44.77.60.60).

Religion

Eglise St-Germain-l'Auxerrois

2 place du Louvre, 1st (01.42.60.13.96). **Open** 8am-8pm daily.

Eglise St-Gervais-St-Protais

place St-Gervais/rue des Barres, 4th (01.48.87.32.02). **Open** 5am-10pm daily.

Eglise de la Marie-Madeleine

place de la Madeleine, 8th (01.44.51.69.00). **Open** 7.30am-7pm Mon-Sat; 9am-1pm, 3.30-7pm, Sun.

Synagogue

13 rue Pavée, 4th (no phone).

Shopping

British & American Pharmacy

6 rue de Castiglione, 1st (01.42.60.72.96). **Open** 8.30am-7.30pm Mon-Fri; 9am-7pm Sat.

Hôtel du Louvre

place André-Malraux, 1st (01.44.58.38.38).

Louvre des Antiquaries

2 place du Palais-Royal, 1st (01.42.97.27.00). **Open** 11am-7pm Tue-Sun.

Theatres

Comédie Française

Salle Richelieu, 2 rue de Richelieu, 1st (01.44.58.15.15). **Box office** 11am-6pm daily. **Tickets** 70F-190F; 65F concs; 30F limited visibility.

Opéra National de Paris Bastille

place de la Bastille, 12th (08.36.69.78.68). **Open** *box office* 130 rue de Lyon 11am-6.30pm Mon-Sat. *Guided visits (01.40.01.19.70).*

Théâtre Musical de Paris

1 place du Châtelet, 1st (01.40.28.28.40/recorded info 01.42.33.00.00). **Box office** 11am-7pm daily; *phone bookings* 10am-7pm Mon-Sat. **Tickets** phone for details.

Théâtre de la Ville

2 place du Châtelet, 4th (01.42.74.22.77). **Box office** 11am-7pm Mon; 11am-8pm Tue-Sat; *telephone bookings* 11am-7pm Mon-Sat. **Tickets** 95F-190F; half-price on day of performance, concs.

Chronology of rule

Louis VII	1137-1180
Philippe II, Auguste	1180-1223
Louis VIII	1223-1226
Louis IX, 'St-Louis'	1226-1270
Philippe III	1270-1285
Philippe IV	1285-1314
Louis X	1314-1316
Jean I	1316
Philippe V	1316-1322
Charles IV	1322-1328
Philippe VI	1328-1350
Jean II	1350-1364
Charles V	1364-1380
Charles VI	1380-1422
English Rule	1420-1436
Charles VII	1422-1461
Louis XI	1461-1483
Charles VIII	1483-1498
Louis XII	1498-1515
François I	1515-1547
Henri II	1547-1559
François II	1559-1560
Charles IX	1560-1574
Henri III	1574-1589
Henri IV	1589-1610
Louis XIII	1610-1643
Louis XIV, 'the Sun King'	1643-1715
Louis XV	1715-1774
Louis XVI	1774-1793
Republic	1792-1798
Napoléon Bonaparte (Consul)	1799-1804
Napoléon I (Emperor)	1804-1814
Louis XVIII	1814
Napoléon I (Emperor)	1815
Louis XVIII	1815-1824
Charles X	1824-1830
Louis-Philippe	1830-1848
Second Republic	1848-1851
Napoléon III	1852-1870
Commune	1870-1871
Third Republic	1871-1939
Fourth Republic	1947-1958
Fifth Republic	1958-

Hôtel de Sully *is a perfect example of a Marais mansion, complete with exquisite statuary.*

Untouched spaces

Christopher Kenworthy

Tapping into the memories of the city via the Latin Quarter.

Start: Mº St Placide, 6th
Finish: Eglise St-Julien-le-Pauvre, 5th
Time: 2-3 hours
Distance: 5km/3 miles
Getting there: line 4 to Mº St-Placide
Getting back: five-minute walk to Mº St-Michel (line 4), Mº Cluny-La Sorbonne (line 10) or Mº St-Michel-Notre-Dame (lines 4, 10, RER B).
Note: opening times of the parks.

I've never believed in past lives, but I keep thinking I used to live in Paris. I even tell people I've lived there, which is a total lie, but I can't stop myself because it feels like the truth. My memories of Paris go back much further than my experience of the place. I found my way around Paris in days, whereas I remain lost in other cities and towns having lived in them for years. I can't speak French until I arrive in the city, and then it becomes fairly easy. There's no definitive explanation for these effects, but I believe there are places in Paris that exude memory.

This walk takes you to a few of the more potent locations. In recent years I've become interested in the idea that places trigger states and provide access to emotions. In Paris there are untouched spaces, locations where some act of melancholy or perception of beauty has stained the place so deeply it never leaves. I could be wrong, but I believe it's impossible to pass through the places on this walk without being moved.

All the locations on this walk have inspired my work in some way. Characters, images, situations and ideas can all arise from the impressions of a space. In Paris there are many rivers of thought and people's memories that can be tapped simply by being present. When people ask me where I get my ideas, I now say 'Paris'. It's best to be here in autumn, just after the fashion freaks leave and everything calms down again. There's more clear light and less rain than at any other time of year; the ideal conditions for tapping the memories of the city.

The walk begins at the St-Placide Métro for no other reason than the pleasure of approaching the Jardin du Luxembourg from the west. From the Métro head south down rue Notre-Dame-des-Champs for a few moments, until there's a left turn on to rue du Fleurus. Even if other walks or frequent trips take you to the Jardin, come to it from this direction for a change.

Cross straight over rue Guynemer, and take the first entrance directly into the Jardin du Luxembourg. Follow the path straight ahead. In the trees to your right, strangely blurred and always a bit distant, is a children's playground that either seems to be abandoned or frothing with activity. I put that down to school hours, rather than anything paranormal. Close to this is a wooden shack that passes as a café. This is the first untouched space. Inside, orange table lamps cast pools of light on the dark wooden tables, making the air outside seem dim and blue, whatever the weather. You're free to go inside, but the best sensation comes from standing close to the west window and looking in. I've found myself remembering many occasions when I've been inside, even

Spaces in the **Jardin du Luxembourg** *may contain the potential for alternative realities.*

though I've never actually crossed the threshold. I've taken other people to this place, and they've had a similar experience. It was this feeling – that a place could offer alternative realities – that was the inspiration for one of my Paris stories, *The Mathematics of the Night*. This café will always be a receptacle of *ennui*.

Now carry on in the same direction, weaving around the ornamental pool in the centre of the garden. It was in this area that the young Simone de Beauvoir used to play with her black hoop, alone; her mother wouldn't let her talk to other children. The French Senate is housed to your left, in the Palais du Luxembourg, courtesy of the Revolution. It was built in the 1620s for Marie de Médicis, Henri IV's widow. They knocked down the Duke of Luxembourg's mansion to make way for the Palais, hoping the new building would be more evocative of Marie's native Florence. Marie was soon exiled to Cologne, and the Palais was recovered by the state, so that, despite its architectural origins, it is now seen as an essentially French building.

Nearby is a charming toilet. You'll find it by the eastern wall of the Jardin, close to the Ecole des Mines. It looks like a door into the wall, but provides a superb experience: scented toilet paper, polite service and even moisturiser. Head to the East Gate, and you'll see some of the most amusing entertainment, in the form of joggers. They're especially abundant on weekend mornings, when they effectively queue around the Jardin, because they all take the exact same route. Only in Paris will you see joggers smoking as they plod around. They take sports fashion to a new level, forgoing Lycra for apparel that looks more like eveningwear. I once saw a woman replete with bangles, earrings, a sort of black dress and a headband, which represented her best attempt to look sporty. She jogged so slowly, in tiny mincing steps, that her boyfriend (dressed like a private detective in a long coat) could keep up with her simply by ambling.

Move on from the jogging path, and cross over boulevard St-Michel, noting that the road has been metalled. The cobbles were peeled up and lobbed during the student riots of 1968, so it was deemed necessary to make the streets weapon free. Perhaps I saw footage of this when I was young, or read about it, but when I first came to Paris, I headed straight for this road, and found it oddly familiar.

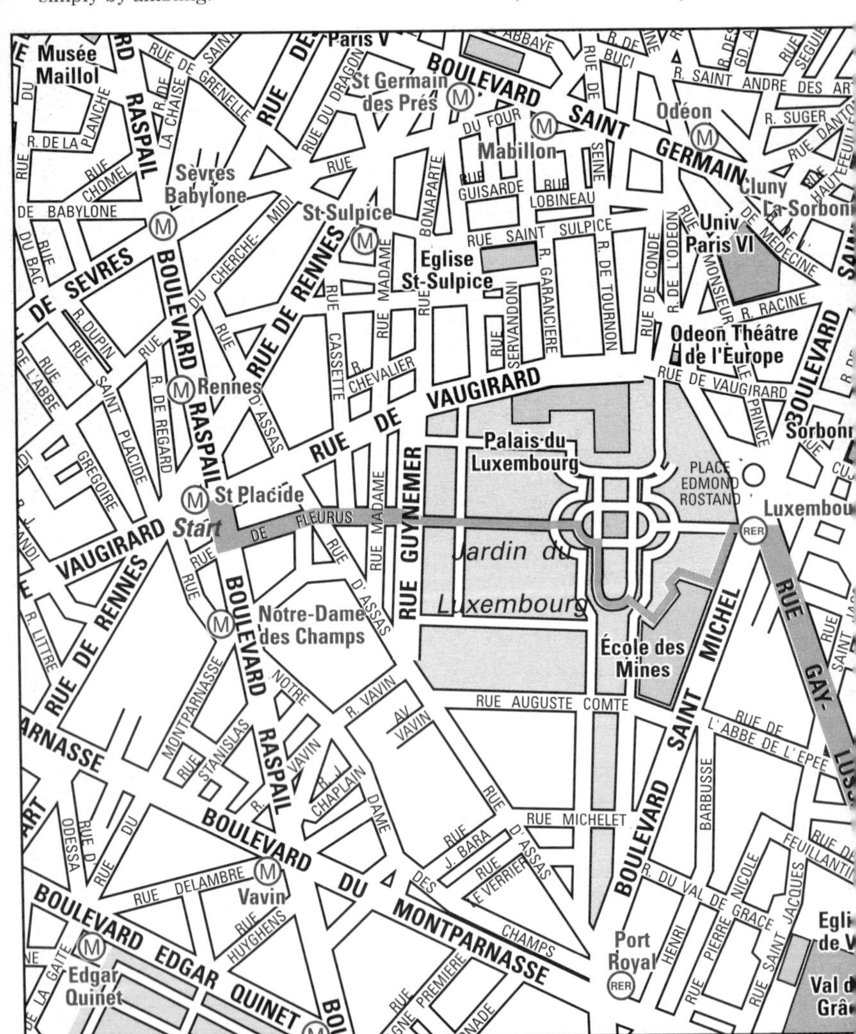

Turn right down rue Gay-Lussac. There was once a hotel down this street which was a 1960s hang out for illegal immigrants, long-stay tourists and a few of those planning the riots. The balconies provided great views of the missile-throwing, and the windows were broken on more than one occasion. It's generally peaceful here, but easy to imagine it riotous. Standing on this street in 1995, I first obtained clear memories of the city's past. I was trying to eavesdrop on a conversation being held by a group of Jewish people, who had gathered on the pavement. Rabin had been assassinated, and something had to be done. Perhaps it was their sense of panic that made me pick up on the events that had occurred there decades before. Now, whenever I stand in here, I'm reminded not of the

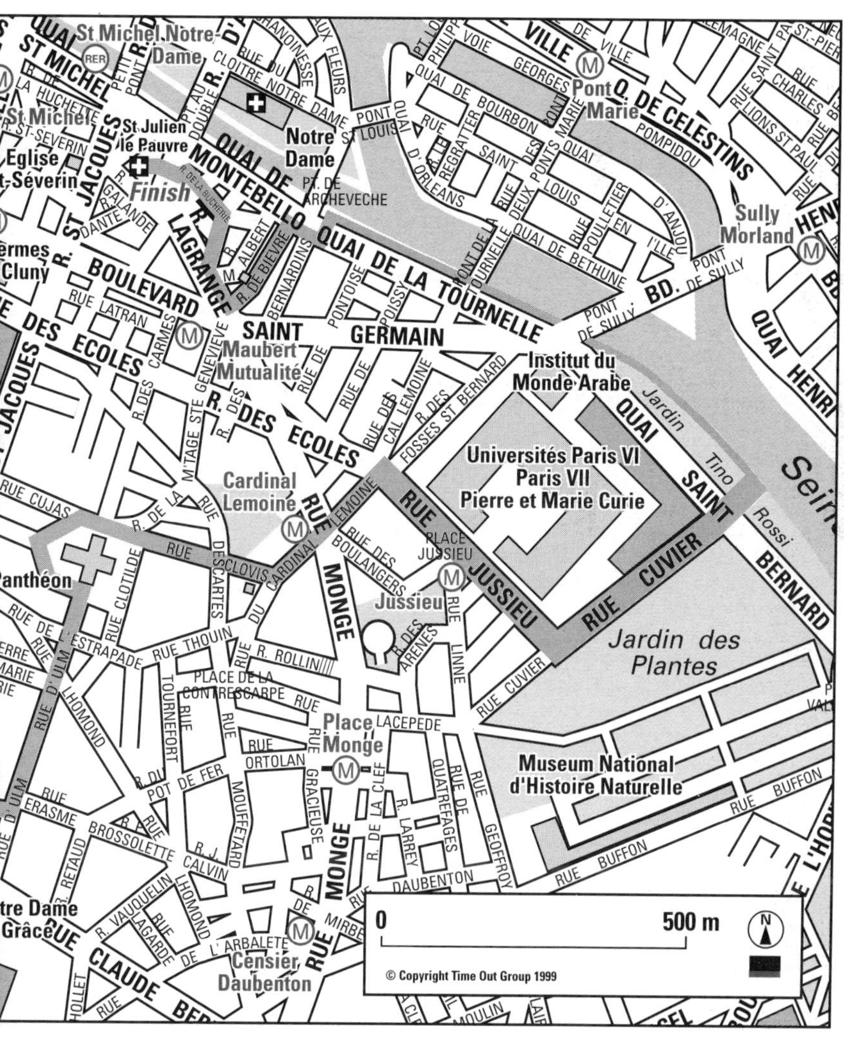

assassination, but of people fleeing, vans appearing from side roads, and of smoke.

Further on, turn left down rue Louis-Thuillier, then left again on to rue d'Ulm and head towards the Panthéon. This is the best street in Paris from which to approach the Panthéon, because you get a sense of the building's size, rather than just a glimpse of the dome. The designer, Soufflot, died of stress before it was completed; one pillar had already collapsed, and he feared the rest would go. His pupil had to patch the thing up with extra walls and pilasters. Originally built at the behest of Louis XV as a commemorative church to Ste-Geneviève, the Panthéon was seized by revolutionaries, who converted it into a necropolis for 'great Frenchmen'. A whole list of subsequent rulers, including Napoléon, changed its use, and it even spent some time as the headquarters of the Paris Commune. In 1885 it was finally declared a national necropolis, when Victor Hugo was interred there.

Sneak around the back to the unusually cool shadows. This is another place to pause and enjoy the sense of space. It's one of those rare locations where you feel as if you're inside a building, even though you're outside. I've never been able to pick up images here, or any sense of story, but there is a strong feeling of sadness, and one that comes from a group of people, rather than an individual.

Head down rue Clovis, where you'll find a remaining stretch of Philippe Auguste's 33-foot-high wall, which was meant to show the boundary of the thirteenth-century city. Surprisingly, it remained valid for 150 years, but then the city felt the need to sprawl and deconstruction began, leaving the section you can see here (and another by St Paul's church in the 4th arrondissement). Then left up Cardinal-Lemoine, and right on to rue Jussieu. Passing the glassy university buildings, you get to see the best dressed students in the world. You can still tell they're students, but they look so much pleasanter than your average Warwick University undergraduate. At the end, turn left down rue Cuvier. The whole of this road is an untouched space. Walk on the side of the road closest to the Jardin des Plantes.

This street is always deserted, filled only with badly parked cars. It's quiet down here, though you can hear the rumble of the city in the distance. I wrote about this street long before I'd ever walked down it. Somehow I'd managed to reach my late twenties before I found out the events in Joyce's *Ulysses* are plotted in a circle around Dublin. Impressed by this, and writing a story about circularity, I thought a ring through Paris was required. For this to work I had to write about rue Cuvier without knowing what it could be like. I described the street as accurately as I could imagine, and was pleased to walk down it a year later and find it was exactly as it should have been: in the middle of Paris, but empty.

At the end of the road, turn left on to the gorgeous quai St-Bernard, glimpsing the Seine. It stinks of traffic and fumes here, and it's murder to cross the road, but down by the river you'll find the Musée de Sculpture en Plein Air in the Jardin Tino Rossi, a grassy bankside garden, overflowing with sculptures. You're a couple of minutes' walk from the exact centre of Paris (marked by a steel plaque in front of Notre-Dame), but there are few locations in the city as peaceful as this park. By the time you reach Pont de Sully, you'll see the Institut du Monde Arabe. This was one of Mitterrand's *Grands Projets*, opened in 1987 to further French understanding of the Arab world. Sadly, Jean Nouvel created a building that looks unapproachable, bringing to mind unsettling clichés of boardrooms and oil deals. Within, however, the building feels gracefully calm. People come here to talk, study and to soak up the atmosphere,

Only by approaching **Le Panthéon** *from rue d'Ulm will you get a proper idea of the building's vast size.*

The **Jardin de la rue de Bièvre** *– a lingering sense of relief and 'memories of two people'.*

which may do more to broaden understanding of the Arab world than the information videos and booklets.

Whatever your exact route from rue Cuvier to Pont de Sully, cross the road by the time you reach the bridge, and head down the steps to river level and walk towards the archway beneath Pont de la Tournelle. As you pass beneath the arch, you will see the most beautiful view of Notre-Dame. Despite being a few moments from the tourist hub, there are rarely many people here. If this place feels familiar, it's because it is. In the past few years it has been used as the main location in *Highlander: The Series*, where the likes of Roger Daltry and that bloke from Fine Young Cannibals have clashed sabres. Tournelle was also used for the finale of *Les Misérables* and for the dance sequence in Woody Allen's *Everybody Says I Love You*. It even crops up in the occasional soft porn film and countless advertisements. It must be easy to get a licence to film here. There's also a dog-beating man who wanders around here. He's massive and bald, with a sleek grey dog, which he kicks whenever it annoys him. He's there so frequently you can spot him in the background during several episodes of *Highlander*. I thought I heard the dog answer him back once, in English, which was the inspiration for another Paris story, *The Wishbone Bag*.

My obsession with this place may have come from sensing the future, rather than the past. In 1996 I went to Paris with a lover. I took her to my favourite place and we were silent there. I'd never been happier, so it's possible that in all those previous years Tournelle felt special because my future was bleeding back into the moment. A friend insists that I like it because *Highlander* was filmed there and I have this thing about swords, but maybe

One of Mitterrand's Grands Projets, *the* **Institut du Monde Arabe** *has furthered French understanding of the Arab world.*

if you spend some time here, you'll catch the sense of what I left behind.

Walk along the Seine as far as Pont de l'Archevêché, and take the steps back up to street level. Cross over quai de la Tournelle, and head right until you find rue de Bièvre. This is more of an interstice between buildings than a road, but part way down, the buildings back away, revealing the Jardin de la rue de Bièvre. What may have occurred here I can't guess, but I can usually sense something like relief. I have memories of two people, who were friends for a long time, looking at each other in a new way.

At the end of the road turn right up boulevard St-Germain to place Maubert, head right up rue Frédéric-Sauton, and then left up rue de la Bûcherie. You're now in a place that's a busy combination of drifting tourists and short-cutting Parisians. Along here you'll find Le Grenier Notre-Dame, the finest vegetarian restaurant in Paris. The seitan with baby potatoes is one of the most blissful meals you could wish for. Downstairs seating is reasonable, but it's worth going upstairs to experience the spiral staircase, which is as steep as a ladder.

At the end of the street you will see the gardens of St-Julien-le-Pauvre. The tree that is held up close to the fence is one of the oldest in Paris, brought here in 1680 from Guyana. If it had been brought any earlier, it might not have survived, because this tranquil spot has a violent past. The first chapel to be built here in the sixth century was destroyed by the Normans 300 years later. The grounds remained unused for another 300 years, but something of the original church must have lingered in the space, because work began on the current church in the twelfth century. It was a popular hangout for sixteenth-century students, but, feeling the need for a riot, they wrecked the place, and it rested dormant for another 100 years, before restoration began. It now serves the Greek Orthodox community.

You have to circumnavigate the church to find the entrance. A fair amount of *Highlander* was filmed here as well, which makes me think the locations manager must have been sensitive to untouched spaces. Whatever. The doors are usually open, and there are occasional concerts here. But the flagstones just outside the entrance are the best place to be; these are the last remaining stones from the Roman road to Orléans. Tourists come and go, wondering whether or not they should be there, but if you pause for a moment, you should find this is a good place to end your walk.

Eating & drinking

Le Barbacane

13 rue du Cardinal-Lemoine, 5th (01.43.26.37.01). **Open** noon-2.30pm, 7pm-1am, daily. Closed two weeks in Sept. Tropical décor and a menu based on Martinique and Guadeloupe cuisine.

Le Buisson Ardent

25 rue Jussieu, 5th (01.43.54.93.02). **Open** noon-2pm, 7.30-10pm, Mon-Fri; 7.30-10pm Sat. Closed Aug. A popular, refreshing and modern market menu bistro offering fine dishes.

Buvette des Marionnettes

Jardin du Luxembourg, 6th. **Open** *Sept-May* 8.30am-6.30pm daily; *June-Aug* 8.30am-7.30pm daily.

Chieng Mai

12 rue Frédéric-Sauton, 5th (01.43.25.45.45). **Open** noon-2.30pm, 7-11.20pm, daily. Closed two weeks in Aug, two in Dec. Delicious Thai food.

Flowers Café

5 rue Soufflot, 5th (01.43.54.75.36). **Open** 6am-midnight daily. Fine view of the Panthéon out front, cosy banquettes inside.

Fogon St-Julien

10 rue St-Julien-le-Pauvre, 5th (01.43.54.31.33). **Open** noon-3pm, 8pm-1.30am, Mon-Sat. Closed one week in Sept. A fine array of paella dishes in an intimate setting at this Spanish restaurant.

Le Grenier Notre-Dame

18 rue de la Bûcherie, 5th (01.43.29.98.29). **Open** *summer* noon-2.30pm, 7.30-11pm, Mon-Thur, Sun; noon-2.30pm, 7.30-11.30pm, Fri, Sat; *winter* noon-2.30pm, 7.30-10.30pm, daily.

Les Quatre et Une Saveurs

72 rue du Cardinal-Lemoine, 5th (01.43.26.88.80). **Open** noon-2.30pm, 7-10.30pm, Tue-Sun. Closed two weeks in Sept. A vegetarian gem with only organic ingredients.

The flagstones outside the **Eglise St-Julien-le-Pauvre** *are from the Roman road to Orléans.*

Le Rallye
11 quai de la Tournelle, 5th (01.43.54.29.65). **Open** 8am-2am Mon-Fri; 9.30am-2am Sat, Sun. Cheap beer and simple hot dishes in this down-to-earth caff.

Tarazoute
18 rue du Cardinal-Lemoine, 5th (01.44.07.29.50). **Open** noon-3pm, 7-11.30pm, Mon-Fri; 7-11.30pm Sat. Closed Aug. Welcoming venue specialising in North African food.

La Tour d'Argent
15-17 quai de la Tournelle, 5th (01.43.54.23.31). **Open** noon-1pm, 7.30-9pm, Tue-Sun. Haute cuisine overlooking Notre-Dame. Book in advance.

Parks

Jardin du Luxembourg
place Auguste-Comte, place Edmond-Rostand, rue de Vaugirard, 6th. **Open** *summer* 7.30am-9.30pm daily; *winter* 8am-5pm daily. *Children's playground* 10am-dusk daily. **Admission** *children's playground* 14F children; 7.50F adults.

Jardin des Plantes
place Valhubert, rue Buffon or rue Cuvier, 5th (01.40.79.30.00). **Open** *Grande Galerie de l'Evolution* 10am-6pm Mon, Fri-Sun; 10am-10pm Thur. *Ménagerie (01.40.79.37.04) Apr-Sept* 10am-6pm daily; *Oct-Mar* 10am-5pm daily. **Admission** *Grande Galerie* 40F; 30F concs. *Ménagerie* 30F; 20F concs.

Jardin de la rue de Bièvre
rue de Bièvre, 5th (01.40.71.76.07). **Open** 8am-dusk Mon-Fri; 9am-dusk Sat, Sun.

Churches & buildings

Eglise St-Julien-le-Pauvre
rue St-Julien-le-Pauvre, 5th (01.43.54.52.16). **Open** 10am-7.30pm daily; *gardens* 8am-dusk Mon-Fri; 9am-dusk Sat, Sun.

Institut du Monde Arabe
1 rue des Fossés-St-Bernard, 5th (01.40.51.39.53). **Open** 10am-6pm Tue-Sun. *Library* 1-8pm Tue-Sat. Café 2.30-6.30pm Tue-Sat; noon-3pm Sun. **Admission** *Building, library* free. *Museum* 25F; 20F concs. *Exhibitions* 45F; 35F concs. **Concerts** (01.40.51.38.14). *Box office* 2-5pm Tue-Sun. No concerts in Aug. **Admission** 100F; 80F concs.

Le Panthéon
place du Panthéon, 5th (01.44.32.18.00). **Open** *Apr-Sept* 9.30am-6.30pm daily; *Oct-Mar* 10am-5.30pm daily. **Admission** 35F; 23F concs.

History in marble

Alistair Horne

The Cimetière du Père Lachaise has been called 'the grandest address in Paris'.

Start: main entrance, Cimetière du Père Lachaise, 20th
Finish: Edith Piaf's grave, Cimetière du Père Lachaise, 20th
Getting there: lines 2 or 3 to Mº Père Lachaise, or line 2 to Mº Philippe-Auguste
Getting back: see above
Note: the cemetery is divided into 97 Divisions, in theory to help locate individual tombs. This walk, however, numbers tombs according to the map we have printed overleaf. For a more comprehensive map of the cemetery, ask at the gate. Note also the opening times of the cemetery.

In the centre of the downmarket east end of Paris there stands a green hill far, far away from the glitter of the *grands boulevards*. Although it is the most visited cemetery in the world, many of the several million tourists who swarm over each year to wallow in French history never seem to get to visit it; yet here rests probably more of France's past than is contained by any other hundred acres of her soil. Within what has long been one of the world's largest cemeteries known to Parisians simply as Père Lachaise lies a varied fortune. Once it was a Jesuit retreat, later a favourite place of dalliance for Parisian lovers, and still later the scene of the most savage blood-letting Paris has ever experienced. Even for non-necrophiliacs, and even if you can remain unmoved by the stories of the legion of French notables tucked away beneath its bizarrely picturesque slabs, in an increasingly frantic city Père Lachaise still offers a sanctuary of peace from which you can get some intriguing off-beat panoramic views of the whole capital.

Here is a true history of Paris, indeed of France herself, in marble and stone.

Back in the twelfth century, the hill where Père Lachaise now sits was an agricultural smallholding that belonged to the Bishop of Paris. There he grew vegetables, wheat and vines – the grapes supplying his own wine press located conveniently close to Notre-Dame. In 1430 it was bought up by a wealthy spice merchant called Règnault de Wandonne; there he built himself a comfortable country house, known as the Folie Règnault (In those days, the word 'folie' did not have the hedonistic connotations it later acquired, but simply implied bucolic surroundings, a derivative of the word '*feuillu*', or 'leafy'.)

Almost exactly 200 years later, the property passed into the hands of the Jesuits, who built a retreat there. Then, in 1675, one of their order – who was called Père La Chaise – became confessor to Louis XIV. (Among other things, Père La Chaise is supposed to have been responsible for persuading Louis XIV to revoke the Edict of Nantes.) Thanks to the bounty of the Roi Soleil, Père La Chaise's estate grew in both size and splendour; for a long time it was known as Mont Louis, in honour of its benefactor. His younger brother, an officer of the Royal Guard, also established himself there in considerable worldly comfort, and the Mont Louis became a favourite excursion for the smart courtesans of Paris, drawn partly in the hope of gaining the ear of the King's influential confessor, partly by the glamour of the *fêtes galantes* given by his brother the Comte de La Chaise. Judging from a contemporary verse –

Sur ces riants coteaux, dans ces joyeux bocages,

Naguère avec l'amour régnait la volupté.

– the Jesuits' domain must have acquired a spicily unecclesiastical flavour, which it retained long after Père La Chaise's death, at the age of 85, in 1709.

With 1762 came the downfall of the Jesuits. The *fêtes galantes* came to an end; the property was sold up, passing through several hands until it was bought by Jacques Baron – who in turn was ruined by the Great Revolution and forced to sell his country holdings to the City of Paris. Meanwhile, within the compressed confines of the old walls of Paris the city elders were being confronted with a progressively hideous problem – over-population of the dead. In pre-revolutionary Paris, almost every parish had its own tiny cemetery; the biggest of which, the Cimetière des Innocents (near Les Halles), measured no more than 130 by 65 yards. As space began to run out, the corpses of the poor were piled into common graves, usually several layers deep, from which an appalling smell emanated to pervade the neighbourhood. When the common graves overflowed, fresh spaces were acquired by disinterring the 'old' bones and heaping them into dreadful charnel houses within the precincts.

One night in 1776, an unfortunate shoemaker traversing the Innocents fell into one of its open graves in the dark; the shock and the stench were too much for him, and the next day he was found dead at the bottom of the trench. Four years later, the common grave at the Innocents collapsed into the cellars of adjacent houses, nearly resulting in the asphyxiation of a number of householders. This was too much, even for Parisians long accustomed to a not so fragrant city. The Cimetière des Innocents was closed down and its mortal remains transferred to the cavernous catacombs from which the stone for old Paris had been hewn.

Félix Faure – *died in action for a redhead.*

But this was still not enough. It required a revolutionary government to cope with the problem, and under the new Assemblée Nationale all graveyards within the city walls were closed down in 1791.

After the lapse of another 13 years, when he had been perhaps more pre-occupied with creating corpses than disposing of them, Napoléon decreed the concentration of the Paris dead into three vast cemeteries to be established beyond the walls (an innovation that was not copied by London until years later). Of these three, the largest was located on the holding that Jacques Baron had been forced to sell; poor Baron himself was among the first to be buried on his own land.

The very considerable eminence provided by the Mont Louis gives Père Lachaise cemetery a remarkable panorama over Paris, once autumn has denuded its heavily *feuillu* avenues. From the chapel

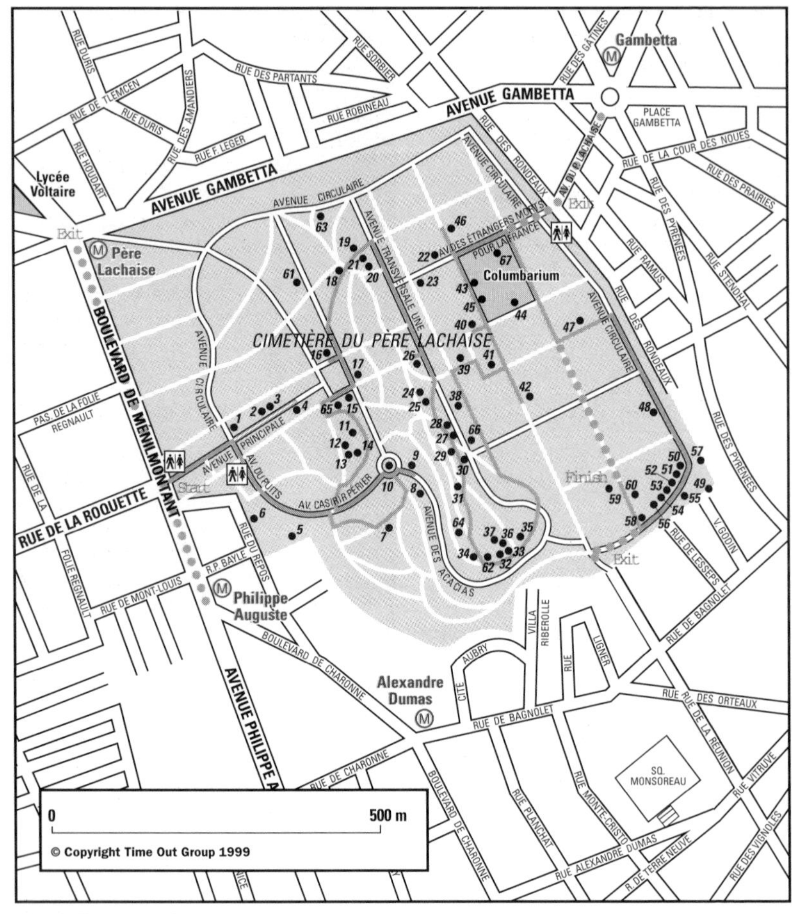

Cimetière du Père Lachaise

1. Colette
2. de Musset
3. Haussmann
4. Faure
5. Héloïse and Abélard
6. Félix
7. Morrison
8. Comte
9. Champollion
10. Périer
11. Bellini
12. Cherubini
13. Chopin
14. Charles
15. Géricault
16. David
17. Thiers
18. Duc de Morny
19. de Balzac
20. Delacroix
21. de Nerval
22. Apollinaire
23. Kardec
24. Corot
25. Daumier
26. Ingres
27. Molière
28. La Fontaine
29. Daudet
30. Parmentier
31. Hugo
32. Davout
33. Masséna
34. Ney
35. Murat
36. Lefebvre
37. Wallace
38. Smith
39. Bernhardt
40. Montand & Signoret
41. Blanqui
42. Noir
43. Duncan
44. Ernst
45. Grapelli
46. Proust
47. Wilde
48. Stein & Toklas
49. Mur des Fédérés
50. Barbusse
51. Willard
52. Eluard
53. Thorez
54. Duclos
55. Marx & Lafarge
56. Ravensbruck
57. Belsen
58. Mauthausen
59. Modigliani & Hébuterne
60. Piaf
61. Bizet
62. Beaumarchais
63. Crocé-Spinelli & Sivel
64. Chappe
65. Talma
66. Hautpoul
67. Callas

built on the side of the original manor of Louis XIV's confessor, you can see the Panthéon, the Sacré-Coeur at Montmartre, the Eiffel Tower and even the pleasant countryside at Meudon out beyond Paris to the south-west. This dominating position also caused Père Lachaise, three times in its history, to become a battlefield. When the Russians attacked Paris in 1814, students of the Polytechnique turned it into a fortified redoubt, but it was carried on the third assault. Fierce Cossacks bivouacked among its tombs, chopping down the trees for their campfires. Père Lachaise came under fire again, briefly, the following year; however, its worst ordeal was during the bitter civil war of 1871.

It was while I was writing *The Fall of Paris* that I first explored Père Lachaise, for it was here that the Paris Commune breathed its last gasp. For a whole week in May 1871, aptly called *'la semaine sanglante'* (bloody week), the Communards had been driven eastwards across Paris by the overwhelming force of Thiers's government troops, burning the city as they retreated.

Among the imposing bourgeois vaults of Père Lachaise the Communards had constructed their last stronghold, defended by their two remaining batteries of artillery and some 200 National Guards, which the Government troops attacked shortly after dawn on 27 May. Bullets and shells splintered the sanctified white marble, blood sullied the pretentious gravestones. After several hours of savage fighting, the last of the defenders was winkled out near the tomb of Balzac, at the centre of the graveyard.

Thiers's troops were in a merciless mood. In a ditch outside the cemetery they had discovered the body of the well-loved Archbishop of Paris, executed as a hostage by the Communards. The next morning, Whitsunday, 147 surrendered Communards were put up against a wall in the eastern corner of Père Lachaise and mown down in reprisal. Over the intervening years the bullet-splattered wall, the Mur des Fédérés, as it is called, marked by a simple commemorative plaque to the Communard martyrs, has become both a touchstone and a highly emotive rallying point for France's left wing.

The Mur lies at the top end of the quite steep hill of Père Lachaise, and we shall – appropriately – terminate our walk near there. But let us start down at the main gate, on boulevard de Ménilmontant, a short distance from the Métro station. Here almost the first grave one comes to is that of the writer, Colette, author of *Chéri*, lying under a stone simply marked but perennially heaped high with the flowers of admirers. Close to Colette lies the body of poet Alfred de Musset, whom excess brought to Père Lachaise at the early age of 47. He was blackballed from the Jockey Club because his horsemanship was below standard, but on his death at least one of his ambitions was realised – that of having a willow tree planted to provide his grave with shade:

Mes chers amis, quand je mourrai
plantez un saule au cimetière,
J'aime son feuillage éploré,
La paleur m'en est douce et chère,
Et son ombre sera légère,
A la terre ou je dormirai.

Every summer evening de Musset's willow used to be lovingly watered by the *gardiens*, however, alas, overshadowed by the large trees that have sprung up around, even before the great drought of 1976 it had begun to assume an ominous sickliness.

Alongside de Musset lies Préfet Georges Haussmann, the nineteenth-century progenitor of modern Paris, admired by some but cursed by medievalists for what he did in the destruction of the old centre of the city. Just across the way is a President of the Republic, Félix Faure, made famous by the amorous exploit which brought him to this resting place. In the middle of the Dreyfus case in 1899, President Faure was in his office while various suppliants awaited his pleasure in the anteroom. Suddenly the shrieks of a woman in great pain were heard; rushing into the holy-of-holies, orderlies were confronted with the terrible sight of a naked President, dead of a heart attack, his hand gripping with the fixity of death the hair of a lusty redhead, in an equal state of undress. The sculpture on top of his grave shows Faure draped in a Tricoleur like a sheet, while his hand seems to be groping the flagpole as if it were his lover. I often feel that the inscription on his grave should read *'mort en brave'* – the conventional wording for a French hero killed in action.

Move back down avenue Principale, and take a left along avenue du Puits. To the right, under shady trees and a Gothic stone canopy, lie two more unhappy lovers, together in perhaps the most famous tomb of all, and certainly the most senior: those two unhappy twelfth-century soulmates, Héloïse and Abélard. After many separations they lie finally reunited, their hands raised in prayer (though there are cynics who doubt the authenticity of what is below). Dating from 1701, an inscription by Héloïse's successor as Abbess of the Paraclete Convent refers tenderly to:

> … *the love which had united their spirits during their lives, and which was conserved during their absence by the most tender and most spiritual letters*…

Then, tucked in under the exterior wall, there is Rachel Félix, the beautiful and sexy actress of Louis Philippe's era, party to what must be one of the most laconic exchanges of love letters on record. After seeing her act, the Prince de Joinville sent round a card: 'Where? – When? – How much?', to which she replied with an equal economy of words that would have delighted any male chauvinist: 'Your place – Tonight – Free.' True to form, her tomb bears simply the inscription 'RACHEL'.

A short distance away, up and to the right of avenue Casimir Périer, is the more recent grave of the pop singer Jim Morrison of the Doors, dead – mysteriously – at only 28, where today a motley crowd of devotees roll spliffs against a backdrop of Doors' lyrics and declarations of love and drug consumption graffitied on to every sign within reach, and in every known language. (Graffiti is, worse than strikes and demos, the greatest plague of modern-day Paris – while on my most recent visit to Père Lachaise, I watched a blowsy Spaniard add her little tribute to the tomb of Héloïse and Abélard in lipstick – as if the indignities done to him in real life were not enough.)

Progressing in towards the centre of Père Lachaise, pass down a few steps to a sunken area where you will find the white stone tomb of the philosopher Auguste Comte. Across the path an obelisk (of course) marks the resting place of the famous Egyptologist who deciphered the Rosetta Stone, Jean-François Champollion. After the extravagant Rond-Point commemorating a fairly dim politician, Casimir Périer, one comes to – on the left – a group of distinguished composers. They include Vincenzo Bellini (though his remains, like those of Rossini, have in fact now been re-interred in their native Italy), Luigi Cherubini and, four graves further along, Frédéric Chopin's ivy-clad stone. In contrast to de Musset's willow, fresh geraniums always seem to adorn his tomb (which is often used as a dead-letter box by clandestine lovers), miraculously renewed year in and year out by anonymous admirers. Chopin shared his mistress, the trousered and moustachioed George Sand, with at least two other denizens of Père Lachaise, Delacroix and de Musset; though Sand herself is buried elsewhere. Acidly she described Chopin as a 'high-flown, consumptive and exasperating nuisance'. A fine epitaph for a lover, indeed!

Among the stars of the musical firmament, Georges Bizet and Pierre

Finally reunited in death, the romantic tragedy of **Héloïse and Abélard***'s doomed love still has resonance among visitors.*

LES RESTES
D'HELOISE ET D'ABELARD
SONT REUNIS DANS CE TOMBE U.

Augustin Beaumarchais, co-author of the immortal *Marriage of Figaro*, are also buried elsewhere in Père Lachaise; Maria Callas embarked on death there, but her ashes were later removed to be scattered in her beloved Aegean (although she is still listed as being in the Columbarium).

It was France that pioneered the first manned balloons, later put to such commendable use during the Siege of Paris, so – appropriately – the inventor of the gas-filled balloon, Professor Charles, lies nearby. At the ascent of Charles's balloon Benjamin Franklin was stung to retort to a spectator sceptical of its usefulness, 'Of what use is the newborn baby?' (Division 71 contains another pair of unfortunate early balloonists, Croce-Spinelli and Sivel – two men who lie together hand in hand, [not a gay couple as far as anyone knows], but intrepid souls who went so high they died from lack of oxygen.)

Nearby is a shaded clearing with seats commanding views over the cemetery. On either side can be found the painters Théodore Géricault, his tomb marked by a bronze relief of somę of his most paintings, including *The Raft of the 'Medusa'*. and Jacques-Louis David, responsible for the heroic portraits of Napoléon. Meanwhile, framing one side of this clearing, in a commanding position at the centre of Père Lachaise, lies a chapel erected by a grateful Municipality of Paris close to the spot where the last Communard cannon fired its final round in May 1871. This colossal pillared mausoleum commemorates the memory of the man principally responsible for the crushing of the Commune, Adolphe Thiers, whose tomb lies adjacent.

Take the chemin Mont-Louis northwards up the hill to a junction of several paths. Few of Père Lachaise's tombs are weirder than the mausoleum tenanted by the Duc de Morny, Napoléon III's natural half-brother, a hyperactive lover and statesman of the Second Empire. It seems to combine every known style from Rome to Armenia, with a suggestion of the Bogumil heretics of Bosnia thrown in, and capped with four protuberances shaped like public drinking fountains or giant golf tees.

In a few yards you arrive at the tomb of another of Père Lachaise's great authors, Honoré de Balzac. 'Friendship and glory

Guards protect the grave of rock icon ***Jim Morrison****, where 'fans' have defaced his tomb.*

Artist **Théodore Géricault** *lies majestically above bronze reliefs of some of his paintings.*

are the only inhabitants of the tombs,' he wrote; he had his hero, Rastignac, bury Père Goriot among the serried ranks of affluent bourgeois that fill the avenues of Père Lachaise. The novel, *Le Père Goriot*, ends with Rastignac gazing down from the heights of the cemetery on the great city lying beneath him like a monster, and issuing his famous challenge:

'Paris, à nous deux maintenant!'

Close by lies Eugène Delacroix in a grand black sarcophagus, but directly opposite Balzac rests Gérard de Nerval (pseudonym for Gérard Labrunie), the eccentric Surrealist poet famous for taking his lobster for walks on a lead. Shortly after his release from a mental asylum, Nerval's body was found hanging from railings on the rue de la Vieille-Lanterne, one of his favourite haunts in Paris. Following avenue Transversale No.1, one of the major routes that run roughly from north to south in the cemetery, and then left up avenue des Etrangers Morts pour la France, you arrive at the resting place of Guillaume Apollinaire, early twentieth century poet who was a close friend of the Picasso and the artistic avant-garde. Badly wounded in the head at the beginning of World War I, he finally died of his injuries in 1918, a considerable loss to French literature.

Just across the way from Apollinaire lies a famous medium of the Second Empire, Hippolyte Allan-Kardec, whose Stonehenge-like monument of hewn stone is kept constantly heaped with flowers by 'believers' – apparently hoping to transfer to themselves his psychic powers.

Returning to avenue Transversale No.1, and swinging now south-west off to the right, is a cluster of great nineteenth-century artists: Dominique Ingres's simple white stone, the black bust of Camille Corot, and behind him, and protected by black chains, Honoré Daumier. (Close by you may also notice an ornate tomb of a bereaved family man, whose sad inscription to his deceased wife, mother and daughter, proclaims: 'This tomb encloses, *hélas*, the three things that made the happiness of a father and a husband.')

At Père Lachaise one is constantly reminded of just how democratic an institution is Death; here, within less than a cortège's length of the functionally non-Christian tombstone of non-believers such as the Communist Party boss from the 1930s onwards, Maurice Thorez (who we'll come to later), are crowded together the opulent vaults of the *haute bourgeoisie*, traditional foes of the French Left. For while the scions of the pre-revolutionary nobility still tend to be interred (like President de Gaulle) in their own country parish churchyards, the remains of the bourgeois *'Deux cent Familles'* fill a large part of Père Lachaise's hundred acres. Row upon row stand the mausolea bearing the hyphenated names of great banking, mercantile and industrial families; taken together they present the greatest agglomeration of architectural eccentricity in all France. Miniature pyramids rub shoulders with Gothic chapels, complete with gargoyles and lacy pinnacles. A reduced Eglise de la Madeleine vies with what seems to be a replica of the Panthéon or a tiny Taj Mahal; another amazing fantasy is a pyramid supported by turtles and displaying on its four sides an ibis, a bullock, a car and a sunburst, the whole *bombe surprise* capped by a giant egg. One tomb imposing by its vastness was commissioned by a dedicated chess player to house an additional 31 occupants – on the grounds that the chessboard holds 32 pieces.

Above all this labyrinth of unrestrained fancies rises the haughty alabaster tower erected by some long-forgotten tycoon, at least half as high as the obelisk in the place de la Concorde. Compared with the extravaganzas in death of the rich *illustres inconnus*, the tombs of the famous writers, artists and musicians already mentioned seem almost indecently simple. For instance, continuing along the path parallel to avenue Transversale No.1, you come across the mighty Molière and Jean de La Fontaine, who, transferred from defunct cemeteries within the old walls of Paris,

A cluster of artists lie close by one another – here **Camille Corot** *guards over his family.*

now rest side by side in two dignified caskets. The same applies to Alphonse Daudet, just across the way, who, from a short distance outside Paris, heard the expiring shots of the Communards as they died inside Père Lachaise. The white marble pilaster-style vase and palm leaf that adorn the tomb of the author of the immortal *Lettres de mon moulin* peek out between two bourgeois family crypts.

Further on you can find the elegantly expressive tomb of the famous scientist, Antoine-Augustin Parmentier (1737-1813), his name for ever associated with the potato (which he introduced to a reluctant France); his shrine is decorated with a plough, ears of wheat and the inevitable basket of spuds, all set in a tiny garden that surrounds the base. Potatoes had hitherto been considered fit only for animal consumption, but Parmentier was so persuasive that troops had to be summoned to guard his own stocks. Several delicious recipes were named after him. (Among the other numerous scientists and explorers also in Père Lachaise is Claude Chappe, the inventor of the semaphore, who when his patent was contested flung himself into a sewer, aged only 42.)

Moving further along beyond Molière and La Fontaine, in a tangle of densely wooded paths above precipitous heights that look down upon Héloïse and Abélard, you pass an illustrious name in Napoléonic history – that of Général Hugo. His son Victor resides at the Panthéon – the highest honour France can accord her *grands hommes*. But the father's grave signals that you are arriving in the Napoléonic section. Here are a cluster of military men – Napoléon's Marshals – names conjuring up all the martial glory of the Empire: a big stone cross for Louis Davout, a column in memory of André Masséna, and a large grey edifice for Michel Ney – shot after the Restoration for his loyalty to the fallen Emperor. Further up the path lies Joachim Murat. Though executed like Ney, Murat's is a new crypt erected by the family, which still thrives to this day; and Jean-Joseph Hautpoul, a commander of the famous cavalry charge at Austerlitz, lies not far from his dashing leader, Murat. The Emperor himself, of course, inhabits his own palatial quarters, built originally by Louis XIV, in Les Invalides.

Among these macho marshals, there also lies the wife of one, Madame Lefebvre, famed to French literature in a wicked caricature of Napoléonic life as 'Madame Sans-Gêne'. Lefebvre was the son of a miller, but, of even humbler origins, 'Madame Sans-Gêne' was a washerwoman who outshone her husband with her blisteringly earthy barrack-room language – barely mitigated when she became a duchess. A plaque on the back of a large white sarcophagus gives her special mention.

Close by the Marshals, in a massive sepulchre, lies an Englishman, Richard Wallace, a considerable benefactor to Paris (and London) during and after the collapse of Louis-Napoléon's Second Empire. Wallace was the bastard son of the depraved Marquess of Hertford, upon whom Thackeray modelled his awful Lord Steyne in *Vanity Fair*. Apart from bequeathing to London the priceless Wallace Collection of paintings – and possibly to atone for his evil parentage – Wallace financed two whole field hospitals during the 1870 Siege of Paris. After that war, concerned at the perennial lack of drinkable water in the city, he donated the elegant fountains still to be seen throughout Paris, and which continue to bear his name, *les Fontaines Wallace*.

Swinging back uphill from the Marshals, in a singularly fitting juxtaposition, along the chemin des Anglais (which runs parallel to avenue Transversale No.1), one comes across the white sarcophagus of a distinguished British admiral who fought Napoléon. Sir Sydney Smith inflicted one of the few early defeats on Napoléon at the Siege of Acre (1799), thus putting an end to his ambitions in the Middle East. Always

an ardent Francophile, despite the wars, Smith returned to live and die in his beloved Paris. Through the assiduous efforts of his biographer, Tom Pocock, Smith's neglected tomb was recently rededicated in a moving Franco-British ceremony in May 1999.

Two blocks beyond Sydney Smith, obscured by two small chapels, but framed by a couple of laurel bushes, lies the immortal Sarah Bernhardt. In less enlightened ages Parisian actresses tended to be rated little better than tarts. Consequently, the great tragedienne Adrienne Lecouvreur (1692-1730), denied access to hallowed ground by the church despite the protests of Voltaire and despite her having been mistress of France's greatest soldier, Maréchal de Saxe, still lies interred beneath the intersection of rue de Bourgogne and rue de Grenelle on the Left Bank. By the nineteenth century, however, French actors and actresses were better treated. Napoléon's favourite, Talma, lies in quiet imperial dignity near the composers we have visited; but 'the divine Sarah' (1845-1923) is housed under a luxuriant tomb of canopied granite. Still stumping the boards though nearly 80 and minus a leg, she acted her final role to perfection, and, literally, to the end, sleeping in her rosewood casket as if to try it on for size. The day of her interment at Père Lachaise was 'such a sight for flowers, followers, and fanaticism as hadn't been seen since Victor Hugo's obsequies' (Janet Flanner, *Letter from Paris 1933-5*), and her grave remains one of the most visited.

In the same division as Bernhardt lie together two more recent luvvies, heart-throbs of mid-twentieth-century France – Yves Montand (born Ivo Livi) and Simone Signoret (born Simone Kaminker).

Heading east up avenue Carette, just a stone's throw from Sarah, you come to the tomb of one of France's principal left-wing revolutionary thinkers of the nineteenth century, the much-imprisoned Louis-Auguste Blanqui. (He spent 33 years inside, at different times; Karl Marx thought him the greatest revolutionary of the century.) It was Blanqui's movement that helped bring about the fall of Louis-Napoléon, and the Commune; after which he was sentenced to life imprisonment, but was released in 1879. A bronze statue of him now lies shrouded in cloth behind a row of fir trees. Turn right along avenue Transversale No.2 and you will confront another eminent figure from the closing years of the Second Empire, Victor Noir. Noir was a well-known journalist shot down in 1870 by an enraged Prince Pierre Bonaparte, a cousin of the Emperor. His death, at the age of 22, provided a cause célèbre and his interment provoked the biggest Republican demonstration that administered one of the final blows to Louis-Napoléon's Empire. Another contemporary of Allan-Kardec, the medium, Noir exudes a special appeal for the sexual fetishist; a guidebook notes of his darkened bronze effigy that 'a certain part of the body shines brightly, thanks to the caresses of sterile women'. Red-top British hacks may find it gratifying that a defunct journalist should be held capable of such wizardry, though it is not entirely clear why.

Antoine-Augustin Parmentier *persuaded the French to eat like a horse – he introduced the potato to their cuisine.*

Retracing your footsteps backwards briefly down avenue Transversale No.2 from Victor Noir, you arrive at the Columbarium Crématorium.

Its bleak rows of plaques record the incineration of such and such an *inconnu* killed in Allied air raids of 1944, though it was once the site of a Muslim enclave established by Napoléon III – always seeking vainly for allies – to please the Turks. Designed (appropriately enough) as a kind of hideous facsimile of Santa Sophia, out of four bogus minarets puff the smoke from the crematorium's busy furnace. A tomb bearing a complete Debrett's entry is that of 'ALI BIN HAMUD BIN MUHAMMAD BIN SAID BIN SULTAN BIN ALI-IMAN SULTAN DE ZANZIBAR';

meanwhile – the Parisians never lagging in contemporary fashion – Père Lachaise today does everything it can to attract the weary bones of Moslem oil potentates.

Hiding within the Columbarium lies Isadora Duncan (No.6796), the American dancer of the 1920s strangled by her own long scarf in an open-top car; the Surrealist artist Max Ernst (No.2102); and the jazz violinist Stéphane Grapelli (No.417). Just across the way is Marcel Proust, discreetly concealed in the smooth black bourgeois family tomb that was erected in honour of his father's prowess as a professor of medicine.

Moving up to the top wall of the cemetery, via avenue Carette, you come across the much-frequented tomb of Oscar Wilde, buried – in his own renowned prediction – as far beyond his means as he had lived. Also penalised for the pursuit of illicit love, in death poor Oscar suffered the same dreadful fate as Abélard suffered in life; some years ago a vandal emasculated the massively hideous Epstein angel that guards his grave. Since then Oscar's manhood has been quietly restored, only to suffer once more. Now, closing the stable door, a stuffy little sign in English and French says:

Do not deface this tomb; it is protected by law as an ancient monument and was restored in 1992.

Poor Oscar!

Passing two blocks along the avenue Circulaire that hugs the outer wall, we reach the grave of two more recent literary partners in the 'Love that dare not speak its name' – Gertrude Stein, patroness of the Lost Generation, and her 'tiny, nimble and mustachioed' lover, Alice B Toklas.

We have now reached the north-eastern heights of the cemetery. Here stands the historic Mur des Fédérés, that focus of the left-wing mythology of France. Over the years since the '*Semaine Saglante*' of May 1871, every Whitsun the Mur has drawn solemn processions to it, sometimes many

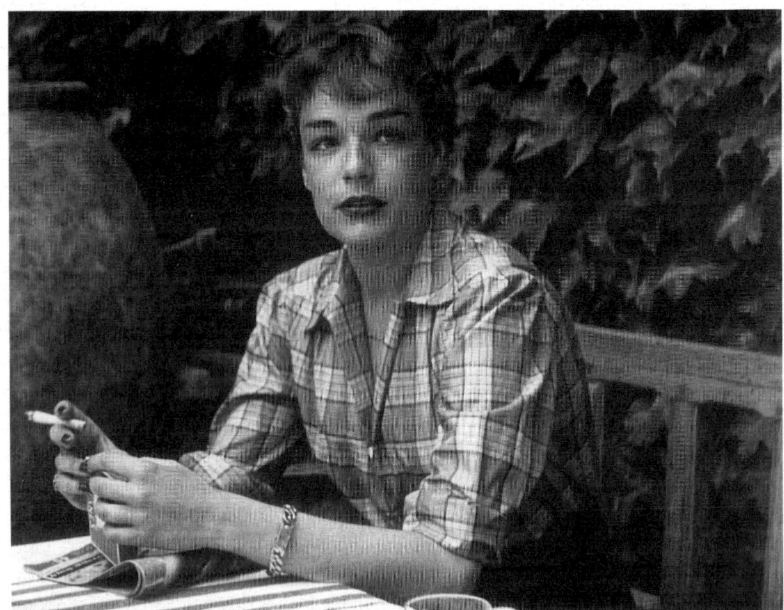

Twentieth-century luvvies also feature – **Simone Signoret** *and Yves Montand share a plot.*

Even in death, **Victor Noir***'s mythical powers attract the attentions of sterile women.*

Oscar Wilde – *constant restoration is needed due to the over-eager attentions of admirers.*

thousands strong and often turning into demonstrations of a strongly topical nature, provoking collisions with anarchists and right-wingers. It was here, in 1935, that Socialists and Communists, marching together for the first time, set the seal on the Front Populaire that was to have so potent an influence upon France's performance in Hitler's Blitzkrieg of 1940. After the war, the annual pilgrimage became the focus of left-wing protest against NATO, against German rearmament, against the French in Algeria and the Americans in Vietnam. In May 1978, the party faithful were bolstered by a Soviet delegation that arrived bearing a gift of the ashes of the last Communard, Adrian Lejeune, who had died in Russia in 1942, aged 95. But, over the Mitterrand years as the appeal of the Left declined, so too has the symbolic magnetism of the Mur. In May 1999, only five rather sad carnations were left marking the event.

With the passage of time, the tombs of France's proletarian heroes have come to cluster around the Mur des Fédérés. Here lie, in succession as you pass, Henri Barbusse, one of the great anti-war novelists of the post-1918 generation; Marcel Willard, the defender of Georgi Dimitrov, who was tried and acquitted of complicity in the Reichstag fire of 1933, later to become Prime Minister of Bulgaria; and Picasso's friend, Paul Eluard, the poet. A highly polished slab of sombre black granite contains the remains of Maurice Thorez, for three long decades from the 1930s onwards the powerful Stalinist boss of France's Communist Party, and those of his long-time Party secretary, Jacques Duclos. Across the path lie the bodies of Laura Marx, daughter of Karl, and her husband, Paul Lafargue – who committed joint suicide in 1911.

Also in this part of Père Lachaise, which has gained the name *'Le Coin des Martyrs'*, are located various memorials to episodes of inhumanity much fresher in human memory. Among grim little plaques honouring the brief lives of young men and women of the Resistance, executed by the Gestapo, there rise grim monuments to the victims of the Nazi concentration camps. The horrors of Ravensbruck, where so many brave French women met their deaths, are commemorated by a pair of manacled stone hands; Belsen by an incredibly powerful group of skeletal figures in blackened bronze, supporting each other and gazing bitterly to the heavens; and Mauthausen, by an austere stone shaft, simply bearing the horrifying statistics of mass murder. It is altogether a corner of unhappiness, these Divisions of Père Lachaise presided over by the Mur.

Moving back in the direction of the centre, you pass painter Amedeo Modigliani buried by a small fir tree together with his lover, Jeanne Hébuterne, who killed herself in grief a few days after he died in agony from meningitis.

Finally, nearby too is Edith Piaf, aka Madame Lamboukas, lying – together with her stuffed rabbit, squirrel and lion – under a simple black stone, which for years was the cemetery's biggest draw. The violet-eyed 'little sparrow', born 'on a *flic*'s cape under a lamp-post', in the impoverished *quartier* of nearby Belleville, had the saddest of lives – but gave delight to millions by her heart-wrenching songs. When she died in October 1963, up to 40,000 fans came to mourn her, including a detachment of men from the Foreign Legion, who had adopted *Non, je ne regrette rien* as their song.

A million visitors a year now come to Père Lachaise, making it one of Paris's four most popular attractions. But how do you get *un booking* (a plot) here? Unless you are very famous, or lucky enough to have a family vault with a *concession perpetuelle* it is by no means easy. The 110 acres of the cemetery are heavily overcrowded by some 10,000 inhabitants, and space is made more limited since a tunnel of the Petite Ceinture railway beneath it collapsed in 1874, showering corpses on to the tracks – following which the whole area was vacated and permanently transformed into an avenue. Furthermore, there are certain criteria required in order to qualify for consideration: those who lived and died in Paris; those who died while staying in Paris; and inhabitants of Paris who may have died elsewhere.

Colossal monuments to victims of man's inhumanity to man stand in **'Le Coin des Martyrs'**.

Then there's the cost. A two-metre-square plot on the edge of a path, in perpetuity, costs 45,000F; 27,500F for a plot elsewhere. A hole in the Columbarium is significantly cheaper – about 10,000F for fifty years. What happens to your ashes thereafter isn't clear.

Nancy Mitford's faithless lover, Gaston Palewski, who was one of de Gaulle's most senior colleagues, confided to me many years ago that he had applied for a shady plot, but had been warned that he could only be put on the 'waiting list'. 'They could not even guarantee me anything with a view over Paris,' he exploded indignantly. How the 'standby' line ever grows any shorter is not quite clear; though Nancy Mitford, teasing Gaston mercilessly, joked at the same time she was sure that 'every once in a while they dig up the old bones, and then grind them up to make cosmetics for Chanel!'

The demand is hardly surprising. Not quite everybody who is anybody has come to rest at Père Lachaise – for instance, Stendhal, Madame Récamier, *'la dame aux Camélias'*, and Heinrich Heine are all to be found up at Montmartre. Nevertheless, Père Lachaise has been called 'the grandest address in Paris'. To be buried there, is, as Victor Hugo once said, 'like having mahogany furniture' (lying in state in the Panthéon, he was himself hardly *mal placé* in death). Apart from sharing the company of so many illustrious sons and daughters of France, it would be difficult to imagine a pleasanter place in which to be laid away than here – with its superb views over Paris and its many bosky avenues that still seem to retain more than a suggestion of the *lieu feuillu* of Règnault the spice merchant. Once upon a time there was a bistro opposite, on the rue du Repos, with the bad-joke name of Mieux Ici Qu'en Face (Rather Here than Over There). But that has disappeared, and – with the exclusion of the sombre reminders of *'Le Coin des Martyrs'* – Death betrays little evidence of his sting in Père Lachaise today.

For many years, an elderly eccentric used to be seen strolling through the cemetery every afternoon at five o'clock, dressed in pre-revolutionary doublet and breeches. Perhaps he was indeed a ghost, but his presence never seemed to disturb the elderly next of kin with their watering cans, or the mothers with gambolling children, and cheerful promenading couples for whom Père Lachaise has become something of a family park. Gossiping nursemaids shackle their prams to the tomb railings, to prevent their charges bowling off down the steep slopes; children clamber happily over the most portentous crypts, as soon as the *gardiens*' backs are turned; and in the strange way that Love and Death represent but two Janus faces of the same head, lovers nuzzle obliviously on benches set in the cool alleys between the tombs – just as when in the times of Père Lachaise himself the courtesans and gallants used to journey out from seventeenth-century Paris to pursue their pleasures on Mont Louis.

Eating & drinking

Chez Luis

92 rue de la Réunion, 20th (01.43.70.33.23). **Open** 9am-1am daily. **Food served** noon-2pm, 7-11.30pm, daily. Closed Aug. A Portuguese café/bar, with a short but authentic menu.

Palais d'Archana

110 boulevard de Charonne, 20th (01.44.64.99.92). **Open** 11am-2pm, 6.30-11pm, daily. Indian kitsch restaurant with a fine range of nan bread.

Le Soleil

136 boulevard de Ménilmontant, 20th (01.46.36.47.44). **Open** 8am-2am daily. Sit outside to catch the rays alongside the local artists and musicians that frequent this café. No food.

Information

Cimetière du Père Lachaise

Main entrance: boulevard de Ménilmontant, 20th (01.43.70.70.33). **Open** *16 Mar-5 Nov* 8am-6pm Mon-Fri; 8.30am-6pm Sat; 9am-6pm Sun. *6 Nov-15 Mar* 8am-5.30pm Mon-Fri; 8.30am-5.30pm Sat; 9am-5.30pm Sun. For information on reserving a plot, contact: *Direction, 16 rue du Repos, 10th (01.43.70.70.33).*

Also in ***'Le Coin des Martyrs'****, a memorial to those who died in Mauthausen, having been transported there from France.*

MAUTHAUSEN

Contributors

Philippe Alexandre is a journalist and political editor. He works for French radio, newspapers and television as a political commentator. He has written a dozen books, among them *Paysages de campagne*, which won him the Prix Aujourd'hui. He was born and educated in Paris near the Jardin du Luxembourg and now lives on the Ile St-Louis.

Chantal Barbe, born and educated in Normandy, taught and lectured all over the world for 17 years. Exiled to her husband's 'village' (the Montsouris district of the 14th arrondissement of Paris), she has fallen in love with the city and now lectures to share her passion.

Jean-Daniel Brèque moved to Paris when he became a full-time translator. Translating into French numerous novels by Poppy Z Brite, Dan Simmons and others leaves him precious little time to concentrate on his own work, although several of his horror stories have found their way into British and American anthologies including *Dark Voices 5*, *Darklands 2*, *Best New Horror 2* and *Love in Vein II*. He is assistant editor of the French science fiction magazine *Galaxies*, and reviews science fiction for *Mauvais Genres*, broadcast by France Culture.

Marie Darrieussecq has lived in Paris for ten years. Although for ever tied to the provinces, having spent the first 17 years of her life by the sea in Biarritz, she loves Paris. For her, the Jardin du Luxembourg is the city's beach. She is the author of *Truismes* (1997), published in English as *Pig Tales* (Faber & Faber), and *Naissance des fantômes* (1998) or *My Phantom Husband* (Faber & Faber) in the UK.

Jean Paul Dollé was born in 1939 and studied philosophy at the Sorbonne. He was very active in student organisations opposing the Algerian war, and in the events of May 1968. He is now a professor at the Ecole d'Architecture de Paris la Villette, and is an adviser to the Ministère de la Ville. He has published several books, including *L'Insoumis*, about the activist Pierre Goldman.

Born in Algeria, writer, journalist and dramatist **Abdelkader Djemaï** moved to Paris in 1993. He is the author of several novels including *Un Eté de cendres*, *Sable rouge*, *31 rue de l'Aigle* and *Memoires de nègre*. He has also written a non-fiction work, *Camus à Oran*, tracing the author's time in Algeria.

Geoff Dyer's many books include *The Colour of Memory*, *But Beautiful* (winner of the 1992 Somerset Maugham Prize) and *Out of Sheer Rage* (a finalist, in America, for a National Circle of Book Critics Award). He lived in Paris for varying chunks of time between 1991 and 1995. Set in the clubs and bars of the 11th, his novel *Paris Trance* is published by Abacus.

Natasha Edwards moved to Paris for all the wrong reasons in 1992 and now lives above the catacombs in the 14th arrondissement. She has been editor of Time Out Paris since 1993, seeking out and writing about, among other things, art, architecture, design and – because the true key to understanding French culture is food and wine – Parisian cafés and restaurants.

Maureen Freely, born in Neptune, New Jersey, in 1952, grew up in Istanbul. She now lives in Bath with an industrial sociologist and has four children and two step-children. Her novels include *Mother's Helper*, *The Stork Club*, *Under the Vulcania* and *The Other Rebecca*. She is a lecturer on the Creative Writing Programme at the University of Warwick. She lived in Montparnasse in the mid-1970s, and has been a regular visitor to Paris ever since.

Born in New York, **Alan Furst** has lived for long periods in Paris. He has written extensively for *Esquire* and the *International Herald Tribune*. Now a full-time novelist, his books – 1930s and '40s espionage novels in European settings – are widely read in the US and the UK.

Antoine de Gaudemar, born in 1951, has lived in Paris since 1968. He has worked in print journalism, radio and television. He is currently editor-in-chief of the leading daily *Libération*, and has been in charge of its literary supplement for the past 13 years.

Sasha Goldman is a film producer who also works in cultural production in different media: theatre events, fine art and publishing.

He has been active with various non-governmental projects and contributes to numerous publications.

Alistair Horne's *The Fall of Paris: The Siege and the Commune 1870-71*, part of *The Price of Glory* trilogy, was first published in 1965 and remains in print today (Papermac). His last book was *How Far From Austerlitz: Napoleon 1805-15* (Macmillan). His *Seven Ages of Paris* is due out in 2000. He has been awarded the Légion d'Honneur for contributions to French History.

Liz Jensen spent four years as a sculptor near Lyon in south-east France, before becoming a freelance writer and the author of two novels, *Egg Dancing* and *Ark Baby*. Her third novel will be published by Bloomsbury in 2000. She now lives in London and the Lot-et-Garonne with her Anglo-French husband and their two Anglo-French children.

Born in Preston in 1968, **Christopher Kenworthy** spent the early 1990s running Barrington Books. Having published Nicholas Royle's Paris-set novel, *Counterparts*, in 1993, he felt it was time to explore the city and spent many weeks there during the next five years. His short story collection, *Will You Hold Me?*, is published by The Do-Not Press. His first novel, *The Winter Inside*, is forthcoming from Serpent's Tail, who have also bought his second. A third novel, set in Paris, is germinating.

Linda Lê, born in Vietnam in 1963, is the author of four novels, including *Calomnies* (published as *Slander* by Nebraska Press 1996), *Voix* (1998) and *Lettre morte* (1999). She lives in Paris.

Nicholas Lezard is a writer and critic, appearing mainly in the *Guardian* and the *Independent on Sunday*. He was born and lives in London, but lived in Paris at various times in the 1980s, and is still a regular visitor. He is currently trying to finish his book, *Fun*, if people would just leave him alone for a minute.

Olivier Morel (Relom) was born in Tours in 1973. He moved to Paris in 1995 and is a contributor to the *bande dessinée* magazine *Psikopat*. He lives in the 10th arrondissement.

Stephen Mudge's profession as an opera singer took him all over the world; a performance of the Mozart requiem at the Salle Pleyel in Paris encouraged him to move to his favourite city, where he began writing. He now contributes articles to various publications, including *Time Out Paris*, and he is the Parisian correspondent for *Opera News*. His first book, *Paris Rooms*, is to be published in October 1999.

Michael Palin is probably the only contributor to have been hit by a fish in Paris. It happened in the Bois de Boulogne while recording *Monty Python's Fish Slapping Dance* for French television in the whacky 1970s. Despite that, he has returned regularly and covered Paris in his latest book and television series *Michael Palin's Hemingway Adventure*. He lives in north London but gets out a lot.

Elisabeth Quin is a film critic for the cable arts channel *Paris-Première*. She appears daily on *Rive Droite Rive Gauche*, presents a weekly programme devoted to short films, and hosts a weekly cinema slot on RTL. She is a committee member of the Deauville Asian Film Festival. She lives in Pigalle and will admit to few links with the criminal underworld, while her links with film date back to her adolescence and her first encounter with *Pépé le Moko*.

Nicholas Royle lived in Paris in 1984/5, teaching English at a *lycée technique* to students who had no interest in the language. He has published three novels (*Counterparts*, largely set in Paris, was followed by *Saxophone Dreams* and *The Matter of the Heart*) and a hundred short stories, and has edited numerous anthologies, among them *The Time Out Book of Paris Short Stories* (Penguin) and *Neonlit: Time Out Book of New Writing Vols 1 & 2* (Quartet). Born in Manchester in 1963, he lives in London. His new novel, due in 2000 from Abacus, will be *The Director's Cut*.

Jeanloup Sieff began taking photographs at the age of 14 and has worked as a fashion photographer for the likes of *Elle*, *Magnum*, *Vogue*, *Harper's Bazaar* and *Paris-Match*. He has had numerous exhibitions and has produced both books and children (Sonia and Sacha). He began writing a novel in 1974, which will probably remain unfinished. He is currently on the look-out for a piano teacher who can teach him how to play like Fats Waller.

Further reading

History, art & culture

Beevor, Antony, & Cooper, Artemis *Paris after the Liberation*
The city during rationing, liberation and existentialism.
Christiansen, Rupert *Tales of the New Babylon*
The Paris of Napoléon III, from sleaze, prostitution and Haussmann's bulldozer to the bloody Commune.
Cole, Robert *A Traveller's History of Paris*
A useful general introduction.
Cronin, Vincent *Napoleon*
A fine biography of the great megalomaniac.
Fitch, Noel Riley *Literary Cafés of Paris*
Who drank where and when.
Littlewood, Ian *Paris: Architecture, History, Art*
Paris's history intertwined with its treasures.
Lurie, Patty *Guide to Impressionist Paris*
Impressionist paintings matched to their exact Paris locations as they look today.
Marnham, Patrick *Crime & The Académie Française*
Quirks and scandals of Mitterrand-era Paris.
Martin, Hervé *Guide to Modern Architecture in Paris*
An accessible, bilingual, illustrated guide to significant buildings in Paris since 1900, arranged by area.
Mitford, Nancy *The Sun King; Madame de Pompadour*
Mitford's biographies, although some years old, are still the best gossipy accounts of the courts of the *ancien régime*.
Johnson, Douglas, & Johnson, Madeleine *Age of Illusion: Art &Politics in France 1918-1940*
Every aspect of the culture of France in an era when Paris was more than ever at the forefront of modernity.
Mann, Carol *Paris Années Folles*
A photographic view of artistic Paris in the 1930s.
Rudorff, Raymond *Belle Epoque: Paris in the Nineties*
Glamorous *fin-de-siècle* Paris.
Salvadori, Renzo *Architect's Guide to Paris*
Plans, illustrations and a guide to Paris, growth, of interest to the general reader as well as to architects.
Schama, Simon *Citizens*
Giant but wonderfully readable account of the Revolution.
Zeldin, Theodore *The French*
Idiosyncratic and entertaining survey of modern France.

French literature

Abaelardus, Petrus & Heloïse *Letters*
The full details of Paris's first great drama.
Aragon, Louis *Paris Peasant*
A great Surrealist view of the city.
Balzac, Honoré de *Le Père Goriot*
All of Balzac's *Human Comedy* deals with Paris, but the story of old Goriot is one of the most acute of his novels.
Beyala, Calixthe *Le Petit Prince de Belleville*
Entertaining chronicle of African immigrants in Paris.
Céline, Louis-Ferdinand *Mort à Crédit*
Remarkably vivid, largely autobiographical account of an impoverished Paris childhood.
Daninos, Pierre *Les Carnets de Major Thompson*
Understand why the French have such odd ideas about the English: the French as seen by a retired English major. Lots of people fell for it when published in the 1950s.
De Beauvoir, Simone *The Mandarins*
Paris intellectuals and idealists just after the Liberation.
Desforges, Régine *The Blue Bicycle*
A vivid, easy-read drama of resistance, collaboration and sex during the German occupation. First of a trilogy.
Hugo, Victor *Notre Dame de Paris*
Quasimodo and the romantic vision of medieval Paris.
Maupassant, Guy de *Bel-Ami*
Gambling and dissipation.
Modiano, Patrick *Honeymoon*
Evocative story of two lives that cross in Paris.
Perec, Georges *Life, A User's Manual*
Intellectual puzzle in a Haussmannian apartment building.
Restif de la Bretonne, Nicolas *Les Nuits de Paris*
The sexual underworld of the Paris of Louis XV, by one of France's most famous defrocked priests.
Queneau, Raymond *Zazie in the Métro*
Paris in the 1950s: bright and very *nouvelle vague*.
Sartre, Jean-Paul *Roads to Freedom*
Existential angst as the German army takes over Paris.
Simenon, Georges *The Maigret series*
All of Simenon's books featuring his laconic detective provide a great picture of Paris and its underworld.
Vian, Boris *Froth on the Daydream*
Wonderfully funny Surrealist satire of Paris in the goldern era of Sartre and St-Germain.
Zola, Emile *Nana, L'Assommoir, Le Ventre de Paris*
These are perhaps Zola's most vivid accounts of the underside of life in the Second Empire.

The ex-pat angle

Hemingway, Ernest *A Moveable Feast*
Big Ern drinks his way around 1920s writers' Paris.
Littlewood, Ian *Paris: A Literary Companion*
Great selection of pieces by all kinds of writers on Paris.
Maugham, W Somerset *The Moon & Sixpence*
Impoverished artist in Montmartre and escape to the South Seas, inspired by the life of Gauguin.
Miller, Henry *Tropic of Cancer, Tropic of Capricorn*
Low-life and lust in Montparnasse.
Nin, Anaïs *Henry & June*
Lust in Montparnasse with Henry Miller and his wife.
Orwell, George *Down and Out in Paris and London*
Exactly what the title says.
Rhys, Jean *After Mr Mackenzie*
Life as a kept woman in seedy hotels.
Royle, Nicholas (editor) *The Time Out Book of Paris Short Stories*
New fiction by British, American and French writers.
Stein, Gertrude *The Autobiography of Alice B Toklas*
Ex-pat Paris, from start to finish.
Süskind, Patrick *Perfume*
Pungent murder in Paris on the eve of the Revolution.

Food & drink

A-Z of French Food A handy pocket glossary.
Masui, Kasuko *French Cheeses*
An illustrated guide to tickle your tastebuds.
Time Out *Guide to Eating & Drinking in Paris*
Over 750 restaurants, bars, brasseries and bistros.
Toklas, Alice B *The Alice B Toklas Cookbook*
Literary and artistic life, and how to cook fish for Picasso.
Wells, Patricia *Bistro Cooking*
Recipes and bistro lore.

Walks for...

Architecture

Philippe Alexandre – the *hôtels particuliers* of the 7th. **Chantal Barbe** – the architectural legacy of the monarchy. **Natasha Edwards** – Guimard, Le Corbusier and Mallet-Stevens are among the architects that feature.

Art

Philippe Alexandre – wander the gardens of the Musée Rodin. **Jean-Daniel Brèque** – finishes at the Musée des Arts d'Afrique et d'Océanie. **Marie Darrieussecq** – a tour of the statues in the Jardin du Luxembourg. **Abdelkader Djemaï** – open house at contemporary artists' studios in Belleville. **Natasha Edwards** – drop in on Henri Bouchard's studio. **Antoine de Gaudemar** – the Surrealists in northern Paris, including Gustave Moreau's studio. **Liz Jensen** – Impressionists' haven of Montmartre. **Christopher Kenworthy** – a sculpture garden by the Seine. **Linda Lê** – a brief visit to the Louvre. **Nicholas Royle** – tracks down the haunts of artist, filmmaker and writer Roland Topor. **Jeanloup Sieff** – his own photographs of graves in the Cimetière de Montmartre.

Cemeteries

Maureen Freely – recalls Sartre's and de Beauvoir's funerals in Montparnasse cemetery. **Alistair Horne** – guides you round Père Lachaise. **Liz Jensen** – takes you on a short tour through Montmartre cemetery. **Nicholas Lezard** – mourns by Beckett's grave in Montparnasse cemetery. **Elisabeth Quin** – tracks down directors in Montmartre and St-Vincent cemeteries. **Jeanloup Sieff** – a photographic tour of Montmartre cemetery.

Eating & drinking

Abdelkader Djemaï – the exotic tastes of Belleville and La Goutte d'Or. **Geoff Dyer** – drink to the gentrification of the 11th. **Maureen Freely** – visits most of the cafés that hosted the Lost Generation. **Alan Furst** – don't miss those exquisite ice-creams. **Sasha Goldman** – samples the best of Jewish fare. **Michael Palin** – Hemingway's watering holes.

Film

Elisabeth Quin – locations from films by the greats such as Carné, Clouzot and Truffaut. **Nicholas Royle** – tracks down the haunts of filmmaker, artist and writer Roland Topor.

Gardens & parks

Jean-Daniel Brèque – follow a blossoming old railway line. **Marie Darrieussecq** – a tour of the statues in the Jardin du Luxembourg. **Linda Lê** – visits both the Jardin du Palais-Royal and the Jardin du Luxembourg. **Stephen Mudge** – a finale in Parc Monceau. **Nicholas Royle** – visits two man-made parks: Belleville and Buttes Chaumont.

History

Philippe Alexandre – recent political traditions exposed. **Chantal Barbe** – the ups and downs of royalty. **Sasha Goldman** – uncovering the history of the Marais. **Alistair Horne** – the past brought to life in Père Lachaise.

Literature

Maureen Freely – traces Simone de Beauvoir's Paris. **Antoine de Gaudemar** – La Nouvelle Athènes of the Surrealists. **Linda Lê** – the walk itself told as a short story. **Nicholas Lezard** – follows in the path of Samuel Beckett. **Michael Palin** – Hemingway's Paris uncovered. **Nicholas Royle** – tracks down the haunts of writer, artist and filmmaker Roland Topor.

Multiculturalism

Abdelkader Djemaï – sample the ethnic diversity of Belleville and La Goutte d'Or. **Geoff Dyer** – goes east to the Arab area in the 11th. **Sasha Goldman** – takes us through the Jewish quarter of the Marais.

Music

Jean Paul Dollé – revisits the jazz greats' haunts. **Stephen Mudge** – opera houses and museums of music.

Nightime

Liz Jensen – the best time for Pigalle's sleaze district.

Parents with children

Jean-Daniel Brèque – green, almost entirely traffic-free, and an aquarium at the end. **Marie Darrieussecq** – toy boats, ponies, lawns and statues in the Jardin du Luxembourg. **Alistair Horne** – tumble among the tombs in Père Lachaise. **Olivier Morel** – short, relatively traffic free, and frequent patches of grass. **Jeanloup Sieff** – track down the graves from the photos in Montmartre cemetery.

Quirky Museums

Natasha Edwards – Fondation Le Corbusier, Musée du Vin and Henri Bouchard's studio. **Alan Furst** – Polish poet Adam Mickiewicz remembered. **Antoine de Gaudemar** – visit the Fondation Boris Vian, the Musée de la Vie Romantique in Pigalle, or the waxworks at Musée Grevin. **Liz Jensen** – blush through the Musée de l'Erotisme. **Stephen Mudge** – the underrated Musée Cernushi and Musée Nissim de Camondo.

Religion

Chantal Barbe – don't miss Notre-Dame or Ste-Chapelle. **Geoff Dyer** – St-Ambroise, a slick new church, and a mosque. **Alan Furst** – the walk ends at the glorious St-Etienne-du Mont. **Sasha Goldman** – historic graffiti in St-Paul, and synogogues in the Marais. **Liz Jensen** – climb up to the Sacré-Coeur for a view over the city, and visit the quirky St-Jean-de-Montmartre. **Stephen Mudge** – high church and metal infrastructure.

Shopping

Abdelkader Djemaï – lively markets at the start and end of the route. **Antoine de Gaudemar** – duck into the passages off boulevard Montmartre. **Linda Lê** – visits several bookshops. **Nicholas Royle** – he just can't resist secondhand bookshops.

Water

Philippe Alexandre – Pont Alexandre III, and a walk along the quai. **Alan Furst** – island hop on the Seine. **Christopher Kenworthy** – walk along the river banks. **Nicholas Lezard** – ends on the spectacular allée des Cygnes. **Olivier Morel** – never leaves the Ile de la Cité. **Nicholas Royle** – criss-cross the Canal St-Martin and see the lake in the Parc des Buttes Chaumont.

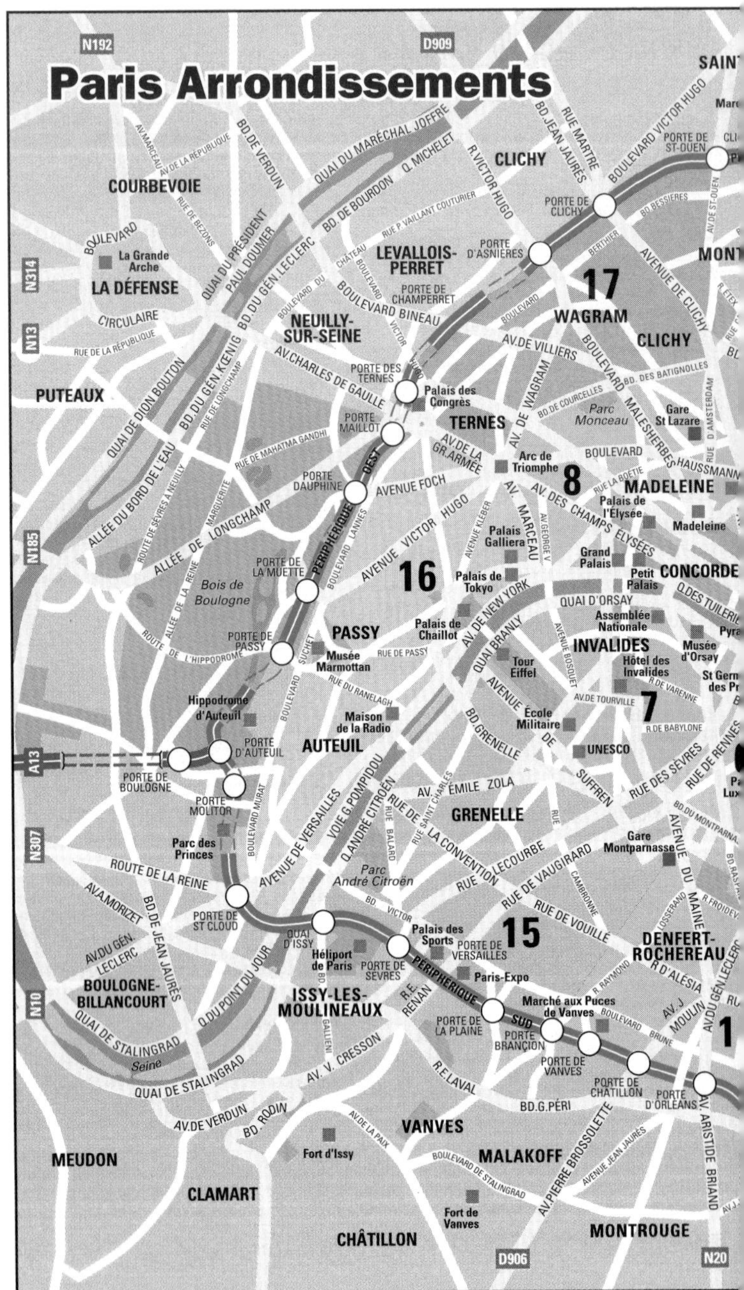

Paris Arrondissements
N192
D909
SAINT
COURBEVOIE
AV. MARCEAU
AV. DE LA RÉPUBLIQUE
RUE DE BEZONS
BD. DE VERDUN
QUAI DU MARÉCHAL JOFFRE
Q. MICHELET
BD. DE BOURDON
QUAI DU PRÉSIDENT PAUL DOUMER
BD. DU GEN. LECLERC
R. VICTOR HUGO
CLICHY
BD. JEAN JAURÈS
RUE MARTRE
BOULEVARD VICTOR HUGO
PORTE DE ST-OUEN
PORTE DE CLICHY
BD. BESSIERES
AV. DE ST-OUEN
RUE P. VAILLANT COUTURIER
LEVALLOIS-PERRET
PORTE D'ASNIÈRES
BERTHIER
AVENUE DE CLICHY
MONT
BOULEVARD
La Grande Arche
LA DÉFENSE
N314
CIRCULAIRE
RUE DE LA RÉPUBLIQUE
N13
PORTE DE CHAMPERRET
BOULEVARD BINEAU
NEUILLY-SUR-SEINE
17
WAGRAM
CLICHY
AV. DE VILLIERS
BOULEVARD MALESHERBES
BD. DES BATIGNOLLES
PUTEAUX
QUAI DE DION BOUTON
BD. DU GÉN. KŒNIG
RUE DE LONGCHAMP
AV. CHARLES DE GAULLE
PORTE DES TERNES
Palais des Congrès
PORTE MAILLOT
TERNES
AV. DE WAGRAM
BD. DE COURCELLES
Parc Monceau
Gare St Lazare
RUE D'AMSTERDAM
RUE DE MAHATMA GANDHI
AV. DE LA GR. ARMÉE
Arc de Triomphe
8
BOULEVARD HAUSSMANN
PORTE DAUPHINE
AVENUE FOCH
PÉRIPHÉRIQUE OUEST
RUE LA BOÉTIE
MADELEINE
Palais de l'Élysée
Madeleine
ALLÉE DU BORD DE L'EAU
ROUTE DE SÈVRES À NEUILLY
MARGUERITE
ALLÉE DE LONGCHAMP
N185
BOULEVARD LANNES
AVENUE VICTOR HUGO
AV. MARCEAU
AVENUE KLEBER
Palais Galliera
AV. GEORGE V
AV. DES CHAMPS ELYSÉES
Grand Palais
Petit Palais
CONCORDE
PORTE DE LA MUETTE
Bois de Boulogne
ALLÉE DE LA REINE
16
Palais de Tokyo
AV. DE NEW YORK
QUAI D'ORSAY
Q. DES TUILERIES
ROUTE DE L'HIPPODROME
PORTE DE PASSY
PASSY
SUCHET
Musée Marmottan
RUE DE PASSY
Palais de Chaillot
QUAI BRANLY
Assemblée Nationale
INVALIDES
Musée d'Orsay
AVENUE BOSQUET
Tour Eiffel
Hôtel des Invalides
R. DE VARENNE
St Germ des Pr
RUE DU RANELAGH
AVENUE DE SUFFREN
AV. DE TOURVILLE
7
École Militaire
R. DE BABYLONE
Hippodrome d'Auteuil
BOULEVARD
Maison de la Radio
AUTEUIL
BD. GRENELLE
UNESCO
RUE DES SÈVRES
RUE DE RENNES
A13
PORTE D'AUTEUIL
PORTE DE BOULOGNE
PORTE MOLITOR
BOULEVARD MURAT
AVENUE DE VERSAILLES
VOIE G. POMPIDOU
Q. ANDRÉ CITROËN
RUE SAINT CHARLES
AV. ÉMILE ZOLA
GRENELLE
BD. DU MONTPARNASSE
RUE BALARD
RUE DE LA CONVENTION
Parc des Princes
N307
ROUTE DE LA REINE
Parc André Citroën
RUE LECOURBE
RUE DE VAUGIRARD
CAMBRONNE
Gare Montparnasse
AVENUE DU MAINE
AV. A. MORIZET
BD. DE JEAN JAURÈS
PORTE DE ST CLOUD
BD. VICTOR
RUE DE VOUILLÉ
LOSSERAND
R. FROIDEV
QUAI D'ISSY
Palais des Sports
PORTE DE VERSAILLES
15
DENFERT-ROCHEREAU
AV. DU GÉN. LECLERC
Héliport de Paris
PORTE DE SÈVRES
PÉRIPHÉRIQUE SUD
Paris-Expo
R. D'ALÉSIA
R. RAYMOND
BOULOGNE-BILLANCOURT
N10
Q. DU POINT DU JOUR
ISSY-LES-MOULINEAUX
R.E. RENAN
BD. GALLIENI
Marché aux Puces de Vanves
BOULEVARD BRUNE
AV. J. MOULIN
QUAI DE STALINGRAD
Seine
PORTE DE LA PLAINE
PORTE BRANCION
PORTE DE VANVES
AV. V. CRESSON
R.E. LAVAL
PORTE DE CHÂTILLON
PORTE D'ORLÉANS
AV. ARISTIDE BRIAND
BD. G. PÉRI
AV. DE VERDUN
BD. RODIN
AV. DE LA PAIX
VANVES
MEUDON
Fort d'Issy
BOULEVARD DE STALINGRAD
MALAKOFF
AV. PIERRE BROSSOLETTE
AVENUE JEAN JAURÈS
CLAMART
Fort de Vanves
MONTROUGE
CHÂTILLON
D906
N20

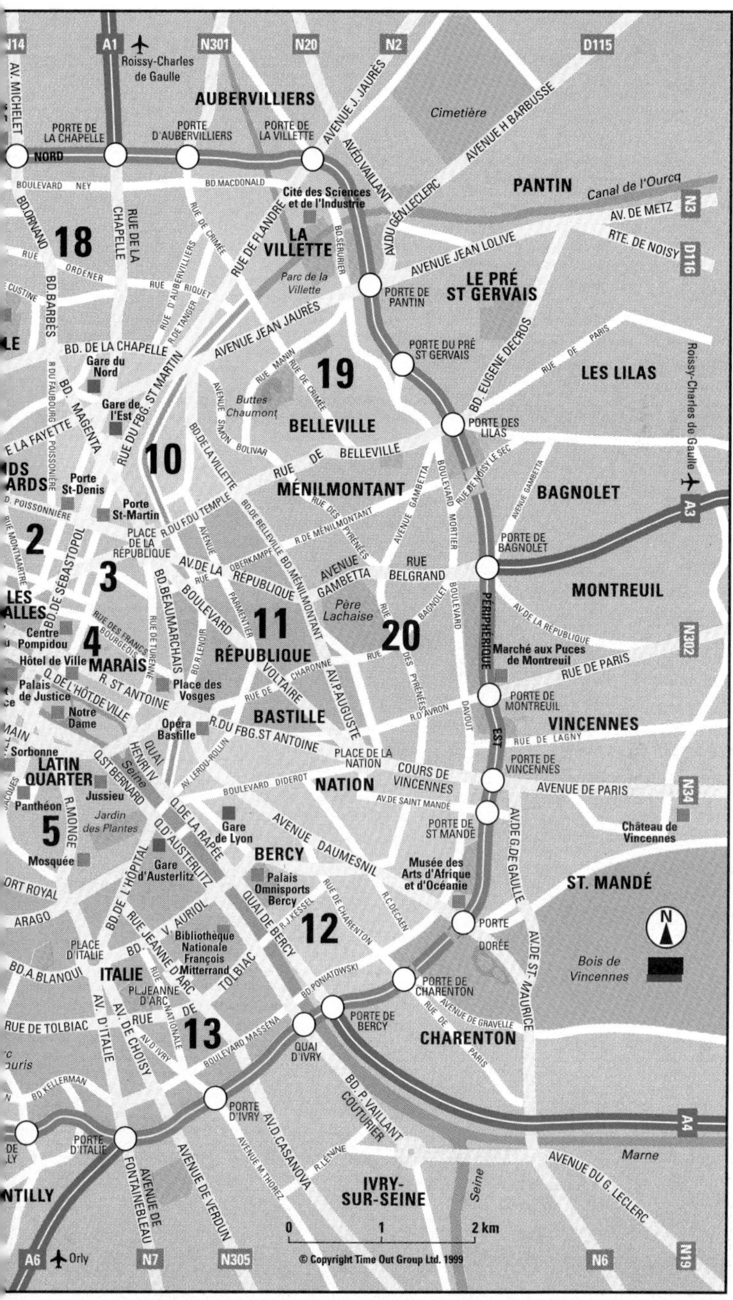
AUBERVILLIERS
PANTIN
LA VILLETTE
LE PRÉ ST GERVAIS
LES LILAS
BELLEVILLE
MÉNILMONTANT
BAGNOLET
MONTREUIL
RÉPUBLIQUE
MARAIS
BASTILLE
VINCENNES
NATION
LATIN QUARTER
BERCY
ST. MANDÉ
ITALIE
CHARENTON
IVRY-SUR-SEINE
18
19
10
2
3
4
11
20
5
12
13
Roissy-Charles de Gaulle
Orly
Cimetière
Parc de la Villette
Buttes Chaumont
Père Lachaise
Jardin des Plantes
Bois de Vincennes
Cité des Sciences et de l'Industrie
Gare du Nord
Gare de l'Est
Gare de Lyon
Gare d'Austerlitz
Centre Pompidou
Hôtel de Ville
Palais de Justice
Notre Dame
Sorbonne
Panthéon
Jussieu
Mosquée
Place des Vosges
Opéra Bastille
Palais Omnisports Bercy
Bibliothèque Nationale François Mitterrand
Musée des Arts d'Afrique et d'Océanie
Marché aux Puces de Montreuil
Château de Vincennes
Porte St-Denis
Porte St-Martin
PORTE DE LA CHAPELLE
PORTE D'AUBERVILLIERS
PORTE DE LA VILLETTE
PORTE DE PANTIN
PORTE DU PRÉ ST GERVAIS
PORTE DES LILAS
PORTE DE BAGNOLET
PORTE DE MONTREUIL
PORTE DE VINCENNES
PORTE DE ST MANDÉ
PORTE DORÉE
PORTE DE CHARENTON
PORTE DE BERCY
QUAI D'IVRY
PORTE D'IVRY
PORTE D'ITALIE
PÉRIPHÉRIQUE EST
NORD
Canal de l'Ourcq
Seine
Marne
0
1
2 km
© Copyright Time Out Group Ltd. 1999

Index

Page numbers in *italics* indicate illustrations.

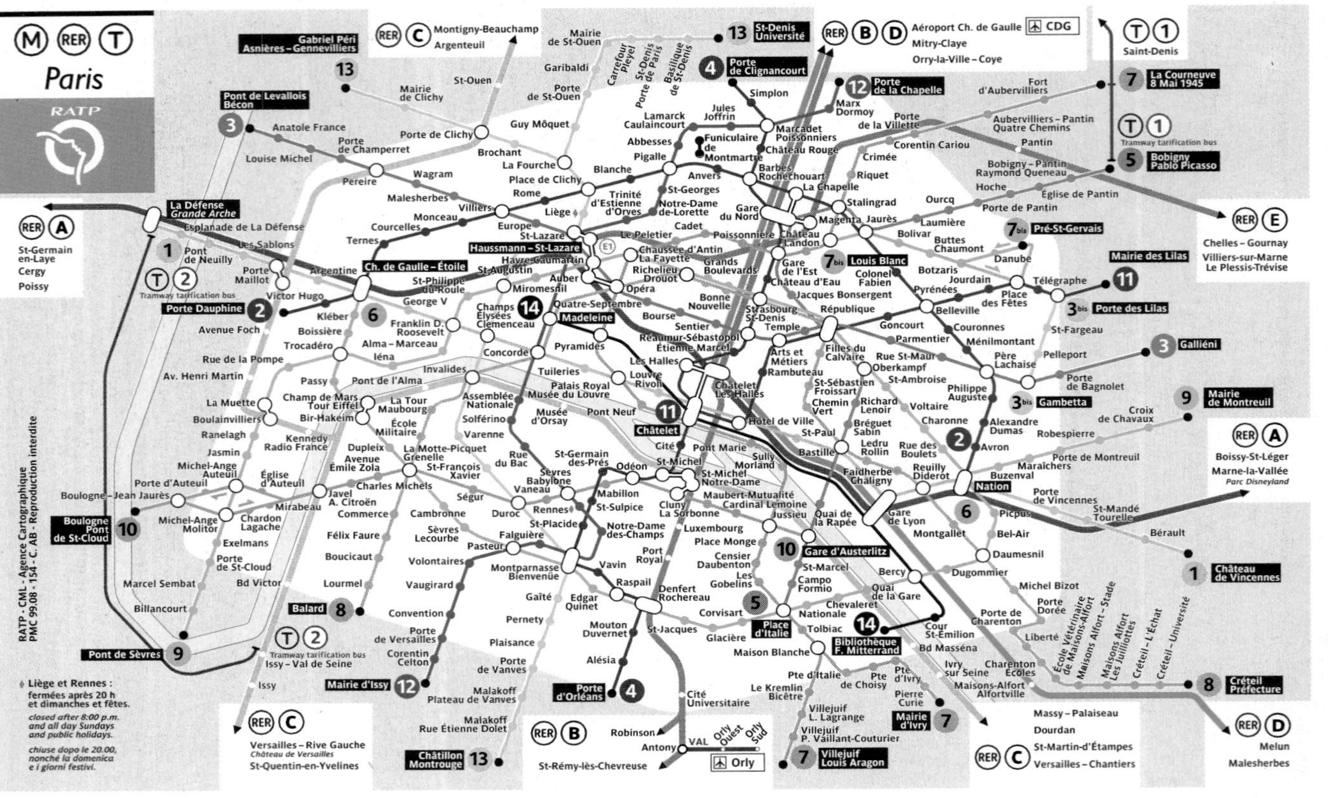

M RER T
Paris
RATP
RER A St-Germain-en-Laye Cergy Poissy
RER C Montigny-Beauchamp Argenteuil
RER B D Aéroport Ch. de Gaulle CDG Mitry-Claye Orry-la-Ville – Coye
T 1 Saint-Denis
RER E Chelles – Gournay Villiers-sur-Marne Le Plessis-Trévise
RER A Boissy-St-Léger Marne-la-Vallée Parc Disneyland
RER D Melun Malesherbes
RER C Massy – Palaiseau Dourdan St-Martin-d'Étampes Versailles – Chantiers
RER B St-Rémy-lès-Chevreuse
RER C Versailles – Rive Gauche Château de Versailles St-Quentin-en-Yvelines
Orly
Liège et Rennes : fermées après 20 h et dimanches et fêtes.
closed after 8:00 p.m. and all day Sundays and public holidays.
chiuse dopo le 20.00, nonché la domenica e i giorni festivi.
RATP - CML - Agence Cartographique
PMC 99.08 - 154 - C. AB - Reproduction interdite